D1299993

REGIONAL SECURITY IN THE MIDDLE EAST

The International Institute for Strategic Studies was founded in 1958 as a centre for the provision of information on and research into the problems of international security, defence and arms control in the nuclear age. It is international in its Council and staff, and its membership is drawn from over sixty countries. It is independent of governments and is not the advocate of any particular interest.

The Institute is concerned with strategic questions — not just with the military aspects of security but with the social and economic sources and political and moral implications of the use and existence of armed force: in other words, with the basic problems of peace.

The Institute's publications are intended for a much wider audience than its own membership and are available to the general public on subscription or singly.

Other Titles in The Adelphi Library

Arms Control and European Security
Edited by Jonathan Alford

Greece and Turkey: Adversity in Alliance
Edited by Jonathan Alford

Nuclear Weapons and European Security
Edited by Robert Nurick

Security in East Asia
Edited by Robert O'Neill

Nuclear Weapons Proliferation and
Nuclear Risk
Edited by James A. Schear

Regional Security in the Middle East

ADELPHI LIBRARY

Edited by
CHARLES TRIPP

Published for
THE INTERNATIONAL INSTITUTE FOR STRATEGIC
STUDIES
by
St. Martin's Press, New York

©International Institute for Strategic Studies 1984

All rights reserved. For information, write:
St. Martin's Press, Inc., 175 Fifth Avenue, New York, NY 10010
Printed in Great Britain
First published in the United States of America in 1984

Library of Congress Card Catalog Number 83-40155

ISBN 0-312-66940-2

Contents

Introduction

In the Middle East the search for agreed principles to serve as a foundation for regional order has proved to be as notoriously difficult as the search for stable foundations for government. These two problems are related. The episodes of fierce conflict which have marked the recent history of the area have not simply been due to a conventional clash of states' interests. More fundamentally, the absence of even the most basic consensus on either the validity of the region's component states or the legitimacy of many of their governments has lent an uncompromising sharpness to regional and domestic disputes. For most of the parties involved there is too much at stake ever to renounce the use of force as the principal means of dealing with these disputes, and the precarious outcome of this has been the tendency to equate security with whatever can be retained for the time being by bluff and coercion.

In the sphere of domestic politics the most radical challenge to the established state authorities of the region in recent years has come from those demanding a specifically Islamic political order. Just such a group was responsible for the dramatic seizure of the Great Mosque at Mecca in 1979, showing that Saudi Arabia, although created by similar forces in the past, was not immune from their contemporary challenge. At the other end of the Arab political spectrum, the Ba'ath regime in Syria has been under similar threat, and since 1979 at least has been locked in mortal combat with the organized forces of the Muslim Brotherhood. The most spectacular testimony to the success of the Islamic radicals in toppling apparently strong regimes is the self-styled Islamic Republic of Iran, even if the ensuing turmoil has made the end result rather more ambiguous. In short, the underlying principles of the state in the Middle East are in flux, and this clearly has grave consequences for any concept of regional security.

One unsettling factor which has caused much of the pressure on Middle Eastern regimes stems from their perceived failure to cope with the challenge of a Jewish state established on land regarded by many in the area as inalienably Arab and Muslim. This lies at the heart of the conflict between Israel and the Arabs. Israel's initial successes have only added to Palestinian resentment and to the dilemma of the neighbouring Arab states. The difficulty now lies in attempting to reconcile mutually exclusive ideas about the final political character of territory claimed with equal determination by both parties.

In a direct military sense the Arab states rather than the Palestinians themselves have hitherto been Israel's principal antagonists. These fronts have produced the wars of the past and cause concern for the future in two particular respects. First, while the quantities of conventional armaments used in the conflict escalate at a disturbing rate, there remains a more troubling possibility that nuclear weapons might one day be introduced. Israel's own fear that such a day might not be far off was dramatically demonstrated by her bombing raid on the Iraqi *Osirak* nuclear reactor in 1981. The second unsettling factor is the prospect of super-power intervention and confrontation, once fighting has broken out in the area, to protect their clients and their interests. This has happened before and the more troubled regional and domestic politics become, the more likely it is to happen again.

These are the themes pursued by the studies in this volume. 'Saudi Arabia's Search for Security' looks first at the underlying components of Saudi politics, and then examines the consequences of their development for the future of the Saudi regime and for Saudi relations with states in the region and outside. A similar approach is used with regard to Syria in the next chapter, 'The Foreign Policy of Syria: Goals, Capabilities, Constraints and Options'. This is an examination of the domestic determinants and the international consequences of the regional policies of this 'front-line' Arab state.

The third and fourth chapters deal with the central Arab-Israeli dispute, with reference to which so much of Syrian policy is worked out. 'A Palestinian State? Examining the Alternatives' addresses the core issue. Its first section looks at the historical background of Palestinian nationalism, and its second examines current proposals for a solution of the 'Palestine Question'. Its third section puts forward ideas for the establishment of a Palestinian state, and assesses the probable repercussions of this for the security of its regional environment. The chapter which follows, 'The Military Threat to Israel', gives some idea of the problem of implementing long-term political solutions when the perception of security within Israel is a product of a sense of immediate military threat. The next chapter, 'A Nuclear Middle East', paints a disturbing picture of the way ahead if purely military solutions to questions of security are allowed to determine the course of events in the Middle East.

The last chapter in this volume, 'Soviet Policy Towards Iran and the Gulf', turns away from events in the Levant to look at the consequences of domestic turmoil and regional conflict in an area since made even more critical by the outbreak of war between Iraq and Iran in 1980. It takes the form of an assessment of the opportunities offered for the extension of Soviet influence in this area by local conditions, and the capability of the Soviet Union, as well as its determination, to exploit them to its own advantage.

Questions of Middle Eastern security raise problems for others outside the region. At the same time they are to some extent amenable to action taken by outside powers. The danger here lies in unilateral intervention to secure narrowly interpreted, short-term interests. However, even in the absence of such partisan behaviour, security cannot be imposed. In the last analysis the outcome must depend on the willingness and ability of the inhabitants of the Middle East to reach workable compromises amongst themselves. Only this will provide a foundation flexible enough to sustain a system of regional security guarantees, and the profound changes of attitude which this demands will constitute the most severe challenge to the peoples of the region in the future.

Charles Tripp

1 Saudi Arabia's Search for Security

ADEED DAWISHA

INTRODUCTION

During the 1970s the system of Middle Eastern political interaction, especially that relating to intra-Arab relations, has undergone a dramatic and fundamental change. The occurrence of military coups, such a feature of Middle Eastern politics in the pre-1970 period, has markedly decreased. The almost universal use of propaganda and subversion has been supplanted by diplomacy as the primary instrument of Middle Eastern political interaction. And pragmatism, even conservatism, seem to have become the primary foreign policy orientations of most, if not all, of the Arab states – a far cry from the 'revolutionary' and turbulent environment which pervaded Middle Eastern, particularly inter-Arab, politics of the previous two decades.

While this change has been precipitated by a number of indigenous and exogenous causes, there is little doubt that Saudi Arabia's emergence as a powerful and consequential regional actor has been a crucial contributing factor. Since the oil price explosion after the October 1973 War, Saudi Arabia has effectively utilized the immense economic leverage her huge oil reserves give to stamp on the area her own brand of conservatism not only by strengthening existing *status quo* regimes, but also by spreading with almost missionary zeal Saudi ideals and principles. Recent events in Iran have pointed in the most dramatic way to the international problems which are caused when instability touches the oil-producing countries of the Middle East. It is in this context that the policies of Saudi Arabia will be of crucial importance for the future.

The purpose of this Paper is threefold. First, it aims to chart the rapid, almost meteoric, rise of Saudi Arabia as a regional power. Secondly, it attempts to explain contemporary Saudi involvement in Middle Eastern and international politics; this will be done by analysing the values, interests, concerns and perceptions of the Saudi decision-making elite. Saudi Arabia's policies at the domestic, regional and global levels, will then be analysed, and her conception of her Middle Eastern and world role ascertained. Finally, the study attempts to identify the various avenues Saudi policy may follow in the next decade, and the potential problems and pitfalls that policy may encounter.

I. THE FORMATIVE YEARS, 1953–73

The 1970s have witnessed the emergence of Saudi Arabia as an influential actor in the contemporary international system. Accordingly, the country's diplomatic and financial activities have acquired a global perspective. However, in the 1950s and 1960s the Kingdom's primary, almost sole, concern was with regional and inter-Arab affairs. Until the 1967 War ushered in the demise of 'radical' politics in the Middle East, the despotically-ruled desert kingdom had concentrated its energies on a defensive battle against the alien socialist doctrines of Nasser's Egypt and her radical allies.

From its very inception in 1926, the Kingdom of Saudi Arabia had been a relatively active participant in regional, and particularly inter-Arab politics. Throughout the 1920s and 1930s Saudi Arabia was involved in a number of disputes with her immediate neighbours such as the Sheikhdom of Abu Dhabi and the Sultanate of Muscat and Oman, and in bitter rivalries with the Hashemite Dynasties of Iraq and Trans-

1

jordan. On the other hand, relations with Egypt were cordial, culminating in a Treaty of Friendship between the two countries in 1936. Saudi Arabia was also a founder-member of the League of Arab States (established in 1945) and a participant, albeit peripherally, in the first Arab-Israeli war of 1948.[1] Nevertheless, the primary preoccupation of the Kingdom's founder and first ruler, King Abd al-Aziz Ibn Saud, was centred throughout his reign on the domestic issues of unifying and developing his country. Vigorous regional activity, and the beginning of Saudi Arabia's international involvement, occurred only after the King's death in 1953, and coincided with the sharp increase in the level of political activity in the region as a whole which reflected the ideological polarization in both the regional and international scenes.

The initial years of the succeeding monarch, King Saud, witnessed a paradoxical coincidence of interest between the conservative kingdom of Saudi Arabia and the revolutionary republic of Egypt, headed by Gamal Abd al-Nasser. Nasser's bitter attacks on the Hashemite Kings of Iraq and Jordan in the wake of the Baghdad Pact were welcomed in Saudi Arabia, given her long-standing rivalry with the Hashemites, and between 1954 and 1957 she closely and loyally followed Egyptian policy, to the extent that one Western observer suggested that the Kingdom was 'on the way to becoming Egypt's most valuable colony'.[2] Indeed a mutual defence pact between the two countries was signed in October 1955, and this was later expanded into the Tripartite Jeddah Pact which included the Yemen. In January 1957 the Treaty of Arab Solidarity was signed by Egypt, Saudi Arabia, Syria and Jordan for a period of ten years. During all the major controversies of this period – over the Baghdad Pact, the Czech arms deal, the nationalization of the Suez Canal Company and the Suez crisis – Saudi Arabia was firmly on the side of Egypt.

At the beginning of 1957, however, Saudi policy began to shift. For a variety of reasons, King Saud was becoming wary of his pro-Nasser, anti-imperialist role, because it was leading to a potential conflict with the United States. In January 1957 he visited the United States and was successfully persuaded to reassess his loyal adherence to Nasserist principles and policies.[3] While no immediate clash occurred between

them, Egypt and Saudi Arabia were beginning to drift apart. King Saud, increasingly conscious of the common interests binding him to the other Arab monarchs, soon began to perceive Nasser and his radical policies as a threat to the Saudi monarchy. It was becoming evident that Saudi understanding of Arab nationalism was markedly different from Egypt's. As one analyst observed:

> To the Saudi rulers, their Arabness was such a self-evident fact that no theoretical elaboration was needed. Being of tribal stock, they thought of themselves as the real, ethnically-pure Arabs. While they recognized the special ties among Arab countries, they attributed them as much to religion and proximity as to Arabism. They did not recognize any mystical links emanating from Arab nationalism. If unity was to be the goal, it should be based on Islam, rather than Arabism.[4]

The first manifestation of the gradual divergence between the two countries occurred in April 1957, when Saudi Arabia dispatched troops to Jordan to help King Hussein against a pro-Nasser coup. The disagreement between the two former allies was made public when Nasser accused Saud of plotting to assassinate him in order to prevent the formation of the United Arab Republic (UAR) in February 1958. Over the next three years, relations with 'radical' countries such as the UAR and Iraq were strained. At the same time, Saudi-Jordanian relations flourished and were marked by extreme cordiality and intensive co-operation, especially at the military level.

Ideological and political polarization of the Middle East into the 'conservative' camp led by Saudi Arabia and the 'revolutionary' forces under the leadership of Egypt began with the secession of Syria from the UAR in September 1961. The Egyptians perceived the secession as a reactionary move by the Syrian capitalists and feudalists, who were backed by the Saudi and Jordanian kings. Nasser therefore unleashed a bitter ideological and political offensive against 'the backers of the Syrian separatists in the Arab world, particularly Saud and Hussein'. Saudi Arabia immediately responded by intensifying her own campaign against Nasser's socialism, equating it with 'atheistic communism' and describing the Egyptian President as a 'staunch communist who is still as loyal to communism

2

as he was on the day he joined the secret communist organization in Cairo as a junior member'.[5] She also proceeded to undermine Egypt's central position in the Arab world, and, with the help of Egypt's other adversaries, challenged Egyptian dominance in the Arab League by demanding that Cairo should cease to be its permanent headquarters. Saud also presented the Islamic Charter which, in criticizing 'false nationalism based on atheistic doctrine', implied condemnation of Nasser's policies. The year 1962 witnessed a vehemently bitter interaction between Cairo and Riyadh during which radio propaganda was most effectively used. Saudi Arabia also used the holy shrines of Mecca as instruments of her foreign policy – in one instance, demanding that Egyptian pilgrims pay in hard currency (of which Egypt, las she well knew, was very short) and in another refusing to accept the *Kiswa* (the cover for Mecca's main shrine, the holy *Ka'aba*, which Egypt had traditionally provided during the annual pilgrimages) on grounds of the poor quality of the Egyptian offering.

This polarization became complete in September 1962, with the eruption of the civil war in Yemen. Egypt immediately dispatched troops to help the republicans, whereas Saudi Arabia, viewing the war as the inevitable clash between the two ideological poles, uncompromisingly aided the royalist faction with money and equipment. She felt that victory for Egypt in Yemen would constitute a direct ideological and strategic threat to her own political order.[6] Accordingly, she requested help from Jordan and Iran, and followed this by signing a military alliance with Jordan on 4 November. The situation was deemed so dangerous for Saudi Arabia that King Saud was compelled to appoint his more rational brother Prince Faisal as Prime Minister in order to confront the new threat.

After an Egyptian air-raid on the Saudi border, designed to neutralize the source of aid to the royalists, Prince Faisal severed diplomatic relations with Egypt, obtained arms for the royalists from Pakistan and Iran, and asked the United States Air Force to mount a display of strength over Jeddah. Justifying Saudi involvement in the civil war, he declared:

We found ourselves in a position where we had no choice but to act according to our principles,

our religion and our honour . . . Egypt's rulers declared that they had sent their expedition to fight in Yemen to destroy our country and to capture it. We were, therefore, driven into a position where we had no alternative but to defend ourselves. Every state and every country in the world is entitled to self-defence.[7]

The civil war in Yemen lasted for over five years, and the Egyptian troop commitment, increasing from 8,000 in late 1962 to a staggering 70,000 in 1966, had an almost ruinous effect on the structurally fragile Egyptian economy. Apart from very short periods of reconciliation, Saudi-Egyptian relations were extremely hostile, characterized by bitter reciprocal accusations and recriminations.

During this period, Saudi Arabia was reinforcing her position as the leader of the anti-radical, conservative forces in the Middle East. In December 1965, Faisal (who had by now succeeded to the throne) joined the Shah in calling for an Islamic conference. In a pointed reference to socialist principles and doctrines, he proposed that Iran and Saudi Arabia should unite to fight factions and ideas alien to Islam. In January 1966, he visited Jordan and repeated the call for an Islamic summit, to be held later in the year in Mecca. At the same time, he was endeavouring to involve the Western powers more actively in the conflict. He concluded a significant arms deal with the United States and Britain, and launched a vigorous diplomatic drive aimed at alienating the Western powers from Egypt and the radical Arab camp. The Johnson Administration in the United States, already wary of Egyptian-Soviet cordiality, responded by refusing to grant Egypt loans worth \$220 million. It was during these years that the American activity in the area began to constitute a crucial element in Saudi calculations and policies.

The nature and character of inter-Arab relations changed dramatically in the wake of the Six-Day War of June 1967, primarily because of a shift in Egypt's Arab policy. The pre-1967 posture of confrontation was replaced after the war by an attitude of conciliation. This was brought about by three related factors: first, the presence of Israeli soldiers on Egyptian soil caused inter-Arab quarrels to take second place to Egypt's primary post-war objective of 'eradicating Israeli aggression'; second, war-induced economic problems severely limited Egypt's developmental capabilities and imposed on Nasser an Egyptian rather than an Arab orientation; and finally, as a consequence, Egypt's economic well-being gradually became dependent on the financial assistance of the oil-rich reactionary states. This dependence began at the Arab Summit in Khartoum, when Saudi Arabia, Kuwait and Libya agreed to extend annual grants of $280 million to Egypt and $100 million to Jordan to compensate them for the land and revenue loss caused by the June War. King Faisal also reached agreement with President Nasser over the Yemen civil war, with the Egyptians undertaking to withdraw their troops completely within four months. There was a further manifestation of Saudi Arabia's emerging power when Faisal, backed by Hussein, took the leadership of the moderate camp and insisted on attaching to the militantly anti-Israeli resolution which the summit finally produced a clause stipulating that in the effort 'to eliminate the effects of aggression', all possible instruments needed to be utilized, 'including the political and diplomatic'.[8] Freed from her earlier concern with survival against alien doctrines and ideologies, and strengthened by her emerging financial power, Saudi Arabia was beginning to shift from a defensive to an offensive posture as leader of the conservative forces in the area.

During the next two years, the Saudi leaders vigorously endeavoured to strengthen relations with Iran, especially after Britain's announcement of her intention to withdraw all troops from the Gulf area by 1971. The vacuum would need filling and an alliance with Iran, an Islamic state which shared Saudi Arabia's conservative outlook and pro-west orientation, was not only advisable, but necessary.

Overcoming an initial strain in the relationship that followed the Shah's claim to Bahrain at the beginning of 1968, Saudi Arabia made a number of overtures to Iran which resulted in a treaty that delineated the offshore boundaries of the two countries. In November 1968 the Shah paid a state visit to Saudi Arabia, combining it with a pilgrimage to Mecca. In addition to its political significance, that shrewd pilgrimage was acclaimed as symbolizing Muslim unity between the Wahabi Sunni sect of Saudi Arabia and the heretical Shi'a sect of Iran.

Saudi Arabia also began to project an Islamic orientation in her regional activities. King Faisal obstinately rejected the calls of other Arab countries for an Arab summit meeting to discuss the conflict with Israel on the grounds that this should await the outcome of the mission of Dr Gunnar Jarring, the United Nations Special Envoy. Instead, he advocated the convening of an Islamic summit in which the potential of all Islamic countries would be mobilized against Israel. Needless to say, Nasser was extremely antagonistic to what he still perceived as a basically reactionary idea, considering the Arab world and 'Arabism', rather than Islam, as the legitimate and acceptable vehicle for political action. This philosophical divergence between the two leaders was never bridged.

It was the Saudi leaders, however, who scored the initial diplomatic victory. Genuinely concerned over the fire at Jerusalem's Al-Aqsa Mosque in August 1969, and aware of her status as the guardian of Islam, Saudi Arabia used her increasing diplomatic and financial influence in the region and the Muslim world to convene an Islamic Conference in Rabat in September 1969. The conference, which passed a resolution condemning Israel, served to confirm the leadership of Saudi Arabia in the Islamic world. Indeed when an Arab summit was convened three months later, also in Rabat, Saudi Arabia was instrumental in ensuring its failure by categorically refusing to increase her financial support for the Arab confrontation states. Irked by Saudi intransigence, Nasser walked out of the meeting, declaring that the other Arab heads of state were not prepared to participate in the battle against Israel. Although relations between the two leaders were no longer antagonistic, Saudi-Egyptian relations from 1967 to Nasser's death in September 1970, were not congenial.

Sadat's succession to power ushered in an immediate improvement in Saudi-Egyptian relations. Sadat was a devout Muslim, pro-west and conservative in his political orientation, and a man who seemed ready to accept Saudi Arabia's position at the centre of Middle Eastern politics. By 1972, after Sadat had overcome a number of domestic challenges to his authority, Egypt steadily began turning to Saudi Arabia for political consultation and financial aid, at the expense of Libya which at the time was politically linked to Egypt in the Federation of Arab

4

Republics. Faisal was kept closely informed of the gradual deterioration in Soviet-Egyptian relations, and it is interesting to note that the Saudi Defence Minister, Prince Sultan, was in Cairo when Sadat made his dramatic move to expel all Soviet advisers from Egypt in July 1972. In the wake of Sadat's 'electric shock', Riyadh promptly dispatched a military mission to 'study' with the Egyptians the effect of the severance of the Soviet arms supplies on Egypt's military capability. It was decided then that Saudi Arabia would offer the necessary additional financial assistance to help Egypt extricate herself from Soviet political and military influence.

Egypt however, found it difficult to purchase arms from western nations. Consequently, she had to turn again to the USSR, but this time it was no longer necessary to obtain arms on credit. In a meeting of the Arab Defence Council in Cairo in late January 1973, Saudi Arabia authorized the Egyptian leaders to negotiate a massive arms deal with Moscow, to be paid for in hard currency by Saudi Arabia, in conjunction with other Gulf states. In addition, the Gulf states, led by Saudi Arabia, provided Egypt with nearly $500 million in 1973 to bolster her ailing economy. By the end of March, a *de facto* alliance between Egypt and Saudi Arabia had taken place. Sadat was candid about his relations with the rulers in Riyadh: 'There are bilateral contacts and there are indeed positive results from them. It is not the right time yet to disclose these positive results. It is better if we keep them going and if none of our enemies knows anything about them because what ultimately concerns us is the battle, the battle which is before and above everything else'.[9]

Visits by the two leaders were frequently exchanged in the following months and, for the first time, Oil Minister Yamani hinted in mid-April that Saudi Arabia might use the oil weapon if the United States persisted with her support of Israel. Also, for the first time since the mid-1960s, dissonance began to appear in Saudi-American relations. These relations had assumed much greater significance after 1967, when Saudi Arabia emerged as the economic power in the area, and Washington soon realized that the desert kingdom was no longer the weak, and somewhat subservient, client it had been in the previous decade. By the late 1960s the United States was undertaking to modernize the entire Saudi defence sector, and, in 1971, she launched a naval development programme scheduled to last twelve years, involving the supply of vessels, the training of Saudi personnel and the construction of ports. A programme called *Operation Peacehawk*, designed to modernize the Saudi Air Force, is costing an estimated $3 billion. And perhaps most crucial, a private American company was contracted to train four mechanized infantry batallions and one artillery battalion of the Saudi National Guard, the most sensitive part of the Saudi armed forces.[10]

Saudi Arabia became the primary moderate, pro-Western force in the area, consistently advocating moderation inside OPEC and using her resources to sustain and perpetuate conservative pro-western regimes. The relationship, therefore, was mutually beneficial. Saudi Arabia perceived the United States as the guarantor of the Saudi Arabian political order against subversion and disruptive forces in the area. The United States saw the Saudi regime as an influential ally in a strategically and economically important segment of the globe who was willing to demonstrate the kind of ideological attitudes advocated by the United States herself. On his visits to Morocco, Italy, Algeria, Tunisia, Egypt, France, Uganda, Chad, Senegal, Mauritania and Niger in 1972–3, King Faisal consistently preached the perils of Communist and atheist principles. In short, during the latter part of the 1960s and in the early 1970s there was a coincidence of interests between the United States and Saudi Arabia on almost every issue except one – Israel.

The Saudi government was becoming increasingly frustrated by persistent American support for Israeli policies which Saudi Arabia, as well as most Arabs, perceived as blatantly expansionist. Faisal tried to press the United States into taking up a more even-handed attitude to the Arab-Israeli issue after the expulsion of the Soviet advisers from Egypt in July 1972. He emphasized to President Nixon would be in an awkward position if the United States Administration allowed this opportunity to slip by, and he stressed that the justification of American support for Israel by reference to the Russian presence in Egypt was no longer valid. Continued American support for post-1967 Israel would be interpreted by all Arab states as proxy-aggression. This would further alienate the Arabs from the United States government, and would place the pro-American Saudi regime in an untenable position. However, to the increasing annoyance of Riyadh, no such shift in the American approach resulted.

By mid-1973, Saudi Arabia's attitudes towards the Arab-Israeli conflict and the oil weapon were changing rapidly as she became convinced that the United States was not willing to apply pressure on Israel to withdraw from the occupied territories. She was equally convinced that Israel would not voluntarily relinquish these territories – particularly the Holy City of Jerusalem – and that only through a further Arab-Israeli war might the Jewish state be forced to yield them up. In such a situation – and given her limited military capability – Saudi Arabia's most effective contribution to the war effort would be the use of the 'oil weapon'. When Sadat visited Riyadh in August 1973 to report on the preparations for war, Faisal told him that Saudi Arabia was prepared to use the oil weapon this time. The King added: 'But give us time. We don't want to use the oil as a weapon in a battle which only goes on for two or three days and then stops. We want to see a battle which goes on for long enough for world public opinion to be mobilized.'[11]

Ten days after the Egyptian and Syrian attacks on Israeli positions on 6 October, 1973, the Arab members of OPEC met in Kuwait and decided upon a policy of successive 5 per cent monthly cuts from the September 1973 level of oil production, which would continue until Israel withdrew from all occupied Arab territory. Saudi Arabia immediately reduced her level of oil production by 10 per cent. On 4 November, at a further meeting in Kuwait, the Arab oil producers resolved to reduce output across the board by 25 per cent of the September level, but the Saudi cutback was higher still: by mid-November, she had reduced her output by 30 per cent. These primarily political moves were augmented by dramatic increases in the price of oil. From $3·01 per barrel in September 1973, the price shot up to a staggering $11·65 per barrel four months later.[12] The effect on Saudi Arabia's economic power was stunning. Her oil revenue increased from $4·3 billion in 1973 to $22·6 billion in 1974, and her gross domestic product grew by nearly 250 per cent in a year.[13]

By the beginning of 1974 therefore, Saudi Arabia had been propelled by a combination of political and economic factors to a position of pre-eminence and centrality in the area. Her political leadership of the oil boycott, its resultant financial impact on the world economy, and the prominence of her huge oil reserves, had finally transformed the desert kingdom from a rather unimportant client state to a regional power of considerable consequence, whose influence extended far beyond the confines of the Middle East.

II. THE BACKGROUND TO SAUDI POLICY

Values and Attitudes

There were seven fundamental goals in the Second Saudi Five-Year Development Plan for 1975–80. Four were concerned with broad issues of economic and social development, such as increasing economic growth, reducing dependence on oil, developing the physical infrastructure, and improving human resources. The other three, however, had much wider moral and political connotations and were directly related to the basic attitudes of the Saudi political elite and the values of Saudi society. Indeed, the first two goals of the plan were stated as 'maintaining the religious and moral values of Islam' and 'assuring the defence and internal security of the Kingdom'. The third purported to 'foster social stability under circumstances of rapid social change'. Indeed it can be argued that the achievement of this third goal is a necessary pre-condition for realizing all the others.

The most fundamental value of the Saudi regime is security, both in its internal and external manifestations: the defence of the country, by whatever means, against perceived external threat, and the maintenance of domestic, political and social stability. Internally, stability is sought through the vigorous centralization of political control, so that maintenance of the authority of the ruling elite tends to pervade almost all political activity inside the kingdom. While it could be legitimately argued that elite survival through internal political stability is the concern of all regimes, it is a particularly potent impulse in the case of Saudi Arabia for a number of reasons.

In the first place, society and the regime in Saudi Arabia are almost inseparable. The *name* of the kingdom itself attests this fact. The pervasiveness of personalized leadership in Middle Eastern political systems is nowhere more predominant, and the Saudi rulers see their own permanence as an essential facet of the country's survival. Secondly, the country's immense wealth could prove to be a considerable destabilizing factor for its political system. The unequal distribution of wealth, which favours the Royal Family, is bound to create resentment among the other members of society. As long as the country's wealth continues to satisfy the demands of all levels of its society, this particular danger is minimized. However, sudden shifts in world markets, inflationary pressures and new technological breakthroughs could bring about a rapid economic depression that might stimulate societal schisms. Moreover, Saudi wealth has been the primary catalyst of the country's economic and social modernization – a process that could itself be disruptive, because it is bound to lead to clashes with traditional values upon which the fabric of the society and the political system rests. Both these factors make it essential for the regime to maintain strict and effective central control.

In Saudi Arabia, as in other Middle Eastern societies, 'political modernization lags far behind social and economic development. The former would be likely to shake the very core of the power structure, and no regime proposes to bring about its own demise by political reform detrimental to its hold on power. The notion that without a strong centre the whole society may fall apart is no figment of the imagination – no mere rationalization on the part of the rulers'.[14] The Saudi rulers have already begun to experience the destabilizing manifestation of the country's increasing wealth and the disparity between the speed of her economic development and her restricted political liberalization. Seventeen officers and a large number of civilians were tried in October and November 1977 for plotting against the regime, including three Air Force officers tried *in absentia* after flying their planes to Iraq. The objective of the plotters seems to have been the overthrow of the Royal Family and the establishment of a democratic, revolutionary state. These concerns were further heightened by the occupation of the Grand Mosque of Mecca in November 1979 by tribally-based religious zealots.

The Saudi rulers must guard against external threats as well. They are well aware that the country's vast riches may constitute a very attractive target for a covetous and powerful neighbour. The Minister of Information, Muhammed Abdu Yamani, voiced these fears: 'We are a very appealing piece of cake. There are lots of people who would dearly love to get a slice of us'.[15] Saudi Arabia feels this insecurity not only because of her vast wealth, but also because of her strategic position, bordering on such radical states as Iraq and the People's Democratic Republic of Yemen (PDRY) who consider Saudi Arabia as the base for 'imperialist' penetration in the area. Even more worrying is the current instability in the Red Sea and the Horn of Africa. Saudi Arabia could not have welcomed the massive Soviet and Cuban involvement in the Ethiopian conflict, a conflict whose repercussions could easily have rebounded on her. This is why the Defence Minister, Prince Sultan, insisted that all the Saudi regime wanted was 'to keep the Red Sea free from regional and international disputes',[16] and why the peaceful settlement of disputes thus constitutes a primary Saudi goal in the region. Conflicts create instability, which in turn is bound adversely to affect the security of the states in the region.

Security and stability, therefore, are paramount in Saudi thinking and calculations. According to Deputy Prime Minister Prince Fahd, the country's strong man, Saudi Arabia's major concern is that she lives 'in an area characterized by instability'.[17] However, this concern is not confined solely to the Gulf region. Thus, according to Sheikh Ahmad Zaki Yamani, Minister for Petroleum and Mineral Resources:

The security and stability of the oil-producing countries is of the utmost importance not only to the producers themselves but to the world at large. The security of oil supplies, so important to consumer countries is totally dependent on the security and stability of the oil producing states . . . The countries of the world, be they oil suppliers or consumers, have a common vested interest in the security and continuity of oil supplies. Therefore their co-operation in combating any threat to peace in the Middle East is an absolute and constant necessity.[18]

It is therefore easy to understand Saudi Arabia's close relationship with the United States, which is motivated by the 'common vested interests' of the two countries. The interest of neither state would be served by violent disruptions, revolutions, or abrupt changes in the region. Fear of instability also explains Saudi Arabia's almost pathological fear of Communism and of the Soviet Union, perceived as the primary agent of disruptive change in the Third World. As one high government official succinctly put it: 'In the underdeveloped world, we see the threat of radicalism – and we can put our money where the Communists' mouths are'.[19] Finally, the Saudi quest for global stability is clearly manifested in a deep concern about international economic relations, especially as they relate to the western economic crises of the 1970s. In an interview, Prince Fahd explained:

We believe that world economic stability is the most important pillar of world peace . . . The spread of international economic crises distracts efforts to achieve peace in the Middle East. Accordingly, when the Kingdom of Saudi Arabia . . . decided on a 5 per cent increase in oil price against the 10 per cent recommendation of the other members of OPEC . . . it was only taking into consideration the interests of the international community and world stability in the hope that peace would be returned to those regions that have been deprived of peace and, most importantly of course, to the Middle East. We are a part of the world, and we see our oil interests linked to the question of economic peace.[20]

There is no doubt that this almost total preoccupation with security, and hence with global, regional and domestic stability, is a crucial aspect of Saudi attitudes, born of the ruling elite's basic impulse for survival and self-perpetuation. However, it is by no means the only one. Unlike security policy, domestic and foreign policies have been influenced by an equally powerful force, rooted in the historical legacy and cultural traditions of Saudi society as a whole – the religious and moral values of Islam.

The Role of Islam

The influence of Islam is powerful and pervasive, not only in Saudi Arabia but in the entire Middle East. It is the religion of the overwhelming majority of Middle Eastern populations, many of whose values and norms emanate from the inspiration and moral teachings of Islam. Moreover, the position and prestige of Islam as a motivating force is reinforced in the Arab world by the fact that the richest heritage of Arab history is usually traced to the glorious years of the vast Arab Islamic Empire. Consequently, the acknowledgment of the role and influence of Islam in Arab society is not confined, as is sometimes thought in the West, to the traditional, conservative Arab countries, but also affects the Western-oriented and even the revolutionary Arab states. Thus it was at the height of Egypt's radical activity in the early 1960s that a central figure in Egypt's political leadership, Kamal al-Din Hussein, admitted that 'the Arab people believe in the mission of religion (which) is a basic component on which Arab society is based'.[21] Hence, the concept of secularism, vigorously undertaken by the more 'modernization conscious' states of the Arab world, has (not surprisingly) proved to be superficially and tenuously based. For example, widespread and violent rioting greeted the announcement of Syria's secularist constitution in March 1973, with the demonstrators demanding the inclusion of a provision pertaining to the status of Islam as the official religion of the state. The riots subsided only when the Constitution was modified to include a stipulation that the President must be an adherent of the Islamic faith. Similar manifestations of underlying widespread religious fervour and loyalties have occurred in Egypt, Iraq, Lebanon, Libya, Morocco and Sudan. This is because, unlike Christianity, Islam dictates the social, political, legal and cultural system. In the *Sharia*, the Moslems have a law that deals with all constitutional and legal matters and as such is treated, in orthodox Islamic theory, as the only legally acceptable code. Consequently, to the devout Moslem there can be only one legitimate system of government and that is derived from

Islam. Conflict with the Western concept of secularism is therefore inevitable, and the frequency with which it has occurred since independence testifies to the immense influence of Islam in Arab society.

Islam as a motivator of Saudi policies and purveyer of Saudi-elite attitudes is particularly potent. While other Moslem countries can boast thriving civilizations that pre-dated the advent of Islam – like Pharaonic Egypt, Babylonian Iraq, Phoenician Syria and Lebanon and Achaemenid Iran – Saudi Arabia's cultural heritage and historical legacy is traceable to the Islamic civilization alone. 'For this reason, Saudi Arabian culture, civilization, and socio-political organization are coterminous with Islam. Only when this is understood can the essence of the Saudi policy and the pervasive intensity of the unbroken Islamic continuum be appreciated'.[22]

Part of this cultural and religious awareness relates to the existence of the two sacred cities of Islam, Mecca and Medina, within Saudi Arabia's borders. Not only is Mecca the Prophet Mohammed's birthplace but it also houses the *Ka'aba*, the most venerated building in Islam, traditionally held to have been built by Adam, and rebuilt by Abraham and Ismail. A pilgrimage to Mecca is the duty of every Moslem. Medina is the city in which the Prophet died, and where he is buried; it also contains the tombs of Fatimah, the Prophet's daughter, and of Abu Bakr and Umar, the first and second Caliphs. There is no doubt that the two cities, called by the Prophet Mohammed the Two Sacred Enclaves, contribute considerably to Islam's primordial influence in Saudi Arabia.

This centrality is reinforced by the strict discipline of *Wahabism*, a fundamentalist Islamic sect which preaches the purification of Islam from what it perceives as alien customs and rituals and a return to Islamic doctrines and precepts as they existed under the Prophet Mohammed. It maintains that the cult of sainthood, the worship of saints and holy men, the adoration of their tombs and remains, and other such innovations are contradictory to the true spirit of Islam. In a speech to pilgrims, King Khalid articulated these sentiments by emphasizing the Moslem duty of following in the footsteps of Islam's 'ancestral peers and steering away from innovation that is incompatible with

the Book of God and the traditions of his Messenger'.[23] The penetration of Wahabist principles into the Arabian Peninsula dates back to 1744, when the ruler of the al-Nejd region, Mohammed bin Saud, became a fervent follower of Imam Mohammed bin Abd al-Wahab, the founder of the sect. They were later embodied in the Saudi political and social system by King Abd al-Aziz, the founder of modern Saudi Arabia.

Islamic, particularly the fundamentalist Wahabist, principles permeate the perceptions, attitudes and orientations of Saudi society. Thus according to King Khalid: 'We Moslems, the more we hold fast to these eminent [Islamic] ideas, the better are our prospects to get up and bring the world under our control. On the other hand, the further we veer away from our faith the faster we succumb to factors of decay and start suffering from social and political ills and eventually fall an easy prey to the enemies of Islam who are lying in ambush to attack us'.[24] This is no empty rhetoric. Islamic ideals have contributed considerably to the unique character of the Saudi political system, the most basic premise of which is the inseparability of state and religion. Thus, for example, the entire legal system is 'so steeped in Qu'ranic values that even what appears to be "secular" litigation is adjudicated within the jurisprudence of Islam. There is no corpus of colonial or western precedent to use; the disposition of judges and the precedents used are hence exclusively Qu'ranic'.[25] In this context Prince Abdallah, Head of the National Guard, once unequivocally stated: 'Saudi Arabia has a constitution inspired by God and not drawn up by man. I do not believe there is any Arab who believes that the Koran contains a single loophole which permits an injustice to be done. All laws and regulations are inspired by the Koran, and Saudi Arabia is proud to have such a constitution'.[26] The operational manifestation of this religious penetration into the political system is clearly discernible from an examination of Saudi Arabia's domestic and foreign policies.

Domestically, everyday life is supposed to be conducted according to Wahabist Islamic principles. The consumption and sale of alcohol are strictly prohibited. Blasphemy and adultery are severely, even barbarously, punished. Public leisure centres, such as cinemas and theatres, are

9

universally banned. Education is closely supervised according to Islamic imperatives. And the population is consciously encouraged – and sometimes forced, through the use of the religious police *al-Matawah* – to observe public prayers five times a day.

In the foreign-policy area, Saudi displeasure with laxity among her neighbours has resulted in stricter and more puritanical enforcement of Islamic principles as in the case of Kuwait after King Khalid's visit in 1976. Similar pressures, through the use of foreign aid, have been brought to bear on countries such as Egypt, Sudan and Pakistan: the recent introduction of Islamic laws and regulations in these countries, supplanting long-standing secular statutes and litigations, testifies to the Saudi missionary zeal. In both the domestic and the international arenas, therefore, Islam is far more than a mere rhetorical subject for the ruling elite. It pervades social customs and interactions. It dominates images and attitudes. It motivates policies and is used to justify them. And it embodies the system of values upon which the legitimacy of the regime rests.

Capabilities and Constraints

The Economy

To most westerners Saudi Arabia is synonymous with oil. While it has always been an important part of the country's wealth, since 1974 – when the price of crude suddenly quadrupled – oil has transformed Saudi Arabia into a financial super-power (since the 1973 war it has contributed more than 73 per cent of her Gross Domestic Product). Her oil revenue rose from $4·3 billion in 1973 to $22·6 billion in 1974 and $41·6 billion in 1977.[27] Moreover, her proved crude oil reserves are some 110 billion barrels, with probable reserves of another 67 billion barrels, and much more still to be found.[28] Between 1972 and 1976, the Saudi budget grew elevenfold,[29] with pronounced increases in expenditure on defence, agriculture and industry and transport and communications.

During the first half of this decade, the First Five-Year Plan was in operation, and as a result the Saudi economy grew very rapidly, considerably helped by the explosion in oil prices. The major emphasis of the plan was on agricultural and industrial development and on communications. Two massive dams were built in Wadi

Juzan and al-Abha region, and two major irrigation and land reclamation projects were undertaken. Industrial projects included the Petromin Lubricating Oil Company in Jeddah, a sulphuric acid plant in Daman, expansion of the oil refinery and the steel-rolling mill in Jeddah, construction of an oil refinery in Riyadh, and a long-term programme for the exploitation of mineral resources. In addition, the national road network, a vital component of the economy's infrastructure, was substantially increased to 700 miles of paved roads. Although not all the envisaged projects were finished according to schedule, the First Five-Year Plan was, nevertheless, a striking success.

The Second Five-Year Plan (1975–80) is much more ambitious and, as Table 1 shows, requires an expenditure of $141 billion (a twelvefold increase on the first plan made possible by the massive post-1973 increase in oil revenues). Its primary emphasis is on diversifying the economy by developing new non-petroleum industries and distributing them to the best geographical advantage. The concomitant intended reduction in dependence on oil revenues

Table 1: The Second Five-Year Plan, 1975–80

Programme	Appropriations ($ m)	%
Water and Desalination	9,650	6·84
Agriculture	1,327	0·94
Electricity	1,768	1·25
Industry and Minerals	12,764	9·04
Education	21,009	14·88
Health	4,901	3·47
Social and Youth Welfare	4,150	2·94
Roads, Ports and Railways	6,029	4·27
Civil Aviation	4,205	2·98
Post and Telecommunication	1,197	0·85
Municipalities	15,107	10·70
Housing	4,041	2·86
Pilgrimage	1,416	1·00
Other Development	2,638	1·87
Defence	22,141	15·69
Public Administration	10,816	7·67
Financial Institutions	17,892	12·74
Total	141,051	100·00

Source: Kingdom of Saudi Arabia, *Second Development Plan, 1395–1400 A.H., 1975–1980, A.D.* (Riyadh: Ministry of Planning, 1975), p. 530.

in the long term is witnessed by the projected decline in the hydrocarbon sector's involvement from 86 per cent to 82 per cent over the plan's duration.[30] Another primary goal is to develop further the existing infrastructure by modernizing the presently struggling municipalities and by improving the manpower base through the expansion of education, health and social welfare.

Industrial expansion is dependent upon the development of two major industrial towns – Jubail in the Gulf and Yanbu' on the Red Sea – at an estimated cost of $70 million. These two industrial centres (whose construction is scheduled to continue well into the 1980s and perhaps beyond) are planned around hydrocarbon-processing industries using crude oil and natural gas from Saudi Arabia's massive $10 billion gas-gathering programme. An 800-mile pipeline costing $1 billion is being built to bring crude from the eastern Saudi oil fields to Yanbu', thus linking the Red Sea port with the Gulf oil fields. The projects at Yanbu' include a refinery with a capacity of 500,000 barrels a day, a petrochemical plant and an export terminal for oil and liquified natural gas. In addition to a number of refineries and petrochemical plants, the Jubail Complex will also include an aluminium smelter, a steel mill, several power-generating plants, an extensive telecommunications system, the world's largest water desalination complex, two deep-water ports and an international airport.

Some of these plants are expected to be owned by the Saudi private sector, mainly in joint ventures with Western and Japanese concerns. (Joint ventures have already been negotiated by a number of American companies, including Exxon, Grace and Mobil). This is in line with a conscious policy of stimulating the private sector. Since 1971 the Saudi Government has channelled upwards of $12 billion into the private sector through six special state-owned funds – the Saudi Industrial Development Fund, the Public Investment Fund, the Real Estate Development Fund, the Agricultural Bank, the Credit Bank and the Contractors' Fund. Another effort to encourage the indigenous private sector was the Cabinet's decree of May 1977 that all foreign banks had to sell a majority of their ownership to Saudi nationals within one year. This came six months after the Ministry of the Interior enforced a ban on foreigners

working as local merchants, giving them until the end of 1977 'to wind up their businesses'. This commitment to the private sector and encouragement of economic nationalism clearly shows that the Second Five-Year Plan is not meant to restrict itself purely to economic objectives but is clearly designed to achieve wider ideological and political goals.

While successful in many of its stated objectives, the plan is facing a number of fundamental problems to do with the immense volume of appropriations and the speed with which results are sought. These make its feasibility somewhat questionable. Even Prince Fahd himself has voiced certain reservations about the successful implementation of the plan, given Saudi Arabia's weak economic and administrative infrastructure.[31] The greatest problems lie in the plan's projection of materials and manpower requirements. The original estimates were so ambitious that a considerable gap was bound to occur between planned projects and the availability of the materials for them. This was especially true of construction projects. The unavailability of sufficient materials to start projects has meant that the Saudi planners have been forced to delay or even eliminate some of them. However, due to the absence of a clear guideline of priorities in the plan, this selection process has, on the whole, been haphazard.

The second major problem is the quantitative and qualitative deficiencies in manpower at all levels of the economy. Saudi Arabia's small and under-skilled population simply cannot sustain the ambitious targets of the plan, and importing foreign labour has thus been necessary in order to achieve the envisaged programmes (see Table 2 on p. 14). Indeed, the plan itself called for imported skilled and unskilled labour amounting to more than one-third of the total work force. However, there was no guarantee that such a large number could be available, and even if it were, it would almost certainly introduce a problematic, and probably disruptive, element into Saudi society. Moreover, the need to provide the immigrant labour with somewhere to live would increase the need to import already scarce construction materials, and more foreign workers would have to be imported to build necessary housing and manage the service industries. The result would be more bottlenecks, higher costs and societal disruption.

Whatever development problems she is facing, however, Saudi Arabia is in the fortunate position of having to come to grips with the problems of plenty rather than the problems of scarcity. The economy's limited absorptive capacity and lack of administrative capacity may prove to be constraints on her long-term economic and social development, but this is more than balanced by the broad political influence generated by Saudi Arabia's huge oil revenues, and consequent financial capability. And, as will be seen, the Saudi leaders have proved extremely adept at using this asset.

Religion

As a crucial component of the society's value system, the influence of Islam in Saudi Arabia is pervasive and far-reaching, and it acts both as a motivator of and a limitation on policy. Among the traditionally devout and conservative Moslem population of the Middle East generally, and in Saudi Arabia specifically, Islam has tended to form an effective instrument for gaining and maintaining public support for the ruling elite. This phenomenon has been manifested both domestically within Saudi Arabia and in both the Arab and Moslem worlds.

Domestically, the normative imperatives of Islam in themselves tend to bestow legitimacy on Saudi Arabia's centralized structure of political authority. Islamic law, embodied in *al-Sharia*, is regarded as the Command of God (Allah) and as such cannot be questioned or rescinded by man. *Al-Sharia* is based not only on the Koran, but also on the *Sunna* (the traditions based on the sayings of the Prophet), the *Ijma'i* (the consensus of the Moslem community) and the *Qiyas*, or analogy. The first major decision under the guidance of *Ijma'i* was the election of the first *Khalifa* (Successor) on the death of the Prophet Mohammed. He was given religious and political authority, a decision based on the *Sunna* that 'religious and temporal power are twins'. Islam, through *al-Sharia*, therefore, prescribes the concentration of religious and political power in the hands of one man, *Al-Khalifa*, who is considered as the successor of the Prophet Mohammed. While *Al-Khalifa* as an institution has been politically extinct since the collapse of the Ottoman Empire, the idea of personalized authority and central control still forms an important component of

Islamic cultural values in general and of Saudi society in particular. This religiously-based concept of obedience to the ruler was later reinforced by the pronouncements (*Ijtihad*) of a number of renowned Moslem jurists, theologians and philosophers in the centuries following the death of Mohammed who 'fostered the belief that rebellion was the most heinous of crimes, and its doctrine came to be consecrated in the juristic maxim, "sixty years of tyranny are better than an hour of civil strife".' [32] Such a doctrine, particularly as it purports to be divinely-inspired, is bound to cement the power of the authoritarian and oligarchic regime in Saudi Arabia, the most Islamic of Moslem societies.

Accordingly, the regime uses religion as a unifying agent for the population and as a legitimizing factor for the political leadership. It vigorously reinforces the population's need for religion by encouraging religious behaviour, such as attendance at public prayers, and by the close regulation and supervision of the country's judicial and educational systems. Thus, as stated earlier, church and state in Saudi Arabia are inseparable; legal and constitutional matters are conducted by the *Ulama* (Moslem clergy) using *al-Sharia* as the only binding source of legal discourse. Descendants of the founder of the Wahabi movement, close allies of the Saud family, are usually put in charge of the judicial and the educational systems, and under their influence educational curricula are steeped in Koranic values and imperatives, emphasizing 'religious teachings and doctrine to the exclusion of some liberal arts which might introduce to the people ideas dangerous to the monarchy'.[33] As a result, both the judicial and educational systems have become effective channels for the vigorous dissemination among the population of Islamic dogma, supportive of the regime.

The perceived guardianship of the holy places in Mecca and Medina further legitimizes the political power of the Saudi monarchy by bestowing upon it divine sanction. Not only do the holy places act as potent integrating factors internally, they also accord Saudi Arabia and her rulers much esteem and prestige from Moslems throughout the world, even if, on occasion they impel the Saudi rulers to oppose moves towards a peace settlement in the Middle East, which can cause friction with the United States. To the Saudi rulers, therefore, the annual pilgrimage to

Mecca is of a political, as well as a religious, significance. The pilgrims (719,000 in 1976[34]) come not only from Arab countries, but from places as far away as Indonesia, Malaysia, Afghanistan and Pakistan in Asia, and Nigeria, Mauritania and Niger in Africa. Given the convergence of religion and state in Islamic theory, the religious importance of Saudi Arabia and her rulers has consequential political significance for her foreign policy as well as her domestic policies.

Demography

The tribally-based demographic structure of Saudi Arabia has been an asset to the regime, contributing significantly to the stability of the political system. For centuries, the pattern of political loyalty in the tribal community was hierarchical, with authority focused on the *sheikh*, or tribal chieftain. Assisted by a number of tribal elders and religious personnel, the *sheikh* acted as the central authority, the final arbiter of power and the ultimate dispenser of justice. However, he could not operate outside tribal laws and customs and was as bound by them as any member of his tribe. In the process of transferring the loyalty of the Bedouin from tribe to the nation, successive Saudi monarchs have over the last half-century tended to act, and be perceived, simply as tribal overlords. They have persisted with the custom of making the monarch accessible and available to all citizens. This is nowhere more evident than in the King's *Majlis* (council or audience chamber) in Riyadh. In true tribal fashion, the King, Prince Fahd and other senior princes hold these informal councils, which any citizen may attend, every day except Thursday and Friday (the Islamic weekend). This custom was institutionalized by King Abd al-Aziz in 1952 in a royal decree granting every subject the right of access to the Royal Family, including the Monarch himself. In these gatherings, the ruler is expected to settle disputes, take note of complaints, acknowledge proclamations of loyalty, listen to poetic renderings, or simply take part in general conversation. Monarchical adherence to tribal custom induces loyalty from a population whose demographic structure is dominated by bedouin traditions.

The size of the Royal Family (some 4,000 Princes) is an additional stabilizing factor. Executive levels of government aside, there are princes in all important levels of the administrative structure – the various bureaucratic institutions, the armed forces, the police, the customs and the coast guard. This influence is reinforced by the retinue of *Ikhwa* (brethren) who are attached to princely households, and who invariably act as another bridge between the Royal Family and the Saudi population. The omnipresence of the Household of Saud in the country ensures the effective implementation of policy and, more crucially, provides it with its own widespread intelligence network. The continuing rapid growth of the royal house will undoubtedly further cement its direct control of the kingdom. However, it clear that there are rivalries within the House of Saud, and there is evidence of differences of opinion and even antagonisms between some of the senior princes. These might in the future prove divisive, or even seriously destabilizing.

The Family has also taken measures to guard against threats arising from the changing structures of Saudi society. Under pressure from the rapidly burgeoning technocratic class, which is vigorously supported by the western-educated younger generation of princes, the governmental and bureaucratic structure has been opened up to members of the urban middle class, thus preventing the alienation of this increasingly important and sophisticated group and broadening the regime's base. The most striking manifestation of this new concern was the major reorganization of the Council of Ministers in October 1975. The number of ministries was increased from 14 to 20, and the emphasis in the new Council was clearly on the educated technocratic class. Only eight members were Princes, eleven had higher degrees, one had a bachelor's degree and two were prominent Islamic theologians. Of these doctorates, five were between the ages of 34 and 37 when appointed and had had their degrees no more than five years.[35]

The absorption of the emergent technocratic class into the Saudi governmental structure clearly points to the ability and willingness of the Royal Family to adjust and modify its attitudes to societal developments. The problem, however, is whether the pace of this adjustment can match the breathtaking speed with which Saudi society is modernizing as a result of the country's immense new wealth. In the past, the regime found it comparatively simple to balance the three compatible, even mutually reinforcing, pillars upon which the survival of the Saudi political system rested – family power, Islam and tribal allegiances. However, many aspects of twentieth-century 'modernism' (fast becoming the fourth pillar of Saudi society) are incompatible with these traditional, conservative bases. Thus, while willing to adjust, the Saudi rulers are simultaneously maintaining, and even increasing, their grip on sensitive sectors of the country's political system. In the present cabinet the Premiership and the pivotal portfolios of Defence, Interior, Foreign Affairs and the National Guard are all filled by members of the Royal Family. Similarly the governorships of the country's major provinces are entrusted to Saudi princes. It is also worth noting that the various ministers are considered as heads of department, who have advisory and implementative functions but are at no stage allowed to take independent policy actions. The formulation of policy continues to reside solely with the Royal Family, and particularly with the 'Committee of Senior Princes'. Therefore, unlike other Middle Eastern countries, whose ethnic, sectarian and ideological schisms have made a major contribution to regional instability, Saudi Arabia has suffered relatively little from such disruptions, and the unity of the population and its apparent loyalty to the throne must be seen as a source of strength for the regime.

To some extent, however, quantitative and qualitative demographic weaknesses have seriously constrained the formulation and implementation of policies. Saudi Arabia's small population cannot sustain the wide-ranging industrial and agricultural growth envisaged by her rulers, so that any expansion in the economy must depend on the importation of foreign labour. Indeed, the number of immigrant workers more than doubled between 1974 and 1976, and the Second Five-Year Plan envisages a compound annual rate of growth in immigrant labour between 1975 and 1980 of 21 per cent, compared with a 3·4 per cent rate for the Saudi work force (see Table 2).

In this case, the deficiency is qualitative as much as quantitative. A majority of the population is illiterate, grossly lacking skills. It is for this reason that much emphasis is placed on education in the Second Development Plan. The Plan's educational target entails the construction of some two thousand new schools, thus considerably increasing pre-university enrolment. Nevertheless, because of the extremely weak base, even this ambitious programme will result in only a marginal improvement in the educational level of the population as a whole. Thus, while student enrolment almost doubled between 1971 and 1976 (an impressive achievement in its own right), the number of students as a percentage of the total population only increased from 7·4 in 1971 to 11·7 in 1976. Higher and university education, in contrast, has been relatively adequate. In 1975 some 19,000 students were attending Saudi universities in 1975, and a further 5,108 were pursuing either undergraduate or graduate degrees abroad (this latter number was estimated to have increased to 8,000 in 1976, of whom 4,350 were studying in the United States).[36]

Table 2: Composition of Labour Force, 1975 and 1980

Category	Number of workers				Annual growth rate 1975–80
	1975		1980		
Saudi men	1,259,000		1,470,000		3·1%
Saudi women	27,000		48,000		15·1%
		1,286,000		1,518,000	3·4%
Non-Saudi men	306,000		768,000		20·2%
Non-Saudi women	8,000		45,000		41·2%
		314,000		813,000	21·0%
Total		1,600,000		2,331,000	7·8%

Source: Kingdom of Saudi Arabia, *Saudi Arabia Five-Year Plan, 1975–1980* (Riyadh: Central Planning Organization, 1975), p. 60.

The problem therefore does not lie with education of the top echelon, but with the level below it, where the country's reserves for trained manpower are very thin. As Foreign Minister Prince Saud put it: 'We have science professors without lab assistants and engineers without typists. We have overdeveloped in higher education and are short of intermediate personnel'.[37] However, any planning in this sector is greatly hampered by Saudi social attitudes. Many skilled and semi-skilled professions are considered to be demeaning, so that it is very rare to a see a Saudi plumber or painter, and, when it comes to female employment, it is next to impossible to find Saudi women working as nurses or typists.

Improving the population's qualitative characteristics, therefore, is as dependent on changes in basic social attitudes as on financial investment in education, health and social welfare. Yet, it is worth remembering that the values hampering Saudi advancement are the same values upon which the legitimacy of the regime rests. Efforts to undermine these values and change the attitudes that emanate from them may shake the very foundations of the country's political system. It is upon the resolution of this basic dichotomy that the future of Saudi Arabia may depend.

The Military
Until the late 1960s, the Saudi armed forces, for lack of a manpower base that was adequate either quantitatively or qualitatively, was relatively weak and extremely unsophisticated. The Saudi military capability was almost insignificant, particularly when compared with those of Iran and Iraq. However, by the late 1960s a number of factors had induced Saudi Arabia to embark upon a major arms build-up designed to modernize and considerably strengthen her military capability. Britain's announcement in 1968 of her intended withdrawal from the Gulf area certainly intensified the Saudi sense of vulnerability, coming as it did immediately after the six-year struggle with Egypt over the Yemen. And this sense of vulnerability was appreciably heightened by the impressive arms build-up undertaken by Iraq, whose leaders had more than once publicly declared their ideological antipathy towards the Saudi regime, and by the Shah of Iran's determination to fill the 'vacuum' left by

Table 3: Saudi Forces and Defence Expenditure 1973-9

	Armed forces	Para-military forces	Defence expenditure ($ m)
1973	42,500	n.a.	1,478
1974	43,000	n.a.	1,808
1975	47,000	16,000	6,778
1976	51,500	26,500	9,038
1977	61,500	41,500	7,538
1978	58,500	41,500	13,170
1979	44,500	26,500	14,184

Source: The Military Balance 1975-1976 (London: IISS, 1975), p. 79; *1976-1977*, pp. 79-80; *1977-1978*, pp. 82-5; *1978-1979*, pp. 89-91; *1979-1980*, pp. 94-7.

Britain in the Gulf. Indeed, the Iranian seizure of the three small islands at the entrance to the Gulf in 1971 acted as positive reinforcement for Saudi Arabia's perception of threat. Ideologically, the Saudi government felt increasingly threatened by the Marxist rebellion in the Dhofar province of Oman, and by the support for that rebellion by the Marxist-oriented rulers of the newly-independent People's Republic of South Yemen (PDRY). Additionally, after the June war of 1967, Saudi Arabia began to play a much more active role in the Arab-Israeli conflict, thus making herself a possible target for Israeli retaliatory strikes, and her increasing strategic importance as the world's largest holder of oil reserves served to heighten her sense of military vulnerability. By the early 1970s, especially after the October 1973 War and the subsequent oil boycott, the Saudi arms build-up was accelerated considerably (see Tables 3 and 4), and defence moved to the top of the country's priorities, claiming the highest percentage of expenditure of any programme in the Second Five-Year Plan.[38]

This massive injection of capital has resulted in the rapid modernization of the armed forces. A great number of military complexes are being constructed all over the country, naval bases are being built on the Red Sea and in the Persian Gulf, and a new air base is under construction at Tabuk in the north-west. An impressive variety of armament has been added to Saudi Arabia's arsenal; in addition to the two *Lightning* and two F-5 squadrons, the Saudi arsenal possesses a

15

Table 4: GNP and Defence Expenditure of Selected Middle Eastern Countries 1978

Country	Gross National Product	Defence	Expenditure
		$ bn	% of GNP
Saudi Arabia	64·2	13·17	15·0
Iran	75·1*	7·89*	10·5*
Iraq	15·5	1·70	11·0
South Yemen	0·5	0·06	11·2
North Yemen	1·2*	0·08*	6·6*
Egypt	18·1*	2·81*	15·5*
Syria	6·5*	1·07*	16·5*
Israel	10·5	3·31	24·5

*1977 figure.

Source: *The Military Balance 1978–1979, 1979–80* (London: IISS, 1978, 1979).

HAWK surface-to-air missile system (and has ordered an improved version of it), *Sidewinder* and *Maverick* air-to-air missiles and sophisticated tanks and artillery systems. New acquisitions will include a $10 million tactical missile factory near Riyadh and the extremely capable F-15 *Eagle* fighter, one of the most modern and most sophisticated of United States combat aircraft.

A unique structural feature of the country's defence establishment is the division of the military institution into two separate forces: the regular armed services and the National Guard. The latter, a tribally-based, para-military force also known as the 'White Army', represents a 'family army' which is intensely loyal to the Saudi leadership and which could be relied upon to safeguard the monarchy even if plotters succeeded in infiltrating the regular armed forces, as happened in late 1977.[39] It is composed of Bedouins from the Nejd Province in central Arabia, where the Saud family originated, and its traditions are those of the *Ikhwan* (Brethren), the fanatically religious and fiercely loyal irregular force assembled by the founder of Saudi Arabia, Abd al-Aziz bin Saud. Between 1902 and 1926 he used the *Ikhwan* to consolidate his hold upon Nejd and Hasa, and ultimately to drive the Hashemites out of al-Hijaz. They were then reorganized under the label of the 'White Army' and entrusted with the sole responsibility of safeguarding the Royal Family. The ruling elite trust in this body is such that the defence of the oil fields is entrusted not to the regular armed forces but to the National Guard. Nonetheless, the inherent caution of the Royal Family has produced further elaborate measures to ensure their safety and survival. Both the regular army and the National Guard contain special sections assigned to guard against possible military insurrection: the air force has two counter-insurgency training squadrons, and the King's personal protection is assigned to the Royal Guard, a battalion of hand-picked, meticulously-trained and loyal Bedouins.

The two military establishments are thus meant not only to complement one another in the defence of the country, but also to counterbalance one another in any internal political struggle. The two forces have separate roles, training, logistics, budgetary appropriations, and channels of command – the regular forces fall within the jurisdiction of the Defence Minister, Prince Sultan, while the National Guard is run by the Second Deputy Prime Minister, Prince Abdullah. The American military mission in Saudi Arabia has a complement of 10,000 acting as advisers, trainers and technical experts with the regular armed forces. Alongside nationals of other countries such as Britain, France, Iran and Pakistan, American advisers have been entrusted with training Saudis to use the highly sophisticated weaponry that their country's oil revenues have purchased for them. The same is being done for the National Guard, where 75 American officers, plus 308 American contract personnel attached to the Vinnell Corporation of Los Angeles, have been trying to mechanize four battalions and modernize the entire Guard. The impressively modern headquarters and training facilities of the Guard near Riyadh is some indication of the scope of this vastly expensive modernization process.

However, all this effort and military hardware has not changed Saudi Arabia's status; she remains a second-rate military power. The standing army is very small, the quality of the rank and file remains inferior, and as much as 80 per cent of the $7·5-billion military budget of 1977 was spent on developing the infrastructure rather than on weapons. The money was primarily used 'to put the bases together, give them roads, houses, schools and the trimmings'.[40] One major handicap, apart from the shortage of manpower, is the lack of a modern military tradition: troops who only a few years ago were patrolling the country on camels are now expected to be efficient handlers of sophisticated tanks, computerized missile systems and supersonic jet fighters. A further problem could be the effect of rapid military modernization on the traditional tribal loyalties of a Bedouin army. Moreover, the problem of skills is exacerbated by the existence of a dynamic private sector offering lucrative rewards which are bound to attract the qualified personnel from the armed forces; as a result, all three branches of the armed services are under strength, effective and respected leadership is slow to develop, discipline remains lax, and motivation is low. It is because of this that in March 1977 the armed forces received wide-ranging salary increases of between 20 per cent and 120 per cent. The monthly salary of a private was more than doubled from $240 to $528, and a general's salary increased from $3,150 to $3,620 a month.[41] Moreover, the newly-proposed National Service Programme will, according to Deputy Defence Minister Prince Turki bin Abd-al-Aziz, contain 'attractive financial and moral incentives to encourage young men to join the armed forces in order to achieve full strength, as well as to do away completely with foreign assistance'.[42] Nevertheless the Saudi armed forces continue to lack an offensive capability and, from the evidence so far, there is not much hope that they can acquire such a capability in the years to come. Indeed, the ability of the army to defend Saudi Arabia effectively against some of her regional neighbours is highly questionable, and this acts as a constraint on policy. She dare not push things to the point of open hostility.

III. THE POLITICS OF SAUDI SECURITY

Because of the importance assigned to security and Islam in Saudi Arabia, the Saudi rulers have followed policies designed to safeguard and enforce both. However, since she lacks an effective military capability, Saudi Arabia owes her growing global prestige and influence over regional and international actors to her vast financial resources. Considerably outweighing the economy's absorptive capacity, these resources have allowed her to accumulate large financial reserves that have been used as an instrument of foreign policy.

Saudi Arabia's external assets at the end of 1977, were in the region of $60 billion, or around 25 per cent of the total financial reserves of all member-states of the International Monetary Fund (IMF). Moreover, the earnings on those assets are expected to exceed $8 billion in 1980 and $10 billion in 1981. Indeed, even if oil production is not accelerated, Saudi Arabia's reserves are expected to continue to increase – reaching a staggering $111 billion in 1980, which will constitute about 35–40 per cent of the total projected financial reserves of *all* IMF countries.[43]

This massive capital surplus has made Saudi Arabia a principle source of aid to the developing countries, particularly the Arab and Islamic states; and in 1977 the total value of grants and soft loans she promised to third-world countries was second only to that promised by the United States. As a percentage of her GDP, however, Saudi Arabia's aid is the largest in the world: total grants and loans promised to developing countries increased from $221 million (2·7 per cent) in 1972–3 to $5·7 billion (13·8 per cent) in 1975–6. Indeed, between 1973 and 1975, the Saudi government provided $10·5 billion in foreign aid, of which $6 billion was in the form of gifts and credits to third-world countries (the remainder being loans to international institutions). In order to standardize these ever-increasing foreign aid operations, the Saudi Fund for Development was established; in addition, Saudi Arabia has participated in the establishment of the Islamic Development Bank and the Arab Investment Corporation, which aim to finance development projects in Arab and Islamic developing countries. Saudi Arabia also invested large sums for the Arab Military Industrial Organization (AMIO) but, as a mark of displeasure, withdrew support when the Arab-Israeli Peace Treaty was signed because AMIO was to have based its operations in Egypt.

In examining the direction of Saudi financial assistance, it is significant that the bulk of the aid went to Moslem and Arab countries (see Table 5). Thus, 96 per cent of aid in 1976 went to Islamic countries with 70 per cent going to Arab states. However, Saudi Arabia's financial activities are not confined to foreign aid to developing

17

Table 5: Saudi Aid in 1975 and 1976 ($ m)

Recipients	1957	% of Total	1976	% of Total
Afghanistan[b]	18·3	1·0	7·8	0·4
Bahrain[a]	1·7	0·1	100·0	4·8
Cameroun[c]	17·4	1·0	—	—
Chad[bc]	1·7	0·1	0·1	0·005
Comoro Islands	—	—	2·1	0·1
Congo[c]	—	—	4·1	0·2
Egypt[a]	948·9	53·3	496·8	24·0
Ethiopia[bc]	1·0	0·1	—	—
Gabon[c]	10·4	0·6	—	—
Guinea[bc]	—	—	0·2	0·01
Indonesia	—	—	6·9	0·3
Jordan[a]	49·3	2·8	165·0	8·0
Mali[bc]	16·0	0·9	—	—
Mauritania[ac]	—	—	94·1	4·5
Morocco[ac]	25·0	2·0	—	—
Niger[bc]	13·2	0·7	2·1	0·1
Oman[ab]	100·0	4·6	—	—
Pakistan	74·8	4·2	514·8	24·8
Rwanda[bc]	5·0	0·3	—	—
Senegal[c]	—	—	5·0	0·2
Somalia[abc]	17·2	1·0	22·8	1·2
Sudan[abc]	95·3	5·4	163·5	7·9
Syria[a]	242·2	13·6	189·8	9·1
Thailand	—	—	75·6	3·6
Togo[c]	2·0	0·1	1·1	0·05
Tunisia[ac]	19·5	1·1	—	—
Turkey	10·0	0·6	—	—
Uganda[bc]	5·3	0·3	0·1	0·005
Yemen (North)[ab]	94·8	5·3	121·8	5·9
Yemen (PDRY)[ab]	—	—	100·0	4·8
Total	**1,780·0**		**2,073·7**	
Arab States	1,603·9	90·5	1,453·8	70·1
Islamic states	1,772·0	99·6	1,990·8	96·0
Least developed states	269·2	15·1	418·4	20·2
African states	1,187·5	66·9	789·9	38·2
Non-Arab African states	70·6	4·0	12·7	0·6
Afghanistan, India, Pakistan and Bangladesh	93·1	5·2	522·8	25·2

Islamic states shown in *italic*   *a* Arab state   *b* Least developed   *c* African state
Source: Arabia and the Gulf, 24 July 1978.

18

countries; they are similarly directed at the western developed world and the international monetary system, where she has consistently endeavoured to stabilize international economic relations and to safeguard and bolster the Western economies.

Saudi Arabia, therefore, is using her vast financial assets to achieve the following goals: (1) to aid friendly contiguous states against disruptive influences in order to ensure the stability of her own immediate milieu; (2) to participate in the economic and military development of other Arab states, especially those confronting Israel; (3) to help *status-quo* powers repel Soviet and Communist influences; (4) to encourage Moslem states to re-establish and/or reinforce Islamic norms and values in their political and social systems; and (5) to safeguard and bolster the free-market competitive economic systems of the 'free world'. These goals have determined the thrust and direction of Saudi policies as they have unfolded in three separate, yet interdependent, fields of activity; the Arabian Peninsula and the Red Sea area, the Middle East region, and the international system.

The Arabian Peninsula and Red Sea Area

Saudi Arabia is without question the dominant power in the Arabian Peninsula,[44] being the largest, wealthiest and (apart from North Yemen) most populous country in the area. In the wake of the October 1973 War she became more active in asserting this dominance, particularly towards the much smaller and more vulnerable Gulf states. By the mid-1970s the states in the area – with the notable exception of South Yemen – had come to accept Saudi Arabia as the major agent for ensuring stability in the Peninsula. In order to establish and reinforce this relationship, the Saudi rulers made frequent visits to those Gulf states in which 'Gulf security' was the primary item of discussion, an initiative undertaken by the late King Faisal. The momentum was maintained by King Khalid and Prince Fahd, however, and eleven months after his succession to the throne, King Khalid, accompanied by a large delegation which included the Ministers for Foreign Affairs, Defence and Aviation, and Communications, visited the Gulf states of Kuwait, Bahrain, Qatar, Oman and the United Arab Emirates. Sheikh Zayid of Abu Dhabi was quoted as saying that 'a Saudi initiative is required to assure stability and security in the Gulf',[45] a statement which amounted to an admission by the sheikhdoms of Saudi Arabia's ascendancy in the area.

To ensure the permanence of this role the Saudi rulers, immediately after the October 1973 War, launched a vigorous diplomatic initiative to settle all the outstanding disputes, which might disrupt the stability of the area. Endeavouring to set a precedent for other Gulf states, Saudi Arabia settled her own frontier dispute with Abu Dhabi in September 1974, abandoning a long-standing claim to the Buraimi Oasis in return for territorial concessions by Abu Dhabi on the other borders between the two countries. Riyadh seems to have concluded that there was little point in trying to defend the area against external 'aggression' or internal 'alien' ideologies and influences, if frontier disputes continued to impede co-operation among the states of the region and the co-ordination of their policies. Prince Fahd emphasized the urgency of this concern in an interview in 1976, when he confided that a major priority of Saudi policy in the Peninsula was 'the speedy resolution and liquidation of all border conflicts and problems. This includes the completion of the delineation of boundaries between the Sultanate of Oman and the United Arab Emirates, the settlement of the continental shelf boundary between Saudi Arabia and Kuwait, and the settlement of the dispute between Qatar and Bahrain over the island of Hawar'.[46] That by the end of 1978, these long-standing disputes either had been settled or at least had ceased to be major irritants testifies to the vigour of Saudi Arabia's diplomacy and to the increasing influence she exerts over her immediate environment.

In conjunction with her efforts to settle the outstanding border disputes among the Gulf states, Saudi Arabia also endeavoured to strengthen the ability of the mainly conservative, pro-Western regimes of these states to counteract any internal or external threats to their survival. It must be remembered that the majority of the neighbouring Gulf states have always contained the seeds of potentially serious internal dislocations. For example, of Kuwait's one million inhabitants only 40 per cent are indigenous: as much as 25 per cent are Palestinian, Egyptians and Iranians constitute a further 16 per cent, and the rest of the population consists of substantial communities of Iraqis, Jordanians, Indians and Pakistanis.[47] Similarly, only a quarter of the populations of Qatar and the United Arab Emirates could be classified as original inhabitants of the area, the rest being made up of other Arabs (particularly Palestinians, Egyptians and Yemenis) and of Iranians, Indians and Pakistanis. Similar problems are encountered by Bahrain, where an influential segment of the population is of Iranian stock and there are serious Sunni-Shi'ia sectarian divisions.

Given these internal schisms, the Saudi rulers seem to have decided to strengthen the *internal* security systems of these states. Contacts with other Gulf states on this matter were started as early as 1974, but operational co-operation began in earnest only after the visit of Prince Nayef, the Saudi Minister of the Interior, to Bahrain, Qatar, Oman and the United Arab Emirates in October 1976. Six months later, Kuwait entered the security consultations, and by the end of 1979, Saudi Arabia had succeeded in co-ordinating the activities of the various intelligence organizations and in establishing Saudi Arabia as the central overseer of security activities in the area.

In trying to bolster traditional and moderate rule in the Gulf states, the Saudi rulers have vigorously discouraged any efforts by these states to liberalize conservative political and social systems. This is in keeping with the belief that such liberalization would ultimately lead to dissension and dislocation, and that centralization of political authority is an essential prerequisite for the maintenance of stability. Furthermore, western-style democratic practices are perceived as alien to Islamic principles, with their primary emphasis on the unity of religious and temporal power residing within a strong central decision-making institution. Thus, it is now widely accepted that Saudi pressure was instrumental in the dissolution of the Bahrain National Assembly in August 1975. Although King Khalid later denied Saudi involvement, it is interesting to note that, almost immediately after the denial, Saudi Arabia extended $350 million in aid to Bahrain.[48] Moreover, during his visit to Kuwait in March 1976 King Khalid is known to have voiced his concern over the degree of freedom enjoyed by that country's Parliament and press. There is no doubt, therefore, that the Kuwaiti ruler's decision to dissolve the National Assembly on 29 August 1976 and to suspend two newspapers, *al-Watan* and *al-Tali'ah* (both known for their radical, pro-Palestinian views), was undertaken with the blessing and active encouragment of Riyadh. Fearing a spillover of possible political upheavals in the fragmented Gulf societies, Saudi Arabia has insisted on the maintenance of centralized rule and the adherence to strict Islamic guidelines by the governments of the smaller Gulf states. These demands have contributed considerably to the increasing conservatism and fundamentalism of the Gulf's regimes.

Saudi Arabia's vigorous efforts to stabilize the Peninsula have naturally led to virulent anti-Soviet and anti-Communist policies. Indeed, her hostility to Communism verges on paranoia. This is because she sees Communism as diametrically opposed to her two primary values: she believes it to be both disruptive (aiming to undermine the conservative *status-quo* powers, such as Saudi Arabia) and atheistic (and, consequently, anti-Islamic). On taking office as Deputy Prime Minister in 1974 Prince Fahd gave a direct and personalized vision of his priorities, later reported in the *New York Times* of 23 December 1977: 'I intend to get the Russian Communists out of Somalia. My policy will be to help the moderate forces in Southern Yemen. I will help the Sudan resist Communist subversion.' Saudi financial aid in the Peninsula has thus been used to counter Communist influences and tendencies.

One Gulf state that had fought Communist insurgents for long periods was Oman, and, although the Marxist uprising in the Sultanate's Dhofari province had collapsed by December 1975, Saudi Arabia increased her aid to Oman so as to insure against its re-emergence. Saudi aid to Oman in 1977 included $97 million for roads, $250 million for defence, $100 million for developing copper resources, and $100 million for the development of the Dhofari province; other development loans and grants have gone to Oman's fishing industry, oil production, airport construction and improvement, and communications.[49] By the end of 1979, Saudi aid to Oman was expected to total $3 billion.

Similar aid was instrumental in persuading North Yemen to expel a considerable number of

20

Soviet advisers and reduce her reliance on the USSR. Indeed, the extensive Saudi aid has included responsibility for balancing the North Yemen's budget and alleviating her payments deficit, as well as for large-scale subventions to her armed forces. In order to ensure Sana'a's compliance with its dictates and demands, Riyadh has supplemented the economic incentive with indirect pressure on North Yemen's central authorities by manipulating a number of powerful Yemeni tribes that receive financial assistance from Saudi Arabia. Consequently, long negotiations between North Yemen's President Ibrahim al-Hamdi and the leaders of the Hashid and Bakil tribes had to be conducted through the good offices of Riyadh. Not surprisingly, Riyadh was thought to be implicated in al-Hamdi's assassination by local tribesmen, particularly as the murder occurred the day before the President (who had become increasingly irked by Saudi influence in his country) was due to travel to Aden to discuss possible unity measures with the Marxist-oriented regime of South Yemen. In fact, Saudi influence over North Yemen was such that after al-Hamdi's assassination his successor, President Ghashmi, felt obliged to confirm his new cabinet with the Saudi rulers. In late 1979 North Yemen turned again to the Soviet Union for arms and advisers because Saudi Arabia had slowed down supplies of American arms.

There have even been efforts to entice the Marxist South Yemeni regime. In return for an end to Aden's support for radical movements in the Arabian Peninsula, Saudi Arabia promised $25 million for South Yemen's five-year plan and over $100 million for other projects.[50] Additionally, she agreed to finance the expansion of the oil refinery in Little Aden and to supply the necessary crude. Since South Yemen is one of the poorest Arab countries, almost completely without natural resources, the Saudi rulers must have been more than surprised when Aden refused the offer. If anything, South Yemen stepped-up her 'disruptive' activities, culminating in the assassination of the pro-Riyadh, North Yemeni President Ghashmi, in June 1978. In retaliation, Saudi Arabia sponsored the unprecedented Arab League decision to impose sanctions against a member country with the suspension of financial and technical assistance to South Yemen. She must have realized, however, that isolating Aden would only increase its destabilizing tendencies and its dependence on the Soviet Union. Consequently, she quickly responded to Iraqi mediation during the Baghdad Summit in November 1978, and this resulted in a considerable lessening of tension between the two ideologically polarized neighbours. Nevertheless, intensified hostilities between North and South Yemen in the spring of 1979, and the consequent general mobilization of Saudi forces has exposed the inherent limitations affecting both Saudi power and its ability to ensure the stability of the Arabian Peninsula.

Relations with Iraq
Another area in which Saudi foreign policy has encountered problems has been in relations with Iraq. Indeed, Baghdad's mediating role in the dispute between Saudi Arabia and South Yemen in November 1978, was rather ironic, since Iraq, with her avowedly radical Ba'athist ideology, had always been a source of deep concern for Saudi Arabia. While not strictly speaking a part of the Arabian Peninsula, Iraq has nevertheless been actively involved in the political interactions of the region, and policies such as her irredentist claims on Kuwait, her support for the Marxist Dhofari rebels in Oman, her affinity with the South Yemeni regime, and her antipathy towards Saudi Arabia's conservative, 'pro-American' attitudes, having been perceived by the Saudi rulers as destabilizing to the area. In this case too, Riyadh has discovered that it was quite impotent to effect a reorientation in Iraqi attitudes or policies, primarily because, as an oil-rich state in its own right with a powerful military machine, Iraq could withstand more successfully the traditional Saudi financial and diplomatic pressures. Improvement in relations between the two countries was therefore dependent not so much on Saudi initiatives as on changes in Iraq's outlook. There is thus little doubt that the gradual normalization of Iraqi-Saudi relations during 1978 occurred as a result of fundamental modifications in Iraqi attitudes primarily brought about by indigenous factors. Power struggles within the Ba'ath Party leadership, disquiet in the armed forces, and the increasing alienation of the large Shi'ia community from the Sunni ruling elite (given a dramatic boost in January 1979 by the Iranian revolution) seem to have convinced the Iraqi

leaders that the pursuit of radical and revolutionary policies in the Arabian Peninsula would ultimately affect their already turbulent domestic situation. Saudi Defence Minister Prince Sultan paid an official visit to Iraq in April 1978, and, after talks with President Bakr and Vice-Chairman of the Revolutionary Command Council Saddam Hussein, he declared that there were 'no points of disagreement on any topics discussed'. The Iraqis confided that agreement had been reached 'to remedy problems of common concern'. Immediately after this visit Saudi Arabia despatched Planning Minister Hisham Nazèr to Teheran, reportedly to convey to the Shah the willingness of Iraq and Saudi Arabia to establish with Iran 'a form of co-operation in the fields of defence and security to meet any future developments in the region'. Similarly in June 1978, the Iraqi Information Minister confirmed that Iraq, Iran and Saudi Arabia were co-operating to safeguard oil routes.[51] Immediately after the fall of the Shah in January 1979, Iraqi Interior Minister Izzat Ibrahim al-Douri, an influential member of the Ba'ath Party's Command and Iraq's Revolutionary Command Council, spent seven days in Saudi Arabia discussing Gulf security.

Saudi concern over possible disruptive influence extends beyond the Arabian Peninsula to the Horn of Africa and the Red Sea area, and it was heightened with the eruption of hostilities between Somalia and Ethiopia, especially since Ethiopia was actively supported by Cuban forces. For Saudi Arabia this heralded the entry into the area of the forces of 'international Communism', with its total opposition to the two cherished values of regional stability and the preservation of Islam. In a visit to Sudan, Prince Saud al-Faisal, the Saudi Foreign Minister, spelled out this concern: 'Existing problems in the Horn of Africa should be solved through peaceful means and by the states in the region themselves without any foreign interference . . . Foreign presence in the Horn of Africa is one of the factors leading to instability and insecurity in the region . . . The kingdom is doing its best to bring about security and stability in the Horn of Africa free from big power rivalry and foreign presence'.[52]

Notwithstanding her protestations, Saudi Arabia did interfere. In her efforts to counteract the spread of 'Communist influences', she used her financial power, coupled with her 'American connection', to entice Somali President Siad Barre to sever his country's connection with the Soviet Union. Thus, Saudi Arabia reportedly gave Somalia $400 million in return for the expulsion of Soviet advisers. However, Somali defection from the Soviet camp was hardly likely to ease the tension between Somalia and the newly-installed, Soviet-backed, Marxist regime of Ethiopia.

The Saudi government maintained active support for Somalia in the latter's war with the Cuban-backed Ethiopian forces – support which took the form of economic and diplomatic assistance and the financing of arms shipments to the hard-pressed Somali forces. For example, it was reported that in February 1978 over thirty ships carrying arms and ammunition arrived in Somalia, and that most of these supplies had been paid for by Saudi Arabia; indeed Somalia received over $200 million from Saudi Arabia for the purchase of arms during this period.[52] Nor was Saudi Arabia reticent about her involvement. On 20 February 1978, King Khalid publicly called on Arab League members to support Somalia by providing her with effective assistance, saying that Saudi Arabia had already provided Somalia with moral and financial aid, and that he was prepared to provide further aid, so that Somalia could continue her war against Ethiopia. This was followed by a visit from Foreign Minister Prince Saud al-Faisal to Teheran for the purpose of co-ordinating Saudi-Iranian policy towards the conflict in the Horn of Africa. However, Saudi policy met with very little success, as the Somali war effort soon collapsed – a further example of the limitations of financial power when not accompanied by an effective military capability.

Saudi policies in the Arabian Peninsula and the Horn of Africa have been almost exclusively designed to strengthen traditional and conservative forces and to undermine the spread of what are perceived as 'disruptive' practices and 'destabilizing' influences. Shrewd use of diplomacy and financial power, in addition to Saudi Arabia's prestige as the foremost Islamic country in the area, did generate success on numerous occasions, but the failures only went to show that the leaders of a country with a small population which lacks an effective military capability cannot expect to have their own way all the time, especially when confronted by equally obstinate leaderships with their own ideological commitments. Indeed Saudi Arabia can probably go no further than she already has in her attempts to influence the foreign and security policies of her neighbours.

The Middle East Region

Saudi Arabia's foremost concern in this area is the resolution of the Arab-Israeli conflict. This emanates from the commitment to the principle of stability, and Riyadh has consistently considered the continuing Arab-Israeli conflict as a destabilizing force in the region which, if not settled quickly and equitably, would lead to major eruptions in the entire area. The Saudi concern manifests itself in two ways. In the first place, Saudi Arabia is now strategically vulnerable to Israeli air attacks. During the wars of 1967 and 1973 Saudi Arabia was perceived by Israel and the Arab world as a peripheral actor, but her increasing involvement in inter-Arab affairs, and particularly her financial support of the three Arab 'confrontation states' (Egypt, Syria and Jordan) has propelled her into the centre of Arab-Israeli activities. With the recent Saudi order of F-15 *Eagle* fighters from the United States, and the construction of an air base on Tabuk (in the north-west of the country, within striking distance of Israel), Israel might very well consider Saudi Arabia a legitimate target in any future war. Riyadh is well aware that its air defence system would not be able to counter the highly efficient Israeli Air Force, and it is therefore very much in Saudi Arabia's interest to work towards a peaceful resolution of the Arab-Israeli conflict. The Saudi rulers were among the first Arab leaders to accept the legitimacy of Israel, provided she withdrew from the Arab territories occupied after 1967. To Saudi Arabia, East Jerusalem is an occupied Arab city that must be handed over to the Arabs as a condition of any future settlement of the conflict: when asked about Saudi recognition of Israel, King Khalid replied that, before this could happen, 'Israel must be asked if it will withdraw from the occupied Arab territories, including Jerusalem. This town must regain its previous status under Arab sovereignity'.[54] This concern over the fate of Jerusalem is natural, given the country's commitment to the protection of Islam, for Jerusalem ranks as the second holiest city in Islam, after Mecca. The City houses the Dome of Rock from which, in the traditions of Islam, the Prophet Mohammed ascended into Heaven. Consequently, in addition to her (no doubt genuine) desire to safeguard the Islamic status of Jerusalem, Saudi Arabia cannot afford to be seen by Arabs and Moslems alike to be abandoning the struggle to restore the revered Islamic shrine to Arab sovereignty. It is thus explicitly stated that the pan-Islamic Secretariat for Islamic Affairs will continue to co-ordinate the activities of its 22 member states from the Saudi city of Jeddah, but only until the 'liberation of Jerusalem'.

The Palestinian issue provides another dimension of Saudi involvement in the Arab-Israeli conflict. Riyadh has consistently argued that, as long as the Palestinians do not have a state or at least a homeland, they will continue to act as a destabilizing agent in the area. Since 1973, Saudi Arabia has endeavoured to strengthen the moderate wing of the Palestine Liberation Organisation (PLO) by providing the Al-Fatah guerrilla group and its leader Yasir Arafat with considerable financial support, thus undermining the more extreme groups (most of them avowedly Marxist), such as George Habbash's Popular Front for the Liberation of Palestine (PFLP). This policy has the added advantage of enhancing Saudi Arabia's credibility and prestige in the eyes of the Arab/Moslem world, since she can be seen to be actively involved in upholding the Palestinian cause. Her problem, however, is that the perpetuation of the conflict, which she attributes to Israeli intransigence, has undermined the position of the Palestinian moderates and strengthened the extremists' argument that Israel is innately aggressive and expansionist, and as such, seems to understand only the language of force. Since 1975, therefore, the Saudi rulers have argued that the achievement of stability in the area is intrinsically and inexorably linked with progress towards a resolution of the Arab-Israeli conflict, but that peace will not be attained as long as Israel and the western world persist in dealing with peripheral issues, rather than tackling the core of the problem, namely the 'legitimate rights of the Palestinian people'. Thus, in the wake of the American Defense Secretary Harold Brown's visit to Saudi Arabia in February 1979, Foreign Minister Prince Saud al-Faisal insisted 'without a solution to the Palestinian problem, there is no hope of restoring stability . . . in the region. This is what we told Harold Brown and what we have continually stressed to our American friends'. To Riyadh therefore, 'the Palestinian case constitutes the basis of the conflict in the Middle East, and a just peace cannot be achieved, except through withdrawal from all the occupied territories, including Jerusalem, and recognition of the legitimate rights of the Palestinian people, including its right to statehood and self-determination'.[55]

Full-hearted Saudi support for the Palestinian cause was also meant to deflect the attacks mounted by the more militantly anti-Israel Arab regimes against Saudi Arabia's moderate posture. The public espousal of the Palestinian cause has tended to be an important factor in the competition for leadership, a competition which has plagued relations among the various Arab regimes since the 1950s. It was hardly a surprise, therefore, when Riyadh expressed its unequivocal support for the Palestinian guerrilla assault on 11 March 1978, in which an Israeli bus was seized and over thirty Israelis killed. The attack was described by Radio Riyadh as a 'bold move' and one which 'would serve to remind Israel and the rest of the world that the Palestinians exist and that a just peace in the Middle East is vital'.[56] Indeed, when Israel retaliated by invading Southern Lebanon in the same month, King Khalid felt compelled to despatch a strongly-worded message to President Carter urging him and his government to stop Israel's 'flagrant aggression' against Lebanon.

Although her importance began to emerge in 1967, it was the quadrupling of the oil prices in 1973 and 1974 that brought Saudi Arabia to the forefront of Arab politics. As the largest producer, it was natural for her to assume the mantle of leadership of the Organization of Arab Petroleum Exporting Countries (OAPEC). Later her massive subventions to the Arab states, particularly the so-called confrontation states, made her a pivotal actor in the Arab-Israeli conflict. This assumption of Arab leadership resulted as much from Saudi Arabia's own initiative as from the perceptions and activities of the other Arab countries. Thus, in order to explain the sudden normalization of American-Egyptian relations after Secretary of State Kissinger's visit to Cairo in January 1974, President Sadat embarked upon a diplomatic offensive in the Arab world which began in Riyadh before going on to Damascus and other Arab capitals. It was indicative of Saudi Arabia's burgeoning regional importance that, although President Assad of Syria had been Sadat's ally and 'brother-in-blood' during and after the 1973 October War, the first Arab leader to hear the details of the Sadat-Kissinger talks was not the Syrian President but the late King Faisal. The same Egyptian strategy was pursued after the signing of the Sinai Accord in September 1975, when General Husni Mubarrak, the Egyptian Vice-President, went to Riyadh to receive the all-important Saudi blessing. He delivered a detailed message from Sadat to King Khalid and then held a series of discussions with the King and other members of the Saudi monarchy in Taif. Indeed, Egypt openly admitted that Saudi Arabia's approval of the agreement had been obtained before Dr Kissinger embarked upon his mission. There is little doubt that the primacy of Saudi Arabia in Egyptian calculations and policies related in no small measure to the fact that between July 1974 and June 1975 she injected over $1,200 million into the Egyptian economy.

Similar financial contributions to other Arab countries, such as Syria, Jordan, Morocco, Tunisia and Mauritania, and to the PLO have spread Saudi influence throughout the region. And the Saudi rulers have proved themselves adept at exploiting this influence in order to promote their own policies and political attitudes. Saudi pressure upon Syria during the latter's intervention in Lebanon's civil war was a case in point, since it was Saudi Arabia's decisive intervention that halted the Syrian advance against the Palestinian and Moslem forces in Lebanon in October 1976. The Saudi leaders despatched a personal envoy to Damascus with 'an urgent and explicit message' to President Assad to attend a mini-summit in Riyadh with the leaders of Egypt, Kuwait, Lebanon and the PLO. Reluctant to antagonize their paymasters any further, the Syrian leaders accepted the invitation, and on his arrival in Riyadh President Assad declared that he had ordered his troops to stop fighting as a 'gesture of good will to King Khalid'. Moreover, the successful conclusion of the Riyadh Summit, in which the Saudi role was paramount, brought warm Syrian praise for the Kingdom 'in spearheading diplomatic efforts to end the conflict and preserve the unity of Lebanon'. Assad's acceptance of a cease-fire and his subsequent reconciliation with President Sadat, with whom relations had been extremely strained for over a year, were accompanied by a Saudi promise to reactivate the annual financial subsidy to Syria and compensate her for the economic loss incurred by the high cost of the intervention.[57]

More recently the way in which diplomatic activities after the Camp David Accord were centred on Saudi Arabia emphasized her importance. Immediately after the Egyptian-Israeli agreement was announced on 17 September 1978, a PLO delegation led by Abdul Mohsen Abu Maizer, a senior member of the PLO Executive Committee, arrived in Saudi Arabia and had talks with Prince Fahd. On 21 September, Secretary of State Cyrus Vance started a two-day visit to solicit Saudi support for the Accord. On 26 September President Assad of Syria arrived to discuss the 'evolving situation' with Prince Fahd, and the Syrian news agency said that the talks took place 'within the framework of the wise Saudi policy which always seeks to unify Arab ranks'.[58] On the same day, Egyptian Deputy Premier Hassan Tuhami, accompanied by an adviser to King Hassan of Morocco, flew to Geneva for talks with King Khalid, who was receiving medical treatment there, and four days later King Hussein of Jordan visited Saudi Arabia.

While undoubtedly enhancing the country's prestige, and consequently its influence over Arab and Middle Eastern politics, this growing regional and international status has also had its disadvantages. It has propelled Saudi Arabia into the forefront of the anti-Zionist Arab crusade, and thus increasingly compelled her to take militant stands and make uncompromising policy pronouncements on the issues of the Palestinians and Jerusalem. She cannot now revert to the passive, peninsular-oriented posture of the 1950s and 1960s, yet her growing involvement within the wider Middle Eastern context goes against her innate conservatism and her natural tendency towards moderation. This contradiction is proving to be an increasing source of trouble for Saudi foreign policy. The dilemma was evident during the Baghdad Summit of November 1978, called to discuss Arab response to the Camp David Accord. As the acknowledged guardian of Islamic and Arab rights, Saudi Arabia could hardly object to the Summit's vigorous condemnation of President Sadat's 'capitulationist' policies, yet she was loth to endorse any political or economic measure that might undermine the moderate, anti-Communist and pro-American Egyptian regime. Thus, while emphasizing that the Summit was unanimous in rejecting the Camp David agreements, Prince Fahd simultaneously insisted that there had been a consensus against policies that 'would harm the Egyptian people who had made considerable sacrifices for the Arab cause', while an official statement on behalf of the Saudi Council of Ministers deprecated the Egyptian-Israeli peace treaty, declaring that 'all decisions aiming to resolve the conflict must be taken within the framework of Arab legitimacy as defined by the resolutions of the Arab summits'.[58] Saudi Arabia's reluctance to sever diplomatic relations with Egypt nearly caused the collapse of the March 1979 meeting of Arab Foreign and Economic Ministers in Baghdad before, bowing to the constraints imposed by her growing status in the Arab Islamic world, she reversed her position and was obliged to endorse the passing of political and economic sanctions on Egypt. It seems likely, therefore, that, as Saudi Arabia's regional influence increases, the problems and contradictions surrounding the formulation and implementation of her foreign policy will become increasingly difficult to reconcile or resolve, and she will become as much the prisoner of circumstances as the leader or arbiter of the region.

Saudi Arabia and the International System

Since the mid-1970s Saudi influence has transcended the immediate region and spread to other parts of the international system. Like her increased Middle Eastern prominence, Saudi Arabia's growing international importance, particularly in the Third World, has been a function not only of her own initiative, but also of the perceptions of other countries.

Saudi Arabia's global activity, like her inter-Arab involvement, has been guided by her commitment to the two overriding values of stability and Islam. Thus in her relations with the developing world, Saudi Arabia has tended to favour Islamic or anti-Communist regimes and organizations. Pakistan, for example, was

LIBRARY OF MOUNT ST. MARY'S COLLEGE

the most favoured recipient of Saudi aid in 1976, even surpassing Egypt (see Table 5 on p. 18). In return, Pakistan has tended to comply enthusiastically with Saudi demands for the introduction of Islamic law into her legal system. Similar Saudi pressure has resulted in the incorporation of certain Islamic principles into the legal systems of Bangladesh and Mauritania, and other countries such as Chad, Gabon, Niger, Senegal, Somalia and Indonesia have been urged to do the same.

Besides the encouragement of Islam, the other basic focus of Saudi foreign policy has been demonstrated in a vigorous effort to contain, and wherever possible retard, the spread of Communist influence in the Third World. Pursuit of this objective in Somalia, North Yemen, South Yemen, Egypt and Sudan has already been mentioned, but even more indicative of Saudi Arabia's anti-Communist zeal has been her support of non-Arab, non-Islamic Zaire. In March 1977 a rebellion erupted in the Shaba province of Zaire which was actively supported by the Marxist regime of neighbouring Angola. It soon became obvious that the regime of President Mobutu Sese Seko was unable to restore order. Some 1,500 Moroccan troops were quickly flown to Zaire aboard French transport planes to stop the advance of the rebels, and by the end of April the rebels had been pushed back into Angola. Saudi Arabia was the major financier of the operation. Mobutu survived another invasion in Shaba fifteen months later, and this time he was helped by the direct intervention of French and Belgian paratroopers. However, realizing that his country needed to institute widespread economic reforms if stability were to be maintained, he embarked upon a visit to Riyadh, after which the Saudi rulers agreed to supply oil and financial assistance to shore up Zaire's faltering economy. Riyadh also urged the moderate, pro-Western African countries to organize a 'defence system' for the continent to combat 'outside interference'.[60]

Saudi involvement in Zaire and other third-world countries illustrates that when the two principal values are mutually reinforceable, the resulting foreign policy action is predictable; thus, it would be almost inevitable for Saudi Arabia to fight the spread of Communist influence in the Arab world, since this would further the causes of Islam and stability. How-ever, there have been instances of Saudi foreign involvement that have suggested a clear conflict between the two values. (One glaring example is the intermittent diplomatic and financial support accorded to the Moslem secessionists fighting against the conservative pro-American President Marcos of the Philippines.) After the Pakistani election crisis of 1977, Saudi Arabia supported the opponents of President Bhutto, and thus helped to ensure his downfall. It could be argued that this support contributed to the instability which pervaded Pakistan during the period of power struggle; however, this was due to the political orientation of the opposition, which was distinctly more Islamic and conservative than Bhutto's.[61] On the other hand, Saudi Arabia clearly supported the secularist Shah during November and December 1978, in the latter's struggle against the Iranian Moslem clergy. These examples indicate that neither the anti-Communist nor the Islamic instinct takes permanent precedence over the other, but that adherence to one at the expense of the other is dictated by pragmatism and politics.

In the wider context of the East-West divide, Saudi Arabia, motivated by her two primary values, places herself firmly in the Western camp. The industrialized countries of the West have, since 1974, been absorbing the bulk of Saudi trade at an ever-increasing rate. A great proportion of this trade is done with the United States, but Western Europe and Japan also absorb their share. By the end of 1977, therefore, the Saudi Monetary Agency's international holdings included well over $15 billion in western Europe, particularly in France, Switzerland and Britain.[62] For example, British exports to Saudi Arabia rose from $800 million in 1976, via $1,200 million in 1977, to $1,460 million in 1978. Similarly, British imports from Saudi Arabia grew from $1,960 million to $2,200 million between 1976 and 1977, and to $2,240 million in 1978.[63] Saudi Arabia has not been backward in exploiting her financial power over Western Europe in pursuit of her own ideological orientations. In fact some instances could only be described as blatant interference in the domestic concerns of other countries. For example, before the March 1978 French election there were widespread predictions of a significant increase in the left-wing vote, and even of the possibility of a socialist or socialist-dominated administration. Responding

26

to this, Riyadh made public its intention to postpone the conclusion of a large arms deal, allegedly involving hundreds of millions of dollars, until the political tendencies of the new government had become clear. Indeed, almost immediately after the electoral success of the French Right, King Khalid made an official state visit to Paris, during which Prince Saud, the Foreign Minister, emphasized that Saudi funds, estimated by the French press to be around $5 billion, would continue to flow into France.

The American Connection

Notwithstanding the consistent growth in Saudi Arabia's ties with Western Europe, her most crucial concern continues to be the maintenance of friendly relations with the United States. Because of the United States' role as the leading *status-quo* and anti-Communist global power, there is a natural coincidence of political and strategic interests between the two countries. Furthermore, the Saudi ruling elite sees the United States as the guarantor of stability in the region and the protector of the House of Saud, since it is well aware that the prospect of radical, nationalist or leftist elements overthrowing the ruling family, and thereby controlling the oil supplies to the United States and the Western world, is almost as unacceptable to Washington as it is to Riyadh. To the Saudi rulers, therefore, it is the American attitude to the Royal Family that defines and determines American policy towards Saudi Arabia and the region – and that is the strongest political and strategic commitment they could want. Yet it is clear that Saudi Arabia is reluctant to be seen to be moving too close to the United States. She is unwilling to provide forward bases and does not want an increased American presence in the country. Above all she cannot allow herself to become totally isolated in the Middle East by demonstrating unequivocal support for American policies in the region.

The United States, for her part, considering Saudi Arabia an effective agent through which to achieve her strategic objectives in the area, can only welcome her almost missionary zeal in trying to halt Soviet or Communist incursion into the area, as witnessed by her initiatives in South Yemen, Somalia, Eritrea, Zaire, Egypt and the Sudan. This has led some American policy-makers to suggest that 'Saudi strategic objectives resemble those of the United States more closely than those of any other country'.[64] In defending American sales of the F-15 fighter planes to Saudi Arabia, Secretary of Defense Harold Brown, testifying before the Senate Foreign Relations Committee, emphasized the Administration's positive view of Saudi Arabia's role and policies:

Saudi Arabia stands for peace and moderation in the Middle East . . . Saudi Arabia consistently demonstrates its friendship toward the United States. The government of Saudi Arabia has shown high statesmanship in a series of difficult decisions over the past few years in placing its own immediate self-interest subordinate to the health of the world economy. Its political influence, both in world affairs and in the Middle East, has been for moderation. In sum, there are many factors of enormous economic importance which we have in common with Saudi Arabia.[65]

Reinforcing these political and strategic affinities are the multi-faceted economic ties which increasingly draw the two countries together. While Saudi Arabia has a vast network of trade relations with western Europe and Japan, there is no doubt that she considers the United States to be her major trading partner. Partly because of undoubted American technological and scientific supremacy, but mainly due to the political judgment of the Saudi leadership, American-Saudi economic relations have blossomed considerably since the October 1973 War. The basis of this growth was spelled out as early as 1974 by Saudi Oil Minister Sheikh Zaki al-Yamani:

Our priority is to industrialize Saudi Arabia and to diversify its economy. Investment by Saudi Arabia towards achieving its end will benefit the United States from whom we will need to import capital goods and technical expertise. . . . The need for oil in the United States and the need for technological expertise in Saudi Arabia provides a natural starting point towards intensified co-operation aimed at serving the best interests of both countries . . . which would reflect not only a marked benefit to our individual economies but also to the world and its stability as a whole.[66]

Four years later, Sheikh Yamani's prescriptions had been successfully translated into concrete policies. At present, Saudi Arabia supplies more than a quarter of United States imported energy needs, and some 85 per cent of her accumulated financial surpluses are held in dollars. Nearly $35 billion of Saudi foreign assets are thought to be in American government securities, with an additional $24 billion invested elsewhere in the United States, and the Joint United States-Saudi Committee for Economic Co-operation is presently in charge of contracts worth over $650 million. The United States is Saudi Arabia's largest trading partner, and, despite increasing oil imports, the trade balance remains in her favour. At least 90 per cent of Saudi military needs are supplied by the United States, and in 1977–8 this generated an income to American companies of some $8 billion.[67] The Bendix Corporation helps to maintain the regular army; the Vinnel Corporation is building a new National Guard; AVCO Corporation trains the Coast Guard; TWA virtually keeps the national airline flying; and Lockheed and Raytheon are indispensable for air defence.

The importance to Saudi Arabia of the growing US-Saudi partnership is clearly shown in her recent policies. For instance, although the revenue from an average oil output of 8 billion barrels a day in 1978 already exceeded the absorptive capacity of the country's economy, in response to urgent American appeals the Saudi rulers increased output by 25 per cent during the period from November 1978 to February 1979, so as to offset the cutbacks in Iranian output. This allowed the United States to avoid having to institute stringent domestic energy-saving measures. Similarly, in early July 1979, in the wake of the OPEC meeting in Geneva, Saudi Arabia raised her oil output to 9·5 million barrels per day to offset the shortages in the American market. Against the wishes of most members, Saudi Arabia reaffirmed this policy at the December 1979 OPEC meeting in Caracas, Venezuela, which ended in deadlock and effectively instituted a two-tier price system.

In April 1978, Saudi Arabia had insisted on postponing the proposed informal meeting of OPEC countries (at which many OPEC members had been hoping for a decision to raise oil prices to compensate for the decline in the dollar) in order to allow time for the dollar to recover.[68]

Later in 1978, Prince Fahd endeavoured to give the American currency a further boost by expressing his belief that 'the dollar was the most important international currency' and that his 'definite information was that the dollar would return to its former strength soon'. Moreover, Saudi Arabia 'has rejected the proposal for replacing the dollar [for oil pricing] with a basket of currencies, and had opposed oil price increases unless there were exceptional circumstances'.[69] During 1977 and 1978, Saudi Arabia on a number of occasions extended the maturity of her American financial investments in order to support the stagnating United States economy and the weakening dollar.

The culmination of all this activity came in 1978, when Saudi Arabia won the long and sometimes bitter struggle to obtain the sophisticated F-15 *Eagle* fighter. She could easily have acquired the more than adequate French *Mirage* 2000 and 4000 without the need to resort to the fierce lobbying she had to undertake in Washington,[70] and without having to comply with the restrictions the United States imposed on the use of the F-15. To the Saudis, however, the purchase of the American plane carried political rather than strategic significance: it represented a continuing American commitment to Saudi Arabia for at least the decade in which the planes would be delivered, the infrastructure built, and a training programme fully established. In other words, the Saudi rulers felt that, at least during this period, the United States was bound to act as guarantor of their regime.

Saudi Arabia's behaviour within OPEC since 1973 is further testimony to her almost obsessive concern with the interests of the United States, in particular, and the health of the Western World in general. Not only was Saudi pressure instrumental in lifting the oil embargo on the United States in March 1974, but a year later, it was again Saudi Arabia who stood almost virtually alone against moves by the other members to institute a co-ordinated programme of cutbacks in oil production in order to maintain the price, and to index-link oil prices so as to maintain their value in real terms.[71] This moderate stand was maintained at the September 1975 OPEC meeting in Vienna. Sheikh Yamani came to that meeting advocating a continuation of the price freeze, at least until January 1976, in order to assist the emerging signs of recovery in some of the major Western economies still suffering from the effects of the post-1973 recession. However another faction of OPEC, led by Iran, demanded a 15–20 per cent increase, with no commitment to any period of freeze therafter. Yamani insisted that Saudi Arabia would on no account accept such an increase, and, if the other members were to increase their prices, she would not only keep her own prices frozen, but would also allow her production to rise in accordance with market demand. The prospect of Saudi Arabia cutting into the other producers' markets with her huge surplus capacity caused an inevitable softening in the positions of the hardline OPEC members, and a compromise emerged involving a 10 per cent price rise with a commitment to maintain the new price until 30 June 1976, when it was to be reviewed again. When that time came the 'hawks', after a stormy session, again ended up by bowing to the demands of Saudi Arabia, backed by the United Arab Emirates (UAE), to freeze prices until the end of 1976. The Kuwaiti Oil Minister confided that 'some members thought that the position of Saudi Arabia and the UAE should be ignored, and that other members should raise the price of their oil. [However]. there was no point in raising prices in the face of Saudi and UAE opposition, [for] there can be no OPEC without Saudi Arabia'.[72] For his part, Prince Fahd emphasized that Saudi policy 'was aimed at helping the nations of the world overcome their economic difficulties'.[73] In this particular instance, a complete dislocation of OPEC was narrowly averted.

It was becoming obvious, however, that the widening gulf between Saudi Arabia and the majority of OPEC members over price and production levels was bound to lead to a parting of the ways; and indeed the inevitable confrontation occurred in the December 1976 Conference in Qatar. For the first time in its history, the organization emerged from the meeting hopelessly split. This split was exemplified by a two-tier system of pricing: Saudi Arabia and the UAE opted for a 5 per cent increase over the whole of 1977, whereas the rest of the organization decided to increase their prices by 10 per cent from January 1977, and by a further 5 per cent at mid-year. The Saudi decision naturally attracted bitter denunciations, not only from the militant members such as Iraq, Libya and Algeria, but also from that erstwhile supporter of the United States, the Shah of Iran. However, Saudi Arabia considered it was more important not to retard the faltering world economic recovery, since a new recession might precipitate Communist gains in a number of European elections. According to Sheikh Yamani, 'we are extremely worried about the possibility of a new recession, worried about the situation in Britain, Italy, even in France and some other nations, and we do not want another regime coming to power in France or Italy'. Asked whether he meant the Communists, he replied, 'Yes' adding, 'the situation in Spain is not so healthy either, and the same applies to Portugal'.[74] However, he also told a press conference immediately after the conference broke up: 'I want you to know that we expect the West to appreciate what we did, especially the United States'.[75]

In the next three meetings, Saudi Arabia, by adamantly refusing to sanction any price increase, succeeded in keeping the price freeze throughout 1977 and 1978. This meant that during these two years oil prices remained stable in the face of continuing inflation and a decline in the value of the dollar which, according to Kuwaiti sources, wiped out 30 per cent of OPEC's real revenues.[76] By December 1978, therefore, the pressure to raise prices, put on Saudi Arabia by other OPEC members, had increased considerably. This was reinforced by the cutbacks in Iran's oil production as a result of the growing unrest there.

OPEC's December 1978 meeting in Abu Dhabi produced an annual price rise of 14·5 per cent, to be effected in four phases. Here again it was in response to Saudi Arabia's prompting that 'phasing' was introduced; even so, Sheikh Yamani declared himself to be unhappy with the increase, but said that the Iranian situation had made it very difficult to argue for moderation. The weakness in Saudi Arabia's position continued throughout the first quarter of 1979, since exceptionally high prices were being obtained for oil sold on the 'spot' markets, giving oil companies massive instant profits on oil bought at the official price. As individual member states proceeded to increase prices unilaterally, Saudi Arabia called for an urgent meeting 'to regulate consumption and stabilize prices to save the world from possible economic relapse'. However, at the extraordinary meeting held in Geneva on 26 and 27 March she was compelled to go along with the other members in bringing forward to the second quarter of 1979 the price increase which the December meeting had originally programmed for the fourth quarter. It is clear that, while Saudi Arabia failed to dissuade the other members from imposing additional surcharges on the officially increased price, she had decided to hold the price of her own oil for the rest of the year. However, at the OPEC meeting of 26–28 June 1979, she did agree to raise the price of 'Arabian Light' by 23·7 per cent to $18 per barrel. This last-minute compromise between Saudi Arabia and her more militant partners, agreed upon in order to avoid a complete collapse of the Organization, involved a minimum price of $18 per barrel, at which the Saudi 'Light' was pegged, and a maximum price of $23·50 per barrel, applying to Libyan, Algerian and Nigerian oil, with the other oil-producing countries selling their crudes at around $20–22 per barrel.

As the year progressed, the position of Saudi Arabia grew increasingly weaker, particularly after the Iran's government cut that country's oil production from some 10 per cent to 6 per cent of the Western world's consumption. In previous years OPEC members had refrained from cutting production and, as a result, Saudi Arabia could keep prices down by flooding the market with her own production. However, with the substantial Iranian cuts, Saudi Arabia's spare capacity of, at the most, two million barrels a day was insufficient to maintain market stability. With demand far outstripping supply in the latter part of 1979, over a quarter of OPEC's oil was being sold on the spot market or at spot-market-related prices which were running at between $35 and $45 a barrel. By early December 1979 the Saudi oil price of $18 a barrel looked ridiculously low and was perceived by the other members to be based not on any economic rationale but on purely political criteria relating to a long suspected Saudi–American understanding. Thus, a week before the scheduled December 1979 OPEC meeting, Saudi Arabia announced a 33 per cent rise for her light crude to $24 a barrel. The Saudi leaders were gambling that the sheer size of the increase would bring the other OPEC countries into line, reduce selling on the spot market and ease the pressure for production cuts which could have adverse effects on the American and Western economies. At the meeting in Caracas, Venezuela, however, the Saudi gamble failed, leaving the organization's price system in disarray, with only Saudi Arabia, Venezuela, Qatar and the UAE holding out for a base price of $24 a barrel. Other members went for significantly higher prices, ranging between $80 and $40 a barrel.

While it is true that, in comparison with other OPEC members, Saudi Arabia continued to work for moderation, it is also true that by mid-1979 she was no longer showing the same resolve in confronting the other members of OPEC in order to protect Western and American interests. This perceptible decrease in enthusiasm could be partially attributed to frustration with the West's seeming inability to cope with its economic problems. Riyadh was certainly distressed about the reluctance of the American Congress to pass an effective energy bill which would reduce the United States' wasteful consumption of oil, and it also frequently voiced misgivings about the continuing social and economic problems of Western Europe. In all probability, however, the cooler attitude towards Western interests related more to Saudi perceptions of American attitudes to political events occurring in the area during 1978 and 1979, than to disenchantment with the West's political and economic laxity. The apparent impotence of the United States in the Somali-Ethiopian conflict, her unwillingness to come to the Shah's rescue in Iran and the heavy-handed way in which the Carter Administration endeavoured to pressure Saudi Arabia and Jordan, the foremost pro-American Arab states, into supporting the Camp David agreements and the Egyptian-Israeli treaty, all seem to have contributed to a Saudi reassessment of the country's policies and political orientations. But what hurt most was that neither the United States nor Egypt consulted Saudi Arabia before entering negotiations over a Middle-Eastern peace settlement.

An important part of this reassessment concerned Saudi relations with, and attitudes towards the Soviet Union. As we have seen, Saudi Arabia has tried vigorously to counter Soviet influence on many fronts, and her hostility to the Soviet Union has frequently led her to an exaggerated perception of Moscow's allegedly 'conspiratorial' intentions in the area.

Thus, in a series of statements in the Spring of 1978 Sheikh Yamani said that he expected the USSR to become a net importer of oil by the mid-1980s, adding that her actions in the Horn of Africa, together with her involvement in Afghanistan, indicated the importance of the Gulf and its oil fields in the eyes of the Communist super-power. To Yamani, these destabilizing developments 'were only the first step, to be followed by others'.[77] By early 1979, however, Saudi official statements and pronouncements relating to the Soviet Union had moderated considerably. Indeed, in March 1979 Foreign Minister Prince Saud insisted that: 'The lack of diplomatic relations does not mean that we do not recognize the Soviet Union or the importance of the role it plays in international relations. Quite the opposite. We have, on more than one occasion, expressed our appreciation of the *positive* attitudes adopted by the Soviet Union towards Arab issues' [my italics].[78]

It is, nevertheless, unlikely that this incipient flexibility and moderation was meant to signify a fundamental change in attitude by the Saudi rulers. It seems rather to have been a manifestation of growing exasperation with American policies in the Gulf area. The modification in Saudi Arabia's public posture towards the Soviet Union was therefore a tactical rather than a strategic policy reorientation – merely a temporary adjustment in response to conditions in the international environment. Even if some ties were to be established with the Soviet Union and the Socialist bloc, Saudi Arabia will continue to be resolutely anti-Communist because of her commitment to stability and Islam. Her outspoken criticism of the Soviet invasion of Afghanistan is an example of this. Because of the fundamental importance of these two values, radical shifts in Saudi Arabia's foreign policy, particularly in relations with the super-powers, seem unlikely in the near future.

IV. PROSPECTS

The stability of Saudi Arabia, and indeed of the peninsula as a whole, has been viewed with increasing concern in the wake of the Iranian revolution, and particularly after the attack on the Grand Mosque in Mecca. As a *status-quo* power pursuing moderate and pragmatic policies, Saudi Arabia constitutes a crucial western interest in the area, and as such, the maintenance of the Saudi regime has been a primary objective of the foreign policies of the United States and the Western world in general. There can be no doubt that a mass uprising in the oil-rich, pro-Western kingdom would be a major blow to the West, and it is therefore hardly surprising that Western circles have become apprehensive about the possibility of the Iranian revolution repeating itself in the more exposed and seemingly less secure Saudi kingdom.

It could be argued, however, that these fears are somewhat exaggerated, and that the danger of Saudi Arabia undergoing the kind of upheavals which befell Iran is, at present, minimal. The conditions that contributed to the Iranian eruption are not found in Saudi Arabia. In the first place, the Saudi population is one-eighth of Iran's so that it was possible for all levels of society to benefit from the dramatic post-1973 increase in the country's wealth. The Saudi government, with its massive surpluses, has been able to undertake wide-ranging social projects (such as housing, free education and medical services, irrigation systems, transport and road improvement) and, unlike its counterpart in Teheran, could extend the benefits of these projects right down to the lowest levels of Saudi society. It has, moreover, been extremely successful in impressing upon the people that the considerable progress in their social and economic conditions is due entirely to the monarchy's beneficence, and therefore that any threat to the Royal Family jeopardizes the interests and well-being of the Saudi population. Thus, although a wide disparity between the upper and lower levels of society does persist, the standard of living of the poorer Saudis has improved to such an extent that they now seem to identify their interests fully with the preservation of the Saudi monarchy.

Another important difference between the Iranian and Saudi cases can be found in the role played by the religious establishment in the political system. A major contributing factor to

31

the Iranian revolution was the mounting resentment of the Shi'ia *mullahs* against a secularist monarch intent on curbing their political role and influence. This does not apply in the Saudi case, where the political system is consciously steeped in Koranic values, and where the religious establishment is constantly consulted and made to participate fully in the decision-making process.

Finally, although the Saudi political system is undoubtedly authoritarian, even archaic, it is nevertheless based on tribal tradition and has its own peculiar brand of grass-roots democracy. As has been mentioned earlier, the Royal Family, through the institution of the *Majlis*, have constantly made themselves available to the public. They have thus ensured that the population has access to them, and that communication between the rulers and the ruled is maintained. This is in stark contrast to the situation that existed in Iran, where the Shah increasingly isolated himself from his public and their problems and aspirations.

There are, however, clear dangers resulting from the rapid modernization process that the country is currently undergoing. It is difficult to predict the eventual effect of this societal transformation on the population's traditional allegiances and society's existing system of values; it could very well affect the country's stability by undermining the very same social patterns and cultural values that underpin the legitimacy of the monarchy. The Saudi rulers, however, seem well satisfied that the chances of serious societal dislocation resulting from rapid modernization are at present slim. Oil Minister Yamani has observed that rapid change was bound to produce tension, but he has said that he believes it would take at least another generation to bring about substantial material revolution to bring about substantial social change. Ghazi al-Gosaibi, Minister of Industry, insisted that the strong influence of family and religion would see the people through the transformation, and these sentiments were echoed by Minister of Planning Hisham Nazer, who described the institution of the family as 'the arsenal of Islam which will defend the Saudis against the corruptions of the modern world'.[79]

It remains to be seen whether these unifying forces, which stem from the very roots of Saudi society, can combat the undoubtedly disruptive effects of this rapid modernization, but there are no indications at present of an impending e plosion. Thus Prince Naif, Interior Ministe could boast in 1977, 'we never had more th 250 political prisoners at any time, and v released the last 63 two years ago'.[80] This mig sound as if it were a standard princely clai but few would strenuously contest it. Indeed, US State Department report released by t Senate Foreign Relations Committee in Febr ary 1978 concluded that arbitrary political arre in Saudi Arabia was neither practised nor co doned, and that there was no evidence of in viduals being imprisoned for their politic beliefs. The report continued that torture w not sanctioned or practised, and that clos trials had rarely been held in recent years.[81] could thus be safely argued that at least in t foreseeable future the Saudi rulers have ve little to fear from their own population.

If the above conclusion is correct, then hc can the attack on the Grand Mosque in Mec in November 1977 be explained? It is importa at the outset not to exaggerate the size, t popular following or the wider ramificatio of the operation. The attack was led by a religio zealot who, with some 250 followers infiltrat and occupied the Mosque at dawn prayers the first day of the fifteenth century of t Islamic calender, proclaiming himself as t *Mahdi*, (the awaited Messiah). It took the Sau security forces two weeks to defeat the rebe killing 75 and capturing 170, their own casualt being officially put at 60 dead and over 2 wounded.

There is no doubt that the relatively lo duration of the military confrontation a the resultant high casualties conferred on t occupation an importance out of all prop tion to its actual significance as a manifestati of general revolutionary potential in the count Had it not been for the Mosque's complex syst of subterranean passages and the natural luctance of the government forces to use hea fire power inside the most venerated mosque Islam, the attackers would have been clea more swiftly and with far fewer casualti Furthermore, while a few of the gunmen w Egyptian, Kuwaiti, Yemeni, Pakistani and Mor can students, the vast majority were Saudi B ouins belonging to the Otaiba tribe, which i plied that support for the siege was only limi and tribally based. During and after the seiz

32

of the Mosque, there were no reports of disturbances, unrest, or even unease, in the major cities, or among the agricultural Bedouins, and there has been no decrease in domestic or foreign investment as a result of the attack.

Perhaps more ominous for the regime were disturbances, unconnected with the siege of the Grand Mosque, which occurred among the predominantly Shi'ia population of the Eastern province in November 1979. During *Ashoura* (the period of annual unrest and intesne religious mourning in Shi'ia Islam, which effectively symbolizes the divide between Sunni and Shi'ia) riots, in which a dozen people were killed and a large number wounded, were reported in a number of small towns near the main oil installations in Dhahran and Dammam. While there is little doubt that the Shi'ia element of the population has become more restless in the wake of the Iranian upheavals, its revolutionary potential in Saudi Arabia is very limited, since it constitutes no more than 12% of the total Saudi population. Moreover, having lagged behind the rest of the population, it is only now beginning to gain financially from the oil boom which has taken place in the Eastern province. Removal of grievances should gradually decrease any disruptive or destabilizing tendencies they may have at present.

Finally, in order to lessen the likelihood of future manifestations of discontent, the House of Saud, as it had done in the past, quickly responded with its usual mix of reformist and authoritarian measures. The government has said that in the Third Five-Year Plan there will be a lower level of capital expenditure and slower growth, and there seems to be a move to concentrate on rural rather than urban development. Corruption is to be more closely scrutinized, and the King has already banned some of the senior princes from engaging in commercial enterprises. At the same time, the expected introduction of women into the country's labour force seems to have been shelved and there have been reports that the religious police, *al-Matawah*, has recently become far more diligent in the execution of its duty.

Thus, while limited and localized in their effects on the general stability of the regime, the events in Mecca and the Eastern province seem to have had considerable impact on the Royal Family. Depending on what lessons the regime learns from these events and how it continues to respond to them, the attack on the Grand Mosque and the demonstrations in the Eastern province could be seen in the long run to have strengthened the regime, rather than weakened it. For the time being, therefore, any discontent among the Saudi population seems neither deep enough nor widespread enough to constitute a real danger to the stability of the Saudi regime.

However, the same might not be true of the immigrant labourers who have been working in Saudi Arabia for many years. As we have seen, the 1975–80 Five-Year Plan calls for nearly a three-fold increase in their number, and, if current trends continue, one in every three workers employed in Saudi Arabia will be a foreigner by the end of 1980. On the whole these workers, many of whom are radical Shi'ia Yemenis, have been excluded from the considerable state benefits available to Saudi nationals, and, with their numbers constantly increasing, and their social and economic position deteriorating in relation to the indigenous population, the immigrants have come to represent a growing source of concern for the Riyadh authorities. As a frustrated community with mounting grievances, they could become a potent destabilizing agent in Saudi domestic politics. It was hardly surprising, therefore, that when a Saudi Communist Party was clandestinely formed in November 1975, its leadership declared that it would concentrate much of its activity 'on the workers from abroad'.[82]   The Saudi authorities have consequently endeavoured to tighten their control over the immigrant community, and this seems, if anything, to have heightened existing tensions. In the autumn of 1978 a number of clashes occurred between immigrants and the Saudi security forces, with reports of thirty people killed and 120 injured in one riot, and a newspaper editorial denounced 'recent attacks on security forces by foreign elements who were being checked for proper identification'.[83] It thus seems clear that, as long as immigrant workers continue to be excluded from the full social and economic benefits and opportunities the state extends to Saudi nationals, such friction is bound to manifest itself in a growing confrontation that may eventually undermine the stability of Saudi Arabia's social and political systems.

Strictly speaking, however, the immigrant

workers do not constitute an internal threat to the regime, for foreign nationals can always be deported if they are perceived as such. The bulk of this community consists of unskilled labourers who can be easily and quickly replaced by workers from other countries, with few adverse effects on the development plans. Thus, for example, placid and more conformist workers from Pakistan, Baluchistan, the Philippines or South Korea could, if the need arose, take the place of radical Yemenis. In all probability, such a move would receive the overwhelming support of the indigenous Saudi population.

If these conclusions make it appear that all is well internally, there remain a number of problems on the horizon which, if ignored, may shake the complacency of the Royal Family. There is widespread corruption; there is a high degree of materialism which rides uneasily with the spiritual commitment to Islamic ideals; there are strains within the Royal Family and a degree of actionalism; and there may soon come a time when the pursuit of wealth alone no longer satisfies the aspirations of the Saudi populace. In Kuwait, the merchants are beginning to challenge the political power of the sheikhs, and it would be surprising if the commoners in Saudi Arabia did not also seek a measure of political power in the years to come. Much will depend upon the willingness of the Royal Family to allow some levers of power to leave their hands. Permanent division of the country into first- and second-class citizens by birth could incite disaffection among the lower strata of society, exerting pressure that could ultimately lead to a civil explosion.

In addition to these possible sources of disruption, attention is focused on external threats aimed at destabilizing the Riyadh government. Given Saudi Arabia's experience of the Nasser-backed republican revolution in North Yemen in the 1960s and her intense antipathy towards the Marxist regime of South Yemen, it is only natural that she considers the southern border to be her most vulnerable strategic point. In explaining the decision in early 1979 to withdraw the Saudi contingent from the Arabe Peace-keeping Force in Lebanon, Foreign Minister Prince Saud told the Lebanese Prime Minister 'Just as you are burdened with your problems in the south, we also have a southern problem at the Saudi-Yemeni border'.[84] The great un-spoken fear is that the two Yemens might merge and, with a combined population of nine million present a formidable challenge to Saudi Arabia. Such a merger would be all the more ominous because the more dynamic and better organized Marxist leadership of South Yemen would be bound to emerge as the dominant political authority. A major strategic objective of the Saudi regime has therefore been to prevent the unity of the two Yemens at all costs. As was pointed out earlier in this Paper, it appeared more than coincidental that North Yemen President Hamdi was assassinated the day before he was due to travel to Aden to discuss possible unity measures. Saudi Arabia will no doubt continue to exploit her influence with the influential tribes of North Yemen to try to frustrate any efforts to create a united Yemen. However, as she has discovered elsewhere, there is a limit to her ability to manipulate events in other countries, and the Royal Family must consider the possibility of confronting a Soviet-backed, Marxist-led united Yemen in the future.

A further possible threat, in the context of any future Arab-Israeli confrontation, is that of a Israeli air attach against Saudi oil fields. With her increasing regional and international influence, her considerable financial support for the Palestinians and the Arab confrontation states, and her publicly-declared hostility toward the Egyptian-Israeli accords, Saudi Arabia is no longer considered by Israel as a peripheral actor in the Arab-Israeli conflict. Consequently, the strike against the very source of the Arabs growing regional and international power must be a very tempting proposition. Even with the recently purchased (but as yet undelivered) F-15 fighters, Saudi Arabia can hardly expect to stand up to the efficient Israeli Air Force.

Another threat could arguably come from her radical northern neighbour. Iraq, led by the socialist, left-wing Ba'ath Party, and having often declared hegemonial ambitions towards Kuwait and ideological antipathies towards Saudi Arabia, has long constituted a major destabilizing threat to the Saudi regime. Paradoxically, however this threat has receded noticeably in the wake of the Iranian revolution. The majority of the Iraqi population belongs to the Shi'ia sect of Islam, and might therefore come to look upon the Iranian *mullahs*, rather than the minority Sunni government in Baghdad, as its moral and political leaders. This potentially explosive domestic situation in Iraq has been exacerbated recently by the re-emergence of Kurdish secessionist activities after the fall of the Shah. As a result, the Iraqi regime has become very reluctant to indulge in disruptive regional operations. Instead it has increasingly endeavoured to pursue moderate and co-operative policies towards its southern neighbours. Indeed, Baghdad has even been willing to consider the hitherto much-derided notion of a Gulf security system as a possible policy option. It might in the past have considered such concepts as 'regional alliances' and 'filling the power vacuum' to be reactionary efforts aimed at maintaining American influence in the area, yet it was interesting to note that, in the wake of the Shah's deposition, Iraw was beginning to consider such concepts quite seriously. In April 1979, Saddam Hussein, the most influential figure in the Soviet-backed Iraqi regime, made this startling statement:

> We must take up arms against any foreigner, regardless of his colour, who may violate Arab sovereignty. In this context, we do not differentiate between a progressive, or a Zionist, or a Frenchman. Nor do we differentiate between American and Soviet. Irrespective of the formal friendly ties it may have with some of us, the Soviet Union, and it is a friend of Iraq, cannot be allowed to occupy Saudi territory. This is because Saudi land is not outside the Arab map, and what applies to it applies to the rest of the Arab countries.[85]

Present indications, therefore, suggest that the hitherto potent Iraqi threat to Saudi stability has considerably decreased.

A further reason for Iraq's moderation towards Saudi Arabia relates to the obvious need of the radical Arab regimes to close ranks with their conservative counterparts in order to confront the Camp David Agreements and the Egyptian-Israeli Treaty. To a large extent, therefore, the pursuit of co-operative policies towards Saudi Arabia was implicitly contingent on her adoption of a militant stand against the policies of President Sadat. And it is here that Saudi Arabia might ultimately face the greatest challenge to her survival, for an adamant opposition to the Camp David Accords could potentially erode the hitherto strategically overriding relationship between Saudi Arabia and the United States.

In February 1979, Senator Frank Church Chairman of the Senate Foreign Relations Committee and a well-known supporter of Israel, admonished Saudi Arabia for allegedly being more of a detriment to peace than the United States was willing to admit. He said that the projected sale of the F-15 fighters should be reassessed and suggested that Saudi Arabia should be told that a 'special relationship could not be a one-way street'.[86] The White House immediately disassociated itself from this highly partisan speech, but the Senator's remarks nonetheless served to highlight the painful dilemma in which Saudi Arabia now finds herself. A perceptible coolness in the 'special relationship' inevitably followed, and this was accompanied by rumours of schisms within the Royal Family and tension inside the armed forces. Whatever the truth of these reports, there can be no doubt that in the summer of 1979, an intense debate regarding Saudi-American and Saudi-Arab relations took place within the ranks of Saudi Arabia's ruling elite.

The choice facing Saudi rulers is both difficult and very consequential. One the one hand, they cannot condone the Egyptian-Israeli Accord for fear of alienating the Arab world and undermining their country's legitimacy, which is based on its status as the guardian of Islam and Islam's holy places. On the other hand, they are clearly unwilling to adopt a militant stance and thereby run the risk of weakening the moderate regime of President Sadat[87] and, more importantly, of losing crucial American political and strategic support. Obviously, Saudi Arabia would prefer not to have to choose between these two alternatives, for both are intrinsically linked to the survival of the Saudi regime itself. Yet only if there were a dramatic breakthrough in the Egyptian-Israeli negotiations on the West Bank, Jerusalem and the status of the Palestinians, would Saudi Arabia be extricated from her dilemma. Otherwise, a clear-cut choice will have to be made in the end, and in making that choice the House of Saud will face the gravest crisis it has yet had to meet.

NOTES

[1] For a good analysis of Saudi policies during that era, see George A. Lipsky *et. al.*, *Saudi Arabia* (New Haven: HRAF Press, 1959); and H. St John Philby, *Saudi Arabia* (London: Benn, 1955).

[2] Lipsky, *op. cit.*, p. 201.

[3] See Erskine Childers, *The Road to Suez* (London: Macgibbon & Kee, 1962), pp. 120–21.

[4] Ghazi A. Algosaibi, *The 1962 Revolution in Yemen and its impact on the Foreign Policy of the UAR and Saudi Arabia* (unpublished London University Ph.D. thesis, 1970), p. 272.

[5] British Broadcasting Corporation, *Summary of World Broadcasts, Part IV, The Middle East*, 5 March 1962, p. 3.

[6] For analysis of Egyptian perceptions, see A.I. Dawisha, 'Intervention in the Yemen: An Analysis of Egyptian Perceptions and Policies', *Middle East Journal*, vol. 29, no. 1 (Winter 1975); and Dawisha, 'Perceptions Decisions and Consequences in Foreign Policy: The Egyptian Intervention on the Yemen', *Political Studies*, vol. 25, no. 2 (June 1977).

[7] Quoted in Algosaibi, *op. cit.*, p. 313.

[8] British Broadcasting Corporation, *Summary of World Broadcasts, Part IV, The Middle East*, ME/2559/A/2.

[9] Alvin Z. Rubinstein, *Red Star on the Nile: The Soviet-Egyptian Influence Relationship Since the June War* (Princeton, N.J.: Princeton U.P., 1977), p. 243.

[10] More information can be found in Peter Mangold, *Super-power Intervention in the Middle East* (London: Croom Helm, 1978).

[11] Mohamed Heikal, *The Road to Ramadan* (London: Fontana, 1976), p. 266.

[12] The best analysis of the oil crisis can be found in *Daedalus*, vol. 104, no. 4 (Autumn 1975).

[13] *The Middle East and North Africa 1976–1977* (London: Europa, 1977), p. 608.

[14] R. K. Ramazani, *Beyond the Arab-Israeli Settlement: New Directions for US Policy in the Middle East* (Cambridge, Mass.: Institute for Foreign Policy Analysis, 1977), p. 42.

[15] *Newsweek*, 6 March 1978, p. 13.

[16] *Events*, 3 December 1976, p. 17.

[17] *Newsweek*, 6 March 1978, p. 18.

[18] *Middle East Economic Survey*, 12 December 1975, p. 4.

[19] *Newsweek*, 6 March 1978, p. 13.

[20] *Events*, 22 April 1977, pp. 18–29.

[21] UAR, *The Proceedings of the Unity Talks* (in Arabic) (Cairo: National Publishing House, 1963), p. 409.

[22] Ralph Braibanti and Fuad Abdul Salem al-Farsy, 'Saudi Arabia: A Developmental Perspective', *Journal of South Asian and Middle Eastern Studies*, vol. 1, no. 1 (Fall 1977), p. 9.

[23] *The Economist*, 10 December 1977, p. S34.

[24] *Ibid.*

[25] Braibanti and al-Farsy, *op. cit.*, p. 25.

[26] Quoted in Abbas Kelidar, 'The Problems of Succession in Saudi Arabia', *Asian Affairs*, vol. 65, no. 1 (February 1978), p. 29.

[27] *The Middle East and North Africa 1977–1978*, (London: Europa, 1978).

[28] *The Economist*, 10 December 1977, p. S13.

[29] Kingdom of Saudi Arabia, *The Statistical Indicator,*

1976 (Riyadh: Ministry of Finance and National Economy, 1976), p. 47.

[30] *Arabia and the Gulf*, 7 November 1977, p. 8.

[31] *Wall Street Journal*, 17 September 1976, pp. 1–2, 10.

[32] Hamilton Gibb, 'Constitutional Organization: The Muslim Community and the State', in Majid Khadduri and Herbert J. Liebesny (eds), *Law in the Middle East* (Washington DC: Middle East Institute, 1955), p. 15.

[33] Ali Hassan Alyami, 'The Coming Instability in Saudi Arabia', *New Outlook*, September 1977, p. 21.

[34] *The Economist*, 10 December 1977, p. S26.

[35] Braibanti and al-Farsy, *op. cit.*, p. 22.

[36] *Ibid.*, p. 19.

[37] *Newsweek*, 6 June 1977, p. 20.

[38] Kingdom of Saudi Arabia, *Second Development Plan, 1395–1400AH, 1975–1980AD* (Riyadh: Ministry of Planning, 1975), p. 530.

[39] *Afro-Asian Affairs*, 22 September, 9 November 1977.

[40] *Newsweek*, 6 March 1978, p. 18.

[41] *Arab Report and Record*, 1977, p. 169.

[42] *Arabia and the Gulf*, 13 March 1978.

[43] *Middle East Economic Survey*, 29 August 1977, pp. 8–10; see also *The Guardian*, 28 September 1978.

[44] The Arabian Peninsula in this context consists of Saudi Arabia, all the Gulf sheikhdoms, the Sultanate of Oman, and North and South Yemen; Iraq is not included in this definition.

[45] *Arab Report and Record*, 1976, p. 195.

[46] *Al-Anwar* (Beirut), 30 July 1976.

[47] Dale R. Tahtinen, *National Security Challenges to Saudi Arabia* (Washington DC: American Enterprise Institute for Public Policy Research, 1978), p. 6.

[48] *Ibid.*; Agence France Presse, 22 March 1976.

[49] *Arabia and the Gulf*, 24 October 1978, p. 5.

[50] *The Middle East*, May 1978, p. 24.

[51] *Al-Thawra* (Baghdad), 18 April 1979; *Al-Ba'ath* (Baghdad), 19 April 1979: *Al-Siyassah* (Kuwait), 19 April 1978; *Arab Report and Record*, 1978, p. 447.

[52] Hsinhua, 10 April 1978.

[53] *Daily Telegraph*, 17 February 1978; *The Middle East*, May 1978, p. 24.

[54] *Arab Report and Record*, 1977, p. 54.

[55] *Al-Hawadith* (Beirut), 2 March 1979; *Al-Nahar* (Beirut), 1 June 1978. See also Prince Sultan's remark to Defense Secretary Brown, that 'regardless of Communist threat, the situation in the area will become more dangerous unless Israel withdraws completely from the occupied Arab territories, including Jerusalem, and grants the Palestinian people the right to self-determination in their own homeland'. *Obaz* (Jeddah), 12 February 1979.

[56] *Arab Report and Record*, 1978, p. 170.

[57] *Financial Times*, 21 October 1976.

[58] *Arab Report and Record*, 1978, p. 690.

[59] *Okaz* (Jeddah), 7 November 1978; *Al-Riadh* (Riyadh), 20 March 1979.

[60] *International Herald Tribune*, 1 June 1978.

[61] Helen Lackner, *A House Built on Sand: A Political Economy of Saudi Arabia* (London: Ithaca Press, 1978), pp. 129–30.

[62] *New York Times*, 9 January 1978.

[63] *Financial Times*, 2 March 1978; *The Guardian*, 14 November 1978; *Financial Times*, 26 February 1979. Given this volume of trade it was hardly surprising when, in a reference to the notorious execution of the Saudi Princess Misha, David Owen, the British Foreign Secretary said: 'Sometimes what governments have to say over individual cases may cause difficulties for our inter-governmental business and financial relations, and therefore to our own prosperity and employment prospects at home . . . [thus] we have to be sensible and try not to provoke unnecessary damage' (*The Guardian*, 2 February 1978).

[64] *New York Times*, 23 December 1978.

[65] *Official Text: US Mideast Arms Proposals* (issued by the United States Embassy Press Office in London, 4 May 1978), p. 4.

[66] *Middle East Economic Survey*, 27 September 1974, p. 12.

[67] *The Middle East*, May 1978, p. 17; see also *New York Times*, 9 January 1978; *Middle East Economic Digest*, 25 August 1978, p. 35; *Arab Report and Record*, 1978, p. 98; and *New York Times*, 11 February 1978.

[68] *Arab Report and Record*, 1978, p. 207.

[69] *Al-Siyasseh* (Kuwait), 23 August 1978.

[70] In her fight against the powerful and pervasive Zionist lobby Saudi Arabia was even obliged to retain a public relations firm at an estimated cost of $165,000.

[71] *Middle East Economic Survey*, 7 March 1975, p. 1.

[72] *Ibid.*, 21 June 1976, pp. 1–2.

[73] *Al-Anwar* (Beirut), 19 July 1976

[74] Quoted in *Arab Report and Record* 1976, p. 762. Prince Fahd also expressed similar views (*Al-Anwar*, Beirut, 22 December 1976).

[75] *Middle East Economic Survey*, 20 December 1976, p. 6.

[76] *Financial Times*, 23 November 1978.

[77] *Ibid.*, 23 June 1978; see also *Arab Report and Record*, 1978, p. 338.

[78] *Al-Hawadith* (Beirut), 2 March 1979.

[79] *New York Times*, 15 March 1978.

[80] *The Guardian*, 21 June 1977.

[81] *Arab Report and Record*, 1978, p. 137.

[82] *Arab Report and Record*, 1975, p. 614.

[83] *Obaz* (Jeddah), 16 October 1978.

[84] *Al-Hawadith* (Beirut), 13 April 1979.

[85] *The Guardian*, 11 April 1979; see also *Al-Destour* (London), 2–6 April 1979, p. 10. A further startling development occurred in June 1979, when the Baghdad regime announced a $300 million aid agreement with the conservative, pro-Western and Saudi-backed government of North Yemen (see *The Middle East*, July 1979, p. 10).

[86] *MEED Arab Reports*, no. 3, 1979, p. 29.

[87] In the wake of the Saudi-Egyptian break that occurred as a result of Camp David, a high Saudi official was reported to have likened Saudi attitudes towards Egypt to 'someone who was forced to amputate a limb in order to keep alive' (*Al-Hawadith*, Beirut, 13 April 1979, p. 14).

2 The Foreign Policy of Syria: Goals, Capabilities, Constraints and Options

ITAMAR RABINOVICH

In early 1982, the Middle Eastern political scene was to a large extent shaped by expectations of the changes that the completion of Israel's withdrawal from the Sinai on 25 April might precipitate, and by the measures already taken in anticipation of these changes. Syria has played a traditionally central role in these developments. As a result of President Asad's boycott of the Fez Arab Summit in November 1981, the Syrian Ba'ath regime was chiefly responsible for the failure of the Saudi attempt to formulate an alternative to the Camp David process that would win a broad Arab consensus. Israel's virtual annexation of the Golan Heights in December 1981 confronted Asad's government with a severe challenge and highlighted the possibility of a Syrian–Israeli war before or after April 1982. And Syria's treaty relationship with the Soviet Union means that such hostilities might lead to a wider international crisis. Finally, the recrudescence of violent opposition to the Ba'ath regime inside Syria in January 1982 has once again underlined a distinctive characteristic of the Syrian polity: the particularly intricate interplay between the course of domestic politics and the conduct of foreign policy.

Asad's Regime: the Formative Years

The political history of the Asad regime can be divided into two well-defined phases: 1970–77 and 1977 onwards. The first were years of growth and success. In 1977 a lengthy crisis began which, as described below, has now entered into its third stage. The initial crisis culminated in the Summer of 1980.[1] The regime then succeeded in forcefully repelling the Islamic opposition's offensive and in restoring a measure of dynamism and resourcefulness to its domestic and foreign policies. But recovery was short-lived and by the end of 1981 President Asad was again faced with an oppressive configuration of internal and external challenges.

During the first, happier, phase of its history the Asad regime won a series of impressive domestic and external successes. Following a long period of endemic instability in Syrian politics Asad succeeded in establishing a comparatively stable and coherent regime. True, the underlying sources of past instability were not fully eliminated and the urban Sunni population continued to denounce the regime as the illegitimate rule of a sectarian Alawi group. But the effective domestic strategy formulated by Asad, his personal leadership, the aura of success and the unprecedented cohesiveness of the new ruling group served to cushion and mitigate the effect of such destabilizing factors.

This domestic success served as a solid foundation for the regime's foreign policy which contributed, in turn, to the regime's prestige and legitimacy. During his first years in power Asad's primary objective was to terminate the state of diplomatic isolation in which Syria found herself throughout the 1960s. This policy led to the formation of the Egyptian–Syrian axis – an essential step in the preparation of the October War.

The military and political circumstances and consequences of that war led to a far more ambitious Syrian strategy which took full shape by 1975. Syria's rulers began to seek hegemony in Syria's immediate Arab environment, a leadership role in inter-Arab relations and in the conflict with Israel and the capacity to manoeuvre between the two super-powers. Occasionally, moments of complacency, they even spoke of taking away from Egypt the role of leading the Arab world as a whole.

This phase of Asad's foreign policy reached its peak in the first half of 1977. By then Syria had won endorsement from the Arab world of her hegemony in Lebanon; together with Saudi Arabia and Egypt she had formulated a unified

The author is Head of the Shiloah Center for Middle Eastern and African Studies, Tel Aviv University.

Arab strategy for a comprehensive settlement of the Arab–Israeli conflict; and she was able to set the conditions under which Asad met with both Presidents Carter and Brezhnev that year. Syria's influence on the course of events in the Middle East was demonstrated in August 1977. The American Secretary of State, Cyrus Vance, announced, on the strength of a Saudi promise, that the PLO would attend a Geneva Conference. But Syrian pressure on the PLO was stronger than Saudi influence and a Geneva Conference could not be convened. This development played an important role in persuading President Sadat that Syria and the PLO had acquired veto power over Arab collective action and that a different strategy was now required.

Domestic Constraints and Foreign Policy

Overshadowed by this aura of success, processes were already at work which a few months later confronted the Syrian Ba'ath regime with a grave and sustained crisis. Like his earlier success, Asad's difficulties were caused by a combination of domestic and external developments. The catalyst for this trend of events was Syria's involvement in the Lebanese crisis.

The Ba'ath regime's military intervention in Lebanon was widely construed in Syria as an essentially sectarian policy – a Christian–Alawi alliance against the Palestinian and Lebanese Sunni Muslims. This perception fanned communal tensions in Syria and the urban population's hostility to the regime. Furthermore, the army's lengthy involvement in Lebanon not only created inflationary pressures but also resulted in internecine squabbling in the regime's upper echelons, and exposed the army – especially the officers, who had previously been isolated within the closed Syrian political system – to the gamut of political opinions circulating in the freer atmosphere of Lebanon.[2] Moreover, involvement in Lebanon led to pressure from Syria's external rivals, primarily Iraq and the PLO: troop concentrations on Syria's borders, denigration of the Ba'ath regime's revolutionary credentials and, most significantly, the encouragement of domestic opposition groups.

Against this background, radical elements in the Islamic opposition to the Syrian regime decided to escalate their efforts to topple it. Fundamentalist Muslim groups had led the opposition to the Ba'ath in Syria since 1964. The urban Sunni population's resentment at being dispossessed by humbler ethnic and religious minority groups of rural background, and the Sunni refusal to accept a ruling group perceived as non-Islamic and irreligious, were most effectively expressed by the Muslim Brotherhood and other like-minded groups and individuals. But the experience of more than a decade showed that strikes and demonstrations could not unseat a regime firmly in control of the army. Hence, like similar groups in Egypt and Iran, and to some extent influenced by their example, after 1976 the radical fringes of the Syrian Muslim Brotherhood resorted to personal terrorism and urban guerrilla tactics aimed at setting Sunni against Alawi. The purpose of the new methods was to neutralize the regime's control of the army and thus bring about its downfall. In the second half of 1979 the radical groups succeeded in instigating widespread civil disobedience in Northern Syria which the regime was unable to quell before the summer.

This chain of events revealed the frail foundations on which Syria's drive in the mid-1970s for regional primacy had been based. A fragmented polity dominated by a minority group could not sustain the burden of an ambitious foreign policy, and was certainly incapable of setting another fragmented house (Lebanon) in order. And as the domestic crisis of the Ba'ath regime continued and then re-erupted, a more perturbing question had to be asked: whether Syria was slipping back to the conditions of the 1950s and 1960s, when endemic instability had undermined her ability to conduct an effective foreign policy.

Constricted Foreign Policy

The domestic crisis of the late 1970s converged with a number of regional developments to produce a state of stalemate in the conduct of Syrian foreign policy. Asad's visions of hegemony and leadership of the mid-1970s had rested on a false evaluation of both Syria's and his own regime's real capabilities, and by the end of 1977 Syria had lost even the capacity to initiate and effect limited foreign policy ventures, and was slipping back into a state of isolation reminiscent of the late 1960s. This state of affairs came to characterize all four major areas of Syrian foreign policy: the Arab–Israeli conflict, inter-Arab relations, the Lebanese crisis and relations with the two super-powers.

Since 1967 Syria's policy in the Arab–Israeli conflict has been governed by the need to demonstrate a credible strategy for regaining the Golan Heights, which the Ba'ath regime had lost in controversial circumstances. As a rule Syria pursued a middle course between those who advocated a political settlement and those who rejected this on grounds of principle. Syria joined Egypt in the October War and in the negotiating process which followed it. In the mid-1970s she distanced herself from Egypt and from the process of settlement, but until 1977 the Israeli issue was overshadowed by the impressive successes of the Asad regime in other spheres of foreign policy, by the Lebanese crisis and by Syria's violent confrontation with the Palestine Liberation Organization.

But by the end of 1977 the Arab–Israeli conflict had taken the centre of the stage again and Asad found himself incapable of responding to the challenges presented by the opening of direct Egyptian–Israel negotiations and by the subsequent Egyptian–Israeli peace treaty in 1979. The meeting held in December 1977 in Tripoli (Libya) by the states which formed the anti-Sadat 'steadfastness front' exposed two major weaknesses in Syria's position. First was the demand made by Syria's more radical partners that she eliminate all ambiguity in her attitude to the issue of settlement by renouncing United Nations Security Council Resolutions 242 and 338. As long as Syria refuses to do that the radical regimes of Libya and Iraq and part of the Palestine Liberation Organization will continue to suspect that Syria's quarrel with Egypt is of a tactical nature and that in more favourable circumstances she might rejoin the settlement process.

The other problem derived from Syria's bitter rivalry with Iraq. This seemed to have been resolved by the short-lived Syrian–Iraqi *rapprochement* that was reached under the impact of the Camp David accords in October 1978 and as a result of Iraq's quest for hegemony in the Arab world. This development was essential to the formation of an effective anti-Sadat coalition at the Baghdad Summit Conference of November 1978. But during the next few months the effort to consolidate the Syrian–Iraqi *rapprochement* and to present a viable alternative to Egypt's military power foundered. The hostility between the Syrian and Iraqi Ba'ath regimes proved to be too profound and by the Spring of 1979 Syria and Iraq were once again at loggerheads.

With Egypt (at least temporarily) outside the Arab pale, and in view of Iraq's hostility (and subsequent preoccupation with Iran), Syria felt militarily exposed to Israel. In Syrian terminology this development was defined as the destruction of the 'strategic balance' in the region and the creation of a 'strategic gap' between Syria and Israel. This was not felt along the Syrian–Israeli ceasefire line as much as in Lebanon where Syria was unable to interfere with Israel's activity. Indeed, the Ba'ath regime was sharply criticized for its failure to resist the massive Israeli invasion into South Lebanon in March 1978.[3]

Still more embarrassing was the gradual implementation of the 1979 Israeli–Egyptian peace treaty and the return during 1979 and 1980 of two-thirds of the Sinai to Egyptian control. While Syria continued to vilify President Sadat and his policies she possessed no political or military means of response, nor could she persuasively point to an alternative strategy likely to bring comparable achievements in the Golan Heights. Occasional references in the controlled Syrian media revealed the Ba'ath regime's sensitivity to the impact that this was having on Syrian and Arab public opinion. The most significant of these was the publication in March 1979 of a series of articles in the Syrian government's paper by Hafez Jamali, a former cabinet member, who, with bitter self-criticism, discussed Syria's record in the Arab–Israeli conflict and argued, among other things, that the Arabs had tended over time to reject peace plans and then to settle on less satisfactory ones.[4]

Asad's failure to organize an effective anti-Egyptian front was also a measure of the decline in Syria's position in inter-Arab relations. The Jordanian alliance, a cornerstone of Syria's military and political posture in the mid-1970s, had been transformed first into an indifferent and then a hostile relationship. Syria resented Jordan's refusal to combat the Islamic opposition to the Ba'ath regime and interpreted the freedom of action granted to Syrian Muslim militants in Jordan as tantamount to support of her enemies. Damascus suspected also that King Hussein, despite his reservations about and criticism of the

Camp David framework, might join it. Jordan in turn saw considerable advantages in replacing her Syrian alliance with an Iraqi one.

A similar deterioration affected Syria's relations with Saudi Arabia and the other conservative oil-producing states. While these states had never been friendly with Asad, they had come to accept his regime as preferable to its predecessor and likely successors. But as Syria's domestic and external problems mounted, and as her mood grew more radical and her sectarian character became more pronounced, the Asad regime became less palatable to Saudi Arabia and her Arab followers.

Syria's rivalry with Iraq has already been mentioned as an obstacle to the creation of political and military alternatives to Egypt. But from a Syrian point of view it was equally disturbing to realize that a shift had occurred in the Syrian–Iraqi balance of power. In the first half of the 1970s Iraq was the weaker party in the conflict, but a period of domestic stability, large oil revenues, a military build-up, the suppression of the Kurdish rebellion and the (temporary) mending of fences with Iran enabled the Iraqi Ba'athists to exert effective pressure on their Syrian rivals during the second half of the decade.

Nor did Syria have comfortable relations with Sadat's other radical opponents. Asad's relations with the Libyan regime of Mu'ammar Gaddafi have been traditionally marked by ambivalence. Periods of co-operation (against Sadat and the US) were followed by periods of tension and hostility. Gaddafi was an occasional supporter of the Islamic opposition to the Ba'ath regime, while, for their part, the Ba'athists tended to regard him with a mixture of suspicion and ridicule. Syria's relations with the PLO were still overshadowed by their conflict over the Lebanese crisis in 1976 and by Asad's attempt to replace Arafat in 1977. Syria's conflict with the PLO was not a mere dispute over questions of policy and orientation. On a deeper level it grew out of Syria's claim that, because of the special historical and territorial links between the Syrian state and Palestine, she was no less a custodian of the Palestinian cause than the PLO. Coupled with Syria's hegemony and her military predominance in Lebanon, this claim presented a serious threat for the PLO. Still, Syria's leverage over the PLO was reduced by the latter's import-

ance for any anti-Sadat front and its skill in drawing support from Syria's Arab rivals. Under these circumstances the PLO managed as a rule to preserve its autonomy, but when vital Syrian interests were involved Syria did not hesitate to force the organization to follow its lead.[5]

The Lebanon issue continued to pose a fundamental dilemma for the Ba'ath regime. Syria did maintain her hegemony in Lebanon, and the long-term prospects for the consolidation and formalization of that position remained good. The Syrian presence in Lebanon provided the Ba'ath regime with the means for controlling the PLO, challenging Israel and Israeli–Egyptian peace, and retaining at least a measure of regional and international influence. But at times the price for staying in Lebanon seemed prohibitive. Thus in the Winter of 1980, at the height of its domestic crisis, the Asad regime found it necessary to redeploy (and withdraw some of) its military units in Lebanon.

The dilemma which Lebanon presented for the Asad regime was further complicated by two developments. One was the intensification of the Palestinian–Israeli military conflict in and from Lebanon. This was desirable to Syria insofar as it challenged the political effectiveness of the Camp David framework. But Syria found it increasingly difficult to stay aloof from the conflict. Consequently, while between 1975 and 1979 Syria and Israel avoided a direct conflict in Lebanon, the Syrian air force began in the Summer of 1979 to engage Israeli planes in reconnaissance or combat missions over Lebanon.[6] The other development was the steady growth in the cohesiveness and power of the (Christian) Lebanese Front under the leadership of the Phalanges. In the autonomous Christian region in Mount Lebanon and along the Lebanese coast north of Beirut the infrastructure of an independent Christian–Lebanese state was being laid. Syria's reluctance to suffer casualties, and Israel's (ill-defined) commitment to the Christians, deterred Syria from a fully-fledged confrontation with the Lebanese Front, but the two were clearly on a collision course.

If the high-water mark of Asad's diplomatic success in 1976 and 1977 was his ability to play off one super-power against the other, his diminished prestige at the end of the decade manifested itself in Syria's growing dependence on the Soviet Union. The Syrian–American dialogue was suspended at the end of 1977, and the Soviet Union resumed her erstwhile position as an indispensable source of military supply and protection as well as of political support and legitimacy for a beleaguered regime. This was clearly demonstrated in January 1980, when Syria was one of the few Muslim countries which refused to criticize, much less denounce, the Soviet invasion of Afghanistan.

Attempted Recovery

The domestic crisis in Syria culminated in July 1980 with an attempt on Asad's life and an open rebellion against his regime. Once the rebellion had been put down, and the immediate threat to the Ba'ath regime's very existence removed, Syria's leaders were able to turn to a more more systematic attempt to revitalize their foreign policy. What resulted was not the formulation of a new ambitious comprehensive strategy, comparable to the ones adopted in 1970 and 1975, for after all the regime was still crippled by the lingering crisis, was uncertain of its general orientation, and faced an inhospitable regional scene. Yet a series of inter-related measures were taken that restored a measure of dynamism and resourcefulness to Syria's foreign policy.

Most significant was the Syrian quest for a formal treaty of friendship and co-operation with the Soviet Union. Earlier in the decade it had been the Soviet Union which exerted pressure on Syria to join Egypt and Iraq, both of whom had signed such a treaty. But this would have been inconsistent with the foreign policy goals and style of Asad, who systematically evaded Soviet pressure. But in 1980 a reversal of perspectives and roles took place. From a Syrian point of view a treaty would do no more than formalize the existing state of affairs and would carry with it considerable advantages. Militarily, a contractual relationship with the Soviet Union could go a long way towards closing the 'strategic gap' with Israel. A treaty could improve the prospects of greater Soviet military aid, might even carry with it a security guarantee to Syria, and, in any case, should enhance the deterrence value of the Soviet–Syrian relationship.

Politically, a treaty with the Soviet Union was to serve as a signal to friend and foe alike that Moscow still considered the Syrian Ba'ath

regime an asset worthy of backing and support. The treaty was bound further to antagonize the US and her friends in the region (Saudi Arabia in particular), but it could also serve as a warning that continued pressure on Syria would only serve to radicalize Syrian politics, bring Syria closer to the Soviet Union, and improve the latter's position in the region. Thus, while in earlier years Asad sought to improve his international position by drawing away from the Soviet Union he was now trying to regain some leverage by drawing closer to her. The USSR, in turn, must have been aware of the liabilities and limitations involved in the new formal relationship with Syria, which explains the lengthy negotiations which preceded the signing of the treaty of friendship and co-operation on 8 October 1980.[7]

Related to this development was the announcement on 10 September 1980 of a (nominal) union between Libya and Syria. Asad must have retained his reservations with regard to Gaddafi's regime, but with his legitimacy challenged so vehemently by his critics, he could use not just the financial but also the moral and political backing of a ruler with such distinctive Arab and Islamic credentials. This backing was made all the more urgent by the decision to sign a treaty with the Soviet Union. Asad – who had himself objected to the idea of such a treaty – expected a wave of criticism and prepared for it by securing Gaddafi's endorsement.[8]

Syria's new alliance with Libya, grafted on to her long-standing relationship with Khomeini's regime, represented in regional terms the emergence of a radical bloc composed of Syria, Libya and Iran. It stood as a rival and an antithesis to the rather loose Iraqi–Jordanian–Saudi grouping which crystallized, too, in 1980. These lines of division overlapped but were coterminous with the pattern of pro-Soviet and pro-American alignments in the region.

The effects of these developments were soon manifested through concrete policy measures. When the war between Iraq and Iran broke out, Syria and Libya supported Iran despite the embarrassment involved in taking the side of the non-Arab party in the conflict. In November, when Jordan hosted the eleventh Arab Summit Conference, Syria boycotted the meeting and was joined by Libya and three other members of the Arab League who either supported the Syrian position or, like the Palestine Liberation Organization, had to toe the Syrian line in any such confrontation.

Most significant, though, was the concentration of Syrian troops along the Jordanian border and Syria's obstreperous threats to wage war on Jordan. This move undoubtedly reflected Syria's irritation with what she perceived as actual Jordanian support of the Islamic opposition to the Ba'ath regime. It could also be seen as a move in the context of the Iran–Iraq war – an attempt to demonstrate the vulnerability of Iraq's major ally. But four other aspects of the crisis seemed to be of particular import: Syria behaved with a confidence which clearly drew upon the new treaty relationship with the Soviet Union; she sought to demonstrate her nuisance value as a central Arab state which, despite its isolation, could disrupt an Arab summit conference and threaten the region's stability, and she conveyed her intention to resist a suspected Jordanian decision to join the Israeli–Egyptian peace process.[9] Underlying Syria's conduct during the Jordanian crisis and in the following months was the sense of strength she derived from the impressive quantitative growth and qualitative development of the Syrian army.

Syria's military build-up in the late 1970s was the one unquestionable practical benefit of her relationship with the USSR. The Soviet Union was hard-put to arrest the progress of the Camp David process and reluctant to provide Syria with a clear-cut security guarantee, but she made up for it by supplying the Syrian armed forces with large quantities of the latest weapon systems. The Syrian military build-up was planned and implemented with a view to meeting the three tasks of the Syrian armed forces: developing a defensive as well as an offensive capability vis-à-vis Israel, defending the regime against domestic opposition, and maintaining Syria's position in Lebanon. Emphasis was put on the development of armoured units, the air force, air-defence systems, and artillery and special forces. By the end of 1980, the Syrian armed forces were estimated to have three armoured divisions, two mechanized divisions, six independent armoured or mechanized brigades, some 395 combat airplanes, 2 missile regiments and several commando and paratroopers regiments. With an army of that size

and with the latest equipment (T-72 tanks and MiG-25s), Asad felt that he could undertake the risk of a military clash with Jordan and even with Israel.

The Lebanese Crisis

The renewed confidence and increased capability evident in Syria's conduct during the final three months of 1980 were underlined by the Lebanese missile crisis, which unfolded in three stages in the Spring and Summer of 1981.

The crisis began with fierce fighting between Syrian troops and Phalangist militiamen who established themselves in the town of Zahle in Eastern Lebanon and tried to link it to the Christian stronghold in Mount Lebanon. The Syrian army then shelled Zahle and Christian areas in Beirut and assaulted Phalangist positions in the Eastern slopes of Mount Lebanon. Israel, who had an ill-defined commitment to the Phalanges, shot down two Syrian helicopters. Syria responded by placing ground-to-ground air missiles in previously prepared positions inside Lebanon's territory, and by reinforcing her missile batteries on the Syrian side of the Syrian–Lebanese border. Israel then argued that this was an infraction of the 1976 tacit agreement to which the US, Israel and Syria had been partners, and threatened to destroy the missile sites. In order to resolve the crisis, the American diplomat Philip Habib began a mediation effort that was interrupted by the Israeli raid on the Iraqi nuclear reactor and by the extensive Palestinian–Israeli clashes in July. It is not known whether Syria's artillery took part in these clashes, but the Syrian ground-to-air missiles certainly constrained the Israeli air force's activity.

Syria's conduct at the early stages of the crisis could be explained purely in the context of the Lebanese crisis. She clearly saw the Phalangist extension into Eastern Lebanon as a challenge to her own position in the country and, in particular, to her hold over its most vital region – the Bekaa valley, which affords Israel one of the two alternative routes for outflanking the Syrian defence line in the Golan Heights.

But Syria's policy soon went beyond a simple response to a perceived Phalangist challenge and should be explained in far broader terms. It revealed, for one thing, a greater sense of confidence, based not so much on a Soviet guarantee as on the numerical strength and qualitative development of the Syrian armed forces. Syria did not seek an armed confrontation with Israel, but she was clearly ready to undertake one if the implementation of her policy so required. This sense of confidence increased in time, when Israel's failure immediately to attack the missile sites and the US mediation style were interpreted in Damascus as signifying a reluctance to engage in or contemplate an Israel–Syria military confrontation.[10]

The exacerbation of the Lebanese crisis in early April coincided with the Middle Eastern tour of Alexander Haig, the then new American Secretary of State. He came to examine and promote his ideas of co-operation among America's diverse allies in the region and of continuing and consolidating the Arab–Israeli peace process after the Israeli June elections. But Syria had no place in Mr Begin's schemes, and he tended to speak derisively about the Ba'ath regime, its relations with the Soviet Union and its role in Lebanon. By triggering a crisis in early April Syria could demonstrate (with anticipated Soviet blessings) that the US was not free to discuss the formation of a pro-Western grouping in the region and the next phase of the Israeli–Arab settlement process without taking Syria into full account.

Syria's original intentions are still a matter of speculation, but the impact of her initiative must have been considerably greater than Asad expected. The missile crisis occurred at a most inconvenient moment for the US – when her Middle Eastern policy consisted more of rudimentary ideas than of detailed concrete plans, when she still did not possess the capacity for a potential confrontation with the Soviet Union, and when she least of all wanted to stand behind or alongside Israel against Syria supported willy nilly by the Arab oil-producers.

The US tried to solve the problem through the mediation mission of Philip Habib. This course of events afforded Syria considerable advantages. Despite her signing of the treaty with the Soviet Union, Syria was negotiating once again with the US – an outcome which demonstrated the difficulty, not to say the futility, of seeking to ignore Syria in planning future moves in the region, and which allowed Syria to inject her point of view into the discussion of both the Lebanese and Palestinian problems.

In Anticipation of April 1982

Although the Syrian–Israeli missile crisis of 1981 has remained unresolved, it has since been overshadowed by several significant developments: the Israeli–Palestinian fighting along the Lebanese–Israeli border and the ceasefire of July; the Israeli elections and the formation of Menachem Begin's second government; and the assassination of President Sadat of Egypt in October 1981.

These developments were given particular significance by the approaching completion of Israel's withdrawal from the Sinai in April 1982. Syria's policy in late 1981 and early 1982 was conducted on the assumption that the Arab–Israeli conflict in its post-April-1982 phase was likely to develop three major potential scenarios. In declining order of preference they could be described as follows. First the crystallization of a new Arab coalition of both moderate and radical Arab states that would undo the post-1977 'peace process' and replace it with a renewed quest for a comprehensive settlement according to Syria's interpretation of that term. Syria's concept of a comprehensive settlement envisaged a complete Israeli withdrawal for less than a peace settlement, a resolution of the Palestinian problem, and Soviet and West European participation in the settlement process. Second, the exertion of military pressure on Israel – preferably by several Arab states, possibly by Syria alone, should such a coalition fail to crystallize. This option would rest on the change in the strategic balance resulting from Israel's withdrawal as well as on Syria's improved military capability. Third, a continuation, at least for a few months, of the pre-April situation.

But Damascus was not the only capital in the region contemplating post-April developments. In anticipation of the same developments measures were also taken by other regional actors – most notably the publication of the Saudi Fahd Plan and the extension of Israeli law to the Golan Heights.

The publication of the Fahd plan and its discussion at the Fez Summit Conference forced the Ba'ath regime to formulate and present an official policy towards the notion of an alternative to the Camp David accords, acceptable to an Arab consensus at an early stage, well before April and under auspices and circumstances initiated by Riad and not by Damascus. Therefore, although some of the elements of the Fahd plan were acceptable to Syria, she chose to play the leading role in obstructing it and in aborting the Fez Arab Summit. This resulted in a strained Syrian–Saudi relationship and exacerbated Syrian isolation in the Arab world.

Far more serious was the Israeli decision to extend Israel's law to the Golan Heights and thus virtually to annex it. The Israeli move, itself taken in anticipation of 25 April, pinpointed Syria's own dilemma. While Asad had been bedevilled previously by his inability to show progress in his efforts to regain the Golan Heights, the pressure to respond effectively to a measure which tightened Israel's grip on that territory was far greater. In the absence of a dramatic political response to the Israeli move, the option of direct or indirect Syrian military measures against Israel before April 1982 had to be given careful consideration. But could Syria risk war with Israel in the political and military conditions prevailing in the Winter of 1981–2? The answer to that question was clearly negative. Yet she had to consider the possibility that she would be drawn into an unplanned war with Israel in the course of a crisis that might easily develop in Lebanon. By this time it had become clear that a new situation had developed in South Lebanon after July 1981. As a result of the PLO's effective shelling of the Northern Galilee, Israel officially declared that a violation of the July ceasefire would lead to a massive Israeli operation in Lebanon, designed to eliminate the PLO's infrastructure in the South and to push it beyond its artillery range.

Syria could hardly afford to sit idle if an Israeli operation of that magnitude were to take place in Lebanon. Her leaders realized that by being drawn into such potential hostilities they would provide the Israeli military with an opportunity to engage the Syrian army under comparatively favourable circumstances. Following this line of reasoning, the Syrian leadership not only suspended its military response to the Golan Law but joined the ranks of those who sought to maintain the Israeli–Palestinian ceasefire in South Lebanon.

The Ba'ath regime's malaise was compounded in February by the recrudescence of the Muslim Brotherhood's challenge. The size of the opposition's organization in Hama and the renewed symptoms of civil disobedience in Aleppo were alarming as such, but their political impact was magnified by two additional factors. One was the fact that the Syrian domestic crisis was made into an issue by the American government. The other was the appearance of recognizable figures abroad as spokesmen for a coherent opposition. Not only the regime's control but its standing and credibility were now being tested.

If Syria had little to expect before the end of April, what options are available to her beyond that date? It seems that the broad alternatives which had existed before the pull and push of the past few months have not changed in essence and that the Asad regime is preparing for them.

Syria's willingness to take part in a prospective Arab effort to replace the Camp David framework with the quest for a comprehensive settlement (compatible with Syria's definition) was most clearly stated in late January by Syria's Minister of Information.[11] In a most instructive interview granted to a Beirut newspaper the Minister explained both his country's opposition to the Fahd plan and its commitment to a form of settlement containing 'elements of peace which if realized would put enough distance between us and the Sadat–Begin form of capitulation'. The Syrian spokesman emphasized that, in return for a full Israeli withdrawal and the confirmation of the full rights of the Palestinians, the Arabs should agree (merely) to the termination of the state of belligerency with Israel.

While this interview was indicative of the preparations made by Syria for the political and diplomatic activity likely to take place in the Spring, the preparations made for the possibility of military clashes were naturally less perceptible. But the option was taken into account.

The Post-April Perspective

On 25 April Israel completed her withdrawal from the Sinai without a crisis in Egyptian–Israeli relations. Nor did a major Israeli operation in Lebanon and a concomitant Israeli–Syrian clash take place, despite the tension along Israel's northern borders in March and April.

Egypt's stated policy – reconciliation with the Arab world without a radical change in the new relationship with Israel – was made more credible by the latest turn of events in the Iran–Iraq war. Iraq's growing difficulties made her more dependent on Egyptian military procurement and, potentially, support. The prospect of an Egyptian *rapprochement* with Iraq and her Arab allies, Saudi Arabia and Jordan, without the latter's insistence on an Egyptian renunciation of the Camp David framework was alarming from a Syrian point of view.

The emergence of an Egyptian–Saudi–Jordanian–Iraqi grouping within the system of inter-Arab relations could among other things abort the formation of the broad Arab coalition which, according to the original Syrian design, should undo the post-1977 'peace process'. In order to prevent the continuation, let alone consolidation, of the Arab–Israeli *status quo*, the pressure was on the Syrian government to resort to direct (Syrian) or indirect (Palestinian) military action against Israel.

The transition to such a new phase need not be the result of a meticulously planned decision. The need to decide on the renewal of the UNDOF mandate and the precarious situation in South Lebanon could provide the opportunity or the spark for a new Syrian–Israeli crisis.

NOTES

Research for the writing of this essay has been facilitated by a Ford Foundation grant administered through Israel's Foundation's Trustees.

[1] See I. Rabinovich, 'Full Circle – Syrian Politics in the 1970's' in G. S. Wise and C. Issawi (eds.), *Middle Eastern Perspectives*, (Princeton, New Jersey: Princeton University Press, 1981), pp. 129–40.

[2] See A. Dawisha, 'Syria in Lebanon – Asad's Vietnam?' *Foreign Policy*, no. 33, 1978–9, pp. 135–50.

[3] Significantly, such criticism appeared even in the Syrian government's newspaper *al-Thawra*, written by a former officer and cabinet member Amin al-Nafuri. See *al-Thawra*, 30 March 1978.

[4] *Al-Thawra*, 23 March and 30 1979 and see Dina Kehat, 'Syria' in Colin Legum and Haim Shaked (eds.), *Middle East Contemporary Survey, 1977–1978* (New York and London: Holmes and Meier, 1980), p. 729.

[5] Walid Khalidi, *Conflict and Violence in Lebanon: Confrontation in the Middle East* (Cambridge, Mass.: Center for International Affairs, Harvard University, 1980), pp. 150–2.

[6] Cf. Z. Lanir, 'Israel's Involvement in Lebanon: A Precedent for an 'Open' Game with Syria?' Tel Aviv University, Center for Strategic Studies, Paper no. 10, April 1981.

[7] See the interviews with Syria's Minister of Foreign Affairs (*al-Nahar al-Arabi wa-l-Duwali*, 13 October 1980) and information (*Monday Morning*, 10 November 1980).

[8] *Al-Iqtisad al-Arabi*, October 1980.

[9] *Al-Mustaqbal*, December 1980. See also, for example Radio Damascus of 24 November 1980.

[10] See the illuminating speech delivered by President Asad on 11 April and the interview with Foreign Minister Khaddam broadcast by Radio Damascus on 15 May.

[11] *Monday Morning*, Beirut, 1–7 February 1982.

3 A Palestinian State? Examining the Alternatives

AVI PLASCOV

INTRODUCTION

The volatile region of the Middle East has undergone five wars in the course of the last thirty years. This chronic instability, caused partly, but not exclusively, by the unresolved Palestinian question has had (and will continue to have) serious implications for the world as a whole. With no solution emerging from the armed conflict between them, Egypt and Israel have opted to settle their differences by peaceful means. Yet the Palestinian issue is now on the agenda between Egypt, Israel and the United States not only because of the Arab commitment to the Palestinian cause but because of the role the Palestinians have acquired in Middle East politics. Despite their military weakness, they are a factor to be taken into account and at least partly to satisfy. They are a vital component of any comprehensive peace formula. Therefore any discussion which isolates the Palestinian question from the political fate of the remaining parts of Old Palestine, i.e., the West Bank and the Gaza Strip, seems pointless because the question needs to be dealt with in its political entirety.

This Paper looks at possible long-term political 'solutions' to the Palestinian question. Discussions of this complicated problem must also refer to the Palestinian experience, for living under Arab control and Israeli occupation not only left its mark on the Palestinian political awareness but created patterns which any assessment of the future must take into account. The first part of the Paper therefore provides a historical perspective, pointing briefly to the main developments relating to the Palestinians since the 1948 war. This historical period will be divided into two, the period prior to the 1967 war, when the Palestinians were living under Arab rule, and 1967 to the present, when most Palestinians have been under Israeli administration. This part of the Paper will describe political and economic developments relating to the area in which most Palestinians live: the West Bank and the Gaza Strip territories, which are being proposed as a possible Palestinian homeland.

The second part of the Paper looks into the options which have been proposed and their implications for regional stability. The 'Israeli Option', which involves either the perpetuation of the present *status quo* or the annexation of the territories in question and the different forms of a 'Jordanian solution' (the return of part or all of these territories to Jordanian control) will be evaluated.

The third part of the Paper concentrates on a 'Palestinian Option' to assess the possibilities for the establishment of an independent Palestinian entity between Israel and Jordan and the political and strategic complexities involved. This part of the study looks beyond the immediate problems posed by the proposed Palestinian autonomy and examines the internal and external conditions under which such a Palestinian entity could come into being and could contribute to 'stability' in the region. These come mainly under two interrelated headings: the political ingredients such a framework must have if it is to satisfy the minimum Palestinian needs; and the minimum security and political requirements of the other states which would be affected, especially Palestine's immediate neighbours, Israel and Jordan.

As an exercise attempting to study the complexities involved in the establishment of such an entity, the Paper does not intend to provide a blueprint for a settlement of the Palestinian question, nor is it concerned with the mechanics of reaching an agreement. Nevertheless, it will be necessary to touch upon some of the more obvious transitional problems involved in getting from an unstable present to a more stable future.

It must be said that the 'solution' proposed here is unlikely to be acceptable to the present leadership in Israel, in Jordan or of the PLO. Yet it may provide a basis on which all could come to reach agreement when the alternatives that each are currently proposing are deemed totally unacceptable to the others. It will require all to retreat from their entrenched positions but, as will be argued in the Paper, concessions of substance will be essential if a more predictable and thus more 'stable' position is to be reached.

Part I: Historical Perspective

I. THE PALESTINIANS UNDER ARAB RULE: 1948 – 1967

The clash between the Palestinian and the Zionist movements under the British mandate developed their respective political awareness. But, while the Jewish community gained in confidence, the Palestinian Arabs were weakened by chronic internal feuds and so were manipulated during this period by the Arab states, especially by Jordan.

The Emirate of Trans-Jordan was created by the British in 1922. It comprised three-quarters of mandated Palestine but was administratively separate from Palestine until 1946, when Britain declared Jordan a sovereign state. Abdullah, then the Jordanian monarch, dissatisfied with the poor, under-developed and geographically isolated Trans-Jordan, strove to widen his domain. He saw the merging of Palestine and Trans-Jordan, as the way to a more extensive state which might provide an outlet to the Mediterranean. His attempts to realise this ambition were resisted by the Jews in Palestine, who had other ambitions. They agreed upon one matter only: there should not be an additional Arab state as envisaged by the United Nations 1947 Partition Scheme. This plan called for the establishment in Palestine of two states – Jewish and Arab – and for the Internationalization of the city of Jerusalem. Whereas the Jews viewed this solution as tolerable, it was totally rejected by all Arab governments as well as by the only recognized Palestinian Arab body, the Arab Supreme Committee for Palestine. Their adamant position was that no Jewish state should be set up on any part of what they regarded as Arab land.

Yet there was a lack of political unity among the Arab states *vis-à-vis* the alternative and this contributed to their failure to prevent Israel's emergence when Arab armies invaded Palestine after the British withdrew in May 1948. In fact, Israel acquired territory more extensive than in the Partition proposal. Jordan, however, had

gained most of Arab Palestine and Abdullah, fearful that renewed hostilities with Israel might result in loss, agreed to cede to Israel territory not taken over by her at the end of the war, but which Israel considered vital to her defence. Israel came to control 77% of pre-1948 Palestine, some 2,500 square miles more than allocated by the UN Partition Scheme. (See Map 1).

Thus, Arab Palestine as envisaged by the UN was divided. Jordan annexed the area to the west of the River Jordan (subsequently designated the West Bank), Egypt controlled the Gaza district, and Israel the remainder.

The Palestinians – refugees and non-refugees – became either Jordanian Citizens (about 800,000), Stateless Palestinians in the Gaza Strip (about 270,000) or Israeli Arabs (about 150,000). Those living in Syria (100,000) and Lebanon (80,000) became Palestinian Refugees.[1] Many Palestinians subsequently found their way to other Arab countries and, later, some emigrated to the West.

The Gaza Strip: Palestinians Under Egyptian Control

The Gaza Strip is 25 miles long and 4.9 miles wide. It could not possibly support the vast refugee population which arrived there and most of those living in the Strip became the responsibility of the United Nations Relief and Work Agency for the Palestine Refugees (UNRWA). Egypt faced difficulties; she wanted to discredit Abdullah and to deprive him of his territorial gains and his claim to represent all Palestinians. If she incorporated the Gaza Strip, this would legitimize Abdullah's annexation of the West Bank (which had never been recognized by any Arab country and was approved of internationally only by Britain and Pakistan). It would prove a serious economic burden, and annexation would make it appear that Egypt rejected the unanimous Arab demand for the refugees' return to their pre-1948

49

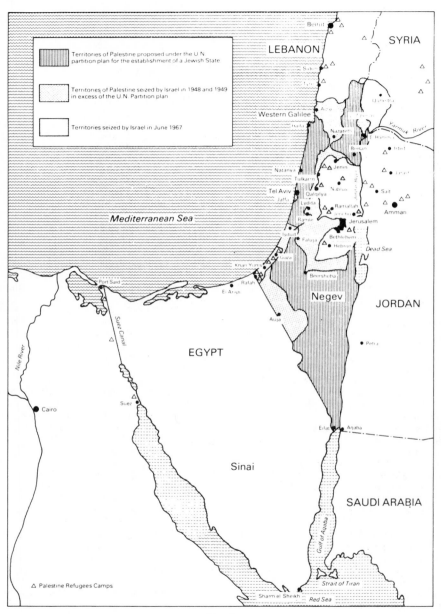

Map 1

homes. It would, moreover, be interpreted as recognition of Israel. Egypt could not appear to betray the Arab cause, and she therefore exercised control over the area. But while appearing to go along with the Palestinians' demands, she did not permit their leaders to have any real power. The first Palestinian government in Gaza was composed mainly of Abdullah's opponents. They declared Jerusalem the capital of Palestine, which Jordan had occupied and later annexed. This 'All Palestine Government' (APG) was manipulated by Egypt against Jordan, but Palestinian support for Abdullah grew even in the Gaza Strip when it became apparent that the Palestinian 'government' was nothing but an Egyptian puppet which was powerless to reduce the disruptive effects of the rigorous Egyptian control. Some Palestinians tried to escape to Jordan but those who succeeded were unwelcome, both because the regime was mistrustful of the Egyptian-controlled Palestinians and because of Jordan's limited economic capacity.

In the mid-1950s, the President of Egypt, Gamal Abd al-Nasser, posed as the champion of the Palestinian cause in order to further his radical Pan-Arab ambitions, and decided to foster military activity against Israel by setting up the *fida'iyun* Palestinian guerrillas. He also used the *fida'iyun* to strengthen subversive elements in Jordan with the hope of damaging British influence there and of bringing down the Hashemite dynasty. Retaliatory raids by Israel, however, exposed Egypt's reluctance to be dragged into a direct military confrontation with Israel.

But despite Egypt's defeat in the 1956 war against Israel and the harsh measures reintroduced by her against the Palestinians following the internationally imposed Israeli withdrawal from the Sinai and the Gaza Strip, the Palestinians continued to pin great hopes on Nasser. Nevertheless, Palestinian pleas to be included in Egypt and later in the United Arab Republic (established in 1958 between Egypt and Syria) went unheard. They were later encouraged by an Egyptian initiative to create a Palestinian Union with Executive and Legislative Councils.[2] However, this body proved as impotent as the APG, being strictly controlled by its founders.

West Bank: Palestinians under Jordanian Rule
Jordan, which had absorbed most of the Palestinians, was the only Arab state to grant them citizenship. This was a source of conflict between Jordan and the other members of the Arab League for a while in the early 1950s, but not between the Jordanian regime and its new subjects. Yet this amounted to incorporation rather than a union between separate states. 'Jordanization' implied absorption of Palestinians, who outnumbered the Trans-Jordanians, into the Kingdom of Jordan. The Jordanian regime in the West Bank was characterized by an extreme reluctance to do anything which might imperil the viability of the enlarged kingdom. Abdullah's dilemma was clear: he had to devise policies which would win Palestinian acquiescence and advance their integration without upsetting the original Jordanian people and endangering his own power base. At the same time he had to make the Palestinians feel that they had taken on a Jordanian identity, while simultaneously supporting their demands to return to their pre-1948 homes. Abdullah's isolation within the Arab world meant that he had to demonstrate his support for the Palestinian cause and his hostility to Israel. Yet he wished to avoid both a distinct Palestinian identity developing within his kingdom and armed conflict with Israel.

Abdullah therefore encouraged 'his' Palestinians – refugees and non-refugees – to take part in the political life of Jordan. Apart from the army, which the Hashemites have always regarded as the corner-stone of their regime, practically all avenues were open to the Palestinians. They came to comprise half the Jordanian parliament and had a large share of members in the government. However, they were not fully trusted and the higher echelons of the administration remained firmly in Jordanian hands.

For their part, the Palestinians had to tread warily. They were politically impotent and fearful. For wealthy Palestinians, the merger of the West Bank into Jordan meant economic and physical security. Even the radical intelligentsia, which had always opposed the conservative regime in Jordan, supported the unification of both sides of the River Jordan on ideological grounds, regarding it as the quintessence of Arab unity and a first step in the removal of what they regarded as artificial differences imposed on Arabs by the imperial powers. Thus annexation was not seriously opposed.

51

Conscious of the symbolic importance of the City of Jerusalem to the Palestinians, the King sought to strengthen Nablus and Hebron economically, and he removed all important offices from Jerusalem to Amman. He refused to grant the City any special status, notwithstanding his historic claim to be its guardian.

At first, many Palestinians were upset by these moves to strengthen Trans-Jordan at the expense of the West Bank, but economic ties now ran through Amman and the merchants soon reorientated themselves. The government encouraged investment in the East Bank and a migration of unemployed Palestinian youth from across the River Jordan followed this economic development. But, since Jordan could only accommodate a fraction of the Palestinian manpower, many young Palestinians emigrated to other parts of the Arab world, taking advantage of the Jordanian passport which proved to be a valuable asset. Palestinians living elsewhere faced serious restrictions on their movements. As the UN provided the refugees' children with education and vocational training this, in turn, enabled the Kingdom to 'export' skilled manpower. These Palestinians proved indispensable in modernizing the Gulf where they earned much higher salaries than in Jordan. The remittances sent home helped to alleviate Jordan's economic hardship and enabled the emigrants' families to improve their own standards of living. Jordan was also happy to export young political radicals, thus allowing the regime to consolidate its hold over the older, more conservative generation remaining behind.

There was sporadic discontent, but West Bank Palestinians hardly ever attempted to organize themselves into a coherent opposition. On the few occasions they tried, internal feuds proved their downfall. Underground opposition parties were formed (which were not exclusively Palestinian), but rarely these called for separation of the West Bank from the rest of Jordan. They aimed primarily at changing the regime's policies rather than the regime itself. They, too, were weakened by their own rivalries and proved powerless beyond organizing demonstrations. Such opposition leaders as there were fled to Syria and Lebanon when the 1957 coup attempt failed and they left behind a political vacuum.

Towards the end of the 1950s, however, the Palestinian question again became an inter-Arab issue. In 1959 Iraq's President General Abd al-Karim Qassem called for the formation of a 'Palestinian Entity'. This was done more to provoke Egypt (by challenging her sole right to speak and act on behalf of the Palestinians) rather than because of a sincere concern for the Palestinians themselves. With this issue dominating inter-Arab rivalries, Jordan changed her official policy towards the Palestinians in 1964 in an attempt to lessen her Arab isolation. She even hosted the first meeting of the Palestine Liberation Organization (PLO) in an attempt to remain in control of Palestinian affairs. But precisely because of the reasons for its establishment the PLO rapidly became an important tool in inter-Arab politics.[3] Thus Jordan hardened her position.

Growing Palestinian helplessness and exasperation with the continuing rifts between the Arab regimes, as well as with the PLO, soon manifested itself in the establishment of another small rival Palestinian organization named *fath*[4] (Fatah) whose leaders managed to gain control of the PLO in the late 1960s. At first Jordan seemed satisfied with Fatah's activities for they embarrassed Egypt and threatened to undermine the main branch of the PLO centred in Gaza. But Fatah incursions into Israel encouraged severe Israeli retaliation against Jordan, forcing her to restrict the political operations of the PLO on Jordanian soil if she was to avoid Israeli raids. The regime also feared that any exclusively Palestinian organization would challenge Jordanian rule over the West Bank and over the numerous Palestinians living on the East Bank. Jordan acted in 1966 and shut down the PLO offices in Jerusalem. In doing so, the regime did not confront serious opposition, for the PLO expressed only muted support for a 'Palestinian Entity' in Jordan. This was partly because the Palestinians feared to support an openly anti-Hashemite movement, and partly because Ahmad Shuqayri,[5] who led the PLO for the first five years, was greatly disliked by many Palestinians, as were his predecessors who were also unknown in Jordan.

Indeed, as far as the Palestinians there were concerned, the question until 1967 was not Palestinian versus Trans-Jordanian, or West Bank versus East Bank, but rather the issue of Palestinian rights within the context of a Hashemite kingdom. The Jordanian regime

52

offered rights to Palestinians individually, but refused to regard them collectively, doing its utmost to suppress a separate Palestinian identity. While the Jordanian regime did not solve the complex problem of its own legitimacy in the eyes of its adopted subjects, it certainly won some measure of respectability and even acceptance. For most Palestinians, expediency and identification with the state went hand in hand. Until the 1967 war, the Palestinians were unable and unwilling to organize themselves as a separatist movement and preferred to concentrate instead on their integration into Jordan.[6]

The 1967 war shattered Palestinian expectations. Not only had Israel managed to destroy the armies of Egypt, Syria and Jordan but she also occupied additional Arab territories, including the whole area known as the remaining part of Palestine, which brought the majority of the Palestinians under Israeli occupation.

II.   THE DEVELOPMENT OF THE PALESTINIAN NATIONAL MOVEMENT: 1967 – 79

Under Israeli Occupation

The 1967 war, according to UN estimates, forced some 150,000 Palestinians from the West Bank to become refugees in the East Bank – half of them for the second time in their lives. Israel allowed only a small number to return to the West Bank under the Unification of Families Scheme. The effect was to further tip the numerical balance of Trans-Jordanians to Palestinians in the East Bank in the latter's favour. Jordan demanded that Israel readmit these refugees into the West Bank and she also rejected Israel's annexation of Eastern Jerusalem. Like all other Arab countries, Jordan condemned Israel for establishing settlements in the territories and called for her immediate withdrawal from all occupied Arab land.

Although Israel and Jordan differed as to the political fate of the West Bank, they enjoyed a degree of economic co-operation and, as in the past, shared the common aim of thwarting any exclusive Palestinian political manifestation in the territories lying between them.

The Israeli authorities kept open the River Jordan bridges for Arab movement to and from Jordan. This benefited all concerned: it enabled Jordan to exercise influence in the West Bank and, for the first time in twenty years, in the Gaza Strip which needed Jordan, now more than ever before, as a gateway to the other Middle East countries. It also enabled the Palestinians to maintain their ties with their relatives. For her part, Israel had an interest in strengthening Hussein's moderating political influence and did not wish to see her markets saturated by West Bank agricultural products and Gaza's citrus fruit.

In order to flaunt her power over the Palestinians, Jordan occasionally closed the bridges or forbade merchandise from certain towns to cross the river. The Jordanian government used the bridges to send salaries and contributions to those on its payroll and to its supporters. Similarly, the Hashemites continued to subsidize some local councils as long as their mayors appeared to be tacitly conforming to Jordanian policies even if, in reality, they staunchly supported the PLO, from whom, up to the mid-1970s, they could not receive economic aid owing to Israel's restrictions. Even Saudi Arabia, who subsidized the PLO heavily, wanted to bolster King Hussein's position by channelling payments to local councils via Amman. Thus in economic terms, the West Bank continued to rely on Jordan.

Israel's attempt to erase any sign of the so-called 'Green Line' (the name given to the 1949 Armistice Lines) had political as well as economic implications. For the first time since 1948, Palestinians from Israel and the West Bank could meet each other freely. This led to the political radicalization of the educated younger generation of Israeli Arabs in the late 1970s, when many of them responded to PLO attempts to recruit them. Until then, they had been purposely ignored by the Palestinians and by all other Arab states, for having remained in Israel as law abiding citizens, thus betraying the Arab cause and granting Israel international legitimacy.

The free traffic across the 1949 Armistice Line and the contact between the two societies had a considerable impact on both the Palestinians and the Jews: the Jews could now visit places of historical and religious significance and the Palestinians could see their former property. Whilst the Israelis rejoiced, the Arabs grieved. But although for most Palestinian refugees the dream of 'The Return' remained, this feeling was soon balanced by a sense of reality and the need to accept the new situation. They flocked eagerly into Israel, thus providing what was to become an indispensable, cheap and unskilled labour force for the Israeli economy. Their standards of living rose, and a building boom took place on the West Bank and the Gaza Strip. Though these territories remained without industries, Israel initiated various agricultural and rehabilitation schemes (especially in the Gaza Strip) and pumped money into the occupied territories via the Palestinian local councils. The Israeli government calculated that the economic boom would keep the Palestinians in work and thereby promote stability and coexistence.

However, the waves of protest in the occupied territories in the late 1960s and the early 1970s reminded all concerned that under the apparently quiet surface there simmered a great deal of unrest. Strikes and demonstrations, initiated mainly by youths in protest against Israel's policies in the occupied territories, were all organized and co-ordinated by the PLO and Palestinian Communists. The process of radicalization became more and more apparent among the students, for whom economic considerations had little meaning. Thus the PLO, functioning from outside the occupied areas, was strengthened and this threatened the more conservative, pro-Jordanian leadership within the territories, which was increasingly seen to be in collaboration with Israel. With no independent power base of their own, the pro-Jordanian leaders had little political influence over developments affecting the Palestinians, as those under occupation always awaited guidance and instructions from Arab governments and the PLO. Hence the fluctuations in the influence of the PLO and the Jordanian government in these territories reflected their respective positions in the Arab world. Both Jordan and the PLO tried to assert themselves as spokesmen for the Palestinians. This competition left its mark on the Palestinians in the occupied territories, as well as in Jordan.

The absence of direct Jordanian control over the West Bank slowed the process of 'Jordanization' and accelerated the development of a distinct Palestinian consciousness amongst the inhabitants, to the benefit of the PLO. However progressive her policies in the occupied terri-

tories, Israel's presence was bound to foster the idea of a national struggle against the occupier. The moderate Palestinians, offered no political concessions by Israel, were pushed aside by the more nationalist elements. Indeed, Israeli policy with regard to the question of Palestinian leadership proved to be counter-productive. By confining local leaders to the handling of municipal affairs only, and leaving general political problems to the Hashemites, she further undermined the conservative leaders' position and, by banning political public meetings, she played into the hands of the PLO which was bound to gain from the absence of any locally organized protest. The PLO thus became the sole co-ordinator of Palestinian unity. The expropriation of land in the occupied territories for security purposes or for the setting up of Israeli settlements only accelerated this trend. Moreover, it was not long before the Palestinians under occupation learned to take advantage of Israeli democracy. The Palestinian press, though censored, enjoyed a previously unknown freedom, whilst that on the Jordanian side became more restricted than ever. The PLO could maintain daily contact with the Palestinians through the media even in the occupied territories where its actions were proscribed.

The Palestinians' hopes rose with the 1973 October war, which was perceived by the Arabs as a victory, regardless of its final military outcome which was in Israel's favour. The Syrian-Egyptian offensive and the demonstration of solidarity throughout the Arab world, culminating in the deployment of the oil weapon, restored Arab confidence, pride and honour. The Arab conference in Rabat a year later declared the PLO to be 'the sole legitimate representative of the Palestinian people' and UN recognition bolstered the PLO's position in the occupied territories.[7]

The Israeli government hoped that a moderate leadership would emerge in the 1976 West Bank Municipal Elections,[8] one which would not adhere to PLO principles and would provide an alternative leadership which could take over certain political responsibilities. Initially, Palestinian participation in these elections was rejected, being regarded by the Arabs as acquiescence in Israel's continued rule over the West Bank but, with Fatah confident of victory, its leaders − unlike the Jordanian government −

authorized its supporters to compete. The results showed a significant drop in the influence of the traditional leaders. The 63,000 voters elected a younger, more assertive and more nationalist Palestinian leadership. PLO supporters, Communists and Ba'athists, running in coalitions called 'National Blocks', came to dominate the councils and in many cases became mayors.

The nationalists' victory stunned the Israeli government. Nevertheless, it ignored the political implications of the vote and continued to regard the municipalities' responsibilities as limited to local affairs. The Israelis, as well as the Jordanians, however, were proved right in believing that daily necessities would shape the town councils' attitudes and that, eventually, they would recognize their need to co-operate with both Israel and Jordan.

However, the Israeli Labour-led governments overestimated the power of economic welfare in bringing the new political leadership to heel and in fostering Palestinian acquiescence in continued Israeli occupation. Ironically, the ascent of Palestinian nationalism came at a time when the Palestinian standard of living was rising. Some Palestinians feared the PLO, but Israel frequently misinterpreted their gratitude and flattery as support for her policies. For the most part Israel ignored the changes that were taking place among the second Palestinian generation, and she underestimated the independence of the young, educated Palestinians who refused to follow in the path of their more compliant fathers. Hence she also failed to recognize the growing influence of the PLO in the West Bank, temporarily satisfied by the periodical political developments which pushed the PLO to the sidelines, and ignoring the growth of Palestinian nationalism which in fact was becoming a force too potent to be dismissed.

This trend was exacerbated under the Likud Government which rose to power in Israel in May 1977. Ideologically committed to the retention of Judea, Samaria and the Gaza District, over which it rejected any territorial compromise, the new Government strove to thwart any Palestinian self-expression. To that end it sought to consolidate Israel's position over these areas through the establishment of many small settlements and the enlargement of existing ones. Deterioration of relations between Israel and the Palestinians became unavoidable because of the conflict resulting from the presence of Israeli settlers in and around Arab cities. Palestinian strikes and other forms of angry protest were quickly quelled by severe restrictions and collective punishments. The cycle of Palestinian violence and Israeli high-handedness culminated in bitter protests against occupation and in favour of the PLO.

In the meantime, the radical mayors also bolstered their own political position, breaking away from the traditional 'division of labour' of handling solely local affairs whilst PLO leaders were engaging in all other matters. Thus the PLO leadership in Lebanon grew ambivalent towards the rising popularity of the mayors: it needed them to co-ordinate political action and strengthen its own position amidst the bulk of the Palestinians over whom it had no control. However, the mayors, with a relatively new sort of power in their hands, might thus prove less amenable to PLO instructions. Moreover, despite its rising popularity among many West Bank and Gaza Strip Palestinians, the PLO did not succeed in undermining Jordan's influence, primarily because of the demographic, economic and political patterns created prior to 1967 which continued to make these Palestinians dependent on Jordanian good-will.

The PLO and the Arab World

Before the imposition of Israeli control, most Palestinians were confused about their identity. Dispersed geographically, with a weak and divided leadership, they were powerless to oppose the regimes which hosted them. They continued to believe that only pan-Arabism translated into a combined military power could return them to their homes. But whether completely isolated from the rest of the Arab world (as in the case of the Gaza Strip) or denied any political voice (as in Lebanon, Syria or elsewhere in the Gulf) or participants in the administration of a country which had adopted them as her citizens (Jordan), the Palestinians eventually grew disillusioned. Arab unity seemed as far off as ever and Arab military power was unstable. Wherever they had come to rest, the Palestinians were looked down on and regarded as a political burden and as potential troublemakers, despite their various assets. Even if the refugees had wanted to assimilate into these countries they were prevented from doing so by Arab regimes which as yet only paid lip service to the Palestinian cause.

The PLO filled the vacuum. Its uncompromising ideological posture, calling for the destruction of Israel and the establishment of a secular democratic Arab-dominated country in her place through armed struggle, appealed widely to the Palestinians. Because it was an umbrella organization embracing several rival Palestinian groups, it was able to consolidate its position. It especially caught the imagination of the younger generation, most of whom were born outside Palestine.

Ironically, the Palestinians were aided by the Israeli occupation of the West Bank and Gaza. Prior to the 1967 war, the idea of a Palestinian entity earned little support among the Palestinians because it seemed to contradict the essence of Arab unity. More importantly, Palestinian unity presented a direct challenge to the Arab states, especially Jordan, until after the Israeli occupation when it was much easier to project the Palestinian cause as part of the struggle against Zionism. It was also only after the Israeli occupation that the Palestinian question could be presented not merely as a refugee problem but as one involving the basic rights of self-determination.

One of the PLO's main aims was to acquire an independent position which would force the Arab states to take it into account[9] by demonstrating its ability to involve the Arab Governments in embarrassing political situations and draw them into military initiatives which, initially, they were reluctant to take.

The only way to focus the world's attention on the Palestinian plight was by engaging in widespread terror. Soon the PLO was receiving arms and training from Libya, Syria and Iraq — all of whom competed for its control in order to manipulate it in inter-Arab rivalries.[10] By a curious reversal the PLO was to gain immensely from the failure of Arab unity, on which it had originally pinned great hopes.

But the PLO's links were not confined to its Arab patrons. It also established political and military relations with the USSR as well as with other international terrorist organizations. This wide range of connections facilitated its operations and boosted its revolutionary image and thus enabled it to put pressure on the Gulf rulers who feared that the PLO would instigate subversive actions. A beaten and frustrated PLO would become less united (benefiting only Israel) and, therefore, less manageable. To unify and strengthen the PLO as well as to influence it, Saudi Arabia subsidized Fatah heavily. This, in turn, enabled it to enlarge its ranks, expand its activities and strengthen its position within the PLO.

Whether or not they approved of its action, no Arab regime could be seen to be opposing the PLO's struggle, especially in view of their own failure to regain the Arab lands. But in Jordan, PLO assertiveness was to lead to the inevitable clash between the PLO and the Jordanian army in September 1970, from which the latter clearly emerged as the winner. This particular conflict served to make other Arab governments aware of the PLO's growing threat.

Deprived of its most vital territorial base in Jordan, which provided direct contact with the Palestinians under occupation and which facilitated military activities in Israel, the PLO searched for a base. Only Lebanon, the weakest of the countries surrounding Israel, could offer the necessary conditions: a fragmented regime, a weak army, and terrain which made it difficult for any military force, Israeli or Arab, to crush the PLO. Upsetting the delicate sectarian and political balances within Lebanon by throwing the country into disarray resulted not only in a *de facto* partition of Lebanon but also in the creation of, in a sense, a 'State within a State'. Lebanon virtually lost her independence. Through military clashes with the Christian Lebanese militia, the Syrian invading forces and Israeli troops, the PLO gained much-needed experience and some degree of cohesion. Its military achievements — much exaggerated — boosted the morale of the Palestinians all over the world. The PLO action, however, added to the growing polarization of the Arab world.

Worried at the way the Palestinians were consolidating their position in Lebanon — with occasional help from Iraq — Syria attempted to 'co-ordinate' (i.e., to restrain) the PLO. Initially she used the Syrian-controlled Palestinian *al-Sa'iqa* forces, a small organization (which was headed by Zuhayr Muhsin but run and armed by Syria) which advocates the creation of a Greater Syria and the making of any liberated Palestinian territory a province of Syria. By early 1976, caught up in an expensive operation which tarnished her forces' image, Syria turned against the Palestinians, whom she had originally come to aid. The bitter memory of the armed clashes between the PLO and the Syrian army and the slaughter of Palestinians in Tel al-Za'tar made the PLO fear Syrian ruthlessness. It took a combined Saudi – Kuwaiti – Egyptian diplomatic effort to save the Palestinian troops in 1977 when the 'Arab Deterrent Force' was formed in Lebanon. This force, however, was almost exclusively Syrian in its make-up.

Thus the war in Lebanon contained lessons for all the parties concerned. The super-powers felt that they would not gain anything by becoming directly involved. The Arab states realized the dangers contained in the increasing strength of the PLO. To Israel it was a reminder that the PLO could not be easily contained either by Arab forces or by herself, unless she physically controlled that region, and whereas Israeli retaliation could harm the PLO, it could not eradicate it. The Israeli invasion into Lebanon in March 1978 only played into the PLO's hands politically, with Israel failing militarily in an expensive operation. Moreover, the attack resulted in the arrival of the United Nations Interim Forces in Lebanon (UNIFIL) to replace the withdrawing Israeli forces. Thereafter, the PLO returned to the attack seeking shelter behind UNIFIL.

Terrorism continued to irritate Israel, and it served as a warning to Arab rulers and the people of the West Bank who sought a position independent of the PLO. It served another political purpose. The Rejectionists also used it to damage the image of the more moderate Fatah leaders by proving that Yasser Arafat's will could not prevail without their consent. The Fatah leadership had to acquiesce in, and at times initiate, certain terrorist operations even if they did not serve its aims internationally, in order to continue to assert its dominant position within the PLO.

Towards the end of the 1970s, the main aim of the 'moderate' section of the PLO – the Fatah – was to influence the Palestinians under occupation and acquire the position of accredited negotiator in any future talks, rather than to continue to use terror for its own sake. This change of emphasis, however, did not mean abandoning terrorism, and military action continued to be part of the PLO's strategy.

The actions of the PLO instilled a sense of pride and dignity in the Palestinian community. It became a symbol of the 'revolution' and a unifying force for *all* Palestinians. Although its military power cannot be compared with that of the Arab states, the PLO has acquired what could be termed 'semi-veto power' over any arrangement which purposely excludes it.

And yet the Iran – Iraq war in the Gulf and the ensuing inter-Arab conflicts, which resulted in the overshadowing of the Palestinian question and the decline of the PLO, demonstrated once again the extent to which the position of the PLO, its own cohesiveness, as well as its subordination to Syrian influence, all depend on fluctuations within the fragmented Arab world.

The Egyptian – Israeli Peace Treaty

Despite President Sadat's courageous visit to Jerusalem, it is clear that the gap between Egypt and Israel on the Palestinian question is as wide as ever. Though the Camp David Accords were at times loosely worded, the Palestinians were provided with an unprecedented opportunity for participation. It was agreed that a new locally-elected Palestinian Self-Governing Authority (SGA)[11] would replace the Israeli civilian and military administration and that the authority for this body would derive from an international agreement involving Jordan, Egypt and Israel. A strong local police force would be set up under the SGA and Israel would relocate reduced military forces in specified locations in the West Bank to provide for Israel's security needs. Provisions were also made in the Agreement for the return of the 1967 Palestinian refugees and for establishing a mechanism for dealing with the larger, more complicated question of the 1948 refugees in a way which would take account of all the relevant UN Resolutions. The question of Jerusalem was left unresolved, with each side reiterating its position. Negotiations on the final disposition of the territories were to begin three years later and were to end two years after that.

But whereas Israel regarded autonomy as 'personal' not 'territorial', that is, to 'people' and not to 'a people', and envisaged these areas remaining indefinitely under her rule, Egypt and the United States believed it to be a transitional phase on the road to some form of Palestinian restricted sovereignty.

Crushed as they are between the millstones of Israel, Jordan and the PLO, the traditional divisions of the West Bank and Gaza Palestinians surfaced once again, even though they were united in their total rejection of the proposed autonomy. But here they were assisted by the Likud's 'hawkish' policies which enabled them to conceal their differences, so contributing to Israel's increasing international isolation. This isolation was demonstrated by the world-wide rejection of the Israeli declaration of the whole of Jerusalem, including the Arab part, as her undivided capital. In that respect, Israel played into the hands of the PLO without the latter having to moderate its own positions. Palestinian intentions of regaining in stages the *whole* of what was once known as Palestine only strengthens the determination of those Israelis who insist on holding on to *all* the territories. Again the Rejectionists on both sides, by adopting a maximalist view, gained ground over their respective moderate parties, thus making it more difficult to break the vicious circle.

Nevertheless, the Egyptian – Israeli Peace Treaty, which accorded Israel the recognition and legitimacy she had been denied since her establishment, is an essential pre-requisite for any agreement to follow. Whether the Treaty will reduce conflict to a more manageable level or whether it will only generate more tension remains to be seen.

Part 2: Proposed Solutions to the Palestinian Question

Two questions must be asked: can the Palestinian issue be shelved politically, while still allowing the Middle East peace-making process to continue? If not, will returning the West Bank to Jordanian control prove a feasible 'solution' to the complicated Palestinian problem? The answer to the first question will focus on the 'Israeli Option' and the second question will focus on the 'Jordanian Option', in an attempt to evaluate the viability of these options.

I. THE 'ISRAELI OPTION'

The Israeli Option is to perpetuate the present situation even if Judea, Samaria and the Gaza Districts are not merged under Israeli sovereignty. Preserving the integrity of most of historic Eretz Israel — the land stretching from the sea to the River Jordan on which the Jewish tribes lived in the days of the Old Testament — would not only satisfy the Israeli notions of historical rights but, by extending political control over these areas indefinitely, Israel would prevent the restoration of any kind of Arab sovereignty and assure her own security. The proponents of this uncompromising maximalist view — essentially, though not exclusively, members of the Herut Party, Gush Emunim and 'hawks' of the opposition Labour Party — refuse to recognize the Palestinians as a people. They reduce the Palestinian plight to a mere Arab refugee problem which needs to be solved within the context of neighbouring Arab countries.

The Different Versions

Maximalists nevertheless differ over the ultimate solution they would prefer to see. There are those who advocate incorporating the 'liberated' areas with their 1,240,000 Arab inhabitants into Israel (which in her pre-1967 borders already harbours over 500,000 Arabs out of the state's 3,900,000 total population), confident that future waves of Jewish immigration would prevent the delicate demographic balance from changing in favour of the Palestinians. Others, worried about the long-term political implication of incorporating this large community (with a natural growth rate of 3.5% per year compared with Israel's Jews

estimated at 1.8%), frustrated by the relatively small number of Russian Jews who prefer Israel to America, and troubled by the growing size of Israeli emigration (which roughly equals that of the Jewish immigration), urge the annexation of these areas *without* granting Israeli citizenship to the Palestinian Arabs. They would deny them the right to vote or to be elected to Israel's parliament but would provide them with some form of limited autonomy. A variation of such autonomy is a 'federation' between Israel and the West Bank [12] which would allow Israelis to settle in the Palestinian 'province' but would not give the same rights to the Palestinians. A further variation envisages an Israeli-dominated federation of Arab and Jewish cantons. [13]

The Settlements — Security and Political Considerations

Most Israelis believe that holding the tiny area of the West Bank as an eastern buffer is a pre-requisite for Israel's defence needs and that such control requires a substantial Jewish presence there. It is obvious, however, that settlements in Judea and Samaria and the Gaza District have a political purpose in that they aim to create *faits accomplis* which would change the demographic balance and geographical composition of the territories in question. [14] They would also break up the contiguity and encircle the densely populated Arab areas situated along the West Bank's watershed. (See Maps 2-4). Similarly, a block of settlements was established along the north-eastern corner of the Sinai Peninsula so as to seal off the thickly populated Gaza Strip from

59

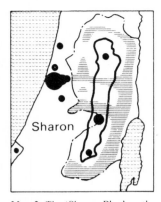

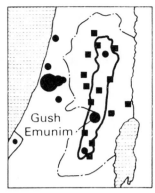

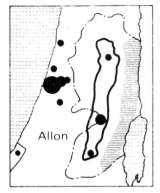

Map 2: The 'Sharon Plan' – the shaded area denotes the Jewish settlements and military preserves in the West Bank (area within broken line) linked by roads to Israel.

Map 3: The sites of Gush Emunim's projected blocks of settlements (black squares) in and around the heavily Arab-populated areas of the West Bank (defined by thick black line).

Map 4: The 'Allon Plan' – the shaded area denotes the Jewish settlement along the sparsely-populated Jordan Valley, with the rest of the West Bank ultimately returning to Jordan.

Source: Erwin Frenkel, 'Settlement without an end' and Samuel Katz, 'Settlement, Strategy and Hypocrisy', *The Jerusalem Post* (international edition), 23 June 1979.

an Egyptian attempt to use the Strip once again as a military launching pad. But whereas the previous Labour governments (which had established the bulk of the settlements) purposely excluded the heavily Arab populated regions from their settlement plans, concentrating mainly on est ablishing points which were regarded as having a strategic importance, the Likud Government sought to put up small settlements throughout the West Bank, being motivated primarily by ideological and political[15] considerations. The main purpose of these settlements is to solidify the option for an Israeli annexation of at least part of the West Bank. The settlements could be incorporated into Israel through municipal and taxation arrangements, which would provide them with an extra-territorial status. Under such jurisdiction they could not become subordinated to any Palestinian Authority which would thereby be deprived of substantial territories. (See Map 5). Accordingly, the more recent Gush Emunim settlements are scattered in the densely populated Arab areas and lack the economic infrastructure and hinterland enjoyed by the flourishing Jordan Valley settlements established by the previous

Labour-led governments on 'state domain'. Thus the main argument within Israel is not over the Jewish people's right to keep these areas but over the feasibility and economic price[16] of realizing these rights in the face of a large and hostile Arab presence.

For their part, the Arabs are outraged by these 'ideological' settlements which exacerbate unrest in the West Bank. The imposition of settlements, which in many cases required the expropriation of privately-owned land, could hardly be conducive to harmonious coexistence. For many Israelis, on the other hand, it is inconceivable that places which were Jewish should become once again 'Judenrein' (i.e. free of Jews). They claim that if peace is to be achieved, Jews cannot be barred from living in their historic land and this suggests that the two communities should not be separated. It is noteworthy, however, that excluding Jerusalem's new Israeli suburbs, there are only some 10,000 Israelis living in some 90 settlements in the West Bank and Gaza Strip amidst the 1,240,000 Palestinians.[17]

Some of these smaller civilian settlements, particularly those situated in the less populated hilly regions, are intended to have a security

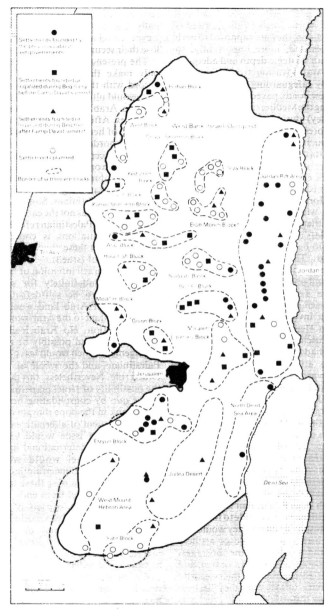

Map 5: Israeli settlements in the West Bank

function as part of Israel's regional defence system. Overlooking the Jordan Valley, as well as certain road junctions, they are supposed to curb guerrilla activities and, more importantly, to provide Israel with strategic depth and adequate warning of an Arab invasion from across the River Jordan. By safeguarding the traffic axes (including the new roads paved by Israel in the West Bank joining the Mediterranean Plains with the Jordan Valley) during the deployment of Israel's reserve forces they are supposed to delay the advance of such an invasion. Although the shallow River Jordan does not constitute a barrier, the terrain is difficult and the East – West roads could be easily blocked, thus allowing time for counter-measures.

However, the Jordan Valley settlements lie in the middle of a wide strip of flat and barren territory and, rather than providing a strategic asset, are powerless to resist any Arab invasion and would have to be protected or evacuated in the event of war. The settlements within the densely populated, hostile Palestinian areas would also demand protection, thus limiting the Israel's Defence Force's (IDF) freedom of action.[18] The Israeli experience during the 1973 war, when Syria invaded part of the Israeli-populated Golan Heights, at times simply by-passing these settlements, tends to prove this point.[19] The IDF had to rush to their defence and this hindered its attempts to halt the Syrian invasion. The evacuation of the women and children was an additional problem.

Moreover, the Jordan Valley settlements could be cut off by a large Arab helicopter-borne force landing between them and Israel. Such invading forces could then control the few eastern cross-roads – crucial for any offensive – and hamper Israeli armour attempting to relieve the besieged settlements. Relief could be further complicated by the local Palestinians, because all the IDF supply arteries that connect the settlements with Israel run through large Palestinian villages.

Even if these settlements were able to fulfil part of their assigned responsibilities, they would still be unable to withstand an air raid or artillery bombardment and could become hostages. Unless these settlements are fully armed and function as fortified army posts their security value is in question; in this case they become military posts, with little of the characteristics of a settlement. However, if mutual military security arrangements are agreed upon, principally in accordance with the Agreement between Egypt, Israel and the US, the settlements would lose their security justification.

The presence of these settlements would not only make the achievement of any political accord with the Palestinians very difficult but they would ultimately compel Israel to control a sizeable Arab minority by increasingly severe measures. After all, Israel has failed to solve the problem of her own Arab population within the pre-1967 borders. Moreover, Israel's consistent refusal to accept the return of the 1948 refugees to her own area on security grounds, regarding them as a 'fifth column', is at odds with a simultaneous drive to take into a greater Israel a much larger number of Palestinians. Similarly, her claim that the West Bank has not the capacity to harbour the 1967 and 1948 Palestinian refugees because of its economic limitations is contradicted by the suggestion that these areas can absorb hundreds of thousands of Israelis.

Thus the Israeli intention of holding on to the West Bank indefinitely for security reasons would seem to be self-defeating. Continued occupation of Arab land would only prove a constant irritant to the Arab world committed to their liberation. No Arab leader, let alone a Palestinian, could possibly be reconciled to an arrangement which would leave over one million Palestinians and the *whole* of Palestine under Israeli rule. Nevertheless, this does not preclude the possibility of Israel perpetuating the present *status quo* by consolidating her control in the West Bank in the hope that, in due course (with the development of alternative energy sources), the Palestinian issue would lose much of its newly-acquired international appeal and that, eventually, Israel would win Palestinian acquiescence. The uncertainties involved in re-linquishing control over these territories would serve to deter Israel from embarking on such a course. With the prospects of the continuing division within the Arab world and a militarily strong Israel, Israel can go on holding on to the territories in question, albeit at the cost of increasing her international isolation and hampering her relations with the US.

But, apart from hindering the peace-making process, continued Israeli rule over these territories is bound to be counter-productive. Annexation would endanger the democratic and fundamentally Jewish nature of Israel.[20] A complex bi-national state has always been vehemently opposed by the vast majority of Zionists, even prior to the establishment of Israel. Rejected by the international community and the Arab world, it would be torn by the continued strife between its Jewish and Arab citizens, threatening the very existence of the Jewish state. The 'Israeli Option' therefore appears to be a recipe for continuing unrest and it will give rise to political and security problems in the future which could prove unmanageable.

II. THE 'JORDANIAN OPTION'

If the 'Israeli Option' (whatever the variation) is based on retaining all of the West Bank, as well as the Gaza Strip, indefinitely under Israel, the 'Jordanian Option' has variants also: the Jordanian version calls for the return of *all* these territories to direct Hashemite sovereignty. The Israeli version envisages the return of *part* of them to Jordan.

Jordanian Version: United Arab Kingdom
Jordanian Objectives
Jordan's isolated geographical position and her political orientation impose powerful constraints on her policy. Wedged between two radical Arab regimes, Iraq and Syria, Jordan was always labelled as a 'Western stooge', following her handling of the Palestinian issue. Her problem continues to be the need to tip the country's demographic balance away from Palestinian domination in order to preserve the foci of power in the hands of the Hashemite dynasty.

The objectives of the present regime in Jordan and those of the PLO are diametrically opposed. This raises the whole question of representation: who has the right to speak on behalf of the Palestinians and who can do so? Jordan's fears are the mirror image of the uneasiness which prevails among PLO leaders. As far as the Hashemites are concerned, a Palestinian state on the West Bank and Gaza may provide a focus of identity for the Palestinians on the East Bank, which in turn may undermine Jordan's authority over more than half of her population. Thus the PLO's existence and actions challenge not only Jordan's right to represent even the East Bank Palestinians, but challenge also the very basis of Jordan as a state. The conflict, therefore, seems insoluble: Jordan has never regarded herself as a mere transitional trustee of the Palestinians – the view of all other Arab countries – and the PLO rejects Jordan's historical and territorial justifications to control both Banks of the River

Jordan. Furthermore, radical Palestinian elements regard a Palestinian – Jordanian revolution in Jordan as a first step to liberating Greater Palestine.[21] After all, Trans-Jordan is seen by many Palestinians, as by Israeli hardliners and the Hashemites themselves, as part of mandatory Palestine. The present Jordanian regime is viewed as an obstacle blocking the struggle for Palestinian self-determination, and is accused of collaboration with Israel. Hence, Jordan's concern for the Palestinian plight stems in the main from the regime's fears for both its domestic position and its status within the Arab world.

Yet any political solution would make the Palestinians on both Banks dependent on Jordanian goodwill. This limits Palestinian choices. There are, for example, some 30,000 Hebronites on the East Bank with property there and families abroad who send their remittances via Jordan. Their dependence on the present *status quo* is quite clear. Moreover, the Jordanian regime, which enjoys considerable support from many East Bank Palestinians, is fully aware of the advantages gained by a Palestinian holding a Jordanian passport. Many Palestinians fear being pushed out of Amman (where they enjoy a high standard of living) to become 'refugees' in their own 'old-new' country – Palestine. They are naturally reluctant to support any political arrangement which will not link Palestine to Jordan.

Jordan's dilemma remains how to grant West Bank Palestinians, should they come once more under her rule, a sense of participation without undermining the very nature of the Hashemite regime and without endangering its control over developments within both parts of the re-enlarged state. To that end the Hashemites will require a camouflaged political formula to grant the Palestinians a limited measure of home rule (in order to justify the concept of a united state)

63

while isolating those who would aim to sever the Jordanian – Palestine connection.

The 1972 Federation Scheme

The Jordanian autonomy plan, which demands a complete Israeli withdrawal and the phased replacement of Israeli forces with Jordanian troops, calls for the name of Jordan to be changed to the United Arab Kingdom (UAK). This is to be composed of two regions: the West Bank and any other liberated territory of former Palestine[22] (presumably the Gaza Strip)[23] to form the region to be known as Palestine (with Jerusalem as its capital) and the region of Jordan on the East Bank with its centre in Amman. Amman would also serve as the capital of the UAK and the seat of the unified executive authority. Each province would have its elected People's Council and government while the supreme authority would remain vested in the Monarch. He would continue to have full control of the army and he would preside over a parliament composed equally of delegates from both regions.[24]

Israel, the Arab world,[25] the PLO[26] and even many West Bank and Gaza Strip Palestinians[27] opposed the plan. But the growing likelihood of the restoration of Jordanian rule over part of the West Bank through agreement with Israel was one of the reasons which compelled the PLO in 1974 to adopt a new 'phased strategy' which called for the establishment of a sovereign Palestinian Authority 'on any liberated territory' so as to prevent it being transferred to Jordan.

Israeli Version: Territorial Compromise

Some Israelis, searching for a way to rid themselves of the Palestinians without having to relinquish their military control over strategic regions in the West Bank, believe that bringing the Palestinians under the *administrative* control of Jordan would satisfy Israel and Hussein's political and security requirements. Such a solution based on territorial compromise, as envisaged by the previous Israeli Labour-led governments, would leave Israel a predominantly Jewish state whilst giving the Palestinians a channel for political expression in a Jordanian – Palestinian state. These principles were embodied in the Allon Plan (named after the late Israeli former Foreign Minister Yigal Allon). Others, like the former Foreign Minister Moshe Dayan, toyed with the idea of a 'functional'

division between Jordan and Israel which would give Israel full military control over the whole of the West Bank and the Gaza Strip, granting Jews the unilateral right to settle there, whilst allowing Arab inhabitants to be linked with, and to participate in, the politics of Jordan and Egypt as their citizens.

Political Calculations

Some Israelis therefore appear to encourage the preservation of a Palestinian identity within Jordan, reasoning that most Palestinians already hold Jordanian citizenship and about 40% of the Palestinian community live harmoniously in Trans-Jordan, the area which originally formed an integral part of Palestine.[28] They argue that it would be unnatural to leave the Palestinian community divided and that therefore it would be logical to 'transfer' the control of the West Bank Palestinians to Jordan. The Israeli assumption behind this argument is that Jordan needs to regain the West Bank, fearing the consequences of an independent Palestinian state.[29] The Israeli supporters of this option predict that the Palestinians would submit to Jordanian control, notwithstanding their current demands for their own separate state, ultimately weakening the PLO. The PLO would then not have the same legitimacy and local backing as it would in a West Bank under 'Zionist occupation'. After all, many West Bank Palestinians, while giving verbal support to the PLO, do fear a PLO-controlled state divorced from Jordan.

The Israelis fear that Palestinian *irredenta* would include demands for the return of Palestinians to Haifa and Jaffa (towns within Israel's pre-1967 boundaries), whereas, under Jordanian rule, the Palestinians would inevitably become immersed in inter-Arab conflicts. In any case, Israel has no desire to undermine Jordan's position, for Israel has always insisted on negotiating only with sovereign states, as such negotiations deal essentially with borders and security arrangements and matters capable of resolution.[30] Therefore, under the Jordanian Option, outstanding political questions (such as the issue of Jerusalem) would seem easier to handle.

Whereas Hussein's grandfather Abdullah regarded himself as 'Jerusalem's saviour' in 1948, Hussein lost Jerusalem to the Israelis in 1967. Taking advantage of Hussein's ambition to restore his lost prestige, Israel offered him a foothold, short of sovereignty, as the Guardian of the Holy Places. Since the establishment in Iran of an Islamic republic and the general resurgence of Islam, Hussein's need to regain his position in Jerusalem is more pressing. Control over Eastern Jerusalem (and Bethlehem) could serve to bolster Jordan's position within both the Arab world and the West, whereas negotiations with Palestinians would doubtless lead to demands for Jerusalem to be their capital, a notion Israel is bound to reject.

A more devious calculation is that Jordan could well absorb Palestinian refugees returning from Lebanon and so weaken the PLO. This could help to restore stability in Lebanon, and would allow Syrian forces to withdraw from Lebanon thus making the PLO there more vulnerable to any future Israeli retaliation.

Security Considerations
Under the Allon plan, Israel would retain a forward defence belt parallel to the River Jordan, controlling both the mountainous ridge and the Jordan Valley below. The heavily Palestinian-populated western regions would be transferred to Jordanian control and access would be allowed via a corridor passing through a sparsely but predominantly Israeli-populated eastern belt which would come under Israeli sovereignty.[1] The West Bank would thus continue to serve as a buffer for Israel, as well as a convenient springboard for the IDF to move into Jordan. To muster American support, Israel argued that from here she could easily defend a pro-Western Jordan from Syria. To gain Jordanian acceptance for this proposal, Israel offered Jordan transit rights through her territory to the sea at Gaza (and Haifa), which would alleviate Jordan's dependence on Syria for an outlet to the Mediterranean. In return Israel insisted that Jordan should be prevented from deploying in the West Bank any forces other than those required to preserve law and order. Because an Israeli demand for the total demilitarization of an independent Palestinian state would probably be unacceptable to the Palestinians (for it might deny the basic concept of sovereignty), a demilitarized western part of a reunited Jordan looks more realistic. Similarly, if Israel ever had to reinvade West Bank territory, seizing part of a country (Jordan) might prove preferable to

occupying the whole of a new Palestinian West Bank state. Retention of a strip of territory between Jordan and most of the West Bank would also make such an operation even simpler.

Limitations and Repercussions
Most of the flaws in the 'Jordanian Option' arise from the new demographic imbalance created by the return of the West Bank to Jordan's control. Already Jordan is crippled by the fact that about half the population of what is now Jordan are Palestinians. Absorbing a further 750,000 or so highly-politicized West Bank inhabitants (or 1.2 million should the Gaza Strip be incorporated as well) would not only make the Jordanians a minority in their own country, but could undermine the existence of the present Jordanian regime. Memories of what nearly happened in 1970 are still clear. Given that King Hussein continues to regard the Palestinians as a security risk, he is unlikely to admit Palestinian refugees from other parts of the Arab world, even if he might be prepared to take back the West Bank. Thus a major component of the Palestinian question would be left unattended to. And the refugees would not be satisfied to have waited all those years in exile merely to become Jordanian citizens nor would many West Bank Palestinians, who have suffered under Israeli rule, be prepared to come back under Jordanian rule. Symbolic gestures will not appease the Palestinians and win their loyalty.

If, however, Jordan proves to be the only partner with whom Israel will negotiate, then the Palestinians may condone the plan, regarding it as only a first step after which all efforts towards Palestinian self-determination would be directed against Jordan. There are also pro-Jordanian elements who approve of a modified version of Hussein's federation scheme, believing that it would place them on an equal footing with the Jordanians and would thus provide for authentic Palestinian expression. They are confident that Jordan has learned from past experience and from the Iranian Revolution and that therefore the Jordanian regime would not impose itself in a way which would endanger its newly-acquired legitimacy – questionable as it may still be – but would prefer a real 'federation' between the two Banks.

Domestic conflict and instability within enlarged Jordan is likely to result from differing definitions of status and aspirations. Moreover, should Jordan eventually become a 'republic' then the Palestinian expectations would rise even higher and they would demand proportional representation. They would also insist on being part of Jordan's armed forces. It would certainly not be in the Monarch's interest, however, to change the basic composition of his loyal Trans-Jordanian-dominated army, which forms the cornerstone of his regime.

Jordanians would have to reassert authority over the West Bank and this could result in renewed clashes between Palestinians and Jordanians and increase uneasiness in both parts of the Kingdom. Jordan has already realized that the association of certain Palestinian interest groups with the government should not be taken as their acceptance of the *status quo*. Moreover, many Palestinians already regard the Hashemites as an obstacle to the realization of their aims, knowing that the Kingdom could not afford to commit itself to the declared Palestinian goals as they would want it to.

The use of force to assert control could prove counter-productive to the Hashemites. Neighbouring Arab states could not remain aloof if Jordan were to smother the Palestinians and this could, in turn, involve Israel. This may threaten all Arab – Israeli agreements, for a move by one Arab country is bound to trigger a series of movements throughout the region, with every Arab regime attempting to prove to the Palestinians (and to each other) that it is the only true custodian of the Palestinian cause.

Finally, the Hashemites themselves, and certainly any radical successors, could grant independence to the West Bank if they considered it more politically desirable. Moreover, should the Palestinians ever gain control of all or part of Jordan, they could be expected to abrogate all former Jordanian agreements with Israel, especially when such arrangements would have been intended to thwart the emergence of any Palestinian entity between them in the first place.

Prospects for the 'Jordanian Option'

Until the signing of the Egyptian – Israeli Agreement, Hussein could never have signed an agreement with Israel unless she agreed to surrender the whole of the West Bank including East Jerusalem. There was one exception to this general condition. As a step on the way, Hussein might have been interested in a partial military agreement. Returning part of the West Bank territory to Jordanian control would probably have prevented an independent Palestinian state from emerging there and might have seriously crippled the PLO. The King could then have been in a position to claim that the military agreement was a first step to the recovery of the *whole* of the West Bank. Full recovery would be followed by an internationally supervised referendum which would enable the Palestinians to choose between having a state of their own and having some form of unity with Jordan. Israel and Jordan both predicted that the outcome of such a referendum would be in Jordan's favour but both tended to agree that it might never be necessary to hold a referendum once Hussein had regained control of most of the West Bank.

However, it seems that this opportunity has long passed. The only time when such a partial solution might have taken place was after the 1973 war, following the precedent set by the Separation of Forces Agreements between Israel, Egypt and Syria. Hussein then argued in secret meetings with Israeli Ministers that, in exchange for Jordan's passivity in the 1973 war, a military agreement should be drawn up in which Israel would cede an area west of the River Jordan. This would have made Jordan the accredited negotiator for the West Bank rather than the PLO, and West Bank Palestinians could have come to see Hussein as their only protector. But the Israeli Labour-led government, under domestic political pressure and insensitive to Hussein's position in the Arab world, rejected the *military* nature of the proposed agreement and would only agree to grant Jordan a limited foothold in Jericho and its immediate environs in exchange for a non-belligerancy agreement. In fact, the presence of the Israeli settlements along the Jordan Valley prevented any accommodation. Hussein's hopes of attending the subsequent Rabat Conference with tangible territorial gains were thus dashed.

Apart from the mid-1974 attempt, Jordan was never in a position to negotiate the future of the West Bank. Those in Israel who advocate the 'Jordanian Option' believe, nevertheless, that time is on their side. They fail to recognize the process of the 'Palestinianization' of the Palestinians, to which Israel herself unintentionally contributed, and fail to understand that Hussein

66

cannot afford to appear to be collaborating with Israel when competing with the PLO over control of the West Bank.

In time the 'Jordanian' possibility has become more remote. The King has realized that Israel does not intend to implement this option, as the growing number of Israeli settlements has shown. Apparently, Hussein has argued that he was being used by the Israelis, for they wanted to enjoy the best of both worlds by keeping him on a leash and playing for time. He could not accept Israel's idea of a 'territorial compromise' which would leave Israel in control of most of the West Bank and leave Jordan with most of the West Bank Palestinians.

In fact, however unpalatable the Israeli occupation is to Hussein, he has come to prefer this to having to absorb even part of the populated West Bank regions. Israel's control would prevent the emergence of a Palestinian entity there and to that end she would probably continue to encourage Hussein's own supporters and enable him to extend his political influence over the West Bank. This would relieve him of the need to pay the political price of controlling it. Hence Hussein was alarmed by the Camp David Accord which would not only make it practically impossible for him to accept anything short of total Israeli withdrawal (including from East Jerusalem), but also it introduced the possibility of the establishment of a Palestinian entity, which he could not afford to be perceived to reject.

The 'Jordanian Option' does not seem to have the ingredients for containing the Palestinian problem, especially when it hinges on a Hashemite regime. The Israeli version of the 'Jordanian Option' lacks the Jordanian partner. Similarly, the Jordanian version is rejected in Israel. With the growing chances of the Labour Party returning to power in Israel, it remains to be seen whether its leaders – the proponents of the 'Jordanian Option' – would persist once it was clear that Hussein did not intend to go back on his maximalist territorial claims or if he were to be replaced by a radical Trans-Jordanian Government which might adopt a hostile posture towards Israel.

Therefore, if neither the Israeli nor the Jordanian 'Options' are politically feasible, the two countries might be compelled to fall back on a Palestinian alternative, previously regarded by both Israel and Jordan as unworkable. For such a 'solution' to materialize and remain durable it would have to meet the minimum essential requirements of all the parties concerned. For the Palestinians that would have to mean a settlement of a host of political and economic questions relating to their plight. For both Israel and Jordan such a 'solution' would have to contain built-in assurances for their own security.

Part 3: A Palestinian State — The Conditions for 'Stability'

As far as this Paper is concerned, the 'Palestinian Option' implies a phased move towards a fully-fledged Palestinian state endowed with most of the characteristics of sovereignty but with certain treaty restrictions regarding its security and political orientations. It would comprise most of the West Bank and the Gaza Strip, essentially along the 1967 borders (as well as any part of the Rafih Salient and coastal Sinai that Egypt might agree to grant Palestine as a gesture), with the eastern part of the 'open' City of Jerusalem as the capital. The problem of the refugees would be solved, primarily, within the Arab world. Such a comprehensive solution would have to be regarded, by all parties concerned, as a *final* settlement of the Palestinian question and the arrangements would have to be guaranteed by both super-powers. *All* outstanding issues and the political and territorial arrangements to settle these problems would have to be agreed and finalized *prior* to the new state's coming into being.

Rather than attempt to reconcile the gap separating the actors concerned by focusing on the present positions held by both sides of the Arab–Israeli conflict, the following Chapters examine the main elements of such a 'solution' and the problems it would raise, the conditions under which such an entity could be established, the advantages and weaknesses of such an option, and its regional implications. This is done not for the sake of predicting how a solution could be arrived at, but in order to examine the complexities involved in a 'Palestinian Option'.

I. THE PALESTINIAN STATE

Boundaries

Until the Peace Treaty between Egypt and Israel was signed there were no *de jure* boundaries between Israel and the Arab states surrounding her. The different types of boundaries, as well as the border regimes which accompanied them, were almost all a product of wars. Jordan, however, was always the exception. It was the only Arab state in 1949 to surrender land to Israel which that nation had not occupied in the war. While the border linking Israel and Trans-Jordan north and south of the West Bank has not given rise to disputes, the line separating Israel from the West Bank has been, and will continue to be, one of the main bones of contention between Israel and the Arab world.

Many Palestinians are aware that the most they can expect at present is a Palestine consisting of the West Bank and the Gaza Strip defined by pre-1967 borders. Whereas these borders roughly overlap the 'international lines' between Israel and Syria, Egypt and Lebanon, in the case of a future Palestine these are merely arbitrary lines.

The only internationally sanctioned borders which the Palestinians could accept more readily are those of the 1947 Partition Plan — a scheme they rejected out of hand at the time, confident then of being able to control the whole of Palestine. Such borders differ substantially from the 1949 Armistice Lines.

Palestinian support for the 1947 Partition Plan stems from the fact that such borders would give them more of Israel and deny Israeli control over the Upper Galilee in the north and the 'Small Triangle' in the east — both regions now heavily populated by Israeli Arabs. Furthermore, such borders would allow territorial contiguity between the Palestinians and Egypt, through Auja (Nitzana) and with Syria (through the al-Hama enclave east of the River Jordan). Syria would certainly welcome this definition of Palestine for it would provide her with direct leverage over both Palestine and Israel. For those reasons alone, Israel would reject the 1947 Partition boundaries (which she regards as invalid anyway) as a basis for negotiation and

68

turn to the 1949 Demarcation Line as a more desirable framework.

Minor Border Rectifications

Most discussions of the establishment of a Palestinian state advocate the 1967 border lines as boundaries. However, certain border rectifications should be made in the long-term interests of all parties concerned, and the 1949 Armistice Line which does not coincide with the international border should provide a basis for rectification. Any border changes would, of course, prove painful for both sides and will not be easy to carry through against opposition.

However, certain readjustments of the 1967 border line will have to be incorporated into the Peace Treaty if the Palestinians' minimum political needs as well as the Israeli and Jordanian security requirements are to be met. Reconciliation of these must be based on the principle of reciprocity. The issues include the problem of Jerusalem, the ninety or so Israeli settlements in the West Bank and the Gaza Strip, the frontier villages on both sides of the border, a route connecting the West Bank and the Gaza Strip and control over the sources of water. One such deal might allow Israel to maintain control over certain observation posts above the Jordan Valley in return for Palestinian political rights in Jerusalem or for limited areas *west* of the 1967 border. Israel could retain the Latrun road to Tel Aviv and its eastern environs (see Map 6) and, in exchange, compensate Palestine's border villages by granting them small pieces of Israeli territory. This could ease somewhat the economic problems of the Palestinian frontier villages which since 1949 have suffered from an acute shortage of land.[32] Alternatively, Israel could grant those villagers the right to cultivate at least part of what was their land without it being returned to their direct control – as was agreed in the 1949 Armistice Agreement,.but this was never implemented. Another exchange might involve the transfer to Palestine of a number of Arab villages situated along the border in the Tulkarm-Qalqilya area – the region closest to the Mediterranean and thus the most sensitive to Israel's security.

Whatever happens, for the sake of defending her vital security interests, Israel must remain in control of strategic points in the West Bank. These should include the high ridge of hills

Map 6: Greater Jerusalem

overlooking the Israeli – Palestinian border in the north-western region of the West Bank, as well as certain Israeli settlements, such as Gush Etzyon (which overlooks the Jerusalem-Hebron road). In addition, continued Israeli military presence in the mountains above the Dead Sea and especially deep in the north-east in the hilly regions overlooking the Jordan Valley are indispensable for Israel's security providing her with strategic positions which control the routes from the Jordan River both eastwards and westwards.

Another precondition for stability is that the border should be left open. Economic co-operation between Israel, Palestine and Jordan would cement and strengthen the delicate and fragile political relations between these states.

The Capital – East Jerusalem

The question of Jerusalem is charged with emotion. As a psychological and symbolic issue it poses unique problems. It remains the corner-stone of any comprehensive Middle East settlement. Religion, ethnicity and politics are all inter-related. Most sensitive of all the problems is, of course, that of sovereignty. Both Jordan and Israel have consistently ignored the UN call for the Internationalization of Jerusalem and its surroundings. Jordan, as noted earlier, downgraded the status of the eastern part of Jerusalem when it was under her control, transferring functions to Amman, but Israel has turned New Jerusalem into her own capital. The latter's unilateral decision has never been accepted by the world as a whole. Similarly, Israel's annexation of East Jerusalem and its environs after the 1967 war was rejected and her recent moves have given rise to widespread international protest.

The Muslim world (not only the Arab world) will insist that East Jerusalem comes under Arab sovereignty. Unless the issue can be resolved, no wider agreement seems likely, for Israel's position on this matter is also clear: Jerusalem is regarded by most Israelis – regardless of their political orientation – as their indivisible, eternal capital in which the rights of all religious communities to worship in their own Holy Places would be preserved. It has not been forgotten by the Jews that, before 1967, Jordan refused to implement the 1949 Armistice Agreement which provided for free Israeli access to the Jewish Holy Places in East Jerusalem. Thus the gap between the two sides is difficult to bridge.[33].

Although it might be desirable to avoid the establishment of two municipalities or even a borough system in an attempt to bypass thorny debates over territorial rights, this may prove to be the best alternative available. There have been suggestions that Greater Jerusalem should be turned into one county within Israel in which the size of the Arab population roughly equals that of the Jews. Local Arab and Jewish 'quarter councils' which would handle solely municipal and community matters, would then be established. Others argue that such a new, enlarged Jerusalem should gain a super-municipal status as a 'free city' similar to that of Tangiers. This would call for an overarching municipality with a rotating mayorship. As far as the Arabs are concerned, Jerusalem's status could then resemble that of Mecca and Medina. Neither of these cities are Saudi Arabia's capital but they are revered as holy. Nablus could then serve as the Palestinian capital.

But any legalistic discussion which regards the issue as a mere question of freedom of worship and omits the desire of the Palestinians to make Jerusalem their capital is short-sighted. Despite the fact that neither under the British Mandate nor under Jordanian rule was Jerusalem the centre of Palestinian political activity,[34] and despite the secular nature of Palestinian nationalism, Jerusalem has become a Palestinian national symbol under Israeli annexation.[35] Thus a formula is called for which enables the Palestinians to declare East Jerusalem as their capital while leaving the city fully open. The Arab part could gain a legal status similar to that applied to the Vatican. The dangers and difficulties are not hard to see. Re-division, like that which exists in Berlin, could not be excluded as a possibility. Closed borders and customs between Israel and Palestine and conflicts over the provision of services and distribution of resources would complicate any arrangement. If Israel insists on including in Jerusalem all newly-established Israeli settlements surrounding the city as well as the old Jewish Quarter, the Palestinians will demand incorporation of the quarters of Qatamon and Musrara[36] (in New Jerusalem), formally owned by the Arabs but, since 1948, populated by Jews.

Again there is room for some trading of land as a gesture of sincerity, unpopular though this process would be. Assuming all the newly-established Israeli quarters in the Jerusalem district remained under Israeli sovereignty, the abandoned village of Lifta, at the entrance of New Jerusalem, whose population are refugees (many of whom live in al-Bira in the West Bank) could then be returned to Arab sovereignty. The 'Israeli' part of Beit Safafa Arab village, south of Jerusalem, which was divided by the 1949 Armistice Line, could also be returned to the Palestinians and Israel could, in addition, give up part of her share of 'No Man's Land'. Though unequal in land area, such gestures would represent enormous political concessions by essentially equal states and it could alleviate some of the pain which both sides will undoubtedly suffer and win the much needed political acquiescence – a prerequisite to any new form of Arab – Israeli coexistence.

The Israeli Settlements

Another extremely sensitive issue for both sides is the question of the Israeli settlements which have been established in the West Bank and the Gaza Strip since 1967. So long as settlements (and water supply) remain under Israel's control, though not necessarily under her sovereignty, the land available to Palestine would be reduced substantially and a foreign presence would remain. This could threaten Palestinian sovereignty and would thus be intolerable.

Although the settlers living in Hebron or Gush Etzyon base their claims on the fact that they were Jewish settlements prior to the 1948 war, Israel, by denying the 1948 Palestinian refugees the right to return to their places of origin, vitiates the argument. If Israel were to abandon these settlements, international support for the Palestinians' demands to return to Israel would be weakened. Israel might arrange for all evacuated settlements to be given to the Palestinian refugees from Lebanon or Syria, rather than to those living at present on the West Bank, as a token of good will. They have the economic infrastructure to provide for greater numbers later, even though they could not solve the refugee problem.

The debate of the boundaries of the proposed state raises, therefore, two related questions. First, can any Palestinian leadership remain effectively in control and unrivalled in its claim to represent the Palestinians as a whole, while having to shelve officially part of its programme and aspirations? Second, can it isolate those Palestinians who would view such a 'mini' Palestine as only a first step in a greater struggle and who would therefore challenge its authority by demanding further action? These are central questions.

Palestinian Internal Authority
The Palestinians have never governed themselves nor have they ever had a strong and cohesive leadership and even in divided Lebanon they are far from being united. Divisions are deeply rooted in the economic, social and political developments of the first half of this century. However, changes are now taking place. The traditional social framework of clan, village and tribe are now much less important than they were, but the new order is not yet in place. Any incoming Palestinian regime will have the difficult task of bridging the social and political gaps inherent in Palestinian society. Conflicting expectations of the nature of political life and the external orientation of Palestine must be reconciled. Any Palestinian government will face two rather different kinds of opposition – one originating from within Palestine and the other from Palestinian Rejectionists abroad.

At first Palestine is likely to be an unstable republic based on some sort of 'representative' government in a 'participatory democracy' but the record of Third-world consistency is unimpressive and the Palestinian democratic experience might not survive for long. Nevertheless coalitions might form based on ideological differences. The most pronounced conflict is likely to be between the new government and those who would continue to reject the agreement which established the state. Rejectionists would operate mainly, though not exclusively, from abroad and they would endeavour to cripple the new government. They would certainly not feel obliged to abide by any agreements made. Operating from their bases in Lebanon, they would regard Palestine as a useful springboard for waging a continuous struggle against both Israel and Jordan free of the 'supervision' and constraints imposed by other Arab regimes.

Internally, conflict could develop between those 'remaining' under Israeli occupation and refugees returning to Palestine from 'outside'. The present mayors would be unlikely to simply give up their power and status (gained through their open support of the PLO). Unlike the PLO 'officials', they were elected to their posts in 1976 and they will endeavour to hold on to their power. The educated strata of the West Bank and the Gaza Strip (some of whom man UNRWA's senior posts) would probably form the backbone of the new state's bureaucracy and they too would not welcome PLO 'officials'. The local politicians who today are prepared to acquiesce in the PLO's leadership would demand at least an equal share in the running of the new state. 'Who did most for the Palestinian cause?' is a question which will doubtless be at the core of the persisting internal struggle for power.

Radicals, coming mainly from outside, will run into conflict with the local 'bourgeoisie' who prospered under Jordanian rule and Israeli occupation. This 'conservative' upper class may attempt – with Jordanian, Egyptian (and Israeli) encouragement – to assert itself politically in the new state. The PLO fighters are unlikely to consent to such a situation, for the Palestinian struggle is not only to regain the land but also to establish a new kind of democratic society in Palestine (encapsulated in the term *thawrah* [revolution]), which the PLO believes should be totally different from the 'dictatorship' applied by all Arab regimes. Radical Rejectionists would demand nothing less than a Greater Palestine engulfing both Israel and Jordan from where they could export their revolutionary ideals to the rest of the Arab world.

Other political ideologies would be competing for power in Palestine — Communists, Ba'athists, the Arab Nationalists, Syrian Nationalists and the Muslim Brotherhood. Many would look for support from outside. One natural channel would be the Palestinians abroad, who would attempt to influence the Palestinian policies of the Arab governments in their country of residence. Economic conflicts could arise also between the 'indigenous' Palestinians and the 'newcomers'. The West Bank will offer little employment at first and those who return will be competing with those who stayed.

Internal conflict could also arise between Gaza and the West Bank Palestinians, for traditionally the West Bank politicians have tended to belittle their less experienced brothers in the Gaza Strip.[37] The political, as well as physical, gap between the two parts of Palestine may prove difficult to bridge. For example, the 'West Bankers' would probably reject a demand from Gaza to allow a large number of refugees to move from there to East Palestine in an attempt to thin down the population in Gaza. The division of economic resources between the two parts of Palestine will in any case give rise to argument especially if the Strip's relative importance rises because of her access to the sea.

In short, Palestine will have a troubled birth and *any* government will be faced with intractable problems. A precondition for stability is a strong figurehead. Much of Middle Eastern politics hinges on such personalities and only a leader prominent in the struggle for liberation would have the legitimacy to negotiate without being widely perceived as a 'collaborator'. Moreover, only such a politician would have the credentials and personality to confront the Rejectionists 'in the name of the armed revolution'. However, any 'conciliatory' Palestinian government which regards the West Bank — Gaza State as a substitute for other more fundamental objectives will be regarded by the Rejectionists as having 'sold out' to Israel.

It is not always easy to predict alignments and the strength of political forces. However, a hard core of Fatah leaders enjoy massive support among those under occupation who fear that Rejectionism will perpetuate Israel's occupation. Moreover, unlike the other factions, Fatah has among its members in Beirut a number of West Bank politicians expelled by the Israeli authorities. Consequently, the new state may come to be dominated by 'moderate' leftists from the mainstream of the PLO abroad and the West Bank, co-operating with local, more conservative elements.

Only the Palestinians can decide upon the form of internal authority. Nevertheless, both Israel and Jordan have the right to be concerned by the possibility that the political system in Palestine would allow discontented elements to challenge and perhaps overthrow a government which had endorsed a Peace Treaty between Palestine and those two countries. Such a government might be forced (or choose) to radicalize its position by reneging on security arrangements or by raising expectations that further expansion might be possible at the expense of Israel or Jordan or by seeking new alignments which would challenge the delicate foundations on which the Treaty would be bound to rest.

Thus the very process of welding the Palestinians into a state could lead to upheaval which would spill across the borders of the new entity and there are no immediate means by which internal conflict could be controlled. For other countries to install a moderate leadership which would prove acceptable to Palestine's neighbours would contradict the essence of her newly acquired sovereignty. For the UN (or a consortium of nations acting under its auspices) to act as consultants could prove counter-productive as foreign powers would then become the focus of local opposition. The only other possibility is that observers from the Arab League, or the former 'Confrontation States', might assume a supervisory role throughout the implementation of the phased treaty. If the Arab states sincerely wished to maintain the agreement with Israel, they will have to work to encourage the new Palestinian regime to consolidate its position and thus acquire its much needed internal and external legitimacy. An 'Arab Trusteeship Advisory Committee' could assist in the building of the political foundations of the new state. Any internal challenge to the new government would then be tantamount to challenging a much wider body than the Palestinian regime and would, therefore, earn less local support. Such a suggestion would not be without difficulties. It must be assumed that every member of such a 'trusteeship' would seek to pursue his own country's interests and responsibility will therefore be hard to define and harder to implement.

Needless to say, both Israel and Jordan would prove extremely sensitive to such an arrangement which might complicate relations with their other neighbours once the Palestinians tried to hide behind the back of 'trustees'. Both states would prefer a more vulnerable state between them. Only such a status could make the Palestinians more responsible. Any tampering with the Treaty would be an excuse for either Jordan or Israel or both to respond in any way which they considered appropriate. There could be no compromise, delay or debate on such cardinal issues. A Palestinian move to upset the delicate structure would be considered by Jordan and Israel as a *casus belli*, but it may well be the case that the rigid conditions and restrictions likely to be stipulated in the Treaty would themselves work to exacerbate the very tension and instability the parties wanted to avoid.

Security and External Relations
Palestine's future defence posture and foreign orientation will be central to any discussion of a treaty as this involves not only the Palestinian regime's relations with both its neighbours and subjects but also with the rest of the Arab world and the international guarantees which would enable the state to come into being. The first questions relate to the particular status of Palestine: should she be allied, demilitarized, armed but neutral, or subject to international and inter-Arab guarantees, or should she be a state like every other state in the region? It is not what each side would insist upon that is to be discussed here, but rather what types of arrangements would be more conducive to stability and what are the dangers and problems that flow from the various limitations involved.

The Military
Although strictly outside the scope of this Paper, the present debate on this issue may shed some light on the problems. Both Israel and Jordan, who now reject the establishment of a Palestinian

state, argue that her total demilitarization – a minimum prerequisite on their part – could not last, and that it would not be long before Palestine, with external help, turned a police force into an effective army equipped with modern weapons. This development would pose a threat to both states. Another war with all its regional and world-wide implications could follow. The Palestinians aggravate these concerns by arguing that full demilitarization is inimical to sovereignty and that they would require a credible armed force to defend themselves against powerful neighbours.

Three security arrangements could be envisaged which might reconcile the many conflicting interests of the parties concerned. These involve discussion of demilitarization and neutrality – two indispensable and interrelated components which would be closely linked with the appropriate international guarantees aimed both at protecting Palestine's sovereignty and her neighbours' security. The three possibilities are as follows:

– An arrangement which allows Palestine her own fully-fledged armed forces.
– A Palestinian state with a small, modestly-equipped army (with restrictions imposed on its size and equipment) and a police force.
– A Palestine with no army of her own, her territory, air-space and territorial waters *totally* demilitarized, but with a strong, indigenous police force responsible for internal security.

No Limitations on the Military
The Palestinians will find it extremely difficult to accept the concept of total demilitarization as it would be inconceivable for Palestine to have less as a sovereign state than the arms the PLO had at its disposal as a guerrilla movement.[38] The more sophisticated the weapons the PLO receives prior to the establishment of Palestine, the more difficult it will be for the Palestinians to give them up. Moreover, if PLO Rejectionists remain in Lebanon after the establishment of Palestine and receive Soviet arms to face the Israeli, Lebanese and Syrian armies, then it would prove unrealistic to expect the Palestinian state to acquiesce in a situation where the Palestinian Rejectionists would possess arms superior to those of the state. Palestine would, therefore, insist on having her own armed defence force and this would probably have to be roughly half the

73

strength of the Jordanian army.[39] She would also demand a small combat air force, some armour and surface-to-air missiles, not just as a mere token of sovereignty but as an adequate deterrence against attacks from Jordan or Israel.

The obvious difficulty posed by such a sizeable force is that it provides Palestine not merely with a defence capability, but also some capacity for aggression against both her neighbours. Even a small Palestinian force would overlook central and northern Israel and surface-to-air missiles would threaten Israeli air-space. Similarly, control of the hills above the Jordan Valley would grant Palestine a measure of strategic advantage over Jordan. From both an Israeli and Jordanian viewpoint it is highly undesirable that Palestine should be encouraged to strive, from a position of strength, to implement the original Palestinian goals.

Imposed Restrictions on Palestine's Army
Israel and Jordan are likely to argue that, if the Palestinians really want peace, they only require a moderate force for internal security with no armour, artillery, or air force. Both states will also prove extremely sensitive to traffic at Qalandya airport near Jerusalem, the only airfield in the West Bank. They would insist that it be operated solely as a civil airfield, and that no additional runways should be built. Surface-to-air missiles should also be forbidden.[40] Anti-tank missiles would be most suitable for Palestine, enabling even small forces to delay an invasion. In return, Israel might be more flexible in her demands for the restriction of Palestinian naval power and on the demilitarization of the Gaza port. Any build-up of forces in the narrow Gaza Strip is easier to contain than a similar situation in the West Bank, especially when it is obvious that the Palestinians would be unable to transfer arms from one part of their state to the other via Israel's territory.

Yet it is difficult to see how this category differs from the first. History has shown that attempts made to restrict the size of a state's military forces and weapons have rarely worked. The Palestinians will be tempted to enlarge and modernize their inferior armed forces in order to match those of their neighbours and pressures may come also from within the ranks of the Palestinian military elite, who would resent their restricted policing tasks.

Creating a 'licensed' army also invites circumvention. With the consent of Damascus, Palestine could station part of her army on Syrian soil. Furthermore, this would enable Palestinians to open another front against Jordan or Israel if either were to attack Palestine. Conflicts would also ensue over verification of the restrictions.

Within Palestine, control over the armed forces could prove to be a problem with the PLO factions refusing to amalgamate. A faction-ridden army could not protect the state but could bring about civil war or a military coup.

Developing the nation's economy would seem to be more logical than forming an army. This may even be supported by many Palestinians.[41] But Middle Eastern history shows that economic constraints have rarely hindered arms races, especially when both super-powers have transferred weapons cheaply or with credits, in the hope this would give them leverage over their clients. The Arab oil producers may of course help a Palestinian state to purchase arms if they feel it would serve their own interests.

It is obvious that should a Palestinian government decide to purchase arms, there is little to prevent it doing so. And, if it succeeded once, there would be little to prevent it from trying again. Even insignificant breaches of the agreement could prove costly to all parties concerned. Israel still remembers the lesson of the August 1970 Ceasefire Agreement with Egypt which was immediately breached. Egypt moved her anti-aircraft missiles forward. Israel protested but was prevented from acting by the United States who wished to preserve the Agreement. If either Israel or Jordan were seen to be slow to react, then the new state might try to take advantage of this and neither could, therefore, be expected to remain aloof in the face of any Palestinian breach.

Aware of the military power of Jordan and Israel and conscious of the risks involved in having a large army, Palestine may choose not to purchase large quantities of weapons, regarding military inferiority as an asset. She could then call upon other Arab states to come to her aid, whereas a sufficiently strong army might relieve the Arab states of that duty.

If the other Arab states really wish to defuse the Arab – Israeli conflict, they might accept that it is also in their own interest to prevent Palestine from having an army which might drag them into renewed conflict with Israel. A vulnerable

Palestinian state might be far more cautious and responsible than one with a real military capability.

Demilitarization

Palestine could be in a stronger position without an army than with one. There is no real conflict between demilitarization (to be distinguished from Demilitarized Zones which are discussed later) and sovereignty so long as the state can handle her own internal affairs, can maintain internal security and so long as her external security is guaranteed by outside forces. It is one thing to strive for durable independence and another to aspire to a military capability which might cause war. Moreover, it is easier to control an arrangement which stipulates that only police forces are allowed than to verify an agreement which imposes limits on size and quality. What is called for in this case is the establishment of a strong police force — the Palestinian National Guard — whose size and types and quantities of equipment would be limited to that required for keeping internal order.

Facing a police force rather than a properly equipped army could, however, encourage the Rejectionists to take advantage of government weakness to continue the armed struggle against Israel or Jordan with smuggled weapons. Israel and Jordan might then exercise the right to retaliate, should the local government fail to stop such terrorism (or tacitly aid it). However, too frequent retaliation would only expose the weakness of the Palestinian government and make it easier for the Palestinian Rejectionist to undermine it.

One way or another, the phenomenon of terror is unlikely to disappear. The question is therefore how to limit local support for it without playing into the hands of the Rejectionists. To that end, Israel should co-operate with Palestine — as she did with Jordan prior to, and after, 1967 — to help the Palestine National Guard to carry out its tasks. 'Over-reaction' on Israel's part would only make such co-operation more difficult (as again was the case with Jordan) and would present the Palestinian government as an impotent regime which was collaborating with Israel against the Arab cause. Israeli and Jordanian restraint would be essential.

The issue of terrorism shows perhaps more clearly than any other problem how complex the whole arrangement is and highlights three indispensable additional arrangements. The first is the need for a simultaneous settlement of the conflict in Lebanon in a way which will deprive the Rejectionists of a base there. Related to that is the second condition, the full co-operation of the Arab world. The third is the full co-operation of the USSR — the main supplier of sophisticated arms and training to the various Palestinian factions. Without all three, terrorism could still come to dominate the scene. Furthermore, to acquire greater international leverage the Palestinian Rejectionists would not necessarily confine their targets to the Near East. They may spread their action to the most volatile region — the Gulf.

No settlement can be achieved without serious and painful concessions by all sides. If the Palestinians want to establish their state, total demilitarization would be perhaps the heaviest price they would have to pay — not just merely as a sign of goodwill, but as an official expression of their commitment to abide by the Treaty and to regard the borders agreed as *final* rather than *provisional*. Indeed, this may be the only viable 'guarantee' that the Palestinians can give.

A comprehensive settlement which addresses the Palestinian question would also have to include strict security restrictions over the other Arab states and Israel. Such restrictions should apply to numbers of men and types of weapons in particular zones (as with the Sinai arrangements), to the movement of forces and unauthorized arms into demilitarized zones, and to the non-fortification of certain positions. The Treaty, especially, should include undertakings not to interfere with the work of international observers or to obstruct early-warning stations. Yet the terrain on both the eastern and northern fronts prevents the institutionalization of straightforward, flexible, asymmetrical security arrangements of the type established in Sinai. Thus the minimum needed to allay Israel's fears of the Eastern Front would be the total demilitarization of a 20 km-wide strip east of the River Jordan. Similar arrangements are essential in Lebanon, and far more rigid ones are called for on the Golan Heights. In exchange Israel could be expected to demilitarize a symbolic strip on her side. Only under such circumstances could a more stable relationship emerge between Israel and Palestine.

LIBRARY OF MOUNT ST. MARY'S COLLEGE

75

Foreign Affairs: Palestine Neutral not Neutered
(1) For the purpose of the permanent maintenance of her external independence and for the purpose of the inviolability of her territory, Austria of her own free will declares herewith her permanent neutrality which she is resolved to maintain and defend with all the means at her disposal.
(2) In order to secure these purposes Austria will never in the future accede to any military alliances nor permit the establishment of military bases of foreign states on her territory.
(*Federal Constitutional Law of 26 October 1955 on the Neutrality of Austria*).

There are, of course, different types of 'neutrality' ranging from active 'non-alignment' to the passive Swiss example. The type of neutrality adopted is usually determined by external factors. In some cases neutrality is stipulated in the state's constitution – whether originally enforced by external powers or voluntarily endorsed (or both). In others, it is a carefully formulated voluntary principle. The perception and definition of threat either encourages states to accommodate their more powerful neighbours or to increase their defensive capabilities. However, once the principle of total demilitarization is established, then what follows is that the range of choice is limited to that between 'enforced neutrality' and 'self-imposed neutrality'.

There are those who envisage a Palestinian state modelled on the Austrian State Treaty.[42] President Sadat himself has advocated this solution which would bind the state to Jordan and Israel by a peace treaty guaranteeing Palestine's complete neutrality.[43] Such limitations could inhibit certain political developments and supply the necessary justification for any government to continue to pursue a neutral and moderate policy. The proponents of this view believe that the fact that such explicit restrictions were institutionalized in the Austrian case[44] (or voluntarily applied, as in the case of Japan[45]) with no adverse effects, could make the Palestinians more inclined to acquiesce in these arrangements. Neither Austria nor Switzerland derive their security from their rather small defence forces but from their neutral status. Other small states who lie adjacent to powerful neighbours are coming to regard neutrality as the best way to find security.[46] But,

unlike most other states, Palestine is an integral part of a wider Arab world and this introduces a complicating factor. Palestine's permanent neutrality would mean that neither Arab troops nor Arab weapons could be stationed on her soil.

The difficulties of neutrality are its durability and its elasticity. In trying to improve her bargaining position *vis-à-vis* her neighbours, Palestine might follow a 'non-aligned' orientation instead of the 'neutrality' she originally undertook to maintain. Then it is only a short way to 'positive neutralism' and that implies the adoption of a more aggressive policy which might encourage super-power competition by playing one against the other. To that end, Palestine might adopt a 'no peace, no war' policy, hoping that the ensuing 'cold war' might draw in the other Arab states.[47]

This wide range of options demonstrates, perhaps more than anything else, that Palestine's neutrality could not only prove an asset rather than a diminution of her sovereignty, but that this status in itself could become a source of conflict. For it might even benefit Palestine to appear to lose control so as to justify requests for Arab or Soviet aid with Palestinian manoeuvrability being enlarged in spite of, if not because of, her military weakness. She might discover that political capital, not only economic aid, flows more generously when an unpredictable posture is adopted. This explains the concern of not only Israel, but also Arab rulers with regard to the possible consequences of a 'neutralist' Palestine. The latter could easily play one Arab government against another.

Yet in seeking to practice such a posture, Palestine would be constrained by her three neighbours and, fearful of Israel's reaction, she might feel reluctant to invite Jordan to defend her from Israel, unless the political reality across the river changed. Nevertheless, she may still fear having to further compromise her sovereignty by becoming a 'satellite' to a radical Jordan.[48] The Palestinians may also feel uncomfortable with Egypt's influence and her leverage over the Gaza Strip where, unlike the West Bank, she enjoys wide support. It would prove more difficult to withstand pressure from a radical Egyptian government.

A consequent possibility is that the USSR alone (or her surrogate forces) might be called upon to defend the Palestinian state were Jordan or Israel to retaliate against Palestinian infiltration or attempt to police Palestine. Continuing Israeli pressure could then allow the Soviet Union to maintain that she was 'forced' to defend the vulnerable Palestinian state and to step up her support.

A pro-Soviet Palestine might, however, deprive herself of a handsome part of the economic support she would receive from conservative Arab oil-producing countries who would like to sustain their influence there. Palestine may stand to gain more if she is not a Soviet client with predictable pro-Soviet policies. On the other hand, receiving aid from the USSR would not necessarily amount to subservience to Soviet orientation. Moreover, it could well be the case that those supported at present by the USSR would become her critics. For if a comprehensive settlement meant diplomatic relations being established between the Soviet Union and Israel, this would aggravate Rejectionist Palestinians[49] who might find that the Soviet Union does not share their ultimate goals.[50]

The Rejectionists, of course, fear that once a Palestinian state has been created, the Arabs would be absolved from fighting on behalf of the Palestinians. In spite of the fact the PLO managed to bolster its position primarily because of inter-Arab rivalries, the Palestinians themselves suffered greatly because of those disputes and because of Arab – Israeli conflict. Not only did the PLO play no role in the 1967 and 1973 wars but Israeli power forced the Palestinians to lie low during both. One might presume that their sense of vulnerability will persist and that an independent Palestine would be careful not to exceed the limits of her neighbours' tolerance. Yet Israel and Jordan should be careful not to lean too hard on Palestine's already circumscribed sovereignty for fear of giving her an excuse for outside support. After all, the sticks and carrots (i.e., military leverage and economic power) would dictate the substance of relations, despite the mutual resentment and suspicion which would continue to characterize the new coexistence. Stability and security for both sides, regardless of their ideology and orientation, could only be derived if the two sides behave in a predictable manner without demanding additional concessions which would only tarnish the respective regimes and create more internal unrest, thus running the risk of upsetting the entire arrangement.

The question is, therefore, what kind of guarantees Israel and Jordan should seek regarding Palestine's neutrality and demilitarization and what kind of guarantees Palestine would receive in return.

Guarantees

What should be guaranteed, by whom and how, is far from clear. There are many crucial questions: how far can guarantees be relied upon by the recipients? What kind of leverage do the recipients have over the guarantors in the case of default? What kind of deterrents and sanctions are applicable? What kind of guarantees are the parties directly involved likely to demand and what sort of guarantees would the super-powers be prepared to offer to achieve a settlement?[51]

It should again be emphasized that the conflict is not only between Israel and the Palestinians. The resolution of conflict involves the Arab world. Therefore the international guarantees need to cover the Middle East as a whole and as such could not be isolated from relations between the US and the USSR.

Multi-national Guarantees for Protected Neutrality

Palestine would expect guarantees against Israeli or Jordanian military action. Oversight mechanisms must be an integral part of such guarantees. Ideally, both super-powers, the UN, the Arab world and Palestine's two neighbours should all underwrite the agreement. Accordingly, different types of guarantees would be involved. They would include mutual guarantees of non-intervention between Palestine and her three neighbours, Israel, Jordan and Egypt, and sanctions appropriate for breaches of the agreement. A wider set of bilateral and unilateral guarantees should be given by the Arab states surrounding Israel and the super-powers. These guarantees should clearly establish:

– the limits of sovereignty;

– any military and political restrictions accompanying Palestine's establishment;

– limits of interference from outside with respect both to the Arab states and the super-powers.

It is essential that the super-powers bilaterally address questions of the newly-created vulnerabilities of all the states involved. If agreement can be reached (and formally ratified) regarding their responsibilities, this will act as a powerful deterrent to violation.

The UN, too, should become a guarantor, by virtue of the fact that it is already closely linked to the Palestinian issue as a result of various UN Resolutions, Commissions and Relief Agencies. A fruitful avenue to explore would be UN supervision of economic co-operation between the three states. An Economic Agency could not only channel funds into economic projects of mutual benefit but also help to resolve sensitive problems such as water, electric power, trade, customs and currency. Although direct UN involvement of this kind would not constitute a guarantee of security, the constant attention of the UN could raise the price of violation.

US – USSR Co-operation: a Vital Component?

Guarantees would assume that both super-powers have an equal interest in stability in the region. However, this is far from being the case at the moment.

Bearing in mind Soviet intentions and her traditional behaviour in the region, is the USSR indispensable to the peace-making process? After all, Egypt and Israel signed a Treaty in spite of Soviet opposition. The short answer is that purposely excluding her might force the Soviet Union to demonstrate her power by attempting to undermine the Treaty or to create instability. Soviet influence on her clients (as well as on the PLO) should not be belittled. If she does see short- or long-term advantages in supporting the foundations of the new arrangment, at least in the first crucial period, then it would be in her own interest to weaken the Rejectionists. The durability of such a Soviet orientation would depend on what she perceives to be the alternative, and the stakes involved are high.

However, assuming a Soviet wish to become involved, the arrangement cannot hinge solely on her formal agreement to implement the accord. Attempts should be made to involve the USSR so that adherence to an agreement would be in her own interest. It would be against Soviet interests to undermine an arrangement at a time when everybody else – her clients included – is attempting to make it work.

Yet there are also dangers of a too intense involvement of the Soviet Union, for this might raise Palestinian expectations well beyond what could be achieved. The Soviet Union knows,

moreover, that such 'stability' as the Middle East now possesses could easily be replaced by total chaos, over which neither super-power would have control. It is difficult to predict who would then stand to gain. As the USSR has experienced, short-term gains do not necessarily confer long-term advantages.

For the United States, questions of consistency, credibility and the readiness to make use of military capability are important in any discussion of guarantees in the Middle East. It is not what the super-powers say which impresses the local actors. What matters is what they would or would not do, bearing in mind the internal and external constraints under which the super-powers function.

If the US were to vouch for the behaviour of all three signatories of a Palestinian Peace Treaty, the USSR might seek to demonstrate her leverage by trying to undermine the new Palestinian government by presenting it as an American tool. To that end, she might support the Palestinian Rejectionists or encourage upheaval in Jordan.

However, with the stakes involved becoming higher, any Soviet miscalculation could prove costly. If this is understood, a certain 'linkage' might be created between some of the issues and *detente*. Although there are clear doubts about the effectiveness of 'linkage', the new weight of the US Congress in determining American foreign policy ensures that 'linkage' between issues cannot be ignored. Congress would be reluctant to ratify agreements providing the Soviet Union with economic help if the Soviet Union was going back on a commitment to underwrite a Palestinian Peace Treaty.

Nevertheless, it must be realized that there will remain limits to the extent of both super-powers' influence over their respective clients. If anything, reverse leverage is becoming powerful and the US is realizing that being a patron to both Jew and Arab is a difficult task. The USSR has discovered a similar dimension in Syrian – Iraqi (and even Iraqi – Iranian) rivalry. The absence of clear-cut spheres of influence is bound to complicate relations between the super-powers and their clients and, consequently, with each other. Although unthinkable at present, both might come to see that the best way to protect their own interests and to diminish rather than to encourage the prospect of armed conflict in the region could be by physical involvement, by agreement with the local states. After all, with such an array of agreements, the region would acquire no less symbolic a significance as Berlin, where super-power clashes immediately escalate. Moreover, the network of guarantees would encourage the US and the USSR to seek constant contact and crisis management to avoid such an escalation.

Internal Security Arrangments

A clear distinction should be drawn between guarantees (which define the *casus belli* and the conditions under which intervention is called for) and monitoring, which is the daily policing of the implementation of the Peace Treaty.

Monitoring, while essential, would doubtless prove a sensitive issue. For many Palestinians, the presence on their soil of foreign observers would hurt their national pride and self-respect. For the Israelis, having in any case little faith in international observers, it would mean the presence of a force which could limit their freedom to retaliate — inspection will therefore be a source of provocation. Yet observers can neither prevent either party from preparing for an assault nor can they act to repel it. The most they can do is to provide early warning of an impending attack and alert the guarantors to prevent action and restore peace. The dangers are that observers would become bogged down in trying to trace terrorists and in preventing them from mounting attacks across borders with their credibility probably tarnished as a result.

Theoretically, policing of a demilitarized Palestine could be carried out by some com-bination of the following monitoring forces:
- Israeli or Jordanian;
- Israel and Palestine's National Guard together (with or without Egypt and Jordan);
- Israel and Jordan (with or without Egypt);
- an all-Arab force;
- the United Nations;
- a Soviet — American force.

Israel believes that the presence of the Israeli Defence Force (IDF) in Palestine is not only a guarantee against any Palestinian military action but a deterrent to invasion from the east. In times of peace, however, the value of such a presence is questionable. The obvious military advantages would not seem to outweigh the political dis-advantages. Israeli forces would become a focus of Palestinian opposition and would weaken the Palestinian government's legitimacy, which may

prove counter-productive to Israeli interests. If border changes allowed Israel to retain some strategic positions both on her border with Palestine and in regions overlooking the Jordan Valley (see page 23), there would be no need to station troops in Palestine. The terrorist threat, which Israel is bound to live with under whatever arrangement, would, as now, be deterred by the threat of punishment.

Another undesirable solution is an Israeli — Palestinian force. Such co-operation would brand the new Palestinian government as a collaborator. Of course a degree of co-operation will be essential to prevent escalation of conflict along their common border and the mutual defence pact must establish modes of co-operation like those agreed between the Egyptian and the Israeli armies.

The inclusion of Jordan might also cause difficulties. Although Jordan is used to handling Palestinian subversion or terrorist action, she is unlikely to win Palestinian consent to this arrangement. However disguised, the presence of Jordan would be likely to provoke opposition, as would the presence of Egypt.

An all-Arab force consisting of Jordanians, Egyptians, Saudis and Palestinians could both aid the Palestinian government in controlling the Rejectionists within the country and grant it the legitimacy it needs for such action. It is difficult to see the local population actively aiding terrorist groups against such a wide Arab consensus. However, this option also has flaws. For one, Israel is unlikely to consent to the stationing of *any* Arab troops in Palestine for she fears being surrounded by powerful Arab states. Israel would want Palestine to remain exposed. Moreover, a foreign Arab force on Palestine's soil might encourage the Palestinians to feel that they were being backed by the Arab world. If conflict occurred between the Palestinian Rejectionists and the all-Arab force, the latter might be reluctant to act and would thus be ineffective. The experiment of the Arab Deterrent Force in Lebanon is evidence not only of that but also of the close relations that emerged between Syria and the PLO, despite the fact that their interests were incompatible in many instances. But there are other reasons why the presence of such a force is undesirable. The dangers of escalation if Israel entered Palestine to retaliate would be clear and would complicate

79

Israel's relations with those particular Arab states – which would, again, suit the Rejectionists. On the other hand, it might be possible for the Palestinians to argue that they could not be held responsible for the Arab force's actions. Nor could they easily order its withdrawal.

The Palestinians would obviously favour the presence of UN troops in Palestine for they enjoy great support in the UN and they have come to regard UNIFIL as a political and military 'buffer' against Israeli retaliation. But not only did UNIFIL fail to stamp out terrorism, it also failed to prevent Israel from acting against the PLO. Nevertheless, Palestinian support for the UN may stem also from a feeling that UN forces would prove a less permanent proposition. In fact, since it was installed in the Middle East in 1949, the UN has never had the capability to enforce the Armistice regimes it was supposed to maintain, as events leading to the 1967 war have proved, or to deter war. UN forces had failed earlier to prevent the *fida'iyun* infiltration or Israel's retaliation. Nevertheless, the UN observers could perform some useful functions,[52] though they are basically ill-placed to be effective militarily.[53] Only the super-powers have real influence in that part of the world.

Thus, even if to many Israelis it may suggest greater constraints on their own actions and an undesirable tolerance of Palestinian actions (which could also mean that Israel will run into conflict with both the US and the USSR), it is conceivable that Israel, Palestine and Jordan – distrusting each other and placing little faith in UN or other forces or in super-power verbal 'assurances' – will seek to involve both super-powers in a monitoring capacity. That would entail constituting a Soviet – American 'peace force' to act as a buffer between each of the parties[54] to be stationed in certain observation and other strategic posts[55] (such as Qalandya airfield, Gaza's port, or Jerusalem).

As a confidence-building measure, some of these internationally-supervised observation posts should be manned and inspected by civilians from all local parties, in addition to their Soviet – American civilian teams. Together they would also inspect the traffic across the River Jordan and the territorial waters in order to attempt to prevent the infiltration of terrorists and the smuggling of arms into Palestine. All information gathered by such surveillance must be provided to all concerned, for the purpose of such machinery is to be a credible channel for the quick processing of complaints. In addition to these jointly controlled observation posts, Palestine's neighbours would retain their own sensors, provided perhaps by the guarantors.

The super-powers, however, would probably be most reluctant to agree to such an active role which calls for their physical presence in the region. This would not only establish unprecedented modes of involvement in Third-world disputes, but it could also result in conflict between them. Yet it may prove to be the only condition acceptable to all the parties under which Palestine could be established.

Economic Viability

The attachment between the four economies — those of Israel, Jordan, the West Bank and the Gaza Strip – could lay a solid foundation for the proposed settlement. One of the main questions which would trouble Palestine would be her economic weakness. She would seek to strengthen her relations with the Arab world and the West, hoping to be granted financial assistance, but no economic development of any magnitude could take place without the co-operation of her neighbours. The cultivation of goodwill, together with pragmatic economic interest, would probably allay much of the friction and diminish, though not eliminate, the possibilities for the eruption of hostilities. How could the arrangement between the countries concerned be institutionalized, so as to strengthen economic interest and facilitate a process whereby each partner would have stakes in the well-being of the other's economy? New types of economic links could develop. These could include: heavy Israeli government and private investments in these territories; industrialization of the West Bank; Palestinian private investments in Israel's economy; open Arab markets for Israeli goods; and development of tourism. No matter what the final political answer, the West Bank and the Gaza Strip would continue to depend economically on open borders with both Israel and Jordan: with Israel as a source of potential employment and access to markets; with Jordan for exporting products to the Arab world. Closing the borders with her neighbours would seriously affect her own economy and could result in acute unemployment in Palestine, the political consequences of which would deter any Palestinian government, whatever its ideological inclinations. Correspondingly, Israel would face severe economic problems should the many Palestinians now working in Israel be denied access. Jordan would also be affected by a closure of borders.

The question of whether or not the new entity would be economically viable is not all that important. It would be political rather than economic decisions which would give birth to certain 'solutions'.[56] Nevertheless, any political arrangement will contain economic components which would have a bearing on Palestine's room for manoeuvre; those who argue against, and especially those who argue for, the establishment of an independent state stress the ill-defined 'economic viability' argument as a further justification for their position.[57] There are no clear-cut answers to the potential problems that could be raised.

One of the issues that will be politically acute will be the division of water between the three states. Israel's water reserves inside the Green Line, which depend also on water from the underground aquifer of Samaria, are constantly diminishing. Incorrect deep drilling on the western slopes of the West Bank could salinate the water (through the seepage of sea water). With the rise in the Palestinian standard of living (which will increase domestic consumption), the development of irrigated agriculture[58] and the establishment of industry in Palestine, Israel's water problems will increase. The Palestinians would have only a limited reservoir on which to draw and the position will become even more acute once the Syria – Jordanian Maqarin Dam begins to cripple the western part of the Jordan Valley towards the mid-1980s. Unless the problem of water allocation is resolved through regional co-operation, it is bound to lead to crisis.

Regional co-operative ventures could be extensive. They include: nuclear water desalination; 'resuscitation' of the mineral-rich Dead Sea (whose southern part is doomed to evaporate unless water reaches the River Jordan) to turn it into a huge solar-energy lake; the revival of agriculture in the western part of the Jordan Valley; co-developing the ports of Aqaba and Eilat in the south; water and sewage reclamation; and improved drainage. Some of these problems could be solved by a canal leading through the 25 miles or so separating the Jordan River from the Mediterranean. The differences in height could provide cheap hydro-electric power and compensate the Dead Sea for the loss of water from the River Jordan.[59] Such a canal could start from the Gaza Strip via Israel and down to the valley. Of course, this calls for long-term cross-border co-operation which could demonstrate how the most acute problem could have long term advantages.

Co-ordination in agriculture, as well as industry, is essential to avoid unnecessary competition. Palestine would probably want to export most of her farm produce either for hard currency or for energy from the Gulf states. In any case, Palestine's natural resources are poor, and raw materials for industry would have to be imported.[60]

The Israeli occupation has boosted, in an economic sense, both the relatively backward West Bank and Gaza Strip and the more advanced Israeli economy. However, the time when the Palestinians could easily better their lot – mainly through employment in Israel – is over. With a higher standard of living on the West Bank and with the impact of the Israeli rate of inflation, more Palestinians now invest in the Jordanian economy and many emigrate to the Gulf. There are obvious economic interdependencies which can help lay the foundation for a 'common market' economy and thus facilitate a *de facto* 'confederation', or (as Israel's former Foreign Minister, Mr Abba Eban, prefers to call it) a 'community' between the three states. Separate development could prove economically costly.[61] Many delicate economic problems lie ahead, all of which, although susceptible to co-operative solution, have political facets which will demand a great deal of caution, patience and sensitivity if the Palestinians are not to feel that their economic vulnerability might be used as a political weapon.

Population

Palestine's population would consist of the present inhabitants of the West Bank and the Gaza Strip, Palestinians returning from abroad and Palestinians staying abroad, who would nevertheless opt for Palestinian citizenship and who would probably form the bulk of it.

Refugees Returning to New Palestine

These would include the 1967 refugees who now live in the East Bank and a certain number of the 1948 refugees. The first category could be easily absorbed. Half of them are indigenous West Bankers. Some of the 1948 refugees, who fled from the Jericho area refugee camps during the six day war, would, in any case, prefer to remain in Jordan.

The approximate numbers of 'returnees' can only be guessed. One Palestinian source has suggested that some 610,000 Palestinians, mainly refugees, would opt to live in the new state within the first five years. [62] The same source argues that about 683,000 Palestinians would remain in the Arab countries, either because they have property there or because they would fear the loss of their rights to their original homes in Israel if they settled in Palestine. Those who have no property would return eagerly unless they suspected that they would earn a far lower income in Palestine than at present. But such estimates are obviously premature as the numbers wishing to return will depend on the political atmosphere at the time, on the agreed terms of compensation and on the form of economic assistance such 'returnees' would be entitled to receive from their new government. Much will also depend on the provisions made by the other Arab states for those who would prefer to remain in their countries.

No role should be given to the UN in regard to repatriation and compensation. UNRWA should be terminated the day Palestine is established. The essential services that UNRWA has been providing would be transferred to the new authorities and UNRWA's former personnel would provide a ready-made infrastructure for the Palestinian Ministries of Interior, Health, Education and Welfare. Having a country of their own, the refugees would immediately gain citizenship and would become the sole responsibility of their new government, which would have to handle all aspects of integration and compensation. This is not simply a symbolic act. Winding up UNRWA's operations was always associated by the refugees with the solution of the Palestine question. The ration card has always been regarded as the refugees' 'passport back to Palestine'. Many refugees would certainly fear the dissolution of UNRWA, believing that this would mean no more free education or health care. In that respect they are backed by UNRWA's staff who, naturally, are uneasy about losing their status and jobs. Thus assurances would have to come from the Palestinian government to allay the refugees' anxiety. New internationally-backed economic projects could be set up to provide for the integration of trained youngsters. It should not be forgotten that, contrary to the popular view, Palestinians are hard-working and skilful and have the experience of building the economies of other Arab states. [63]

The shortage of housing could hinder the task of absorption. Most schemes revolve around the idea of the new government setting in train building projects, funded by foreign aid, by dividing part of the domain it inherits between the refugees. Each family should be entitled to choose between receiving a plot of land and building materials or being compensated for its property in Israel. The existing refugee camps in the West Bank, which are by now either suburbs of certain towns or well-equipped villages, could be turned into proper settlements. Their inhabitants would be able, if they so desired, to build houses on the land where their shelters are situated. They would have title deeds to these tiny but valuable plots of land (a small part of which was Jewish property prior to 1948), [64] which they could also sell. Although it would be desirable to encourage refugees to leave the existing camps, not all would do so. The older generation would want to continue to live with their relatives and friends, [65] while the younger generation would probably leave the overcrowded camps and move into neighbouring towns. Special housing projects should be set up for young married couples as part of the large economic projects to be established. The over-populated Strip would require much attention.

As mentioned previously, the refugees from *outside* the West Bank and the Gaza Strip could be offered those settlements Israel would evacuate in the West Bank, the Gaza Strip, the Rafih Salient, the Sinai and the Golan Heights. [66] Owing both to their political symbolism and to the tangible benefits they offer (housing, agriculture and industrial infrastructure), these settlements would, ultimately, prove to have immense value as an Israeli bargaining chip for peace rather than as a security asset in times of war − as they were originally intended to be.

Return of Refugees to Israel

If the issue of the return of refugees to the new state of Palestine is essentially an economic one, it is dwarfed by the insurmountable political difficulties contained in the possibility of the return of many of them to Israel. Whereas the Palestinians will insist on the full implementation of the UN principle that any refugee who wished to return to his place of origin should have the right to do so, Israel will totally reject that right, regarding this as the price the Arabs should pay for Israel's agreement to the establishment of Palestine. Admitting the refugees would be seen as a security threat and further complicate Israel's demographic problem. It would also leave the Palestinians divided *between* states, which would seem to contradict the idea of having a homeland for the Palestinians. Israel also maintains that, since the number of Jews from Arab countries who were forced to leave their homes and property[67] roughly equalled (at the time) the Palestinian refugees from Israel, then it is for the respective Arab states to absorb the Palestinians as Israel did the Jewish refugees.[68] Naturally, this argument has never been accepted by the Arab states and has been rejected out of hand by the Palestinians. But then the plight of the Jewish refugees was never acknowledged by the Arab states, at least in a manner which would take into account those refugees' desire to remain in Israel.

Thus a compromise needs to be formulated which will address the dauntingly complicated refugee problem in its entirety, with both sides making concessions. It has been suggested that, unless a certain number of refugees are admitted into Israel, no comprehensive solution to the Palestinian question is possible. Israel could be expected to absorb about 60,000 refugees. This number would be even lower than the East Jerusalem Arabs who would then come under Palestinian sovereignty.

But it would be for Israel to say who would be admitted and where the refugees would be settled.[69] Refugees would not be able to return to places which are now populated by Israelis or regarded as security regions.[70] Israel could agree to integrate a certain number of refugees in the Arab villages they left, depending on their absorptive capacity. She could also license some refugees to return to the ruins of the very few old Arab villages remaining.[71] The return of the refugees would be phased and Israel would be expected to assist them in their integration — perhaps with a special international fund set up for the purpose.

Refugees Preferring to Remain Outside Palestine

Only a limited number of refugees would be able to leave their present localities, at least in the first period — and many would not want to leave. This issue touches upon a host of political and demographic problems, given that the establishment of Palestine would raise hopes or create sharp dilemmas for the Palestinian diaspora.

Although a Palestinian government would not tolerate any internationally-imposed restrictions on the size of its population, Palestine will have to set an annual limit on immigration for fear of being saturated by unemployed refugees. Therefore it should be stipulated in the Peace Treaties that no Arab government should be allowed to exercise a deliberate policy of expelling Palestinians. What the refugees want is the free *choice* to live within or outside Palestine. The Rejectionists apart, there would be many Palestinians (mainly of the older generation) who would prefer to be compensated and remain in their present places (with or without Palestinian citizenship) rather than go back to Palestine. Another problem could be created with those emigrating from Palestine after receiving compensation or selling their newly-given land. Equipped with a newly-acquired Palestinian citizenship, an immense psychological asset, living outside Palestine would now have a different meaning.

As in the past, one of the main problems would centre around the thorny question of entitlement for compensation, namely, who is in fact a refugee. Employing the widest and most flexible definition of the refugee status and having a generous rate of compensation would lessen the political tension surrounding this issue, making it possible for the Palestinian government to handle more easily the question of absorption and compensation.

The burden of the refugee question should be borne by all parties concerned. The Arab countries who had a Jewish minority (like Iraq, Egypt and Syria)[72] should contribute their share by paying the equivalent of the present value of the Jewish property confiscated there after the Jewish exodus in the 1950s to a special Arab-supervised Foundation (including the Palestinian Government) from which the Arab refugees would receive their compensation.[?³] Israel should be one of the main contributors to this Foundation.

Yet the refugee question is not, and never has been, simply an economic problem. The original phased Arab strategy which aimed at bringing about Israel's eventual liquidation is encapsulated in the Arabic term *al-Awdah* (The Return),[?⁴] to which the Palestinians are still committed. The 'Right to Return' is regarded as the natural, inalienable right of every Palestinian refugee to return to his own home (Israel) or, if he wishes, to be compensated and remain elsewhere. This principle of 'free choice' has been reiterated in all UN Resolutions on this subject since 1948. No Palestinian government could give up this right. Thus a new (and probably radical) government would doubtless claim that a territory within the 1967 borders could not possibly absorb the refugees wanting to live there. The presence of a large Palestinian population is necessary initially to create a viable political entity[?⁵] and as a guarantee against being swallowed by Israel in the future.[?⁶] More importantly, it would give Palestine a position of strength from which to demand the next phase: the 1947 Partition Scheme. To that end, some Arabs urge Palestinians to learn from the achievements of Israel. Israel was a nation of newcomers which managed to survive against all odds and then expand to enable other waves of immigrants to enter. Hence, there are dangers contained in a 'solution' of the refugee question, as well as in a settlement which purposely leaves this problem unsettled. In both instances, refugees' expectations could destabilize the new state and the entire arrangement. It would remain to be seen whether the Rejectionists' appeal would be considerably weakened once a large segment of the refugees is satisfied and fearful of losing its new status.

II. IMPACT ON THE ARAB WORLD

Beyond their public expressions of support for Palestinian rights, the Arab regimes are divided over the issue of the form the solution to the Palestinian problem should take. Prominent among the proposals are different types of 'federations', not only as a reflection of the yearning for Arab unity but also as a means of reining in such a new entity.

'Federations' and 'unions' in the Arab world emerge not from economic necessity or from a genuine common political quest but rather as a manifestation of provisional common interests to demonstrate power and leadership in the name of Arab unity. All such frameworks, however, tend to expose the growing polarization between inherently unstable Arab regimes. Coalitions do not last. While the Ba'athists in Damascus and Baghdad were at odds, for example, 'revolutionary' Syria and 'reactionary' Jordan were officially attempting to establish a 'union'. Conversely, in late 1980 Syria made threatening advances towards Jordan − now allied with Iraq.

Another reason for the tenuous nature of such 'federations' is the fact that the more powerful party seeks to assert itself over its partner or partners. Mutual suspicion and envy replace the spirit of unity. Nevertheless, it is worth looking at the elements that might contribute to a new form of coexistence in the region, for clearly past experience shapes the political considerations of the Arab States.

Because they support the idea of a Palestinian entity for different reasons, ideas about it are far from similar. For some it would enable them to rid themselves of the Palestinians. Lebanon, for example, wholeheartedly supports the establishment of Palestine for this reason. Others are motivated by different sets of considerations. Egypt and Saudi Arabia want to relieve themselves of the political burden of their commitment to the cause of Palestine (not the Palestinians), while Syria and Iraq see the settlement as a means of furthering their conflicting interests in the Arab world. The political aspirations of the latter states deserve closer examination.

The Link with Syria and Iraq
With regard to Syria, the point of departure is Lebanon. Some Arab states became increasingly troubled by the fact that the entire Arab *status quo* had been changed by Syrian intervention there and questions were raised as to Syria's political intentions. Concern that the old

'Greater Syria' (*suriya al-Kubra*) idea was being realized caused some uneasiness. This plan called for the unification of Palestine (i.e., 'Southern Syria' *(suriya al-Janubiyah)*),[77] Jordan and Lebanon under Syrian hegemony. The other conflicting aspiration, dating back to the early days of the present century, envisages the establishment of a union encompassing all those countries under Iraqi leadership in 'the Fertile Crescent'. The basic differences between the two schemes shed some light on the historic mutual suspicion existing between Syria and Iraq. Although Iraq may be happy to see Syria entangled in Lebanon, she is nevertheless apprehensive about the implications of Syrian expansionism and is further troubled by the thought that Syria might acquire an advantageous position in a future Palestinian state. Both radical states support Palestinian Rejectionist groups such as the *al-Sa'iqa* (founded, armed and controlled by Syria) and the Arab Liberation Front (ALF) (the Iraqi counterpart) but only Syria will be in a position to offer 'her' Rejectionists sanctuary across Israel's borders. Syria is close to (but not contiguous with) Palestine, which Iraq would find difficult to match.

To both Syria and Iraq Jordan is, therefore, important as a gate to Palestine. Jordan could become a focus of Syrian – Iraqi rivalry following the establishment of a Palestinian state and will find it difficult to stay neutral. Syria would prefer a weak and insecure Jordan on her flank, and would be troubled by any Jordanian attempt to seek Egyptian or Iraqi assistance. Syria and Iraq would also fear an Egyptian role in Palestine through the Gaza Strip. And, to complete the circle, Egypt would be uneasy if Syria were to dominate Palestine for this would bring Syrian influence closer to Egypt and further isolate Jordan.

Yet despite this complex pattern, all fear, each for their own reasons, that things might get out of control. A radicalized Palestine might derive part of her power − like the PLO − from inter-Arab rivalries and could drag the Arab world into yet another war with Israel for the sake of the recovery of the 'other parts' of Palestine. Syria would feel more vulnerable than Iraq and so more nervous. Israel could hardly be expected to occupy Iraqi territory, whereas she is still holding Syrian land. On the other hand, despite the fact that the present Palestinian attitude to Egypt is distinctly hostile, Palestine might feel quite comfortable with an Egyptian umbrella, even if the more obvious link is with Syria. 'Federation' with Syria could appeal to land-locked Palestine rather than a union solely with Jordan. A Jordanian – Palestinian 'federation' might be riddled with mistrust, whereas the Palestinians would feel more secure and less isolated were the Syrians or Iraqis to be included, regarding each of the more powerful states as likely to constrain the other and to deter Jordan from upsetting the delicate balance. Any Jordanian intervention in Palestinian affairs would then be regarded as undermining Syria's or Iraq's custodianship over the Palestinians.[78]

The real justification for a 'federation' is military, in order to give Palestine some security against Israel. Any Israeli attack on Palestine would then be regarded as an attack on the 'federation' as a whole. It would lead to the formation of an all-Arab policing force which would further deter Israel. The Palestinian government could regard Syrian support also as a way of diminishing the influence of the Rejectionists. Other Palestinians justify their support for Syrian involvement on the grounds that a weak state would tend to encourage division within the Arab world to the advantage of Israel. Some Palestinians have supported a 'tripartite union' based on the traditional connections between Syria, Jordan and the Palestinians.[79] Even some East Bank Palestinians approve such a federation,[80] though others press for complete independence.[81] The latter warn that such external protection will have its price.

The Gulf States

Ironically, the states who have suffered the economic burden, the political scars and the loss of lives in Arab wars with Israel are also relatively poor. And the Gulf states, who are more remote and rich, applaud and fund the conflict. They are quite comfortable with this 'division of labour'. However, their wealth, which gave them considerable political power, has been achieved with foreign labour, often highly politicized Palestinians. This leads to considerable ambivalence on the part of the Arab Peninsula Sheikhdoms. They need the Palestinians, but they are constantly reminded that the Palestinians expect their weight to be thrown behind the Palestinian cause and they fear a consequent entanglement.[82]

They know that financing PLO activities not only does not make them immune but, in fact, strengthens the very forces they fear.

Yet the Gulf is, and will continue to be, the main source of livelihood for the bulk of the Palestinians. Most Palestinians will continue to try whole-heartedly to integrate into their respective countries. Whatever the final resolution of the Palestinian question, Kuwait for example would not be regarded by the Palestinians living there as a mere transit station. Twenty per cent of her one million-strong population are Palestinian immigrants (with their offspring) who are now firmly established. Other states in the Gulf have a smaller proportion because families remain behind.

So long as the Palestinian question is unresolved, however, it is difficult for the Palestinians to demand rights similar to the indigenous population of their host country. Resettlement outside Palestine has always been viewed as 'collaboration with the Zionist state' and therefore unthinkable. The painful choice of returning to a Palestinian state or remaining outside does not yet have to be made, but it is extremely likely that a large share of these Palestinians would prefer to remain in the Gulf, despite the resentment they are facing from their Arab brethren there.

For their part, the governments in the Gulf states aim to replace immigrants holding jobs at the higher echelons with qualified locals. They are also striving to prevent immigrants from purchasing property and acquiring local citizenship. Needless to say, there are wealthy Palestinians who have managed to by-pass these restrictions and it would prove extremely difficult for these governments to send many Palestinians home. This would probably result in those who stayed being compelled to radicalize their position in order to demonstrate both their leverage over the local regimes and to justify their rejection of the Peace Treaty — which they will probably regard as a betrayal and a submission. This could bring about the conflict the Arab governments want desperately to avoid.

Palestine's limited absorptive capacity would also make it more difficult for the oil-producing countries to 'encourage' the departure of many Palestinians, despite the fact that this could be quite an effective weapon against subversive elements, as well as against the Palestinian

government.[83] Palestine's economic vulnerability could allow these conservative regimes to moderate Palestine's external policies. Though some Arabs fear this burden, Saudi Arabia currently believes that this would enable her to acquire greater control over the Middle East. (It should also be said, however, that a Qadhafi-type regime emerging in the Gulf could facilitate a movement in the opposite direction.)

Thus, given Palestinian expectations and the political ambitions of the Rejectionist states — at present Libya, Syria, Iraq and, perhaps, eventually, Jordan — Palestine's real neutrality becomes a necessity for the other Arab states. Yet the emergence of new Arab regimes, inter-Arab developments and international changes could all produce different policies and varying alignments with respect to Palestine. The chronic instability prevailing in the Arab world makes it difficult to deduce future trends. Even if some of these states doubt the wisdom of having a Palestinian entity in the region, they know that their choices are limited. Refusing to absorb the Palestinians, and thus raising their expectations of a homeland, has proved to be a counter-productive measure on the part of the Arab states who now have to grapple with problems of their own making.

Some Arab rulers seem to appreciate that a 'Jordanian option' is not viable. Although it could be one way of extracting the West Bank from Israel, Jordanian rule could not solve the Palestinian problem. They do hope, nevertheless, that Palestine's geographical position and consequent dependence on both Jordan and Israel would introduce an element of moderation in Palestine's policy. They might even approve the formation of a Palestinian state on condition that Palestine join in a 'federation' voluntarily with Jordan, *after* being granted independence but they might insist that the substance of this link be decided . *prior* to Palestine's inception.[84]

Jordan's Dilemma
Palestine's Leverage over Jordan
The transformation of the Palestinian entity into a territorial unit may undermine Jordan's very legitimacy. If the new state speaks for *all* Palestinians (regardless of their place of living and citizenship), this could mean that Jordan would cease to represent even those Palestinians

remaining in the East Bank. Although she dismisses non-Jordanian statistics concerning the size of the non-Palestinian population, Jordan's demographic composition is her Achilles Heel.[85] Her nightmare is that, once the Palestinians are granted a state, their old aspirations would seem more realizable, and that this would result in internal upheaval in Jordan between Palestinians and Trans-Jordanians, with the former being assisted by either Syria or Iraq. Thus external conflicts could exacerbate Jordan's internal problems and, conversely, contentious domestic issues might strain Jordan's relations with at least one of her neighbours.

Wherever their stronghold, the Palestinian Rejectionists would seek to cause conflict between Israel, Jordan and Palestine. Infiltration would trigger border clashes and the ensuing chain reaction would probably culminate in large-scale Israeli retaliation, however much all might attempt to avoid conflict. Such a chain reaction is likely to result in Jordanian repression against Palestinians within her borders, if not against Palestine, enabling the Rejectionists to present the Jordanian regime as collaborating yet again with Israel against the cause of Palestine. If the Rejectionists' sanctuary was in Syria, Jordan would worry that the latter might lend support to incipient underground Palestinian networks inside Jordan whose aim would be the overthrow of the Hashemites. These fears will always be at the core of Jordanian – Palestinian relationships. For the Palestinians remaining in Jordan, the painful choices contained in the issue of dual loyalty could be accentuated by Palestine's radicalization, particularly if Palestine were to manipulate border tensions for internal reasons: the regime might try to deflect internal criticism and bolster its position by highlighting disputes with Jordan. To topple the Monarchy, the Palestinians would need to receive backing from radical Jordanians (especially within the military) as well as from Syria, Iraq (or, perhaps, even Israel). Once in power in Jordan, there would be no reason for the Palestinians to conform to previous bilateral agreements between Jordan and Israel, especially those made to the detriment of the Palestinians. The Rejectionists make no bones about their ultimate goal. They oppose the establishment of a separate Palestinian entity alongside Jordan, and

view both the Jordanians and the Palestinians as one people,[86] admitting that only 'the requirements of a specific historical phase demands concentration of all efforts towards Palestine.'[87]

Jordan's Leverage over Palestine

Nevertheless, are there elements which could work to Jordan's advantage? Jordan could saturate Palestine with hundreds of thousands of Palestinians, even if that tended to destabilize not only Palestine but Jordan herself. Similarly, Jordan would be the gateway for the new entity to the rest of the Arab world which, in turn, will make Palestine rely, to a large extent, on her neighbour's goodwill. Moreover, militarily, Palestine will be at Jordan's mercy and Palestinian insecurity (and fears of Israeli retaliation) could force Palestine to turn eastwards for help. Jordanian patronage would have to be accepted. This would allow Jordan to dictate terms. She might decide to send her forces to Palestine's aid. Alternatively, Jordan may withhold help in order to demonstrate that Palestine's best defence is having good relations with her neighbours.

The Jordanian army, in which Palestinians do not enjoy the powerful positions necessary for a *coup d'etat*, is loyal to the Hashemites and wants to perpetuate the *status quo*. Both the minority and Bedouin elements who man the highest echelons of the military would regard defending continuity in Jordan as protecting their own survival. For them 'patriotism' is tantamount to personal faithfulness to their King. Their opposition to the PLO in September 1970 not only revealed their hatred for the Palestinians but their military superiority over them. There is no reason to believe that the Trans-Jordanians would willingly accept Palestinian domination and, so far, 'those in Jordan who supported the Jordanian entity have shown an incomparably greater degree of consistency, intransigence and readiness for sacrifice than those who opposed it'.[88]

Some Jordanians, however, might come to favour a strong Palestinian government on the grounds that it would soon learn to appreciate the constraints involved. A weak leadership, based on narrow support, would always be a target for the Rejectionists. Moreover, a strong nationalist government could handle opposition in a far more effective way than the relatively powerless conservatives. What Jordanians fear is a Palestinian move to set up a 'federation' with Syria or even Iraq, directed in the main against Jordan and Israel. This would seriously limit Jordan's ability to put pressure on Palestine and could, in turn, subject her to Iraqi or Syrian pressure. If Iraq and Syria remain at odds, then Jordan might seek to strengthen her ties with the country which is not allied to the Palestinians and she might aim to have close relations with Egypt as a counterweight to the radical states. Paradoxically, Jordan has recently sought to strengthen her ties with neighbouring Iraq despite, or perhaps because of, her radicalism. This was intended to strengthen the position of Jordan within the Arab world and among the Palestinians, as well as to improve her bargaining position with the United States whose resolve was generally perceived to be weakening. Of course, this does not mean that, given a settlement, Jordan would not insist on American guarantees similar to those granted to Israel but she is likely to be more flexible in her external relations.

Links between Jordan and the USSR are still based on the 1968 Cultural Co-operation Agreement with some additions.[89] This is primarily because the Jordanian regime does not want to appear to be carrying the burden of serving Western interests in opposing the Soviet presence in the Middle East. Hussein presumably believes that Jordan can only gain if he can play off the super-powers against each other. His Western orientation must not therefore be taken for granted but nor will he permit the USSR unrestricted access. In so doing, he might hope to convince the Soviet Union that they would benefit more by working through him rather than by encouraging subversive action against him. Maintaining ties with the USSR and (perhaps China) could also strengthen Jordan's position *vis-à-vis* Iraq and Syria. Hussein seems confident that only such a 'positive neutralism' would provide him with a firmer American commitment to his security. But he also must realize that military hardware and economic aid could hardly prevent internal instability.

Jordanians believe that whatever will be the formal nature of the links between the two Banks, Jordan must now concentrate on developing her 'own' region as a national unit. Crown Prince Hassan and others who support this school of

thought are likely to favour an intact 'Jordan for the indigenous Jordanians', having a Jordanian-initiated Palestinian entity lying to the west which would depend solely on Jordan and seek to be federated with her after independence. After all, the new entity probably could not afford to jeopardize its own tenuous foundations by severing its relations with Jordan. Rather, it would opt for maintaining positive ties with the regime in Amman.[90] Then, Jordanians suggest, a 'confederation' could be established but subject to Jordanian conditions.[91] This could even result in strengthening the more moderate Palestinians. The Jordanians take comfort from the fact that many Palestinians favour a link of some kind with Jordan. These are found mainly in the upper classes on the West Bank, on the East Bank and even in the Gaza Strip.

But what troubles Palestinians (apart from the economy), when considering future links with Jordan, is the question of sovereignty. Thus many Palestinians would like to enter into a new sort of union *after* independence, bargaining with Jordan on an equal footing and with mutual respect. Such a gradual evolution would be healthier than a Jordanian-imposed 'federation' – even if they ultimately amount to almost the same. Other Palestinians fear that Palestine would be destined to be once again the junior partner of such a 'confederation' or 'federation' if either ever came into being, and they would feel far more confident in joining a wider union which would include Egypt. The proponents of this arrangement are found mainly in the Gaza Strip.

Jordanian Choices
The new reality would contain new problems for Jordanians which would involve painful decisions. Jordan would insist first that all 1967 refugees should move across the river; next would probably follow many of the 1948 refugees who had not established themselves economically in Jordan. Many of those who migrated over the years to the East Bank would wish to go back. Most still have families on the West Bank and they might find it cheaper to live there than in Amman. This gradual exodus would doubtless be encouraged by the Jordanian government. All these moves would ease Jordan's demographic problems. Jordan would also have to decide whether the remaining Palestinians could continue to hold Jordanian citizenship (and

passport). This would not merely be an expression of Jordanian chauvinism aimed at antagonizing the Palestinians and 'their' government across the river, but an administrative adjustment to the new political situation.

One possibility would be to allow those acquiring Palestinian citizenship in place of Jordanian to vote in Palestinian elections. That would provide for a political outlet westwards, venting part of the pressures contained in the situation of Trans-Jordanian – Palestinian enforced coexistence within the East Bank. Jordan would now have some leverage over 'her' Palestinians, who could be expelled to their own country, something which she could not previously do.

Jordan might nevertheless decide that it would prove useful to have prominent Palestinians as members of the Jordanian Parliament, Senate and even Government, for this might encourage Palestinian moderation in Jordan and they might serve as intermediaries of the new Palestinian government. It would also indicate, however, that Palestine would not represent all Palestinians and this could prove to be a source of friction. Obviously, Jordan would prevent the existence of any Palestinian organization designed to maintain a Palestinian identity in Jordan.

Another related issue is that of the Palestine Liberation Army (PLA) unit which is at present stationed on Jordanian soil and which has functioned under her auspices. This army could be dissolved, kept as a special unit in the Jordanian armed forces, or transferred to Palestine to become part of her own new police force.

Finally the 'open bridges' policy could prove Jordan's best political instrument for this would allow her to control the flow of people, imports and exports and tourism. Jordan could thus make clear to every Palestinian the extent of her importance and it would remind Palestinians of the limits of their independence and the penalties involved in failure to adhere to what had been agreed.

It is almost inevitable that Palestine, sandwiched between Israel and Jordan (who would both insist on strict implementation of the Treaty and who would share the same interest in thwarting anything which arose between them to threaten their security), would be forced to depend increasingly on her Arab neighbour. If ever Israel comes to believe that a Greater Palestine composed of both Jordan and the new state would suit her better than an unpredictable small state, this will be despite the long-standing compatibility between the interests of Israel and Jordan dating back to the 1940s. Israel might then actively promote the idea of a Greater Palestine, at the expense of Jordan.

III. THE IMPLICATIONS OF A PALESTINIAN STATE FOR ISRAEL

The establishment of a Palestinian state is regarded by most Israelis as a threat to Israel's very existence. It follows that the attainment of 'tranquillity' and the shedding of the heavy political burden of the Palestinian problem will be at a high price.

Although the occupation of the Gaza Strip and the West Bank did not prevent Palestinian terror – which at first operated primarily from the East Bank and thereafter the Lebanon – Israel feels more secure if she is in control of them. But greater than the fear of terrorism is the fear that the West Bank could become a springboard for an attack by the militarily powerful Eastern Front. Israel fears an alliance between Syria, Iraq and the Soviet Union and has learned from history to trust no other country as far as her security is concerned.

The recognition of the PLO not only by the East but increasingly by the West worries Israel. The PLO is showing no signs of moderation. It still rejects Israel's *right* to exist, and announces its intention of 'liberating the *whole* of Palestine'. A West Bank – Gaza Strip state as a necessary first phase in this strategy further troubles her. Furthermore, such a state could not contain all the Palestinian refugees who might wish to return. [92]

To all these dangers are added the fears that Arabs in Israel will demand to be incorporated territorially in a Palestinian state. These fears are valid. Israel argues that because the creation of a

89

small Palestinian state could not possibly *solve* the Palestinian problem, it can only be seen as a step on the road to the destruction of Israel. A Palestinian state means war, not peace to Israel. These perceived threats deserve further elaboration.

Threats to Israel

There are political risks and military dangers threatening Israel's survival. The political risks arise between Israel and the Palestinians; the military dangers involve the Arab world as a whole. The Soviet Union is regarded as playing a role in both.

The following quotation encapsulates the dangers perceived by Israel:

'If we find that our forces cannot ameliorate the enemy and throw it into the sea, then we will take this into consideration. We will then have to wait and work by stages . . . One must not adhere to the policy of "all or nothing". We would not have succeeded in Tunisia if we had done so. Every step which took us nearer to the goal we accepted . . . If we confine ourselves to passion, we will stay hundreds of years like this, reiterating the slogan of the usurped homeland.'[93]

Long-term Palestinian Aspirations

Though pledged to the recovery of *all* the land formerly known as Palestine,[94] the PLO's various groups hold divergent views of the way to achieve this ultimate aim.[95] The classification of these power groups as 'moderates' and 'extremists' is somewhat misleading, because the written constitution of the PLO — the Palestinian National Charter — binds all the groups.

The Rejectionists within the PLO, including certain elements within Fatah itself, call for a continued armed struggle. Negotiation implies recognition of Israel, and recognition is something they are not willing to extend under any circumstances. They also fear that, once a Palestine is established from the West Bank and the Gaza Strip, the Palestinian commitment to the recovery of the remaining parts of old Palestine — now the state of Israel — would dwindle.[96]

The 'Moderates' (who are a major component of the Fatah) advocate diplomacy as the way to establish a sovereign state in the West Bank and Gaza or even a 'Patriotic Authority' (*Sulta Wataniyah*) on any liberated part of Palestine. Both stages are regarded as provisional. The ultimate goal (*hal da'im*) remains the establishment of a Secular Democratic State.[97] Following a West Bank – Gaza interim state, the 1947 Partition Plan would be implemented and all Palestinian refugees would thereafter return to their places of origin. Israel would wither and die as a result of political attrition and armed conflict.

It is assumed, however, that once the PLO is called upon to participate in a dialogue, it would fragment. Moderates and Rejectionists would acquire a totally different meaning: the former would be those acquiescing in any arrangement which granted the Palestinians an independent state roughly contained by the 1967 boundaries in exchange for their commitment to regard it as an *ultimate* solution to the Palestinian Question and the recognition of the *right* of Israel to exist as a Jewish state. The Rejectionists would doubtless do their utmost to abort such a compromise.

In any event, both groups believe that an Arab-dominated Secular Democratic State, in which Jews, Christians and Muslims would coexist peacefully, is an inevitable product of a phased implementation, which will parallel many revolutionary political and social changes in Israel and the Middle East as a whole.[98] They believe that social tensions between the two halves of Israeli society — 'Western Jews' and 'Oriental Jews' — will come to the fore once Israel is not threatened by the Arab world and that, therefore, peace would fragment Israel from within. They assume that the frustrated 'Oriental Jews' will eventually return to their places of origin and that this would change the numerical balance in favour of the Palestinians, thereby ending Israel's existence as a Jewish state.[99] This argues for temporarily shelving the military option in favour of a superficial calm after the establishment of Palestine.

Although 'Moderates' may be underestimating the cohesion of Israel's second generation which transcends social barriers, the dangers are real. Irredentist Palestinian demands will persist, echoed eagerly by refugees within, and particularly outside, the new state, encouraged by the success of the first phase of the Palestinian strategy. The new government, instead of resigning itself to the new reality, may be unable to control irredentism and it is easy to imagine the ensuing chain reaction. The danger for Israel is that Palestine would become a new Lebanon, especially if Lebanon were to remain the Rejectionists' haven.

Arabs in Israel: Threat of Secession
The establishment of a Palestinian state will raise the expectations of the Arabs in Israel who might insist on being incorporated into the new state in accordance with the 1947 Partition Scheme, which would include a large part of the Israeli territory they populate. Israel, like Jordan, has a demographic problem. Arabs within Israel may reach one million by the year 2000 – roughly equal to the projected West Bank Palestinian population.

Today there are 650,000 Israeli Arabs (including East Jerusalem's 160,000 inhabitants) and this is 17% of Israel's total population. These Arabs populate three main regions inside pre-1967 Israel: Galilee, the 'Triangle' (the area adjacent to Tulkarm – Jenin – Nablus in the West Bank) and the Negev. Half of them live in the Galilee, Israel's northern province, which is divided equally between Jews (307,200) and Arabs (286,900). The Upper Galilee, however, is dominated by Arabs. An Israeli plan to 'dilute' this heavily Arab populated region with Jewish settlements was shelved because the Government devoted attention solely to populating the occupied areas. Only one new settlement was established in the Galilee between 1967 and 1977 whereas over ninety settlements were established in the occupied territories. From Israel's point of view this policy was self-defeating. It will be far more difficult now to embark on a policy of 'Galilee's Judaization', because this would require the expropriation of more Arab land, an issue which has already given rise to sharp protests amongst the Israeli Arabs as recent attempts to establish tiny settlements in that region have demonstrated.

The process of 'Palestinization' of the Arabs in Israel has intensified since the 1967 war because, for the first time since Israel's independence, no border has separated the West Bank and Gaza Strip Palestinian communities from their brothers living inside Israel. Many Arabs within Israel have increasingly identified themselves with the PLO. They have come to feel themselves 'second class' citizens particularly as a result of the rapid growth of higher education among the young and frustrated Arabs. It is a young population. Some 75% of the Israeli Arabs are under 30 years old. Contrary to expectations, the rise in the Arabs standard of education did not bring moderation or growing acquiescence. Thirty years of being Israeli citizens has not reconciled the Arabs of Israel to being willing members of that state.[100] The status of the Arabs within Israel is likely to trouble Israel increasingly, whatever the final outcome of the Palestinian issue.

Israel will therefore oppose changes to the 1967 border on a *mutual* basis because she fears that such an arrangement would bring renewed demands from Israeli Arabs for the implementation of the 1947 Partition Scheme. Any future Palestinian government which made representations on behalf of its 'trapped branch' in Israel and insisted on incorporating this territory into Palestine, regardless of the peace agreements, would be bound to elicit an angry reaction from Israel.

Once a Palestinian state is established, the Israeli Arab problem might subside. Peace might take the sting out of their plight and enable Israel to overcome her suspicions and alleviate many of their problems by incorporating them more into government.[101] Urbanization could proceed and, in due course, even the Upper Galilee might look somewhat different demographically if Israel continued the process of Judaization there, but that would mean full compensation for expropriated land.

The most optimistic view is that, if the principle of symmetry were applied, Israeli settlers could live on the West Bank under Arab sovereignty and have the same rights and duties as Arabs would have in Israel. Israel would desist from expropriation, fearing the consequences for her settlements beyond the border. And so a predominantly Jewish state would exist next to a predominantly Arab state.[102]

Certainly the problems of the Arabs in Israel cannot be ignored as they have been. It seems unlikely that many Israeli Arabs would opt for moving from Israel to Palestine, yet Israel will probably reject the idea that Israeli Arabs, remaining in Israel, could vote in Palestine and so also be able to vote in Israeli municipal, but not parliamentary, elections (in a similar capacity to that of the East Jerusalem Arabs who still hold

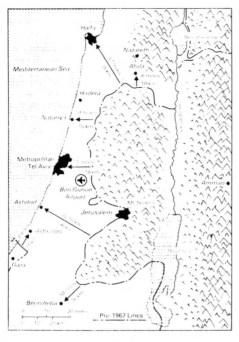

Map 7

Jordanian passports even though Jerusalem was annexed to Israel). Israel would wish to prevent the further deepening of dual loyalties of her own Arab population.

Nevertheless, this possibility should also be examined, for there are no easy remedies when trying to address the complicated and dangerous question of the political identity of Israel's Arabs. Providing an outlet for this kind of pressure, despite the political dangers that may ensue, would probably outweigh the dangers of ignoring the changes that have taken place amongst Israeli Arabs.

Danger from the Eastern Front

Undoubtedly this is the most serious and immediate danger for the survival of Israel were Israel to relinquish control over the area west of the River Jordan. Not only do Israelis fear that Palestinian aspirations might give rise to terrorist infiltration, which the new state may be reluctant or unable to control, but they also fear the old

Arab dream of using this area as a springboard to attack Israel's heartland. In view of the region's topography, this is a real threat.

Israel's vulnerable waist is flat with no barriers between the Mediterranean and the foothills of the West Bank. At points this waist is only 9 to 15 miles wide. (See Map 7). Most of Israel's population and most of her industrial infrastructure are concentrated in the narrowest part of this strip[10] in an area no larger than London and New York together. An invasion from the Eastern Front could easily cut the country in two. The West Bank can be traversed by modern armour in a few hours (as Israel proved in the 1967 war) as can the Golan Heights which are devoid of natural obstacles. Control of even part of the West Bank could give an attacking Arab force the ability to strike at Israel's central and northern airfields and dominate her airspace and thus seriously hinder Israel's defence capability.

Jordan, despite the fact that she has the longest borders with Israel, has never been perceived as a threat by Israel. This would change once a Palestinian state was established and Israel would then be more sensitive to what occurs in the East Bank, especially in any demilitarized region adjacent to the River Jordan. If Jordan were to move her forces to the eastern side of the Jordan valley or if arms were to enter Palestine from Jordan, Israel could be expected to retaliate against Jordan, as such a situation would prove intolerable for her.

Another set of potential dangers would arise if the Palestinians seized control of Jordan or if Jordan were invaded by one or more of her other Arab neighbours. If the Palestinians received Arab support in a take-over of Jordan, they would come to possess a secure base and a modern army (the Jordanian Arab Legion). Syria or Iraq might be invited to safeguard Arab interests and station their forces east of the River Jordan as well as along the Syrian – Israeli border. This would constitute a grave threat to Israel.

Israel believes that Iraq's accumulation of arms, the purchase of tank-transporters and the paving of new highways towards Jordan and Syria are all directed mainly towards her. Iraq could be expected to send westwards between 3 and 4 times as many tanks and troops as in 1973. This could be a way for Iraq to assert herself as the leader of the Arab world, a position to which she aspires. However, the recent war between Iran and Iraq, in which the latter's performance has been far from impressive, could mean that in the next few years Iraq might prove reluctant to become entangled in a large-scale prolonged war elsewhere in the Middle East. Without Iraq the Eastern Front would not be a serious threat to Israel, despite Syria's newly acquired strength and Jordan's military growth. Moreover, Jordan might be reluctant to consent to the presence of a large Syrian or Iraqi force on her soil which, apart from putting the onus on Jordan, might prove difficult to get rid of once the war is over (as Hussein's experience with Iraq in the late 1960s demonstrated). But with the addition of Iraq (with or without expeditionary forces from other Arab states), the Eastern Front of the mid-1980s would produce a much more serious potential threat to Israel than it has been in the past,[104] for such a force could launch several offensive efforts simultaneously along the extensive and vulnerable border.

Certainly the gathering of all these forces would give Israel ample warning. She could retain the option of launching a pre-emptive strike or waiting for the other side to make the first move (assuming the co-guarantors remained aloof). The entry of Syrian or Iraqi forces into parts of western Jordan would be regarded as a *casus belli* and result in an Israeli invasion of Palestine or even parts of Jordan. Certainly, Israeli forces would move forward to control once again the crest of the Palestinian hills overlooking the Jordan valley so as to forestall the danger. Israel would probably then have the capability to either slow an eastern invasion or to take the battle to Jordanian or Syrian soil. Syria in particular would have to guard against an Israeli attack via Lebanon.

Thus much would come to depend on Egypt's behaviour. Certainly Egyptian participation would complicate things for Israel and she would then have to rely on the United States to restrain Egypt. For should Egypt move into the Sinai this would force Israel to face in two directions. And with the military modernization of the Arab armies in the 1980s, the very existence of Israel could be endangered.

Arms transfers to such a volatile region are destabilizing[105] for the possession of arms can make the military option more attractive. The super-powers appear to believe that supplying arms gives them political influence over their respective clients but there is little evidence to show that such influence can be used to restrain clients intent on war. Given the enormous revenues at its disposal, the Arab world can purchase more or less what it likes. Western Europe is also only too eager to make a profit from the sale of arms and Israel is particularly concerned that Iraq's new connection with France will lead to Iraqi possession of nuclear weapons. This might deprive Israel of her ability to deter the Arabs from launching a war with the aim of bringing about her liquidation.

Israel will continue to need to match the might of all her adversaries at once. Moreover, an Israel confined to her pre-1967 boundaries would suffer strategic disadvantages which would demand some margin of overall military superiority. The Arab states are unlikely to tolerate an adverse strategic balance. It is hard to see how it would be possible to alter this progressively deteriorating situation without co-operative restraint by the arms suppliers to peg capabilities at a level which would make aggression an unattractive option.

The 'Soviet Threat'

The Soviet Union, as the main arms supplier of Israel's adversaries, has always been regarded as a menace by Israel. She has felt threatened by the deep Soviet involvement in the military affairs of her client Arab states. Israel suspects that the Soviet Union would use a Palestinian state to advance her own interests at the expense of the US. She would be well placed, whether or not she became a co-guarantor of a treaty, to undermine the fragile Peace Treaty and reactivate the Arab – Israeli conflict, either directly through Palestine or indirectly by backing the Rejectionists. Soviet patronage would only encourage the Palestinians to continue the armed struggle against Israel (and against Jordan) and to present new political demands.

The forms of Soviet involvement could either be by proxy or through the presence in Palestine of numerous Soviet advisers. Furthermore, Soviet support for Palestine might also allow her to topple an 'unco-operative' Jordanian regime. Arms could then flow to the Palestinians through a radical Jordan or through Gaza Port. An electronic surveillance system established in Palestine by the Soviet Union would certainly hinder Israel's defence capability.

Such turbulence would allow the Soviet Union to work on the American tolerance threshold. Israelis are becoming sceptical about American resolve to stand up to Soviet pressure. By 'borrowing' the arms that she has supplied, the USSR could rapidly project her own forces in order to deny American access. Moreover, Israelis fear that Palestine would no longer be overawed by the strength of the IDF once Soviet forces were stationed on Palestinian soil.

The counter-argument is that an Israel surrounded by Soviet clients becomes indispensable to the West as the only foothold in the region from which to counter Soviet expansionism. This would give Israel the pivotal role in US strategy that she desires, for she believes that the only border the USSR would recognize is one which might bring a direct confrontation with the US. Israel might thus come to regard her ability to trigger off a chain reaction involving both super-powers as her main strategic asset. A daring Israel could make life extremely uncomfortable for both super-powers, perhaps especially for the Soviet Union. The latter might not wish to run the risk of encountering Israeli retaliation which could embarrass her[106] and prove counter-productive, especially if such retaliation involved the US. This is where the tiny size, relative isolation and topographic conditions of Palestine might serve to constrain Soviet action.

It might be assumed that the Peace Treaty would inaugurate a new era, not only between the local parties but between themselves and external forces. Since the establishment of Israel, the changing interests of the external forces have determined their association with the local actors. This is likely to continue in the future. However, the role of outside powers is starting to be affected by their clients. The Soviet Union is finding it hard to maintain good relations simultaneously with two countries which are in confrontation with each other, such as Syria and Iraq or Iran and Iraq. Each will consider that Soviet support for the other is directly opposed to herself. Limitations of Soviet influence are enforced, furthermore, by the fact that she only backs certain Arab states and this deprives her of any political leverage over Israel. The US, by appearing as the patron of both sides, forces even the most radical elements in the region, the PLO included, to regard her, unlike the USSR, as an indispensable interlocutor.

Israel and the Soviet Union have already found themselves siding with the same party (Ethiopia) against the US and Egypt in the Horn of Africa. There is therefore a glimmer of hope that, if the USSR became party to a comprehensive Peace Treaty, she would re-establish diplomatic relations with Israel (if this had not already happened). If, as part of a guarantee, the USSR were to allow Russian Jews to emigrate freely to Israel, this would certainly bolster Israel demographically. Israel, for her part, would have to become more flexible in her attitude to Soviet actions in the region and an element of trust would have to be involved for she would fear that the USSR might try to take advantage of Israeli flexibility.

American Guarantees to Israel

Israel will seek tangible and enforceable guarantees from the US to compensate her for the loss of strategic depth. Such guarantees should detail operational responsibilities (not merely refer to them in vague terms) and would state when Israel would be free to act as she saw fit without fear of losing US backing. The guarantees would also detail the conditions under which the US would agree to defend Israel. These principles would be embodied in a formal Defence Pact between them. Israel will seek an American commitment to respond within 24 hours to an Israeli appeal by sending military aid and troops if Israel desires. To be convincing, such a commitment should not require Congressional approval, implying a wording similar to the NATO Treaty.

Ideally the Defence Pact should be linked to a wider Soviet – American agreement in which the super-powers would undertake not to interfere with Palestine's neutrality.[107] If the Soviet Union were to abrogate her part of the Palestinian Treaty, the United States would be forced to retaliate.

Israeli demands will be set high, for Israel's best defence is her own strength which would not make her depend on her ally's capability and will to act, especially once their mutual interests are no longer compatible. Hence she will wish to retain the right to take unilateral action and will require the US to ensure that Israel is always stronger than any possible combination of Arab states, including Egypt. Furthermore, Israel will seek from the United States one or more special satellites for her own independent observation of the Treaties and she will also expect to be given any information concerning the verification of the respective security arrangements which the US herself obtains so as to detect violations. Finally, Israel will expect substantial American economic aid.

Israel's Future Defence Posture: Back to Pre-emption?

Whereas Israel felt constantly threatened within her pre-1967 borders, her post-1967 boundaries made her feel more at ease. She could threaten Arab centres of population rather than vice-versa. Her territorial gains gave other strategic advantages: rather than being threatened by Syrian forces on the Golan Heights, she now controlled part of this mountainous ridge overlooking Syria; occupation of the West Bank enabled her to control the areas east of the River Jordan and movement into and out of the area; and her border with Egypt was now marked by the Suez Canal and the Gulf of Suez, with the Sinai serving as a buffer (which also proved indispensable for large-scale training and manoeuvres).

Thus Israel was provided with ample warning time and she could afford to adopt a new doctrine of static defence, abandoning the emphasis on a first strike. She had the space to engage and tie down any Arab invading force far away from Israel and the post-1967 lines came to be regarded as 'secure borders'.

Yet it was inevitable that Israel's attempts to perpetuate this *status quo* would be regarded by the Arabs as continuous aggression and that their attempts to regain their lost land would be perceived by Israel as a threat to her security. Israel's definition of 'secure and recognized borders' was bound to be totally rejected by the Arabs. Hence these borders could not provide Israel with the security she yearned for.

The 1973 war brought home to Israel that even with 'secure' borders, the cost of the war was unbearable. Yet the belief persists that, had Israel been without the Sinai buffer or the Golan Heights, she would have been destroyed. That war also inflicted great damage to one of Israel's most vital assets – morale. Questions began to be raised regarding Israel's defensive doctrine and tactics.[108]

The Israelis realized that the Arabs had reached a new understanding of the political gains to be achieved by limited war even when they were ridden by faction. Static defence of Israel, good intelligence and air power could not, in combination, prevent these limited gains. The Separation of Forces Agreements which followed in Sinai and the Golan Heights and the Interim Agreement with Egypt taught the Israelis that they could live with some previously unthinkable territorial changes. The Egyptian – Israeli Peace Treaty, based on Israel's agreement for total withdrawal from the Sinai and the dismantling of all Israeli settlements there, made many Israelis realize that, with adequate security arrangements, Israel's security was not automatically at risk if a 'small' Israel could receive in return the legitimacy and recognition, she always longed for.

Yet the demilitarization of the Sinai provides some assurances against an Egyptian attack which will be practically impossible to replicate elsewhere. Withdrawal to the pre-1967 borders implies a need to return to the previous pre-emptive doctrine. Such a doctrine entails rapid and powerful armoured Israeli offensives capable of penetrating deep into Arab territory in conjunction with massive air raids.[109] No longer would a 'small' Israel be able to absorb the first wave of a surprise assault far away from Israel's centres of population. Moreover, she would suffer from congestion and would be deprived of early warning from surveillance stations she had previously set up deep in the Sinai and on the Golan Heights.

Early warning is always regarded as indispensable for Israel for she relies heavily on her ability to mobilize reserves, the main component of the IDF, in time to meet an attack. While it is true that those reserves would have less distance to travel, mobilization for any length of time is economically disastrous. It follows that the tolerance threshold to Arab military build-up would be very low for an Israel within pre-1967 borders. In 1967 mass mobilization and pre-emptive action derived from a sense of intolerable threat. Though a clear distinction must be made between a war of attrition and all-out war, the fact that Arab artillery could shell Israel's urban centres and most of her military installations, even from areas east of the Jordan, would be regarded by Israel as a new threat.

95

Sophisticated conventional weapons alone will ensure that 'secure borders' will be a chimera. 'Secure borders' require *mutual* recognition.

Only clear-cut military superiority might enable Israel to deter the Arab states from low or high level aggression by threatening condign punishment. But as Middle East history has shown, even that may not suffice.

A war would not necessarily be confined to the Near East or to conventional weapons. In an attempt to force super-power intervention to stop the war when she had the upper hand, Israel might decide to attack Saudi Arabia. She may even be encouraged to adopt the posture of a 'crazy state' to compel the super-powers to appease Israel rather than the Arabs. It is in this context that an Israeli nuclear capability would be relevant. No Israeli government would hesitate to take advantage of its superiority in the nuclear field if Israel's cities were bombed or if an Arab invasion were to threaten the state's existence.

None of this would make one optimistic that greater stability would follow from an Israeli withdrawal to the pre-1967 borders. The return to a pre-emptive doctrine would be a return to the knife-edge situation in which the consequences of *failing* to act to destroy the forces threatening Israel would appear more dire than the likely consequences of acting swiftly. Furthermore, the penalties likely to follow any delay in acting decisively will be more severe as Arab strength increases and as modern technology provides the means for the very rapid application of military force. Needless to say, the prospect of regimes in the Middle East coming to control nuclear weapons would only complicate the entire picture.

CONCLUSIONS

The Regional Dimension

Central though it is, the Palestinian question is only a part of the Arab – Israeli conflict. This conflict is not over the issue of a Palestinian state – a demand which surfaced only after the 1967 war when Israel came to control the Palestinians – but over Israel's existence, in whatever borders, as the embodiment of Zionism. The all-Arab commitment to the cause of Palestine (not to the Palestinians as such) is a manifestation of their rejection of Israel's right to exist as a Jewish state in the Middle East. Although the Palestinians have been socially suppressed, economically exploited, and politically manipulated by the Arab regimes, *the cause of Palestine*, which symbolized their degrading defeats, shaped Arab hostility towards Israel. So long as the Arab world does not fundamentally alter this approach and does not recognize Israel's right to exist, no settlement can come about. Conversely, without a 'solution' to the festering Palestinian question and the with-drawal of Israel to roughly the 1967 borders – especially once this principle has been established in the Egyptian – Israeli Agreement – no comprehensive settlement is likely to materialize in the Middle East.

Thus the Palestinian question can only be solved as part of a general peace between Israel and the Arab world. As such, it would need the blessing not only of the Palestinians but of most of the Arab world, including all the states surrounding Israel and pivotal forces such as Saudi Arabia. Such a peace treaty would also help to crystallize a new consensus among the Palestinians, whose reactions are traditionally determined to a large extent by the dimensions of inter-Arab politics. Both sides would have to overcome their sense of insecurity and be willing to make previously unthinkable concessions if they were to take the courageous and painful steps necessary for compromise.

The Egyptian – Israeli Peace Treaty has changed the nature of Middle Eastern politics and has created a new atmosphere: the mutual fears, hatred and deep-rooted suspicions have been at least partly assuaged. The vicious circle was broken by unprecedented concessions made by both parties. Failure to address the Palestinian issue could, however, endanger the whole process of peace-making – the separate peace which Israel has been pursuing is a mirage. Regardless of the contempt that many Arabs have for the Palestinians, no Arab regime would risk abandoning them, not only because of the rest of the Arab world's commitment but also because they know that no agreement can last as long as the plight of the Palestinians continues.

The fact remains that both the Israelis and Palestinians will have to exist side-by-side. The question is *how*?[110] Israel is there to stay and the Palestinian question will not resolve itself or go away. As argued here, a binational state is not conceivable owing to the diametrically opposed interests of the two peoples and their national awareness. Nor would one people accept minority status under the other.

On the face of it, the 'Jordanian Option', if it could be implemented, might promote greater stability in the region and would place the Palestinians under firm Arab control. Yet Jordan could not solve the Palestinian predicament and the inevitable tension between Palestinians and Jordanians would probably destabilize the whole region.

The only other possibility is something along the lines of the theoretical model described here, namely a move to a fully-fledged and independent Palestinian state. Obviously such a solution has shortcomings and limitations. It would seem, however, that a Palestinian entity limited in certain respects by Treaty and guaranteed by outside powers is the least undesirable of the alternatives. Like the other proposed solutions, such a Palestinian state may be strongly irredentist. But, unlike the other alternatives, it would provide the Palestinians, for the first time in their history, with their own country. Therefore, the question is not whether a small Palestinian state can solve the Palestinian problem in its entirety, but rather what are the various alternatives facing the local actors when confronting a limited range of choices – none of which can offer a fully satisfactory remedy to this troubling and complicated problem?

For both Israel and Jordan, the establishment of a Palestinian State is linked to their very existence. For the Palestinians and the rest of the Arab world, it would mean that territorial and other claims must be shelved in exchange for a militarily-restricted but sovereign Palestine. Only on such a basis can an agreement between Israel and the Arabs provide the Palestinians with a state of their own, Israel with the 'security' she is longing for, and her neighbours with their land. Borders must be mutually recognized and open if

there is to be renewed vitality. New military technology tends to diminish the value of 'buffer zones' and the virtues of 'strategic depth', and it is only predictable behaviour and good will – not the security arrangements as such – which can provide the parties with security. Yet, because the settlement will be fragile, security arrangements are of paramount importance.

The return of occupied lands to their respective owners and a final settlement of the Palestinian question in all its aspects could reduce Arab motivation to engage in conflict with Israel, but it would also increase the risks for Israel. She would be exchanging concrete territorial assets for verbal commitments. The question haunting Israel is whether Arab readiness to settle might not be replaced in the future by new territorial demands (owing perhaps to regime changes) or by a temptation to squeeze a more vulnerable Israel. No guarantee exists which can entirely remove that fear.

Palestinian actions would depend largely on the positions taken by the neighbouring Arab states and these would not necessarily be homogenous. It is difficult to assess how these states would react if the Palestinians threatened to upset the foundations of the agreement. Much would depend on timing. The fact that Israeli withdrawal from Syrian territory would take about five years would probably make Syria reluctant to do anything which could jeopardize her chances of regaining her lands without war during that time. Once Israel's neighbours were in control of their lands (when the phased process of Palestine's establishment would need to be finalized),[111] the incentive for them to disrupt the process, with the prospect of a full-scale war happening at a time not necessarily of their choosing, would be lower than when Israel controlled their lands.

But the possibility of another Arab – Israeli war remains and this may have little or nothing to do with Palestine. Though the balance of power will probably remain in Israel's favour and Israel could strike at Arab targets beyond the neighbouring Arab states, these factors alone will not prevent an eruption of renewed hostilities whether by accident or design. The agreement should endeavour, therefore, to assure the parties concerned that no change of the *status quo* could be made without affecting the super-power relationship. Should they realize that their mutual relations depended on a settlement being kept, they may be willing to prevent the deterioration of relations arising from the actions of clients. The prospects of instability in the Middle East could have serious consequences for the world as a whole.

The arms race would nevertheless continue. Terms such as 'manageable' or 'controllable' would prove as meaningless as before. But a detente between Israel and the surrounding Arab countries might permit a less volatile and therefore more 'balanced' instability which would limit both the forms and range of conflict, although it would not remove the causes of instability.

But one thing is clear. A comprehensive settlement of the Arab – Israeli conflict would not provide stability for the Gulf. Palestinian self-determination tends to be regarded as a panacea for resolving all the most complicated political questions. If the Palestinians can be satisfied, it is argued, much of the instability in the Middle East will go away. Yet the volatile Arab world is imperilled by forces within it, which are completely unrelated to the Arab – Israeli conflict – as indeed the war between Iran and Iraq has demonstrated. Instability in the Gulf could be triggered by over-rapid or ill-judged modernization, inter-Arab conflict and super-power competition. Tension will continue in the Middle East with the threat of war never very far from the surface, regardless of any political arrangement over the Palestinians. Nevertheless, the solution of the Palestinian problem would doubtless remove one of the main sources of tension.

Between the 'Israeli Hammer' and the 'Jordanian Anvil'

However, much of the new reality in the region would depend on whether Palestinian ambition would be satisfied with a somewhat restricted state or whether it would be regarded simply as a means for moving towards the original Palestinian goals. Although many Palestinians would begin by viewing the new arrangement as a transitional phase, possession could prove attractive and the possibility of losing a tangible asset might make them reconsider the political alternatives of an uncompromising and unpromising endless struggle. The stubborn Rejectionists could prove to be the real Pales-

tinian enemy rather than Jordan or Israel, and consequently their isolation may grow. Many who now support the Rejectionists may become more pragmatic as has often happened in the past. What an underground organization can afford to do or say, a state cannot. Moreover, once guerrilla leaders have succeeded in forming a state, history shows that they tend to change in many respects. It could be wrong, therefore, to assume that there will be no change in political aspirations in the future for, at present, while the Palestinians have nothing of their own, they have nothing to lose and everything to gain. Should they achieve independence, the stakes for the Palestinians would be very high. The price they may be expected to pay for breaching the Agreement may be a deterrent. At risk will be their opportunity to complete the process of becoming masters of their political fate. Terror cannot destroy Israel nor can it alone gain the Palestinians their aspirations. The danger of terrorism is not so much the damage it causes but the chain reaction it can trigger. At present it strengthens Israel's intransigence and tends to recruit world-wide support for the idea of restricted sovereignty. The Palestinians are unlikely to wish to supply Israel with a reason for reinvading Palestine. It would take Israel only a very few hours to assume control over a relatively defenceless Palestine. Palestinian action would thus be restrained by their lack of faith in the super-powers' ability to stop an angry Israel retaliating for any Palestinian terror.

Israel's eastern border stayed quiet in the 1973 war because the Palestinians and Jordan feared that, should war break out there, the fate of Nablus and Hebron would be like that of Jaffa and Lydda in 1948 and that, before long, their inhabitants, too, would become refugees.[112] The sense of being at Israel's mercy would tend to deter any Palestinian government from violating an agreement. An exposed Palestine would be far more cautious than one which has an international force behind which to hide. Furthermore, Israel would have powerful economic leverage over Palestine. At a price to herself, she could cause massive unemployment in Palestine by closing the border and she could also sever the West Bank (i.e. East Palestine) from the Gaza region (West Palestine). Jordan would have similar leverage. The options open to her would be either unilateral punitive action, such as closure of the borders, or perhaps a Jordanian invasion approved by Israel, which could bring Palestine once more under Jordanian control.

This type of coexistence is encapsulated in the term 'Finlandization'. Palestine's room for manoeuvre would obviously be severely constrained and this would probably colour her relations with both Israel and Jordan. Logically, Palestine's desire ought to be to protect her own independence through friendly relations with those two countries.

In the final analysis, the Palestinian question cannot be solved in total isolation from Jordan. However far-fetched this may seem at present, mainly owing to Hussein's pro-Western orientations, in the long run, demographic, economic and political developments may combine to bring about a major shift in Jordan's political balance. By virtue of the role it plays in the East Bank, the sizeable Palestinian majority in Jordan could lead to her 'Palestinization' and thus lay the foundations for a new form of coexistence between the Palestinians and Israel. Despite the fact that the Palestinians view the West Bank as the core, and not the periphery, of any Palestinian state, once the Palestinians ruled the East Bank, the West Bank and the Gaza Strip, the new Greater Palestine might acquiesce more readily[113] in demilitarizing her own West Bank — to Israel's satisfaction[114] — while maintaining an army on the East Bank. Greater Palestine could also then absorb more of the refugees. Even the issue of Jerusalem might then be easier to handle.

As to the more immediate future, Israel would be well advised to call from a position of strength for the establishment of a phased and restricted Palestinian state. Politically this would force the PLO to come into the open and expose its real intentions or deprive it of at least part of the backing it enjoys among Palestinians under occupation, among moderate Arabs and in the West. If Israel waited until she was appearing to 'acquiesce' in American pressure,[115] this would be perceived by the Arabs as weakness and would only encourage them to increase their demands.

Time is not on Israel's side. She must realize that it is in her interest to rid herself of this burden, providing she can arrange matters to ensure her security. This will involve both guarantees and assurances from the US that she is willing to maintain Israel's qualitative edge over the rest of the Arab world. After all, Israel's ultimate security cannot rest solely on Arab goodwill or on super-power guarantees. The risks for Israel should not be minimized — if she ever brings herself to permit the establishment of a Palestinian state — for there will be many uncertainties in such a new form of coexistence.

Provided with the opportunity to establish a state, the Palestinians could prove to themselves and to the world whether they really want to build a homeland of their own for future generations with the co-operation of their immediate neighbours, or whether, by engaging in hazardous political games, they are willing to risk the destruction of all they have sought for so long to create.

NOTES

[1] There are various estimates of the size of the Palestinian community scattered throughout the world. Their numbers range today between 2.8 and 4 million. The main reason for this dispute centres around the numbers of the refugee population which comprise two-thirds of the Palestinian community. In June 1978, UNRWA put the number of registered refugees at 1,757,269, nearly a third of whom were living in camps. These include the refugees displaced from the West Bank, the Gaza Strip and the Golan Heights in the 1967 war: East Bank, 892,561; West Bank, 314,257; the Gaza Strip, 350,114; Syria, 323,435; and Lebanon, 211,902.

[2] See Hussein Abu al-Namel, *Gaza Strip, 1948 – 1967: Economic, political, sociological and military developments* (Arabic) (Beirut: The Palestine Research Centre, 1979), pp. 192-201; 335-44.

[3] Syria, Egypt and Iraq recruited some Palestinians to their armies and in 1964 had Palestinian units which were called the Palestine Liberation Army (PLA) though in fact they remained in their previous formation under the respective countries' control rather than commanded by the newly formed PLO. For further reading see Sara Bar-Haim 'The Palestine Liberation Army: stooge or actor' in Gabriel Ben-Dor (ed.), *The Palestinians and the Middle East Conflict*. The International Conference held at the Institute of Middle Eastern Studies, University of Haifa, April 1976 (Israel: Turtledove Publishing, 1978), pp. 173-92.

[4] The name was adopted by reversing the abbreviation of the organization's name — *Harakat Tahrir Filastin* (Palestine Liberation Movement) to meaning 'Victory' or 'Conquest'. One of the Fatah's prominent leaders Salah Khalaf (known as

'Abu Ayad') said in his *A Palestinian without an identity* (Arabic) (Karima Print Kuwait, 1978?) p. 61 that the Fatah was established as early as 1958 (in Kuwait). Its military operations, however, did not start until 1965 (see Ehud Ya'ari, *Fatah*, (New York: The Dial Press, 1971)).

'A Palestinian refugee who was consecutively a member of the Syrian delegation to the UN, Under Secretary for Political Affairs of the Arab League, Saudi Arabia's Minister of State for UN Affairs and Ambassador to the UN and the Representative of the Palestinians at the Arab League.

'For further reading see Avi Plascov, *The Palestinian Refugees in Jordan 1948 1957*, (Frank Cass: London, 1981).

For further reading on Jordan's maneouvres after the Rabat summit, see Asher Susser 'The status and position of Jordan in the Arab – Israeli conflict since the Yom Kippur war' in Alouph Hareven and Yehiam Padan (ed.) *Between War and settlement: the Arab - Israeli conflict since October 1973*, (Tel-Aviv: Bitan Modan Publishers; The Shiloah Centre for Middle Eastern and African Studies and Zmora, 1977). pp. 70-78.

'In the Gaza Strip no municipal elections had taken place since 1946, and the respective mayors were nominated to their posts by the existing authorities, Egyptian up to 1967 and Israeli thereafter.

For a discussion of the PLO's strategy see Gabriel Ben Dor 'The Institutionalization of Palestinian Nationalism 1967 1973' in Itamar Rabinovish and Haim Shaked (ed.), *From June to October, The Middle East Between 1967 and 1973*, (New Brunswick: Transaction Books 1978). The Shiloah Centre for Middle Eastern and African Studies, Tel Aviv University.

" For a detailed analysis of the mutual relationship between the PLO and the Arab states, see the relevant Papers in Gabriel Ben Dor (ed.), *The Palestinians op.cit* in note 3 and Fuad Jaber 'The Arab regimes and the Palestinian Revolution. 1967 – 1971' in *Journal of Palestine Studies*, Vol. II, No. 2, Winter 1973, pp. 79-101.

'For a detailed analysis of the problems involved in establishing such an autonomy and its ramifications – see Brig. Gen. (Res.) Aryeh Shalev, *The Autonomy – Problems and Possible Solutions*, Centre for Strategic Studies, Tel Aviv University, CSS Papers No. 8, January 1980.

' A study carried out by the Jerusalem Institute for Federal Studies (JIFS) listed no less than thirteen types of such frameworks with different variations, (see Meir Nitzan, *Proposed federative arrangements in the Land of Israel 1917 - 1977* (Jerusalem: JIIS. 1978). For further reading see Daniel J. Elezar and Ira Sharkansky, *Alternative federal solutions to the problem of the Administered Territories* (Jerusalem: JIIS. 1978).

'' See Raanan Weitz *Peace and Settlement, Outline Plan for rural and urban settlement in Israel* (Jerusalem: Jewish Agency for Israel, 1978) pp. 4-5. Another version is proposed by Israel Peled which calls for a Cantonal division similar to the Swiss model (unpublished paper dated 3.7.78).

'' This 'buffer' in the Jordan Valley was planned in 1967 to be composed of 30 settlements housing some 17,000 Israelis and a townlet to be populated by 1977 by 15,000 inhabitants. Today there are in the Valley some 23 settlements with far less population than envisaged originally.

'' The settlements around Jerusalem and the envisaged 'satellite towns' encircling the Holy City are supposed to lay the foundation for a Greater Jerusalem. This area is to be surrounded by an additional 'safety belt' of settlements stretching from Gush-Etzyon to Bayt-Horon via Ma'aleh-Edomim (which is situated between Jerusalem and Jericho).

'' There are no official published figures as to the current Israeli expenses over the settlements beyond the Green Line. A recent study, however, suggested they amount to 8% of the total budget of 1980 - 1. (See Zvi Sholdiner 'The real cost of the settlements' in *Ha'aretz* Daily, Tel Aviv, 25.7.80). The Israeli public was already disenchanted by the Government's spending vast sums on the settlements at a time when Israel's inflation reached 150% and the Government was cutting back on essential services.

' Israeli Government figures, however, argue that there are 18,000 Israelis living there. Moreover, Government officials believe that in five years time there would be some 110 - 140,000 Israelis living in the West Bank alone in addition to the 10,000 or so claimed to populate that region at present. (*Ha'aretz* Daily, 31.9.80).

'' The first serious debate in Israel over the security value of these settlements took place as late as October 1979 with the hearings and the ruling of the Israeli High Court of Justice on the illegality of the Elon Moreh settlement. The Court ordered the dismantling of the settlement because it had no security justification for its existence and the return of the land to its legal Palestinian owners, who appealed to the Court. The fact that Ezer Weitzman, the Defence Minister, sided with Haim Bar-Lev, one of the former Chiefs of Staff (after whom the Bar Lev Line was named) as well as with Maj. Gen. (Res.) Mattityahu Peled (one of the main proponents of a Palestinian state adjacent to Israel) in arguing – against the position of Refael Eytan, the present COS – that Israel's security needs could be realized by means other than by the establishment of a settlement at the said site, only aggravated the Israeli public.

'' The Arab target was not, as in the 1948 war, to occupy Israeli settlements as such. Accordingly, their tactics differed and, where alternative routes were possible, the Syrians preferred to advance their first wave of armour, rather than to divert and thus split their efforts. Had the Arab invading force managed to reinforce and consolidate its hold on the territories it reoccupied – it could later try to capture the settlements (as happened in the Bar-Lev Line in the 1973 war).

'' A demographic study carried out at Tel Aviv University suggests that in less than two generations the numbers of the Palestinians living within Israel and the occupied territories would roughly equal that of the Jewish population in Israel. For further reading see Moshe Hartman, *The Jewish and Arab Population in Eretz Israel in the year 2000*, Table No. 7 (Hebrew). Tel Aviv University Research Project, 'Criteria for Defining Secure Borders'. No date.

'' See the Palestinian National Council (PNC) Resolutions of March 1971; January 1973; and June 1974. Also interviews with Na'if Hawatma the leader of the Popular Democratic Front for the Liberation of Palestine (PDFLP) in *al-Yawm*, Beirut 22.1.74; *Shu'un Filastiniyah*, Beirut, September 1975 and interview with George Habash the leader of the Popular Front for the Liberation of Palestine (PFLP) in *al-Hadaf*, Beirut 3.6.78.

'' The clause 'and all other Palestinian territories' was probably included in the UAK scheme in reference to Hussein's continued commitment to the Cause of Palestine, so as to allay Palestinian fears and win the occupied inhabitants' support. The East Bank Palestinians, however, were *not* mentioned in the plan.

Hussein was on record later emphasizing 'We do not differentiate between Gaza, the West Bank and the East Bank'. (Interview in *al-Nahar*, Beirut, 24.8.72.)

For the full text see *Amman Radio* 15 March 1972.

See Ahmad Baha al-Din 'An objective attempt to analyse King Hussein's proposal' in *al-Ahram*, Daily, Cairo, 19 March 1972. Also Zvi Elpeleg, *King Hussein's Federation Plan – Genesis and Reaction*, (Hebrew) Tel-Aviv University: Occasional Papers of the Shiloah Institute, Dec. 1977).

See interviews with Salah Khalaf, Fatah's Central Committee Member in *Filastin al-Thawrah*, Beirut, 12.12.73; 20.2.74 and in *Monday Morning*, Weekly, Beirut 25.2.80.

PLO supporters in the West Bank expressed their rejection of the scheme (see *al-Sha'b* Daily, East Jerusalem and a communique by the Palestinian National Front which appeared in *Filastin al-Thawrah*, Beirut, 13.3.74). Nevertheless a few West Bankers also approved of the scheme: Ahmad Musa Ajwan, *Let us not cut Wood at Night* (Arabic) (East Jerusalem: 1972) in Gideon Weigert *What the Palestinians Say* (Jerusalem: Published by the author, 1974), p. 16.

See Yigal Allon 'Israel and the Palestinians' in *The Jerusalem Quarterly*, No. 6, Winter 1978, pp. 20-40.

See Yehoshua Arieli 'For a Jordanian Solution' – *New Outlook*, May/June 1978, pp. 29-34.

A proposal which fuses together elements of the Israeli Option with the Jordanian Option calls for a combination of an Arab – Israeli shared rule (in the form of a Jordanian/Israeli condominium) with self-rule to the Palestinian inhabitants (see D. Elazar *Shared rule: a prerequisite for peace under the Camp David framework* (Jerusalem: Jerusalem Institute for Federal Studies, 1978).

Most of the Jordan Valley's Arab inhabitants, who were mostly 1948 Palestinian refugees living in three refugee camps adjacent to Jericho, fled in 1967 to the East Bank. And, apart from Jericho town, there are only a few local inhabitants scattered along the valley.

For a discussion of the frontier villages see Avi Plascov, 'The Palestinians of Jordan's border' in Roger Owen (ed.) *Studies in the economic and social history of Palestine in the nineteenth and twentieth centuries* (London: Macmillan and St Antony's, Oxford, forthcoming, 1981).

Numerous works have been written on this issue. For a brief discussion of Israeli ideas concerning this problem and a compilation of issues which form the component of any settlement see Miron Benvenisti, *Jerusalem, the Torn City* (Jerusalem: The University of Minnesota Press (Minneapolis), 1976), pp. 357-388. For analysis on the continued incorporation of Jerusalem in Israel, see Saul Cohen, 'Geopolitical bases for the integration of Jerusalem' in *Orbis*, Summer 1976, pp. 287-313. For a paper on different ideas on 'Internationalization', see Even M. Wilson 'Role of Jerusalem in a possible Arab Entity' in *A Palestinian Entity* (Washington: Middle East Institute, 1970), pp. 58-77. For a proposal of dividing sovereignty, see Lord Caradon, 'Jerusalem: peace begins at the gateway' in *The Guardian*, 27 August, 1979. See also the relevant papers and discussion in *Peace and the Palestinians* (London: Record of Proceedings of a seminar held by the British sectors of the Parliamentary Association for Euro – Arab Co-operation, 1977).

There was little overt Palestinian support in the 1950s to demands made to turn Jerusalem into the 'second capital' of Jordan and those few voices which were aired went unheeded by the Palestinians. Even in the PLO founding-meeting, held in Jerusalem in May 1964, there was no mention of the City's future political status, see Eliezer Be'eri *The Palestinians under Jordanian Rule: Three Issues*. The Harry S. Truman Research Insitute, The Hebrew University of Jerusalem (Jerusalem: The Magnes Press, 1978) p. 62.

See the respective articles in O'Kelly Ingram (ed.) *Jerusalem key to Peace in the Middle East* (Durham, USA: Triangle Friends of the Middle East, 1977).

See, for example, letter by Henry Cattan, a prominent Palestinian, in *The Middle East*, Monthly, London, October 1979, pp. 8-9.

See also Ammon Cohen 'The West Bank – Gaza Connection', *The Jerusalem Post Magazine*, 17 February 1978.

To date, the PLO has at its disposal, in limited quantities, the following weapons: *Tanks* PT-76 Light tks.; T-34/-85; T-54; T-55 (T-62?). *Guns and Howitzers*: 57mm ATK; 40mm AA: 105mm ('borrowed' from the Lebanese army which obtained them from the US); 122mm; and 155mm. *Missiles and Rockets*: SAM-7 (Strella); BM-21 (40 rockets, 122mm, range 11km-20km); *Sagger* (anti-tank missile); RPG-7. *Mortars*: M-37 (82mm); 122mm. APC old BTR. Also Radar equipment. PLO fighters are known to be receiving training in the Eastern Bloc. Their pilots receive training in Libya and their navy personnel are trained by Pakistan (Information extracted from data gathered by the IISS).

Walid Khalidi's article 'Thinking the unthinkable: a sovereign Palestinian state' in *Foreign Affairs*, Vol. 56, July 1978. This is considered to be a carefully charted blueprint of Palestinian demands in future negotiations and suggests two tables on the basis of one-half and one-third of Jordan's military capability, demonstrating the balance remaining in Israel's favour (pp. 704-5).

See also Colonel Merril A. McPeak 'Israel: borders and security' in *Foreign Affairs*, April 1976, p. 440.

See for example, Muhammad Abu Shilbaya, *The Road to Salvation, Freedom and Peace* (Arabic) (East Jerusalem: al-Sha'b al-Tijariyah Print, 1972), p. 78.

See Maurice Stroun and Michele Finger, 'For a permanently neutral democratic Arab Palestinian state bound by an Austrian-like treaty' in *New Outlook*, May/June 1978, pp. 43-46.

See *The Guardian*, 3 July 1978.

See *Austria: Facts and Figures* ('The Constitutional Law on Austrian Neutrality') (Vienna, 1977) Article 1, 1, 2. *The State Treaty for the Reestablishment of an Independent and Democratic Austria* Article 13 (on Prohibition of Special Weapons), stipulates that no assault vehicles, would be possessed, contracted or experimented with, and that the Allied and Associated Powers reserve the right to add in due course other new and more sophisticated weapons.

For further reading see Japan's Defence Agency *Defence of Japan* 1976, pp. 32-33 and *Facts about Japan – National Defence* (Japan: the Ministry of Foreign Affairs, (No. 12-B3, March 1964)).

For further reading see Max Jakobson, *Finnish Neutrality* (London: Hugh Evelyn, 1968).

See Hussein Agha, 'What State for the Palestinians?' in *Journal of Palestine Studies*, Vol. VI, No. 1, p. 7, and Ali al-Din Hilal *Proposals for the Palestinian State*. (Cairo: the

Centre for Political and Strategic Studies in *al-Ahram*, 1978) p. 101.

[48] The bitter memories are fresh in Palestinian minds of the year leading to the 1948 war, when Iraqi and Syrian troops came supposedly to aid the Palestinians against the Jewish inhabitants of Palestine and instead indulged in looting and theft.

[49] For a Palestinian analysis of USSR's policies, see Salah Dubagh, *The Soviet Union and the Palestinian Question* (Arabic) (Beirut: PLO Research Centre, 1968).

[50] For a discussion of the USSR's position on Palestinian statehood, see Galia Golan, *The Soviet Union and the PLO*, *Adelphi Papers* No. 131, (London: IISS, 1977), pp. 3-10.

[51] For a general discussion of the function and reality of guarantees see Shai Feldman *Outside guarantees and regional security*, Paper presented in the IISS 23rd Annual Conference (to be published shortly).

[52] Such as observing at certain points the 30-mile-long corridor connecting the two parts of Palestine via Israel's territory – a route the Palestinians would probably insist on being regarded as an international free-way if not part of their own territory.

[53] Yet many West European observers believe that, given appropriate funds and arms, the UN peace-keeping forces are the 'cement' to any Middle East arrangement (see for example, Anthony Verrier, 'Who will keep the peace?' – *Jewish Chronicle*, 13 October 1978 and Valerie Yorke, 'Palestinian Self-Determination and Israel's Security', *Journal of Palestine Studies*, Vol. VIII, No. 3, Spring 1979, pp. 22-23).

[54] George Ball advocated the stationing of American soldiers between Palestine and Israel in sensitive points and establishing US Navy bases in both countries as American assurances (see his article 'America's interests in the Middle East – The dangers for unlimited support for Israel' in *Harper's*, 21 September 1978).

[55] It is not inconceivable that the super-powers would avail themselves of the option to blow up the main arteries of communication from the Golan Heights into Israel and from Jordan into Palestine (and Israel's heartland). This would require the prior agreement of all the parties concerned, but explosives could be laid deep in the ground near where these roads cross demilitarized zones adjacent to the borders. Guarded by armed Soviet and American forces, the devices would be operable only by consent of both co-guarantors. In the event of a surprise attack by one or a number of states, the super-powers would, upon request of those attacked, retain the option, if all other modes of persuasion failed, to slow down the assault, compensate for the vulnerability of those attacked and create time for resolution of a crisis.

[56] See also Brian Van Arkadie, *Benefits and burdens: a report on the West Bank and Gaza Strip economies since 1967*, (New York: Carnegie Endowment for International Peace, 1976).

[57] Richard Ward 'The economics of a Palestinian Entity' in *A Palestinian Entity*, (Washington: the Middle East Institute, 1970), pp. 106-109; Vivian Bull, *The West Bank – is it viable?* (Lexington, Massachusetts: Lexington Books, 1975); Elizabeth Collard and Rodney Wilson, 'The Economic potential of an independent Palestine' in *Peace and the Palestinians, op. cit.*, in note 33, pp. 136-141; Elias H. Tuma and Haim Darin-Drabkin, *The Economic Case for Palestine* (London: Croom Helm, 1978) (and their respective articles in *New Outlook*); John Stebbing 'The Creation of a Palestinian

Arab state as part of a Middle East settlement' in *International Relations* (The Journal of the David Davis Memorial Institute of International Studies, Vol. VI, May 1979, pp. 507-517).

[58] It is interesting to note that in the West Bank less than 5% of the cultivated land is irrigated compared with 45% in the Gaza Strip (mainly citrous) and Israel, see John Stebbing *The Creation of a Palestinian Arab State op. cit.*, in note 57 (Reprint) p. 15.

[59] For maps describing another project joining Haifa with Beit-She'an (in the northern Israeli part of the valley, see Yair Anavi and Rino Tsror 'The Jordan Rift: This could happen in 1990' in *Monitin* magazine (Hebrew) (Tel-Aviv) No. 20, April 1980. See also Uri Davis, Antonia Makes and John Richardson 'Israel's Water Policies' in *Journal of Palestine Studies*, No. 34.

[60] For further reading see Arie Bergman, *Economic growth in the administered areas 1968 – 1975* (Jerusalem: Bank of Israel, Research Department, 1975).

[61] For a discussion of the role of the existing various local Palestinian institutions, see Emil A. Nakhleh, *The West Bank and Gaza Towards the making of a Palestinian State* (Washington DC: American Enterprise Institute Studies in Foreign Policy, 1979) 65 pp.) Also John P. Richardson, 'Developing Palestinian Institutions' paper presented at the Conference on Constructive Alternatives – *New Outlook*, August – September 1974, pp. 38-52.

[62] See *Filastin al-Thawrah*, Beirut, 1 January 1978, p. 139.

[63] For further reading see Nabil Shaath 'High level Palestinian manpower' in *Journal of Palestine Studies*, Vol. 1, No. 2, Winter 1972; Ibrahim Abu Lughod, 'Educating a Community in Exile: the Palestinian Experience' in *Ibid.*, Vol. II, No. 3 (Spring 1973); Muhsin Yusuf 'The potential impact of Palestinian education on a Palestinian state' in *Ibid.*, Vol. VIII, No. 4 Summer 1979.

[64] See Appendix No. 8 *Map of Palestine, Land in Jewish Possession* (as of 31 December 1944) in A. Plascov, *The Palestinian Refugees, op. cit.*, in note 6.

[65] Many refugees have managed throughout the years to purchase land, in many cases adjacent to the camps, with remittances sent by their sons working in the Gulf.

[66] Both Egypt and Syria should be encouraged to cede for this purpose the Israeli-evacuated settlements in their territory.

[67] See also PLO official Sabri Jiryis', article in *al-Nahar*, Daily, Beirut, 15 May 1975.

[68] For further reading see Yaacov Meron, 'The "complicating" elements of the Arab – Israeli conflict' in *Indian Socio-legal Journal*, India, 1977, pp. 1-28.

[69] The following rules could be applied: prior to their admittance all refugees would be subject to security vetting; refugees could only apply as family units so as to prevent split loyalties; once granted Israeli citizenship, they would have to be law-abiding inhabitants in a predominantly Jewish state; they could not be told where Israel intends to rehouse them prior to their arrival; and no applications would be handled beyond a specified date (say three years from the signing of a peace treaty).

[70] A different proposal advocates another manner of handling the question and suggests dividing Israel into two regions: the areas Israel incorporated beyond what was allotted to her by the UN Partition Plan (to where the bulk of the refugees be returned) and Israel of the 1947 borders (to where the return of refugees would be more restricted). (See John Reddaway's

proposed schemes in *Peace and the Palestinians, op. cit.* in note 33). Such a proposal, however, is highly undesirable, for it would, in due course, aid those Arabs struggling for secession along the Partition Lines.

 Lifta village, already mentioned, would be a case in point.

 Syria should also free her Jews, whom she prohibits, to date, from leaving the country. Iraq should allow those Jews who wish to emigrate to do so without imposing restrictions on their assets.

 Britain should be called upon to provide the much needed secret data, still unpublished, concerning Arab property in Palestine and Jewish property in the neighbouring Arab countries where she served as a mandatory power. France could assist with regard to Syria, Lebanon and the Maghreb while Italy could help regarding Jewish property in Libya.

 See *Damascus Radio* commentary on 15 February 1977: 'Let us assume for just a moment that, at Geneva the PLO will achieve the right to create a Palestinian national entity on the West Bank and in the Gaza Strip. Israel knows full well that such a mini-state would not have a written constitution and would, therefore, not consider itself committed to any international boundaries. What this means is that the first article of the unwritten Palestinian constitution will be a call for a struggle to return the Palestinian territories on which Israel rests . . . Rosh Hanikra . . . Beit Shean . . . Haifa and Jaffa on the coastal plain – that is, *all* of Palestine, from the Galilee to the Negev, and from the Jordan to the Mediterranean.' Such calls were reiterated by PLO leaders (see Faruq Qadumi's interview to *Newsweek*, 14 March 1977) as well as West Bank politicians (Bassam Shak'ah the Mayor of Nablus in a demonstration against the Camp David accord held in December 1978). In its Fourth Congress held in Damascus between 21-31 May 1980, the Fatah reiterated its original aim of the complete dismantling of the state of Israel: '. . . Al-Fatah is an independent revolutionary movement whose aim is to liberate Palestine completely and to liquidate the Zionist entity economically, politically, militarily, culturally and ideologically . . . The struggle will continue until the Zionist entity is liquidated and Palestine is liberated.' (For full text see *al-Liwa'*, Daily, Beirut, 1 June 1980).

 See Abd al-Aati Muhammad 'The Palestinians in the Arab Homeland' *al-Ahram*, Daily. (The article is a summary of a study held by the al-Ahram Centre for Political and Strategic Studies which provides data concerning the Palestinians throughout the Arab world).

 See Sa'ad al-Din Ibrahim's article on the chances of a future Palestinian state, *al-Ahram*, Daily, 6 January 1978.

 'Palestine is Southern Syria' announced the Commentator on *Damascus Radio* on 22 September 1976, when explaining that the Palestinians would be granted autonomy under such a federation. Syria's President Hafiz al-Asad was also on record regarding Palestine as part of Syria (Interview to the BBC, Winter 1976). The Syrian Version, though never discussed in detail, envisages Palestine as a semi-demilitarized region which provides for the existence of a Palestinian entity without sovereignty with the inhabitants acquiring an Arab identity apart from their Palestinian uniqueness – part of the idea of Arab unity.

 In order to provide Syria with a direct route, by-passing Jordan, and to give the Palestinians an alternative outlet, there are suggestions for granting the Palestinians a small enclave of al-Hama with a corridor passing through the Jordan Valley. This would establish her position *vis-à-vis*

Jordan on a different basis. See Joseph D. Ben-Dak and George E. Assousa, 'A Blueprint for New Palestine' (part of a paper entitled 'Peace in the Near East: The Palestinian Imperative', sponsored by the Stanley Foundation presented at the Conference on Constructive Alternatives in the Near East) – *New Outlook*, August – September 1974, p. 83. Also Farid al-Khatib 'The plan for the establishment of a Palestinian state in the West Bank' – *al-Sayyad*, Weekly, Beirut, 20 June 1974. But owing to the Syrian advantages contained in such a link, it is unlikely to be accepted by Palestine's neighbours.

 See an article by the late Dr Hamdi Taji al-Faruqi, 'Why a Palestinian State' – *al-Quds*, Daily, East Jerusalem, 13 December 1976. It is noteworthy, that following the 1967 war, he was perhaps the first notable on the West Bank who came out in full support of a Palestinian state on the West Bank and Gaza coexisting with Israel. He did not change these views despite the shelling of his house by the PLO in December 1967.

 In December 1976, when Syria and Jordan were negotiating a union, a delegation of East Bank Palestinians met the leaders of the Syrian Ba ath Party and called for the establishment of a Union Council of 450 representatives in which all Palestinians living in the Arab world would be represented. (*al-Ra'i*, Amman, 16 December 1976).

 See an article by Muhammad Abu Shilbayah in *al-Anba'*, Daily, Jerusalem, 17 December 1976 in which he attacks al-Faruqi who was known until then for his long-standing support of an independent state.

 For further reading see Avi Plascov, *Gulf instability – Sources of intra-state Conflict*, chapter VI: 'Immigrants and politics'. IISS Occasional Papers (Farnborough, Hants: Gower, forthcoming).

 A few Arabs interviewed depicted the Palestinian diaspora in the Middle East as a 'cancer' amidst certain Arab countries which will become an 'octopus' once the Palestinians have a state of their own. (See also Farid al-Khatib's article on the Arab bloc against a PLO-led Palestine (when he describes the Lebanese position) in *al-Sayyad*, Beirut, 2 September 1976.

 See *al-Ahd*, Qatar, 6 December 1977, pp. 21-22.

 Reacting to both Israel's Foreign Minister's declaration that Jordan is a Palestinian state – and to Dr George Habash of the PFLP who said that '70 per cent of Jordan's population are Palestinians', Amman Radio revealed the following details regarding both the Palestinian and Trans-Jordanian population: 'The total number of the Palestinian people inside the occupied Palestinian homeland and outside is about 3,200,000. About 1,850,000 of these continue to live in the Palestinian homeland, in accordance with the following demographic distribution: (1) About 1,200,000 Palestinians reside in the occupied West Bank and the Gaza Strip. About 650,000 Palestinians live in the part occupied in 1948. (2) About 700,000 Palestinians live in Jordan: 500,000 in other Arab countries and about 190,000 in the diaspora . . . The demographic situation in Jordan confirms that the rate of Palestinian presence is not as much as one-third of Jordan's population. The last population census in Jordan confirmed this rate, indicating that Jordan's population without the Palestinians is 1,600,000'. (This is a highly exaggerated figure – Avi Plascov).

'In addition to the fact that these statistics contradict the above-mentioned Israeli and Arab allegations . . . a demographic situation does not define the identity of land. The Arab Gulf states are the best example of that . . .' (Amman

103

Home Service 19.00 gmt 30 June 1980. Summary of World Broadcast (SWB) ME/6460/A/6).

[86] See the PNC Resolutions of March 1971, January 1973 and June 1974.

[87] See the PNC Resolutions of 18th Plenary Session, Cairo, March, 1971.

[88] Uriel Dann, *The Jordanian Entity in changing circumstances, 1967 – 1973*. Occasional Papers Series, The Shiloah Centre for Middle Eastern and African Studies, Tel-Aviv University, August 1974, p. 2.

[89] During his visit to Moscow, Crown Prince Hassan revealed that the two countries were about to expand their co-operation beyond Soviet assistance to vocational training, village electrification and mineral extraction – see *Moscow Radio* in Arabic 17.00 gmt, 19 October 1978 – BBC, SWB SU/5948/A4/3. In September 1980 Jordan was first visited by Soviet military experts.

[90] See *Filastin al-Thawrah*, 6 February 1974.

[91] See interview with Jordan's Prime Minister, Zeid al-Rifa'i in *al-Diyar*, Weekly, Beirut, 13 December 1974.

[92] In the words of Ahmed Shuqayri, the first head of the PLO, 'How can such a micro, jelly-state accommodate the native Palestinian population of the West Bank plus the 1,000,000 on the East Bank and the 300,000 refugees in Syria, the 450,000 in Lebanon, the 200,000 in Kuwait, the 70,000 in Egypt and the 50,000 in Saudi Arabia?' *Monday Morning*, May 1980, p. 32.

[93] President Bourguiba of Tunisia at a Jericho Palestinian Refugee Camp, 3 March 1965. Amman Radio 20.05 gmt 3.3.65 (*Daily Report*, Foreign Broadcast Information Service (USA) MA/1801/A/3).

[94] Compare the Fatah's 4th Congress Resolutions of May 1980 *op. cit.* in note 74, with previous PNC's Political Programmes and with the Rejectionists' Programmes. (For a comparison on the basis of the 1977 programmes – see Appendix 1 in Israel Altman 'The Palestine Liberation Organization' in Colin Legum and Haim Shaked (ed.) *Middle East Contemporary Survey*, Vol. One 1976 – 77, The Shiloah Centre for Middle Eastern and African Studies, Tel-Aviv University (New York and London: Holmes and Meir Publishers, 1978) pp. 181-208.

[95] For further reading see Yehoshafat Harkabi, *Palestinians and Israel* (New York: John Wiley and Sons, 1974) and his articles on this subject.

[96] For a detailed discussion of those rejecting the establishment of a West Bank State – see Hussein J. Agha, 'What State?' *op. cit.* in note 47.

[97] See Resolutions of the PNC, Cairo, June 1974 – Items 3 and 4 (this programme is considered the corner-stone of PLO policy despite more extremist resolutions which were drafted thereafter). For an analysis of the strategy behind this measure see Fuad Faris, *A Palestinian State*! in Middle East Research and Information Project (MERIP) Reports No. 33, USA, December 1974, pp. 3-27.

[98] See for example Ali al-Din Hilal, *Proposals op. cit.* in note 47, pp. 118-119.

[99] See for example Wahid Muhammad Abd al-Magid, *The Arab Jew in Israel*, (Arabic) al-Ahram Centre (Cairo, 1978).

[100] A recent study funded by the Ford Foundation carried out by Sami Samuha of the Jewish – Arab Centre in the Haifa University in Israel revealed that in 1978 – 79 some 50% of the Israeli Arabs did not recognize Israel's right to exist; 64% regarded her as a racialist state and 59% demanded the implementation of the 1947 Partition Plan's which would make most of them citizens in a Palestinian Arab state. (It should be pointed out that these tendencies were far more explicit among the young educated 'second generation' born mainly after Israel was established. As reported in the Israeli press, however, a similar study carried out by Khalil Nakhalah contradicted the above conclusions. (*Ha'aretz*, Daily, 10.8.79).

[101] The villagers of Iqrit and Bi'ram – the 'internal' Arab refugees who live within Israel but are prevented (despite promises to the contrary) from living on their own land which they vacated willingly in the 1948 war – could be invited to return to their places of origin. Likewise the Bedouins' plight should be addressed as well as that of the Druz.

[102] See Ze'ev Hirsch, 'A Fruitful Symmetry' in *The Jerusalem Post*, 18 November 1979.

[103] From the north they are: Haifa (population 227,000), 21 miles; Hadera (35,700), 11 miles; Hertzeliya (82,400), 9 miles; Tel-Aviv (354,000), 15 miles; Petah-Tikva (107,000), 1.8 miles.

[104] See Brig. Gen. (Res.) Yehoshua Raviv, *The Arab – Israeli Military Balance (in view of the Israeli – Egyptian Peace Treaty)*, Centre for Strategic Studies, Tel-Aviv University, CSS Papers No. 7, February 1980, p. 79.

[105] For a study of past attempts and ideas for future arms control measures – see Yair Evron, *The Role of Arms Control in the Middle East*, Adelphi Papers No. 138, (London: IISS, 1979), 42 pp. Also his chapter in *The Future of Arms Control: Part III. Confidence Building Measures* (ed. Jonathan Alford), Adelphi Paper 149 (London: IISS, 1979).

[106] The lesson of the Israeli air force, which showed little inhibition when bringing down five Soviet aircraft over the Sinai in the war of attrition, is still fresh in the latter's mind.

[107] The former President of the World Jewish Congress, Dr Nahum Goldman, suggested that such neutrality should be applied to Israel as well, so as to neutralize both states, in exchange for international guarantees and other local arrangements, see *Die Zeit*, 12 July 1979, and 'True neutrality for Israel' in *Foreign Policy* No. 37, Winter 1979/80.

[108] For further reading see Maj. Gen. (Res.) Aharon Yariv (ed.), *Secure Borders*, Proceedings of Panel Discussion, Centre for Strategic Studies, Tel-Aviv University (CSS Papers No. 2, October 1978).

[109] See Yisrael Tal, 'Armour: Myths and Reality', *Ha'aretz*, Daily, Tel-Aviv, 20 October 1974 and his 'Israel's Doctrine of National Security: Background and Dynamics, in *The Jerusalem Quarterly*, 4, Summer 1977, pp. 44-57.

[110] For a discussion of the various scenarios regarding the future of the Palestinians see G. Ben-Dor *The Palestinians and the Future of Middle East Politics: A Tentative Exploration of Some Alternative Scenarios*, Paper prepared for the international conference on 'The Middle East and the West Towards the End of the 20th Century', Center for Advanced International Studies, University of Miami, February 12-14, 1980.

[111] Although this Paper has not discussed the mechanics of reaching a settlement, it is strongly advocated that the whole phased agreement should not begin to be implemented until *after* the last neighbouring Arab country signs the Peace Agreement and begins the process of normalization with Israel. The period of transition should last 5 to 7 years throughout which Israel's military would be present in certain

strategic zones primarily, but not exclusively, in the range of hills overlooking the Jordan Valley. The most desirable place to begin would be with the first phase of the establishment of a new state in the Gaza Strip. The area has little of the emotive power or strategic importance of the West Bank and there are only a few Israeli settlements there which would make progress easier.

[112] See Moshe Dayan's article 'We and the territories' Arabs' – in *Ma'ariv*, Daily, Tel-Aviv, 18 June 1976.

[113] PLO thinking has undergone a certain evolution since the days when its supporters Walid Khalidi, Audah Butrus Audah, Klovis Maqsud, Ghassan Kanfani and others, critized the Egyptian Ahmad Baha al-Din's proposal for the establishment of such a Palestinian state to be composed of Jordan, the West Bank and the Gaza Strip (but as a first stage) for it would have meant recognizing Israel – an inconceivable thought in the 1960s. The latter's proposal and his answers to these are all published in his book: *A Proposal for a State of Palestine* (Beirut: Dar al-Adab, 1968).

[114] Instead of co-operating with the US in opposing the Syrian involvement in Jordan in 1970, Israel could have assisted the PLO in taking over that country. There are those who argue that, if Israel were to help the Palestinians to take Jordan over in the future, this might guarantee Palestinian reciprocation, once satisfied with sovereignty.

[115] See George Ball 'How to save Israel in spite of herself' in *Foreign Affairs*, April 1977, p. 459.

4 The Military Threat to Israel

COLONEL ANDREW DUNCAN

Introduction

In this paper I intend to make a *tour d'horizon* around Israel's borders; on each front I shall consider the security situation today, the potential threat and the potential implications of a peace settlement in the Middle East for Israeli security. In this last respect it is assumed that a comprehensive settlement, including internationally guaranteed safeguards, has been achieved in return for Israeli withdrawal from occupied territory. I shall not attempt to analyse the threat in terms of numbers of men, tanks or other equipment; the broad details of the military balance are already well known and, in any case, many less quantifiable factors such as standard of training, intelligence, command and control, logistics and morale contribute as much to combat capability as do numbers of men and weapons. I shall concentrate rather on geography and terrain and on current military problems. I shall attempt to avoid involvement in purely political matters (although Israel's political and economic policies are as likely to affect security in the long term as are purely military factors). I shall try to consider matters from a strictly military viewpoint (on the improbable assumption that political problems can be solved if security can be assured) but from time to time political comment will be unavoidable.

Defence Policy

Before describing the main elements of Israeli defence policy, it is necessary to emphasize that there are two distinct and separate threats to Israel's security. This, though obvious to practitioners of Middle East affairs, is often confused by others, including a good many Israelis. The first, and traditionally the most dangerous, is the conventional threat posed by the Arab states and their massed tank armies. The second is the day-to-day threat of terrorist activity and civil disturbance. Like most terrorist campaigns, the activities of the Palestine Liberation Organization

Colonel Andrew Duncan, was British Defence Attaché in Tel Aviv from July 1977 to June 1980.

(PLO) are more designed to win the propaganda battle than to cause serious casualties; often terrorist raids are made purely to provoke the Israelis into reacting (or rather over-reacting), which, in its turn, often leads to international condemnation of Israel with the initial provocation conveniently forgotten.

To meet these two threats, the conventional and the terrorist, requires different military measures, different types of forces and different types of training. It is probably true to say that the Israel Defence Force (IDF) is organized, equipped and trained pre-eminently to defeat the conventional threat, and deals with what it considers the lesser threat on an 'as and when required' basis using, whenever possible, its existing weaponry with little additional training. In the argument over the return of occupied territory, the distinctions between the two threats tend to become blurred; considerations which support the retention of territory often receive much more attention than those which point to the expediency of withdrawal.

Israeli policy to meet the conventional threat is based on three principles: delay, mobilization and counter-attack. First, delay must be imposed on the attacking enemy by the relatively small and predominantly conscript ground forces and by the superbly trained and virtually all-regular air force, so as to give time for mobilization to take place. Mobilization affects the whole country, as national service entails a minimum of three years' full-time service for men and two years for women, followed by a reserve commitment to the age of 55. The final principle is to counter-attack, using the reserve formations which are probably three times the size of the standing army, with the aims of ensuring that the battle is not fought on Israeli soil, of destroying the maximum amount of enemy equipment so that they will not be in a position to attack again for a good many years, and to gain ground which can later be used as a bargaining factor in negotiations leading to an armistice agreement. In the present state of affairs a pre-emptive attack is not considered necessary on military grounds, nor is it considered a political option purely to defend occupied territory. However, should the territories eventually be returned then pre-emption would undoubtedly again become an essential option in defence policy.

Israeli counter-terrorist policy was formerly based on the biblical principle of 'an eye for an eye' (though a better description of the normal level of Israeli counter-action might be 'a dozen eyes for a tooth'). In January 1979 a new policy was adopted, which allowed the IDF to attack any known terrorist concentration or training base before a potential cross-border raid could be launched. This policy, despite the adverse international and (after the raids on the Iraqi *Osirak* nuclear reactor in June 1981 and the PLO headquarters in Beirut) internal criticism it attracts, is claimed to be highly successful. Indeed there has been only one cross-border penetration and no seaborne attempts since the attack on Kibbutz Misgavam in April 1980, other than the ill-fated and short-lived attempts at airborne infiltration employing hot air-balloons and motorized hang gliders. So far as civil disturbance is concerned the IDF normally adopts a low profile in the West Bank and Gaza (Sinai and the Golan Heights are virtually uninhabited except for Bedouin in the former and Druze on the latter and, of course, Israeli settlers). It has often been possible to spend a day in the West Bank without seeing much, if any, evidence of military occupation. However, the reaction to terrorist incidents or civil disturbance is swift and heavy.

I will now turn to the individual areas surrounding Israel and will deal with them in an anti-clockwise direction starting with the Gaza Strip.

The Gaza Strip

The 150 square miles of the Gaza Strip, where over half the population are refugees, were once a hotbed of anti-Israeli terrorist activity. This threat was eliminated in 1971 by the draconian operations led by General Sharon, now the Minister of Defence. To-day the majority of the terrorist incidents in Gaza are of an intra-Arab nature, and a number of suspected collaborators have been murdered. Should the Israelis withdraw, there would be little possibility of an effective conventional force being established in

Gaza. Nor would there be much opportunity for a resurgence of terrorism, as access to the area could be easily controlled (by Egypt across Sinai, by Israel from the sea), and there is no airport. In any event, it would be a relatively simple matter to construct a security barrier of the sort that follows all Israel's borders. The population, which earns a considerable portion of its income by working in Israel, could be opposed to terrorist groups which threaten their livelihood. I see no real security problems which could inhibit Israeli withdrawal from the Gaza Strip.

Egypt and Sinai

Egypt has always had the strongest armed forces of the Arab states and so posed the greatest threat to Israel. But she has posed less of a direct threat since Israel captured the Sinai in 1967. First the Suez Canal separated the two armies. After the armistice agreements following the Yom Kippur War, the Israelis withdrew from the Canal and, until 1980, only a very limited Egyptian force could be deployed east of it. A demilitarized zone, which included the Mitla and Gidi passes over the Central Sinai ridge, was manned by UN Emergency Forces (UNEF II), but the strategic junctions of Refidim (Bir Gifgafa) and Bir Eth Themada remained in Israeli hands. To-day the IDF has withdrawn behind a line drawn from El Arish to Ras Muhammed at the southern tip of the peninsula. By April 1982 the IDF should have withdrawn behind the pre-1967 border, leaving Sinai demilitarized apart from the US-sponsored international force to be based at El Arish and Sharm El Sheikh, and Egyptian forces which will be limited to one mechanized infantry division (restricted to an area whose eastern limit will be a line some 60 kms east of, and parallel to, the Suez Canal and Gulf of Suez) and 4 border-unit battalions. The withdrawal from Sinai, in return for peace on her southern border, poses a number of military, political and economic problems for Israel.

The greatest sacrifice in Israeli eyes is the handing back of a buffer zone which ensured that any battle, on the southern flank, was fought far from Israeli soil. This is not to say that any future war will necessarily be fought astride the border. Any significant breach of the limitation of forces agreement by the Egyptians more than likely would provoke a rapid westward move by Israeli armoured forces. And the Israelis could afford to wait until the Egyptians had significantly breached the peace treaty before advancing into Sinai, thus avoiding the blame for starting any future war. (A number of Israeli observers consider that they will be in a better strategic position after withdrawal than they were when directly facing the Egyptian army across the Suez Canal in 1973.) Any future war would, again, be fought in Sinai but the Egyptians would initially control the junctions of Refidim and Bir Eth Themada, the only points where large-scale armoured forces can swing from one axis to another. The early stages of the war will be fought on the few and relatively narrow routes which cross northern Sinai, and although the IDF would penetrate deeply into Sinai before encountering opposition, their advance will not be as simple as it was in 1956 and 1967.

There will be a loss of early warning, particularly of low-level early warning, although this can be compensated for, to some extent, by the use of airborne warning and control systems (AWACS). The Israeli Air Force will be giving up two of the most modern and best designed military airfields in the world (at Etam and Etzion) but replacement fields are being constructed on the other side, though close to the border. The most serious problem for the Air Force will be the loss of over half its training air space, and a large force of high performance aircraft will have to concentrate its overland training in an area measuring 240 nautical miles (nms) at its longest point and 70 nms at its widest. Thus it will be hard to maintain standards and morale.

The ground forces, too, will lose large training areas, but those remaining available in the Negev are already larger than anything available to NATO forces in Europe.

For the Navy the loss of the base at Sharm El Sheikh will considerably hamper operations in the Red Sea. To reach comparatively open water they will have to transit the 90-mile length of the Gulf of Aqaba–Elat, which is at a maximum 15 miles wide. Admittedly, the Navy will have to patrol less than one third of the coastline than they had to patrol before the withdrawal started, but much of the coastline given up is entirely barren, and there were few worthwhile targets for terrorist attack. Finally, there is a shortage of well-protected berths at the port of Elat, those on the exposed sea wall being untenable in a strong southerly wind. The scope for rectifying this deficiency is severely limited.

On the other hand, there are some advantages to be gained by withdrawal from Sinai. Shorter lines of communication both in war and more particularly in peace will bring a considerable financial saving. Army units stationed on the Sinai border can be redeployed to meet threats in other areas more swiftly. The Navy can commit more forces to protecting the heavily populated Mediterranean coastline of Israel.

There is virtually no likelihood of terrorist activity rising from the Israeli withdrawal from Sinai. Distances are great, the terrain is inhospitable and there is almost no population to provide cover or support for terrorist groups.

There are also economic and political considerations. Economically, there will be the fear of another blockade of the Straits of Tiran, which was a *casus belli* of both the 1956 and 1967 wars. However, the economic importance of the port of Elat is much reduced since the overthrow of the Shah of Iran and the cessation of oil exports from Iran to Israel. On the political front, the main worry is that the principle of total withdrawal may set a precedent which is unlikely to be acceptable in respect of the Golan Heights or the West Bank.

Saudi Arabia

Saudi Arabia has no common land border with Israel, her armed forces are relatively small, and they are spread across a large country. Saudi capacity to take part in an Arab–Israeli war is thus limited. Nevertheless, there are elements in the Saudi forces which Israel perceives as a unique threat. Among these is Saudi acquisition of F-15 aircraft which, if based at Tabuk, would be within 10 minutes flying time of Jerusalem. More generally, the US-provided combination of F-15s (now to be armed with advanced *Sidewinder* missiles), AWACS aircraft, and a fleet of tankers (to provide inflight refuelling for both), is viewed as a serious threat which can be countered only by Israel's own F-15 force. However, the Israeli Air Force would prefer to employ this elsewhere. Israel claims that the operation of AWACS in Saudi air space would enable the Arabs to overlook the whole of her territory. The US denies this, on the grounds that 'terrain masking' would shield a good deal of Israeli territory, and adds that Saudi AWACs will be subject to operational restrictions and, in any case, will be very vulnerable to attack. Whatever the truth of the matter, the destruction of both F-15s and AWACs will undoubtedly come high on Israeli target lists and their presence could make a pre-emptive strike more likely.

The Eastern Front

Despite the lack, at present, of any form of integrated command set-up, Israel sees the combined forces of Syria, Jordan and Iraq, as forming one single front stretching from Mount Hermon to the Red Sea and threatening the whole eastern border of Israel. For simplicity's sake I shall address this area under national headings and will end the section by dealing with the West Bank.

Jordan

The Jordanian armed forces, though relatively small, are well respected by Israel who remembers their effectiveness in the 1948 War of Independence and considers them to be one of the better trained of the Arab armies. There is little threat of Jordanian action south of the Dead Sea, where access to the border along the Arava Valley is virtually non-existent and where there are few worthwhile Israeli targets other than the port of Elat. The main sector where Israeli and Jordanian forces face each other runs from the northern end of the Dead Sea to the Yarmouk Valley which forms the Jordanian–Syrian Border. The terrain on either side of the Jordan Valley is unsuitable for massed armoured movement and heavily favours the defender. On the Jordanian side some six metalled roads lead to the Jordan Valley, all passing through a range of steep hills which rise on average to over 900 metres. These routes could be easily blocked by air attack, and forces operating in the Jordan Valley could find themselves cut off from reinforcement and re-supply. In the Yom Kippur War the Jordanian army made no attempt to attack in this sector, and the only Jordanian troops involved were those committed in the Golan Heights at a late stage in the campaign.

The River Jordan does not present much of a tank obstacle and can be forded at many places. But the approaches to and exits from the river, which now only flows in the centre of what was once a much wider and deeper course, are steep, in many places precipitous, and considerable engineering work would be needed to develop crossing sites. There are probably no more than a dozen potential crossing sites and air superiority would be essential for a successful river crossing. Once across the Jordan an attacker faces a further ridge line which dominates the valley and which must be scaled before any westward advance can be achieved. Only five metalled roads lead from the valley to the line of the Jerusalem–Nablus road and these are all easily defensible. The whole area of the West Bank is covered in steep hills; armoured movement would be slow, and almost entirely limited to roads. Only in the north of the sector are the Israelis vulnerable; here, an attack on the Beit Shean valley would not only be operating in more favourable terrain but also on Israeli, as opposed to occupied, territory.

Jordan, between 1967 and 1970, was the main base for PLO attacks on Israel; one of the reasons for King Hussein's campaign against the PLO in 1970 was the severity of Israeli counteraction, which often caused more damage and casualties to Jordan than to the PLO. Since then the Jordanian Army has been equally as active as the Israelis in ensuring that terrorist attacks on Israel are not mounted across the Jordanian border. But such attacks still occur infrequently.

Iraq

Iraq will clearly be in no position to offer support to an Arab attack on Israel so long as the Iran–Iraq war continues, and even once the war ends a considerable period of time will be required for reorganization, re-equipment and re-training before her forces can pose the same level of threat to Israel as they did before the war. Iraqi forces could be committed either on the Golan or across the Jordan Valley. Israel attaches great importance to the need to observe any Iraqi westward deployment, and a move into the north eastern part of Jordan could be seen as a *casus belli*. Under such circumstances the Israelis could well be tempted to launch a pre-emptive attack with the aim of engaging Iraqi forces in the open desert east of Mafraq, where Israeli superiority in mobile warfare could give them a quicker and better chance of victory than waiting for an attack across the

Jordan. But the difficulties of reaching the selected battle area should not be underestimated.

Syria

The bulk of the Syrian army is normally deployed on the plateau between Damascus and the 1973 Armistice line, where it both faces any Israeli advance and is virtually in its assembly area for an attack on Israel. Since June 1976 a division plus has been committed to the Arab Defence Force in Lebanon. In addition to creating a gap in the Syrian line, the commitment seriously weakens Syria's offensive capability in other ways; these forces are unavailable not only during the period of the commitment itself, but also during both a period of training beforehand and a rather longer period of necessary re-training afterwards.

The Golan Heights, however, must be considered the key operational area for Israeli defence against conventional attack. Not only is the terrain suitable for armoured operations but the distance to be covered before the Syrians can once more overlook Israeli territory is only 12 miles. 1973 was 'a close run thing'. Since then the Syrian forces have been extensively re-equipped by the USSR and others, and have already received several hundred T-72 tanks and some MiG-25 aircraft. Of course, many improvements have been made on the Israeli side as well. Road communications have been much improved both up the escarpment and laterally across it. The Israelis still occupy, despite a westward shift of the 1967 armistice line in 1973, a line of hills (the Tels) which give uninterrupted observation over the Syrian forming-up area and, when conditions are right, as far east as Damascus. The garrison of the Golan is far stronger than it was in 1973 and the stockpiled equipment of reinforcing reservist units is located closer to their operational areas. Israel is unlikely to be caught again.

There is no terrorist activity on the Golan or across the Israel–Syrian armistice line but this is due almost entirely to Syrian policy and Syrian control over the PLO.

What are the possibilities for withdrawal? Israeli opinion is divided. There are those (though the settlers on the Golan are not among them) who advocate the return of the Golan in return for real peace with Syria, but their view may be tempered by the knowledge that peace with Syria, Israel's most intractable enemy, is a long way off. On the other hand, there are those who remember (and nobody is allowed to forget) the time when Israeli settlements in the Hula Valley were vulnerable to Syrian artillery attack. Certainly the IDF will be hard to convince that any withdrawal, even in return for peace, is acceptable. One practical problem would be the necessity to provide land in north-eastern Israel, a highly agricultural area, for defensive positions, camps and training areas. But, despite the recent annexation of the Golan by the Israeli government, a move which has provoked much opposition in Israel, some form of compromise could be worked out which, while returning the bulk of the territory to Syria, would still give the Israelis a foothold on the Golan (a strip a couple of kilometres wide might be sufficient) and deny the Syrians direct observation over the Hula Valley. The returned territory would, of course, like the Sinai, have to be demilitarized with some sort of multilateral buffer force remaining more or less where UNDOF is deployed today (perhaps with a rather more positive mandate).

The West Bank

Until quite recently the level of internal security incidents in the West Bank has not been high, and has normally been considered by the Israelis to be manageable. In the first half of 1980, it had seemed that the situation was deteriorating: the number of incidents was rising and the sophistication of the tactics and the daring of those involved had intensified. However, the signs of a rising scale of terror then faded, possibly as a result of a well-co-ordinated series of car bombs, which on 1 June 1980, seriously wounded the Mayors of Nablus and Ramallah and an Israeli police sapper who was about to defuse a bomb whose target was the Mayor of El Bireh. Those responsible have never been arrested, but the whole attack appeared to be beyond the current competence of the PLO in the West Bank, and there is a strong suspicion that it was the work of Jewish vigilantes. There have been several instances of Jewish vigilante action against Arabs and Arab property, when they felt that IDF reaction to events was not sufficient.

In recent years terrorism either within the West Bank, or committed by West Bank Arabs in Israel, has never been very effective or intense.

110

The highly-publicized events of March 1982 were almost entirely civil disturbances and not terrorism, and the casualties were suffered mostly by the rioting West Bank students. These events should not be overdramatized; there are, in fact, a number of reasons why anti-Israeli activity in the West Bank has not yet reached the scale witnessed in many other countries. First, the West Bank inhabitants have, so far, been rather quiet. (As they say themselves, they have been under military occupation for several thousand years – 'Before the Israelis it was the Jordanians, before them it was the British and before that the Turks etc' – right back to the original Israelite occupation after Exodus.) Secondly, Israeli methods, whether one approves of them or not, generally have been effective in keeping the peace, as is their intelligence system which must employ a widespread net of informers. But Israeli tactics for countering terrorism and civil disturbance are not designed in any way to isolate the terrorists from the rest of the population, and, if anything, have had entirely the opposite effect. No West Bank Arab wishes to remain under Israeli rule, but many will admit that Jordanian rule was even more obtrusive and harsh. They all profess to support the concept of PLO rule, but how many really want to see the return of the refugees who fled from the camps in 1967 and who will expect to be settled on land, already more or less fully utilized, is another matter.

The new Minister of Defence, General Arik Sharon, a former paratrooper and noted hard-liner, has announced, somewhat surprisingly, a fresh policy for the occupied territories. In seeking to create an atmosphere conducive to an Israeli–Palestinian dialogue, the IDF said it would now 'make an effort' not to barge into West Bank schools and universities (the usual scene of anti-Israeli demonstrations), to avoid ordering collective punishments (a normal reaction to terrorist activity or civil disturbance) and to ease up on security checks (an everyday hazard of life on the West Bank). The Military Governor has been replaced by a civilian administrator, Professor Milson. But IDF security operations, and the events of recent weeks, indicate that the new policy may prove, in the end, to be little more than a public relations exercise. And it is probably far too late in the day for such measures to have much effect on the population, nearly all of whom have experienced some indignity during the course of IDF security operations.

Could the Israelis withdraw from the West Bank, or rather can they afford not to? In addressing this question I will examine security considerations alone and will conveniently leave aside political matters such as the creation of a Palestinian State (which is to my mind inevitable), negotiations with the PLO, and the future of Israeli settlements, though these are of fundamental importance in Israeli eyes. Naturally any sizeable conventional force would pose a serious threat. It would overlook Jerusalem and might be able to cut it off from the rest of the country. And there is the threat, which haunts all Israelis, that an armoured force advancing from the area of Tulkarn could split Israel in half by reaching the sea, only 12 miles to the west, in a very short time. But I believe it would require a sizeable force to successfully hold a blocking position across the coastal plain. In many ways the conventional threat from the West Bank is exaggerated by some Israelis. The force that could be maintained there would never approach the size and strength of the other Arab armies, and despite its proximity to the Israeli heartland would never equal the potential threat of the Syrian army on the Golan or even that of the very large Egyptian army on the far side of Sinai. Ezer Weizman, former Minister of Defence, has publicly said he sees no security problem and has pointed out that before 1967 no-one had ever suggested that it was essential to invade and occupy the West Bank in order to ensure Israeli security. A former Chief of Staff has said that the Israeli Defence Forces could safely withdraw from the West Bank so long as they maintained some 3 or 4 military enclaves there. I believe that the present Israeli determination to maintain control over the West Bank is due far more to the emotional ties of Eretz Israel and the right of Jews to live in Judea and Samaria than to true security concerns.

In any case, if by treaty the Sinai can be left largely demilitarized, why cannot the same be achieved in the West Bank? It would undoubtedly be more difficult for any state to accept demilitarization throughout its entire territory, rather than in a border (and largely uninhabited) area. Nevertheless, if peace and an Israeli withdrawal are to be achieved then one must assume that, for some years at any rate, any Palestinian state on the West Bank would be demilitarized, apart from the small arms needed to maintain law and order. Access to the area can only be from Israel or through Jordan, and the task of seeing that heavy weapons are not brought in could be carried out by the UN or some other multilateral force. Some form of control would be necessary at the Jerusalem airport, but apart from this all the controls could be on the far side of the borders of the new state. This might allay Israeli fears that conventional forces could be built up in the West Bank and in due course threaten the nearby coastal urban complex centred in Tel Aviv. The Israelis might insist on retaining some military areas (as provided for in the Camp David agreement) enabling them to regain control over the Jordan Valley in emergency, such as a westward move by Jordanian or Iraqi forces. For example, an enclave astride the Jericho–Jerusalem road and another on the Jiflik–Nablus road would allow them to maintain a limited degree of long-range surveillance over the Jordan Valley. The size and number of these forces occupying them, could be progressively reduced as confidence was established.

Whilst it may be possible to ensure that conventional forces are excluded from the West Bank after Israeli withdrawal, it would be impossible to guarantee that no form of terrorist activity would ever be mounted against Israel from the area. No doubt the border security fence, so carefully obliterated in 1967, could be reconstructed so as to severely limit the possibility of infiltration and the smuggling of explosives into Israel, but the problem of longer range indirect weapons would remain. Presumably the PLO-held BM-21 multi-barrelled rocket launchers, used for the first time in the large-scale rocket attacks in the northern towns and settlements in June 1981, could be kept out. But the man-pack variety of *Katyusha* rockets, however inaccurate, could not fail to hit Jerusalem or the Tel Aviv area. Every plane landing or taking off at Ben Gurion airport would be in range of hand-held SAMs located in the West Bank. Israeli security concerns, after the experience of so many years of terrorism, must be taken into account, and, especially in the initial years, territorial compromise and other confidence-building measures will be essential.

I do not propose to offer any solution to the problem of how counter-terrorist operations in the West Bank could be carried out after Israeli withdrawal, nor suggest which forces should be involved. It would surely be unacceptable to the Arabs for Israeli forces to have the right to operate in the area; and it is hard to forecast which UN members would be prepared to volunteer troops to form a UN force, even if this was acceptable to Israel, for what would be a difficult and thankless task. Enough to say that, given a great deal of understanding and a genuine desire for peace, a military solution could be found. In the final event, the problem might prove smaller than now feared, since the moderates in the new state might well wish to control extreme elements, both to maintain law and order and to avoid any chance of Israeli reprisals. But this is a risk few Israelis would be willing to take. I conclude, therefore, that a military solution is possible but I fear that political considerations are likely to ensure that it is not achieved.

Jerusalem
The future of Jerusalem is probably the most intractable aspect of the whole Arab–Israeli situation, but there are no major security implications. It is true that approximately half the bomb attacks which cause casualties occur in Jerusalem (most others occur in Tel Aviv) but then a large number of IRA bombings took place in Belfast as that was where the most publicity could be obtained. On the other hand, Jerusalem is rarely the scene of civil disturbance (which takes place most frequently in Nablus, Ramallah, Hebron and at Bir Zeit University). The problem is a highly charged mixture of politics, religion and emotion. The strength of Israeli, and Jewish, feeling should not be underestimated; the importance of Jerusalem is fundamental to all Jews.

Lebanon
The Israelis believe that the presence of Syrian troops in Lebanon has opened up the possibility of a new front against them (the Lebanese themselves have not been involved in any war with Israel since the War of Independence in 1948) and that they must earmark forces to counter this threat. In particular they fear a Syrian thrust down the Bekaa Valley aimed at Northern Galilee (the Syrians for their part see the Bekaa

Valley as a route for an Israeli attack on Syria). In my view heavy conventional fighting along the Israeli–Lebanese border is most unlikely. As the Israelis found to their cost in *Operation Litani* the terrain on both sides of the border is most unsuitable for armoured movement, which can normally only take place on a one tank front. Apart from its most northerly end, the Bekaa Valley is surrounded by mountains. To reach Damascus the Ante-Lebanon range must be crossed, while at the southern end the hills of the Arquab block any large-scale movement. The Syrian forces in Lebanon are less of a threat to Israel than they would be in their normal deployment area in the Golan.

The terrorist threat is a different matter. King Hussein's successful action against the PLO in 1970 and the subsequent Palestinian migration to Lebanon were the main causes of the Lebanese Civil War in 1975 and 1976. The outcome of the civil war was the almost total disintegration of the Lebanese government's authority and the introduction of the Arab Defence Force, of which only the Syrians, who made up the largest contingent, now remain. Israeli security concerns led to the unwritten agreement that Syrian forces would not move south of a 'red line' north of the Litani River; this allowed the PLO totally to dominate the area between that line and the Israeli border, with the exception of the few small Christian enclaves close to the border. However, the Israelis preferred this to Syrian occupation of the area. Before March 1978 PLO attacks on Israel were not frequent and were rarely successful. The Israeli invasion of southern Lebanon (*Operation Litani*) was, they claimed, made to counter an increasing PLO build-up in the south, and not just as a retaliation for the seaborne raid on 11 March which resulted in the death of 34 Israelis. When the Israelis finally withdrew, handing over control of the area to UN Interim Forces in Lebanon (UNIFIL), they ensured that a strip, 10 kms wide along the border, was occupied not by UNIFIL but by the militia under Major Haddad, a Christian Lebanese officer, which they had equipped and trained. Although UNIFIL are far more successful in their task than even the Israelis expected, they would be more successful still but for their constant clashes with Haddad's men. PLO attacks on Israel still occur despite the various layers of troops (UNIFIL, Haddad's Militia and the IDF)

which occupy the area between the PLO bases and their targets in Israel. Border incursions are infrequent (the last was in April 1980), and until June 1981 attacks mainly involved the firing of two or three man-pack *Katyusha* rockets, so inaccurate that only towns the size of Qiryat Shemona and Nahariya could be hit whilst the small border settlements were almost certain to be missed.

Border-crossing raids are normally totally unsuccessful in military terms. Firstly they are normally made by a group of heavily-armed and relatively inexperienced young man, their enthusiasm often bolstered by drugs. They tend to home in on a civilian target and take hostages. Without exception they are eventually killed or taken prisoner. The whole affair has the flavour of a suicide mission, but despite the lack of military impact, they do achieve a great deal of publicity and normally provoke an Israeli reaction. One suspects that a different approach to infiltration and a less suicidal objective would still achieve the desired publicity and present the Israeli authorities with a more serious security problem.

Lebanon also provides the PLO with bases from which to mount seaborne raids on the Israeli coast. The IDF has a growing record of intercepting these before they reach the shore, but the detection and interception of the small craft used is difficult and requires considerable effort, round the clock, in terms of radar and other surveillance, and naval craft on patrol.

Today, the PLO forces are becoming increasingly institutionalized and are developing into a form of regular army, which may degrade their ability to carry out successful terrorist operations. At the same time, they are acquiring a growing range of heavy equipment. I doubt that their small force of T-34 tanks will ever be used against Israel, but they represent the thin end of a wedge which could, over some years, grow in size and quality. Far more serious are the BM-21s used for the first time with devastating effect in June 1981. Working individually, on a 'shoot and scoot' principle and firing full salvoes, the rocket launchers managed to hit a large number of northern settlements and caused the virtual abandonment of the town of Qiryat Shemona. The IDF found that they were unable to halt these attacks with artillery and air power, and the only alternatives left were to occupy the area from which the attacks were made or, as was eventually arranged, a ceasefire. The development bodes ill for the future and a repetition could well lead to another Israeli invasion of Lebanon.

To sum up: A conventional Syrian attack on Israel through Lebanon is most unlikely. Traditional terrorist tactics are rarely successful. But the towns of northern Israel are vulnerable to attack, and the PLO now has the means of provoking Israel into military action which, if taken, would only further weaken Israel's international position. In the event of another Arab–Israeli war the PLO could mount a series of harassing attacks along Israel's northern border and thus force the diversion of Israeli infantry from the main battle area.

Air Defence

Any country the size and shape of Israel is particularly vulnerable to air attack from her neighbours. Attack can come from any direction and, apart from Egypt, flight times from take-off to target are short. So far, however, Israel has not experienced any real air defence problem in any of the Middle East wars, and few raiding aircraft have ever reached their targets (the pre-emptive air strikes against Egypt in 1967 and the heavy Arab reliance on SAMs in 1973 are among the reasons for this). Nevertheless, air defence is not neglected. The priority role of the Israeli Air Force has changed, since 1973, from direct support of the ground forces to the counter air battle. The static early warning radar system has been reinforced by *Hawkeye* AWACS, though these may be used more often to control the air battle deep over enemy territory than for conventional early warning. The inventory of the ground-based air defence forces has been strengthened. But the main arm of Israel's air defence remains the fighter force which boasts the best pilots. It is trained to a very high standard with the emphasis on air-to-air combat, and is maintained at the highest state of readiness. The threat of air attack can only increase as the Arab air forces acquire more modern equipment and as their pilot and maintenance crew skills increase, but at present the Israeli Air Force remains vastly superior in every aspect (as witnessed in the several engagements with the Syrians over Lebanon in 1980–81). If anything, Israel is more vulnerable to attack by surface-to-surface missiles than by manned aircraft.

Nuclear Weapons

As yet, nuclear weapons have not appeared in the armouries of the Middle East states, nor do their forces train for a nuclear environment. It is reliably assessed that Israel, if she does not already hold a small stockpile, has the necessary expertise and components available to produce nuclear weapons in a very short time.

However, the fact that it is not certain whether Israel has the bomb or not is a vital part of her security. Should it be known that she had nuclear weapons, then the Arab states would have good reason to press the Soviet Union to provide, or at least promise to make available, nuclear weapons to balance the Israeli threat. On the other hand, the sure knowledge that Israel did *not* possess nuclear weapons would reduce the deterrent value of her forces.

Israel is determined to ensure that no Arab (or Islamic) country shall develop or possess nuclear weapons, and this determination was demonstrated amply by the raid on the Iraqi nuclear reactor. Israel is far more vulnerable to a nuclear threat than any Arab state, with the bulk of her population and industry concentrated in Jerusalem (though this could never be a nuclear target) and on the coastal plain around Tel Aviv and Haifa.

The Risks of Peace

Finally I would like to turn to a different Israeli security issue – the risks of peace. The late President Sadat's momentous visit to Jerusalem started a peace process which, one hopes, will eventually spread throughout the Middle East. The world at large expects this and will be working hard to achieve it however reluctant the participants may be. But for a number of reasons it is possible that peace may pose new security problems for Israel almost as difficult in their way as the present state of 'no war', particularly in the effects a settlement may have on the IDF.

The IDF considers itself to be at war and to have been so for the past 33 years. The constant threat of terrorist activity naturally demands a very high state of readiness in certain units and of surveillance along the borders and sea coast. The size and location of the Arab forces (backed by the spectre of the failures of 1973) also demand a high state of readiness in the standing forces and a fully trained reserve army well practised in mobilization. This situation makes very heavy demands on the officers and men of both the standing army and the reserves. The threat of attack is sufficient motivation for the people of Israel to accept the demands made on them; but how long can this continue as the threat of attack diminishes? There are already calls for a reduction in the length of the reserve commitment, and before long the period of full-time compulsory service may also be questioned. The shortening of both would result in lower training standards and a reduction in combat capability. Loss of motivation could have other effects, including a drop in the number of high calibre young men opting for a full service career. Meanwhile manpower is the least of the Arab armies' worries.

Security is expensive; the IDF spends some 30 per cent of the national budget. For some time economies have been sought and some achieved; but, as every army in the world knows, the ever-increasing cost of modern weapons can never be accommodated by the level of saving that can be made in other areas. As peace becomes more widespread and established the IDF will be faced with additional expenses, necessary to make the day-to-day lot of the soldier more acceptable. The military budget will come under increasing pressure from other government departments and eventually equipment holdings will have to be curtailed. The Arab armies are unlikely to be under such pressure.

Peace with Jordan and Syria is only likely to be possible if the major part, if not all, of the occupied territories is returned. Although a large number of Israelis realize and accept this, there is a growing element who do not and some will resist strongly, even with force, any move towards withdrawal from the West Bank and Golan Heights. The IDF has already been used at El Arish, at the time of the interim withdrawal, and, on several occasions, on the West Bank to halt and physically to move 'illegal' settlers. That Jew should fight Jew is inconceivable to many and it is a traumatic experience for the young soldiers involved. The eventual solution only becomes more difficult as the number of settlers in the territories grow and as they come to resemble more and more the hard-line loyalist community in Northern Ireland. The likely political battles ahead could divide the country as never before and could produce pressures on the IDF for which they are not psychologically prepared.

Conclusion

While it appears from the analysis of the preceding sections that in no individual sector does Israel face a threat with which she cannot cope, the overall threat posed by the surrounding Arab states acting in concert is indeed serious. Heavily outnumbered, the Israelis must rely on the superiority of their command structure, their tactics and the quality of their troops – areas where, however slowly, the Arab armies must inevitably catch up. In 1973 the Arab attack was surprisingly successful. To some extent this success was due to poor Israeli preparedness and to their misreading of the situation. Since 1973 both sides have re-organized, re-equipped and expanded their armed forces, but for many reasons the Arab side has not yet reached the level it attained in 1973, while the Israelis are far stronger than they were then. Time is undoubtedly on the Arab side, but, in my opinion, a great deal of time will pass and possibly several wars before Israel could be defeated militarily.

The author wishes to express his thanks to his many friends in Israel, and elsewhere in the region, who over the years have contributed to his appreciation of these issues. They are, of course, in no way responsible for the views expressed here.

115

5 A Nuclear Middle East

SHAI FELDMAN

The Middle East is on the threshold of the nuclear era. Nuclear programmes now exist in all of the region's important states and these programmes differ in type and stage of progress. Some are civilian, emphasizing scientific research and the production of energy; others are clearly military, aimed at the production of deliverable nuclear weapons. However, differences between

Shai Feldman is a research associate at the Center for Strategic Studies, Tel-Aviv University.

these programmes should not be exaggerated. The routes to nuclear capability are interchangeable; expertise acquired in one path may be used to explore the other. Three questions deserve analysis. How close are the region's states to the acquisition of nuclear weapons? What are the strategic implications of a nuclear Middle East? What are the risks involved in the region's transition from the conventional to the nuclear era?

Nuclear Programmes

Israel's nuclear programme remains clouded in ambiguity. Nevertheless, there is little question but that it is the most advanced in the Middle East. This much has been admitted by Israeli officials and semi-officials on numerous occasions.[1] Much of Israel's nuclear activity revolves around Dimona, a 24-megawatt French-built research reactor which became critical in 1964. Widely accepted assessments are that Dimona can produce plutonium worth about one bomb a year.[2] Other reports claim that Israel has also developed the capacity for uranium enrichment.[3] Such assessments have led observers to conclude that by the late 1970s Israel had constructed some 10–20 nuclear weapons.[4]

Other observers are careful to point out the weakness of the evidence about Israel's nuclear capability. First, there is no sign that the Israeli government has ever made the political decision to convert its admitted nuclear potential to a deliverable military nuclear force. Second, no evidence has ever been provided to indicate the existence of either a uranium enrichment or a plutonium reprocessing plant in Israel.[5] This would explain the lack of evidence regarding the acquisition of fissile material. The result is the ambiguous character of Israel's present nuclear posture.

Notwithstanding their shaky foundation, the numerous reports of Israel's nuclear capability have created a 'preponderance' of evidence. The existence of an Israeli nuclear force has not been shown. However, in the eyes of her neighbours, Israel is clearly regarded as being on the threshold of the nuclear era – if not across it.

Pakistan is farthest from the Arab–Israeli conflict area but is closest to a nuclear capability. Her nuclear programme has been in existence since the early 1960s. Fear of her southern neighbour, India, has been the chief catalyst. Since India's 1974 nuclear test, Pakistan's programme has been dramatically accelerated. Insisting on covering all avenues, she has taken both the plutonium and the uranium routes to weapon-grade material, and a number of alternative paths are being simultaneously pursued along both routes. All in all, Pakistan now has no fewer than five different projects aimed at the production of fissile material.

There are three distinct Pakistani projects aimed at plutonium separation. All are planned to separate the plutonium from the spent fuel (perhaps as much as 200 kg) of the *Candu* power reactor which was in operation between 1972 and 1978 in Karachi. The first is a pilot project acquired in the early 1970s from the Belgian firm *Belgo-Nucleair*.[6] Little is known about the dimensions of the project, let alone the quantities of plutonium already separated therein. The second and largest of the three projects is the French-built processing plant at Chasma. The latter's construction was delayed in mid-1978 when, under pressure of the Carter Administration's non-proliferation policy, France suspended the full implementation of the deal and insisted that crucial components had not been delivered.[7] However, by that time Pakistan had already acquired the plant's specifications, thus allowing her to complete its construction on her own.[8] The third plutonium-separation project is the one closest to yielding weapons-grade material. Adjacent to the Pakistan Institute for Science and Technology (PINSTECH) near Islamabad, the project consists of a 'hot cells' compound. Its dimensions are much larger than those ordinarily associated with research purposes, thus indicating large-scale separation. The project may yield separated plutonium as early as the end of 1981.

Simultaneously, Pakistan is pursuing uranium enrichment. Two distinct projects can be identified. The first is the construction of a large-scale centrifuge enrichment plant in Kahuta, modelled on the Dutch enrichment plant at Almelo.[9] The project required the theft of the plant's specifications from the Netherlands and an impressive covert acquisition drive throughout Europe and North America.[10] The plant may yield up to 50 bombs-worth of enriched uranium a year after its construction is completed. Another Pakistani facility is a more modest pilot project, where enrichment has already begun.[11] Its size is only one-tenth of the Kahuta plant, yet large enough to yield enriched uranium worthy of a few bombs a year. Several hundred tons of natural uranium to be enriched in both projects has been acquired in Niger, directly, as well as through, Libya.

If Pakistan is to become the first Moslem nuclear state, Iraq is most likely to become the first Arab nuclear state. Her efforts date back to the mid-1960s, with the construction of a 2-megawatt Soviet-built research reactor at Tuwaitha, near Baghdad.[12] In recent years, Iraq has dramatically accelerated her nuclear programme; large-scale training of manpower and the purchase of appropriate facilities were conducted in order to establish a scientific and technical infrastructure in the nuclear field.

In 1976 Iraq purchased a complete nuclear research centre from France. The centre is to include a 70-megawatt *Osiris*-type research reactor (called *Osirak*), and a small *Isis*-type reactor.[13] Both are to be fuelled by enriched uranium. France is to supply Iraq with 70 kg of such weapons-grade material, enriched to over 92 per cent.[14] In light of US non-proliferation pressures, France attempted to amend her nuclear agreement with Iraq. An effort was made to persuade the latter to fuel the *Osiris* reactor with the new 'Caramel' fuel, enriched to only 10 per cent – far lower than weapons-grade.[15] As the new fuel is not yet in industrial production, Iraq dismissed the French request out of hand.

Iraq's nuclear programme has thrice been tampered with. On 6 April 1979 the core of *Osirak* was sabotaged at a storage house in La Seyne sur Mer, near the French port of Toulon, on the eve of its shipment to Iraq. By the end of 1979 the reactor's core had been repaired, later to be shipped to Iraq. Then, on 13 June 1980 an Egyptian scientist, Yihya al Meshad, was murdered in Paris. Al Meshad was one of the pillars of Iraq's nuclear programme. The extent to which his death will delay Iraq's efforts is difficult to determine. Later, on 30 September 1980 during the initial phase of the Iraq–Iran war, *Osirak* was damaged again when Iranian bombers, returning from another mission, dropped their remaining load on the nuclear research centre. Some infrastructure facilities were destroyed, but the reactor was only slightly damaged. The nuclear programme was stalled by the departure of the French engineers following the outbreak of the war. With its reduction to a more static war of attrition, their prompt return can be expected. Moreover, during the war, Iraq, an adherent of the NPT, suspended safeguard inspections of her facilities, an important precedent.

The new nuclear research centre provides Iraq with options in both the uranium and plutonium routes to weapons-grade material. In the uranium route, Iraq can divert some of the weapons-grade uranium which the French are to supply under the agreement. France insists she has taken some precautionary measures against such a possibility. One is to make sure that at no time would Iraq have enriched uranium worth more than one nuclear bomb. The other is the pre-irradiation of the enriched uranium, making its handling hazardous.[16] However, French experts themselves admit that these steps are only partial deterrents to the material's diversion. A more effective deterrent is the diversion of uranium, which is a one-shot deal. Once the uranium is diverted, there is no fuel for the reactor. The entire nuclear programme would suffer, and the diversion is likely to be detected.

The plutonium route to fissile material is more promising. 'Blankets' of natural uranium can be irradiated at *Osirak*, thus producing large quantities of plutonium. Moreover, adjustments likely to be made in the reactor's cooling system – to compensate for Iraq's climate – are likely to allow the expansion of the reactor's capacity. This would make plutonium production through blanket irradiation easier still. Separating the plutonium could be conducted with Iraqi adjustments of the 'hot-cell' simulators that are to be provided by Italy under agreement. Taken together, the system may provide Iraq with a feasible nuclear option by the late 1980s.

Libya is the Arab state seeking a nuclear capability with the most fuss and clamour. Lacking a scientific infrastructure in the nuclear field, Libya focuses her efforts on the importation of nuclear bombs. These attempts began in 1970 with Premier Jalloud's trip to China.[17] Jalloud attempted to purchase nuclear weapons, but China refused. He tried again, in vain, in 1975 and 1978.

During the second half of the 1970s Libya's efforts to acquire nuclear weapons had three focuses. The first was Pakistan. Various reports point to Libyan financial participation in Pakistan's nuclear programme.[18] The aid is said to have been offered during Qaddafi's 1974 visit and to have been agreed upon during Jalloud's 1978 visit. In return, Libya is said to expect a sample of the future Pakistani bombs.[19] Other less reliable reports have indicated the planning of a joint Pakistani–Libyan nuclear test in the Libyan desert.[20]

If Qaddafi really expects to receive Pakistani nuclear weapons, he is likely to be disappointed.

Pakistan is unlikely to surrender control over mass destruction weapons to a leader of such ill repute. The political costs likely to follow a possible intelligence penetration of this sort of transaction will be enormous. Yet, a more modest Pakistani contribution to Libya's efforts cannot be ruled out. For example, Pakistan may provide Libya with reprocessing or enrichment services. Libya could thus obtain weapons-grade material, a significant short-cut to nuclear weapons.

The second focus of Libya's efforts was India. Economic co-operation between the two countries developed significantly during the mid-1970s. At that time, numerous Libyan civilian projects were contracted to Indian firms. When the Iranian revolution prevented the shipment of oil to India, Libya agreed to provide her with inexpensive oil. In exchange, Libya expected – in the framework of their bilateral nuclear co-operation agreement – to receive Indian technology for the construction of nuclear weapons. By late 1979 India had made it clear that her reading of their bilateral agreement was different from Libya's. Qaddafi reacted by terminating the shipment of oil to India.[21]

The third focus of Libya's efforts is the Soviet Union, primarily in the realm of energy and scientific infrastructure. In December 1976 the two countries signed an agreement for the supply of a 440-megawatt *Voronesh*-type dual purpose power and desalination reactor. The agreement also calls for the establishment of a nuclear physics centre, including a 2-megawatt research reactor. The Soviet Union insists on applying tight safeguards to such reactors. Thus, they do not constitute a direct and immediate proliferation hazard. Nevertheless, the project would clearly provide Libya with the ability to train a generation of nuclear scientists.

Syria's nuclear programme is still in its embryonic stages. Only in 1976 was a Syrian Atomic Energy Commission established. In 1978 a number of firms in Western Europe were contracted to conduct feasibility studies of possible Syrian investments in the peaceful uses of nuclear energy.[22] In addition, President Assad asked France to supply Syria with nuclear technology. His request was apparently denied. In the summer of 1978 progress was reported in French–Syrian negotiations, but nothing has yet transpired.[23]

In April 1978 President Assad travelled to India, in an effort to obtain nuclear technology and know-how. Syria was apparently seeking short-cuts to nuclear weapons. Some reports indicated that the Syrian–Indian talks were successful, while others reported the exact opposite.[24] Given the Soviet Union's strong commitment to nuclear non-proliferation, Syria's consistent efforts to obtain nuclear weapons from her have failed. Lacking both a scientific infrastructure in the nuclear field and the financial capacity to import one, Syria's current efforts are directed at obtaining a Soviet nuclear guarantee. Unconfirmed reports indicate that such a guarantee was provided as a secret clause to the Soviet–Syrian Treaty of Friendship signed in October 1980.[25] Syria's fear that she would soon face two neighbours with nuclear weapons is the source of her perceived need for such an umbrella.

While the eyes of most observers are directed at Iraq and Pakistan, Egypt may still stage the greatest surprise. There is no evidence of an Egyptian effort to produce nuclear weapons. Yet, in the realm of capabilities as well as in the realm of motivations there is reason to question this widely shared assessment. In terms of capability, doubt is propelled by the fact that, among the Arab states, Egypt has the most developed scientific infrastructure in the nuclear field. Her efforts began in the 1950s; in 1955 the Egyptian Atomic Energy Commission was established and research began immediately into possible uses of radio-isotopes in agriculture and industry.[26]

In 1957 the nuclear research centre at Inshass was established, and by 1961 Egypt had purchased a 2-megawatt Soviet-made research reactor. Since then, Egypt has conducted a massive effort to build a cadre of nuclear scientists. With Yugoslav aid, surveys in search of uranium and thorium in her territory were conducted. These efforts have recently borne fruit, and a Canadian firm was contracted to mine the uranium. In addition, an agreement was drawn up with the United States for the supply of two 600-megawatt *Westinghouse* power reactors. Final ratification is expected to follow the Egyptian Parliament's approval in February 1981 of the NPT. The possible uses of nuclear explosions in a number of civilian projects have also been considered in recent years.

Despite her adherence to the NPT, Egypt could enjoy some advantages if she sought a military nuclear capability. Under the terms of Egypt's nuclear co-operation agreement with India, Egyptian scientists were trained in India's nuclear installations. Some were trained in Trombay, where one of India's small chemical reprocessing facilities for plutonium extraction is located. Egyptian scientists were also present when India exploded her nuclear device in 1974. On 26 January 1978 the two governments signed an agreement to further strengthen their co-operation in the field of 'peaceful application of nuclear energy.'[27]

In the realm of motivations there are three reasons why there may be a greater Egyptian effort to develop nuclear weapons than meets the eye. First, in the framework of inter-Arab competition and Egypt's quest for leadership in the Arab world, Egypt can hardly allow herself to be third to Iraq and Libya in a realm of such enormous strategic consequences. Second, Egypt's leaders have often indicated that they regard Israel as a nuclear state; Egypt is unlikely to tolerate such Israeli superiority for long. Finally, Egypt may well wish to develop the means to deter Libya from possible attempts at nuclear blackmail. As a consequence of his assessment of Qaddafi's personality, Sadat may even regard Libya's possession of nuclear weapons as more threatening than Israel's perceived nuclear capability. All these considerations should lead to some doubts regarding the commonly perceived absence of an Egyptian effort to develop nuclear weapons.

Strategic Implications

In sum, a number of states in the Middle East are clearly on the way to an impressive nuclear capability and may acquire it by the end of this decade. The immediate implication of the ascribed nuclear proliferation is that the potential costs of Middle East wars will increase dramatically. Fear that hostilities may escalate to nuclear levels is likely to deter attacks against nuclear-weapon states. For example, Iraq's invasion of Iran is unlikely to have taken place had Iran been armed with nuclear weapons. As is the case with super-power and medium-power nuclear deterrents, much depends on the credibility of the threat. The threat's credibility, in turn, depends on the political importance of the issues at conflict. Where the state's very existence is endangered, its deterrent threat will be credible. Where more marginal goals are sought, greater doubt would persist as to the threatener's willingness to implement nuclear punishment. For example, it is doubtful that a nuclear-armed Israel could have deterred Egypt from crossing the Suez in October 1973. Yet, with respect to a possible Egyptian crossing of the pre-1967 international border, the deterrent would have been effective. This basic mechanism would persist even if both rivals were nuclear-armed since the relative importance of the issue at dispute determines the parties' willingness to absorb costs. This, in turn, determines their respective willingness to run the risks associated with nuclear threats.

The conclusion is that nuclear proliferation is likely to have a stabilizing effect on inter-state relations in the Middle East.[28] Some wars waged under current conditions are likely to be avoided once potential victims of hostilities become nuclear-armed. The 'common wisdom' about the effects of nuclear proliferation differs widely from the rather benign assessment presented above. A number of grave risks are generally held to be associated with proliferation. Precisely what these are is a question well worth examining.

Irrational Use

The most widely expressed concern about proliferation is that nuclear weapons will be acquired and used by irrational decision-makers. Newcomers to the nuclear club are considered immature, hence both irresponsible and unpredictable. Yair Evron stressed the particular application of the irrationality argument to the Middle East: 'The level of rationality of some of the leaders in the Arab world and the highly irresponsible behaviour of some of the other leaders, suggest that nuclear weapons in the Middle East, far from stabilizing relations in that troubled and tormented region, might in fact lead to the first full scale nuclear war in the world.'[29]

Little doubt should exist that enormous dangers are entailed in the irrational use of nuclear power. Nuclear weapons in the hands of a crazy leader may indeed make for unmitigated disaster. Hence, the problem of irrational behaviour cannot be easily dismissed. There are, however, some dubious assumptions underlying the question of irrationality. One such thought seems to be that under-development is a cause of irresponsible behaviour – else why would the likelihood of irrational behaviour be greater in the Middle East than in the realm of Soviet–American relations? Yet the belief that under-development is linked to irrationality is neither explicitly stated nor even minimally supported. Hence it is not very surprising that in the Third World it is both rejected and regarded as having racist connotations.[30]

Second, assertions with respect to the particular irrationality of the peoples of the Middle East also remain unsupported by evidence. Proponents of the thesis have not made an effort to support it beyond mentioning that Nasser's behaviour in the 1967 crisis is an example of irrational policy-making.[31] The single example of Nasser's miscalculation in 1967 will not sustain a strong association of irrationality with under-development. As Steven Rosen has already pointed out, 'Nasser's 1967 miscalculation in Sinai may look no worse than Truman's misassessment of China's willingness to intervene in Korea, or Kennedy's groundless expectation that the Bay of Pigs incursion would trigger a popular uprising against Castro'.[32] A nuclearized environment may be as subject to miscalculations as a non-nuclear one. But the high price that is associated with mistakes in a sensitive environment also forces the parties involved to reassess their behaviour constantly.

Finally, the assumption that rationality is required for successful deterrence is itself questionable. It is quite possible that for purposes of successful deterrence a more modest demand that the parties manifest a *sensitivity to costs* may suffice. In fact, even Idi Amin and Muamer Qaddafi, the most fashionable examples of irrationality in the 1970s, have demonstrated their sensitivity to costs. The former did his best to mock and discredit Britain but only until the sending of British troops became a distinct possibility. Despite his verbal bellicosity, Amin did not venture to conduct some crazy action against Israel in response to Entebbe. Qaddafi's own sensitivity to costs, again despite impressive verbal aggressiveness, was reflected clearly in 1977. For several months Qaddafi harassed Egypt, along the Libya–Egypt border as well as by covert activities in Cairo. All this stopped,

however, once Egypt moved her Fourth armoured division from the Suez Canal to the Libyan border. Qaddafi was made to see that further harassment would cost an Egyptian invasion, and he proved to be sensitive to such costs.

If sensitivity to costs is a sufficient substitute for the more complex concept of rationality, alarmists about the effects of nuclear proliferation to the Middle East have a more difficult case to make. They must demonstrate that the region's governments are less sensitive to costs than are states presently possessing nuclear weapons. No such evidence is apparent. Although rationality and sensitivity to costs are difficult to prove, statements that those qualities are lacking in the Middle East deserve a great measure of scepticism.

Absence of Second Strike

Another commonly expressed fear is that a nuclear Middle East will be extremely unstable because each of its nuclear states would be able to destroy its rivals' nuclear forces in a pre-emptive first strike.[33] States with small nuclear forces cannot assure the survivability of their forces. Consequently, the region's states will be enormously insecure. If, in addition, they should cherish hopes of effectively disarming their adversary's forces, the consequence would be an enormous and constant temptation to pre-empt. In the absence of second-strike capabilities, a Middle East balance of terror will be extremely unstable. Despite the superficial validity of this argument, the possibility that the region can enjoy a stable balance of terror cannot be easily dismissed. The acquisition of second-strike capabilities would indeed require investments in delivery vehicles so that all potential regional rivals could be reached. However, once such capabilities are acquired, the likelihood of pre-emptive first strikes diminishes dramatically. Moreover, with relatively modest investments, the region's states would be able to improve the survivability of their forces.

The principal source of stability in a nuclearized Middle East will be the enormous difficulties each nuclear state will face when attempting to destroy its rival's nuclear forces. Nuclear weapons delivered against population and industrial centres can impose unacceptable costs even if they operate in an imperfect fashion.

However, nuclear forces must operate perfectly – and with extremely high accuracy – if the opponent's nuclear forces are to be destroyed. Should the attack be carried out in a less-than-perfect fashion, a few of the opponent's delivery vehicles will survive, and the attacker will be vulnerable to nuclear retaliation. The surviving nuclear weapons could then be delivered against the attacker's population and industrial centres, thus imposing unlimited costs even if they operate in an imperfect fashion.

Therein lies the basic asymmetry between the attacker and the attacked: the former's nuclear forces must achieve perfect accuracy and perfect operational reliability if the attack is to be feasible, while the defender can achieve a credible retaliatory capacity with much lower levels of accuracy and operational reliability. This asymmetry, granting a clear advantage to the defender, would dissuade potential attackers from risking 'first-strikes', thus providing the regional balance of terror with stability.

Even small states could affect potential attackers' confidence in the ability to destroy their retaliatory forces. Such states may vary their means of delivery, thus making their destruction difficult; each type of delivery would force potential attackers to develop specific antidotes. The number of weapons possessed may be increased. This would force opponents considering a first strike to multiply their investments; lack of confidence in the operational reliability of their own weapons would require that a number of delivery vehicles be launched against each of the victim's weapons. Providing nuclear forces with mobility will make their detection and destruction an extremely complex proposition. High levels of alert would present potential offenders with the possibility that the victim's forces will be 'launched on attack'. The land, sea and air could be exploited for maximum dispersal; this would also affect the attacker's ability to locate and destroy. Hardening a fraction of the nuclear force would require that the offender achieve extremely high levels of accuracy. Finally, potential victims can do much in the realm of concealment and secrecy to make detection of their forces difficult. Without perfect information as to the location of each delivery vehicle, no attacker could be confident in his ability to destroy the victim's capacity to retaliate. Under such circumstances, potential attackers are likely to avoid risks associated with 'first strikes'.

Catalytic War

Another risk of proliferation to the Middle East is that catalytic nuclear wars may occur. Israel and some Arab state may find themselves drawn into a nuclear holocaust at the initiative of an Arab third party. Syria, Iraq, Libya and the PLO have been mentioned as possible catalysts.[34] Yet, there is reason to question the likelihood of such a scenario. The occurrence of catalytic war requires that a specific party be interested in initiating a process that will eventually lead to general war. But the realities of nuclear war diminish the odds that any party would embark upon such a venture.

The logic of becoming a catalyst of war is that it is an inexpensive strategy for the achievement of desired outcomes. During the long months preceding the 1967 War, Fatah could hope that its behaviour would act as a catalyst to bring about a war between Israel and the Arab states and that the desired outcomes would result without prohibitive costs to the Palestinians. Although with a lower probability for success, Syria could hope for the same. Success in this case is measured not only by whether or not a catalytic war occurred but also by the extent to which the catalyst survived the venture without incurring prohibitive costs. Catalytic behaviour is typical of a party that is sensitive to costs; he is the thrifty one who devises cheap ways to produce desired outcomes. Seen from this perspective, a catalytic nuclear war, especially in the Middle East context, is a contradiction in terms. An Arab–Israeli general nuclear war is likely to involve very high costs to both Syria and the Palestinians. The latter would suffer even if Israel did not retaliate. The odds are very small indeed that, under such circumstances, Syria or the PLO would engineer such a war.

Iraq, Libya and Algeria would remain condidates for catalytic behaviour. However, regardless of their verbal bellicosity, all three have very limited stakes in the conflict. All have contributed financially to the confrontation states and Iraq has contributed a limited size of forces as well. Her actions seem to have been directed more by the wish to improve her position in the Arab world than by any real direct interest in the conflict with Israel. Yet, before embarking on any sort of catalytic behaviour, an Arab state would have to consider that there is a finite probability, even if a small one, that the initiator of the catalytic process would be identified. Detection would expose such a state to nuclear retaliation. *Any* real probability that this could in fact occur should be sufficient to deter a thrifty party from embarking upon such a plan. The enormity, as well as the indiscriminate nature, of the costs of nuclear war contradict the essential logic of catalytic behaviour.

The Risks of Transition

The primary risk of proliferation is not these 'common wisdoms', rather it is the transition from the conventional to the nuclear era. The expected stabilizing effects of nuclear spread assume mature nuclear postures. In the realm of capabilities this assumes a relatively small number of weapons. Because of the limited number of salient targets in the Middle East, not much is required. And, as already mentioned, the capability to deliver these weapons against all regional rivals is also assumed.

A second component of mature postures is that the existence of nuclear capabilities be widely known. This, in turn, requires that nuclear weapons be introduced openly and that all Middle East nuclear states have declared, overt and explicit nuclear postures. Open introduction enhances the credibility of threats and facilitates the elaboration of doctrines for the use of nuclear weapons, thus reducing the likelihood of their misuse. It also allows the development of strategic dialogues between adversaries, thus leading to mutually shared definitions of what is likely to lead to nuclear retaliation and minimizing the possibility that war might erupt through misunderstanding. Moreover, a disclosed deterrent promotes public awareness of the constraints imposed by nuclear weapons. A widely shared appreciation of these constraints is a prerequisite for the beneficial consequences predicted to result from the introduction of nuclear weapons into the region.

The long transition to mature nuclear postures is fraught with dangers. Embryonic capabilities may invite pre-emption, either conventional or nuclear. Yet, even greater risks of transitioning are associated with the existence of undisclosed capabilities. The effects of nuclear weapons must be disclosed to the public; if not consideration of

these effects may not enter into the making of policy choices. The presence of nuclear weapons will be inconsequential if their existence is not known. The likelihood of conventional wars will remain unaffected as will their course. However, disastrous consequences may also occur. A war waged against an undisclosed nuclear state may initially remain unaffected by the unknown presence of nuclear weapons. Yet once the nuclear state begins to lose the conventional battle, it may choose to utilize its nuclear capability. The absence of previous information about the uses and effects of nuclear weapons may lead to the unjustified use of nuclear devices as 'war fighting' weapons. Alternatively, if used as a deterrent, lack of prior socialization may lead an opponent to disregard the deterrent threat, either from ignorance or assuming a bluff. If the threat is ignored, a demonstrative use will be inevitable. This is how undisclosed nuclear postures may lead to nuclear war.

In the Middle East the dangers of undisclosed nuclear postures are particularly relevant. A number of the region's states may develop nuclear weapons without making their capabilities known. Iraq, for example, may wish to keep her nuclear capability unannounced in order to avoid forcing three potentially harmful developments: first, a change in Israeli nuclear posture; second, Iranian and Saudi moves to counter Iraq's capability by developing their own nuclear weapons; third, a Syrian imperative to receive a Soviet guarantee against possible Iraqi nuclear threats. Should other Middle East nuclear states come to share similar interests in postponing disclosure, a perilous transition period will result. With the arena being no longer purely conventional and yet not fully nuclear, confusion would be at its peak. Being unclear as to which 'rules of the game' apply (conventional or nuclear) decision-makers are apt to make mistakes. It could result in a Cuban missile crisis in the Middle East.

The Middle East is about to enter the nuclear era. This much is clear from surveying the nuclear activities of the major states in the region. No greater challenge faces Middle East decision-makers than the management of the proliferation process. It requires that they accommodate themselves to an entirely new conceptual framework. They are capable of making the transition but the task will not be easy. Outside powers could also help, particularly by propagating the new framework and by making immature nuclear capabilities safer. Such action may encourage further proliferation.

However, the enormous perils of transition may now justify greater emphasis on proliferation management, even at the expense of a higher rate.

NOTES

[1] Israel's President Ephraim Katzir was quoted to that effect. See Victor Cohn, 'Israel Says It Could Build Nuclear Weapons', *The Washington Post*, 3 December 1974.

[2] Shlomo Aronson, 'Israel's Nuclear Option'. ACIS Working Paper 7 (Los Angeles: University of California, Center for Arms Control and International Security, November 1977); George H. Quester, 'Israel and the Nuclear Non-Proliferation Treaty', *Bulletin of the Atomic Scientists*, 25 (June 1969): 9.

[3] Robert J. Pranger and Dale R. Tahtinen, *Nuclear Threat in the Middle East* (Washington, DC: American Enterprise Institute for Public Policy Research, 1975).

[4] Arthur Kranish, 'CIA Sees 10–20 Israeli A-Arms', *Los Angeles Times*, 15 March 1976.

[5] P. R. Chari, 'The Israeli Nuclear Option: Living Dangerously', *International Studies* 16 (July–September 1977): 347–350.

[6] R. R. Subramanian, 'Pakistan's Nuclear Posture', *Hindustan Times*, 29 May 1979.

[7] *Foreign Report*, 9 August 1978, p. 3.

[8] *Foreign Report*, 18 June 1980, p. 2.

[9] 'The Bomb Behind the Wall', *The Economist*, 15 September 1979; Don Oberdorfer, 'Pakistan: The Quest for Atomic Bomb', *The Washington Post*, 27 August 1979.

[10] *Foreign Report*, 18 June 1980, p. 3.

[11] Onkar Marwah, 'India and Pakistan: Nuclear Armed Rivals in South Asia'. Paper prepared for the World Peace Foundation Conference on Non-proliferation, Cambridge, Massachusetts (USA), 1–2 May 1980.

[12] Paul Jabber, 'A Nuclear Middle East Infrastructure, Likely Military Postures and Prospects for Strategic Stability'. ACIS Working Paper 6. (Los Angeles: Center for Arms Control and International Security, University of California, 1978).

[13] William Branigan, 'Iraqi Buildup Stirs Concern', *Washington Post*, 27 February 1978; 'How Iraq Lost Its Nuclear Option', *Foreign Report*, 11 April 1979.

[14] *Shield* (Switzerland), 14 July 1978; *Davar* (Israel), 29 June 1976.

[15] Ronald Koven, 'Saboteurs Bomb French Plant Building Two Reactor for Iraq', *Washington Post*, 7 April 1979.

[16] Ronald Koven, 'Iraq Said to Block Nuclear Inspections', *International Herald Tribune*, 7 November 1980.

[17] See Muhammad Hasanayn Haykal, *Al-Ahrām*, 23 November 1973. FBIS, 26 November 1973, p. 6–2. See also Charles Holley, 'Nuclear Proliferation and the Middle East', *The Middle East*, July 1975, p. 19.

[18] See 'The Middle East's Nuclear Bomb Ambitions', *Middle East Newsletter*, 23 April–6 May 1979; Ron Ben Yishai, 'The Moslem World May Have Nuclear Weapons Within 3–7 Year', *Yediot Ahronot* (Israel), 20 April 1979 (Saturday Supplement), pp. 1–2.

[19] *Foreign Report*, 9 August 1978, p. 3; *Arabia and the Gulf*, 9 September 1978.

[20] *Ha'aretz* (Israel), 12 February 1979, cites *Paris Match*; see also *Al-Nahda* (Kuwait), 20 January 1979.

[21] *The Economist*, 17 November 1979.

[22] *Nucleonics Week*, 23 February 1978.

[23] *Al-Sayyād* (Lebanon), 24 July 1978.

[24] See *Newsweek*, 3 April 1979, p. 4; *Al-Ba'th* (Syria), 18 May 1978; *Al-Manar* (Arabic newspaper published in London), 6 May 1978; *Al-Watan al-'Arabi* (Lebanese paper published in Paris), 13 May 1978; *Al-difa'ā al-'Arabi* (Lebanon), August 1978; *Foreign Report*, 31 January 1979.

[25] *International Herald Tribune*, 10 November 1980.

[26] Paul Jabber, *op. cit.* in note 12, p. 11; see also *Akhir Sā'a* (Egypt), 18 April 1979.

[27] Cairo Radio, 26 January 1978.

[28] See also: Robert W. Tucker, 'Israel and the United States: From Dependence to Nuclear Weapons?', *Commentary* 60 (November 1975): 29–43; Steven J. Rosen, 'A Stable System of Mutual Nuclear Deterrence in the Arab–Israeli Conflict', *American Political Science Review* 71 (December 1977), 1367–83; Fuad Jabber, 'Israel's Nuclear Options', *Journal of Palestine Studies*, Autumn 1971; Shlomo Aronson, 'Nuclearization of the Middle East: A Dovish View', *Jerusalem Quarterly*, (No. 2 Winter 1977, pp. 27–44.

[29] Yair Evron, 'Letter to the Editor', *Commentary* 62 (February 1976).

[30] See Sisir Gupta, 'The Indian Dilemma', in *A World of Nuclear Powers?*, ed. Alastair Buchan (Englewood Cliffs, N.J.: Prentice-Hall, 1966), p. 59; Rikhi Jaipal, 'The Indian Nuclear Explosion', *International Security* 1 (Spring 1977): 47.

[31] Alan Dowty, 'Nuclear Proliferation: The Israeli Case', *International Studies Quarterly*, 22 (March 1978): 102.

[32] Rosen, *op. cit.* in note 28, p. 1374.

[33] Raymond Aron, *The Great Debate: Theories of Nuclear Strategy*. (Garden City, New York: Doubleday & Co, 1965), pp. 238–9. Dowty, *op. cit.* in note 31, p. 99; Evron, *op. cit.* in note 29, p. 6.

[34] Yair Evron, 'Some Effects of the Introduction of Nuclear Weapons in the Middle East', in *Israel: A Developing Society*, ed. Asher Arian (Tel Aviv: Pinhas Sapir Center for Development, Tel Aviv University, and Van Gorom, Assem, Netherlands, 1980), p. 116.

6 Soviet Policy Towards Iran and the Gulf

SHAHRAM CHUBIN

INTRODUCTION

The Persian Gulf has assumed great importance for the West in recent years. For the Soviet Union, however, it has long been significant, and there are reasons to expect this sustained interest in her southern periphery to grow in the future. As the Soviet Union becomes a truly global super-power, her interest in unrestricted access to other regions will increase correspondingly. Iran will assume major importance, since not only is her land border with the USSR one of the longest of any Soviet neighbour but she also controls the northern shore of the Persian Gulf and its outlet to the Indian Ocean.

The Organization for Economic Co-operation and Development (OECD) states (Europe, US and Japan) are increasingly dependent on this region (albeit in varying degrees) for material well-being and growth, and this has enhanced its strategic significance for the West. Acutely sensitive to the vulnerability of their energy supplies, these states are also sensitive to the inherent fragility of this reliance. The USSR, equally aware of the volatile and brittle nature of the region, is no less concerned. As a proximate power she may be well placed to exploit (or even assist) upheavals that occur and benefit from the leverage on the West she gains thereby, or to use the region as a buffer in her rivalry with China. But there are also urgent, less opportunist and more direct reasons for her intense concern in the region: resources and religion.

With a declining capacity to export oil, the USSR will become interested in the international energy market in the 1980s. Even if she herself does not become a net importer, she will be deeply concerned to see that Eastern Europe, which will continue to import most of its oil, does so on the best possible terms, with assured supplies at minimum cost. The obvious source will be the Persian Gulf, and Soviet political influence could be the major determinant of the precise terms of oil supply.

The religious dimension affects the Soviet Union more directly. Traditionally she has been interested in the Muslim lands to the south of her, but new factors seem likely to lead to a more concentrated interest in the future. First, within the USSR itself the nationalities question and its religious component are becoming increasingly salient. Because of disproportionately high birth rates, the Soviet Muslim populations of the Central Asian republics will become numerically dominant within the Soviet Union, totalling perhaps some 110 million by the end of the century, or 30 per cent of the total population. In this context, transformations in the states to the south take on considerable potential importance for the Soviet Union. The revenues generated by the same abundance of petroleum which has sparked a strategic interest in the region have also created political and social strains in these countries. Partly as a response to the intrusion of Western culture and rapid modernization, which have acted as a solvent to traditional cultures, a backlash has emerged: a reassertion of Islam, sometimes in fundamentalist form. Given the energy of Islam and its ability to mobilize populations, the implications of such a revival in countries adjacent to her increasingly important Asian republics could be serious for the USSR, since Islam provides an alternative to the Marxist values.

The first pages of this Paper sketch the strategic context within which Soviet policy in the region has unfolded: one of Western retrenchment. Sino-Soviet competition, military parity and growing Eastern bloc interest in Middle Eastern oil are all demonstrable. But even if increased Soviet interest in the region is assumed, it is by no means clear how that

125

interest will be manifested in practice. Chapter II discusses the Soviet perspective towards the region and the relationship with the regional states. Both in attitude and policy, the Soviet Union's approach to Iran is quite different from her approach to the other Gulf states. In terms of depth of interest, the duration of diplomatic links and the importance she attaches to geography and frontiers, her interest in Iran is profound and of long standing. The means of influence available for use *vis-à-vis* a contiguous state are also more plentiful and varied. This has made it necessary to differentiate between the USSR's policy towards Iran and her policy towards the other Persian Gulf states.

The area is useful, too, for an examination of Soviet policies towards a proximate region in an era of growing military power. Considerable space has therefore been devoted to the background and evolution of those policies in Chapter III. Given the dearth of Soviet activities in this region, Soviet policy in specific instances assumes importance; two case studies – the Iran–Iraq dispute (1969–75) and the Dhofar rebellion in Oman (1969–76) – are used to examine and assess Soviet policy. The more general issues of resource-dependence, reactions to regional conflicts, super-power diplomacy in peripheral crises, alliance relationships in a world of complex interdependence, and the interaction of military capabilities and political intentions are also raised, albeit tangentially.

In the light of the endemic instability that characterizes the politics of the Gulf region, Chapter IV deals with the Soviet Union's approach to change. In addition to a discussion of the general attitude, past policy towards Iran, the Islamic factor as an opportunity and a constraint, and the role of the Communist Party as a potential instrument are covered. The second part of the chapter examines these elements in the context of Soviet policy towards Iran during 1978–9, and illustrates the scope and limits of outside powers' influence and the unpredictability of outcomes. The concluding section assesses the record of the conduct of Soviet foreign, economic and military policy in the region in addition to current trends, and sets this in the context of an evolving regional political and strategic setting.

I. THE STRATEGIC SETTING

The Context

There is ample historical testimony for the proposition that the Soviet Union has traditionally been sensitive to developments on her periphery. To perennial concerns of encirclement and vulnerability have now been added the *amour propre* of a super-power – a combination which comprises, in equal parts, an expansive definition of security and a right to predominance in adjacent areas. Iran, as a contiguous state sharing 1,250 miles of common border, has become a 'southern neighbour,' of particular interest. Quite apart from her geographical importance, she has assumed prominence as a potentially weighty factor in Asian politics. As the key link in the West's 'northern tier' for over two decades, she exemplified the success of the West in containing Soviet influence in this region. The steadfast priority which the Soviet Union has attached to breaking this chain on her southern border is often overlooked by those who focus on the Middle East. It is evident, for example, in the pronounced focus of Soviet foreign assistance to these adjacent states. Always predominant in non-aligned Afghanistan, the Soviet Union has, since April 1978, moved to a position of exclusive influence, with a presence in that country that is extensive on all levels.

Less successful with the Western-oriented states of Pakistan and Turkey on either side of Iran, Moscow has found in recent years that persistence may achieve what power alone cannot. Disillusionment in these states with the Western security connection, combined with domestic preoccupations and economic problems, has created new openings for this extension of Soviet influence. The demise of the Central Treaty Organization as a functioning security organization was finally achieved with the advent of a new republican régime in Iran in February 1979.

The growth in most components of Soviet power in the past decade, combined with the changed international system within which it operates, has created a fluid context for Soviet diplomacy. For adjacent states the shadow of Soviet power has been lengthened by its real growth, by its proximity and by the perception of receding Western power. Whether this enhanced power – especially in its military component – is translatable into solid or sustained diplomatic gains for the USSR, remains an open question. But the sense of equality derived from strategic parity undoubtedly has two effects. It buttresses Soviet claims (through the 'equal security' formula) to be accepted as a co-guarantor in many regions, and it increases the incentive for states aligned with the West to come to terms with this new condition by seeking some accomodation with the USSR. In countries where elite perceptions shape foreign-policy orientations, the image of growing Soviet military power undoubtedly matters. By virtue of a diplomatic presence on the peripheries of the Persian Gulf (in Afghanistan, South Yemen and Ethiopia) and of a naval capability, both new departures in historical terms,[2] the Soviet Union has become a new factor in the politics of the region which must be taken into account. At the same time the growth in Soviet military power raises questions as to Soviet attitudes towards its political utility. In Afghanistan Soviet leaders appear to be using military power to achieve political gains.

More equivocal from the Soviet standpoint has been the fluidity deriving from regional political conditions. The enhanced power of some states to use military force to protect their interests as Iran did in Oman, has contrasted sharply with the inhibitions now affecting the use of overt force by the United States. In other cases (like Saudi Arabia) economic power harnessed to a conservative regional diplomacy has complicated the extension of Soviet influence. Furthermore, the fact of increased military power has put at least some (not necessarily symmetrical) restraints on the super-powers in the interest of preserving a measure of détente and avoiding the risks of escalation attendant on competitive intervention.

The sheer intractability of many regional issues to resolution by military force has also constrained this dimension of power, although recent events in Afghanistan have awakened fears for the future. Regional conflicts provide opportunities for exploitation, but undiluted support for one state (e.g., Iraq) threatens relations with others (e.g., Syria and Iran), thus risking entanglement and heavy commitments.

There remain, nonetheless, strong incentives for a deepening Soviet involvement in Iran and the Persian Gulf states which, for analytic convenience, may be classified under offensive and defensive headings, although it is by no means clear that this distinction is recognized by the Soviet Union. On the defensive side is the legitimate interest in stable borders, friendly neighbours and access to nearby areas. On the offensive, is the Soviet interpretation of these interests: for the Soviet Union stable borders mean demilitarized borders, friendly neighbours are compliant states, and access is synonymous with unrestricted or unqualified rights. In practice, security tends to be equated with regional hegemony and this is taken to mean the exclusion of any rival.

Iran's place in the Soviet perspective is indicative. As the only state contiguous with both the USSR and the Persian Gulf/Indian Ocean, she can serve as a defensive buffer, as well as the door into adjacent regions. The importance of a neutral or pro-Soviet Iran defensively is clear – as a safeguard against pressure directed against the USSR during peacetime and, in wartime, as protection for the Soviet southern flank and industrial facilities. A weak, militarily insignificant Iran with loose ties with the West saves the USSR from having to divert military resources from Europe or the Far East to another front. On the other hand, a strong Iran, tightly integrated into the Western security structure could pose a more serious problem for the USSR. Iran's military build-up under the Shah, involving advanced weapons such as the F–14 and AWACS aircraft, a sophisticated electronic intelligence capability, ground facilities available to the West and large stocks of armaments that could be viewed as prepositioned stock for the US, raised questions about a potential Soviet response. Soviet investments in the Transcaucasus and Turkestan Military Districts – 17 divisions, 180,000 men, 4,500 tanks, 2 airborne brigades and aircraft – might have required augmentation.

Also, a compliant Iran could be used 'defensively' from the Soviet perspective to block a distant but emerging threat from Chinese sea-launched missiles in the 1980s or 1990s by denying their launch vessels access to the

Arabian Sea. Less narrowly defined, Soviet interests extend to assured access through Iranian airspace in contingencies requiring a rapid military response. The time and distance saved by such automatic access for airlifts to Africa and by the possible use of Iranian facilities would enhance Soviet influence or capability to intervene more generally.[3]

Finally, the importance of having Iran as a 'friendly neighbour' extends beyond an Iranian denial of bases to other powers, or non-adherence to 'closed political military blocs', to the more positive undertaking of 'sensitivity' to Soviet interests. As the second largest oil exporter (until 1978) with 10 per cent of the world's oil production capacity, Iran is perhaps uniquely qualified to fill the emerging energy deficit of the Eastern European states, which the USSR is increasingly reluctant or unable to satisfy from her own resources. An attractive solution to this problem for the USSR might be to arrange the supply of oil on assured preferential terms from one set of Soviet neighbours to another. This might avoid the serious emerging problem of how East Europe's purchases are to be financed, given Soviet reluctance to see it more heavily indebted to international financial institutions, which are largely influenced by Western governments. In any case the USSR's interest, direct or indirect, in the international energy market is certain to increase in the coming years, as will her renewed interest in those states that are both oil-producers and neighbours.

The China Factor

As China has adopted an increasingly active role in foreign affairs in the past few years, her attention has focused on Asia and on Soviet attempts to encircle her. A natural area for concentration has been Afghanistan, the strategic junction where the USSR, China, Iran and the Indian sub-continent meet, and the country's importance has grown as the politics of south and south-west Asia have become intermeshed. Though land-locked, Afghanistan is an important potential access route, through Iran to the Persian Gulf and through Pakistan to the Indian Ocean. China's interest (like that of Iran and Pakistan) has been in preserving Afghanistan as a buffer, rather than in seeing her integrated into the Soviet Empire.

However the wider aspect of Sino–Soviet rivalry has also affected Soviet policy in the Persian Gulf region, and a number of complex questions must be examined. To what extent has this rivalry influenced Soviet policy, and in what ways? How will continued, and even sharpened, competition be reflected in Soviet policy in the area? Has Soviet policy tended towards more activism and support for revolutionary movements, or towards more conservatism and support for existing regimes? Will rivalry with China and a preclusive interest in forestalling her advances on the Soviet periphery to prevent encirclement tend to encourage yet greater Soviet risk-taking?

The Record of Chinese Involvement

Despite an aid relationship with Yemen dating back to the 1950s, China has only looked to the Gulf seriously in the past decade. In this first phase of her relations with the littoral states she appears to have been motivated by contradictory impulses, the desire to establish ties with existing 'conservative' governments conflicting with the desire to support national liberation movements. In the 1970s, she added formal relations with Iran and Kuwait to those she already had with Iraq, and the establishment of ties with a fourth state, Oman, in mid-1978 gave Peking a greater potential for diplomatic representation among the littoral states than the USSR.

China's decision to establish relations with Iran in particular reflected a basic commitment to give priority to supporting governments which shared her concern for containing Soviet influence by erecting strong barriers in the form of armed forces and regional security arrangements. (The corollary of this was the withdrawal of support for movements which might foster instability in the region and thus be exploited by the USSR. Peking accordingly reduced and terminated her assistance to the Dhofari movement in Oman in 1972–1973.) This interest in Iran as a potential bulwark against the spread of Soviet influence was demonstrated time and again between 1973 and 1978. In June 1973 China's Foreign Minister Ji Pengfei, on a visit to Tehran, endorsed Iran's arms build-up in the light of the 'hegemonist' threat in the region and supported the right of the littoral states to co-operate in assuring security, particularly against subversion assisted by outside powers. These themes were repeated by Vice Premier Li Xiannian in Tehran in 1975, and, later on, Soviet pressure on Iran, criticism of her arms purchases, and Soviet espionage were extensively covered by the Chinese media which contrasted them with Moscow's claims of 'good-neighbourliness'.[4]

In 1978 senior Chinese leaders reiterated their support for co-operation among the Gulf states and registered their interest in Gulf politics. Foreign Minister Huang Hua, visiting Teheran in June, made veiled reference to a common enemy,[5] and in August, Chairman Hua Guofeng underlined this by praising Iran's defence programme, which was being criticized by the USSR. So important had the issue of growing Soviet power and expanding influence become, and the consequent priority attached to developing relations with states in Asia equally concerned by it, that the Chinese leadership failed to assess the domestic stability of their most logical ally in the region, and a glowing report on Iran and the prospects of Sino-Iranian friendship followed Hua Guofeng's visit.[6] The subsequent revolution in Iran was largely attributed to super-power rivalry and especially to Soviet 'offensive' intervention,[7] and the corollary of this was that in strategic terms the loss of Iran was seen as due in part to US weakness.

The Soviet Union has shown great sensitivity to China's growing diplomatic activity in her own backyard (whether in Iran, Romania or Yugoslavia), for this cultivation of states with parallel geopolitical concerns threatens Soviet interests in a more insidious way than do Western schemes. Her criticisms have tended to concentrate on Peking's alliance with 'extreme reaction' and on its support for revitalizing cold-war pacts like CENTO at the expense of 'national liberation movements' and the Soviet Asian security pact project.[8] Soviet diplomacy sought to emphasize to Iran in particular that toying with China would be unfruitful. There were repeated references to those seeking to 'sow the seeds of discord' in Soviet–Iranian relations, and contrasts were drawn between Soviet constructiveness and China's 'unhelpful' attitude on the Iran–Iraq border dispute. Iran was reminded that good relations with neighbours was one of the preconditions for strengthening peace and co-operation (the inference being that good ties with Peking were not a substitute); and China,

accused of trying to expand her influence by supporting the CENTO powers in setting up security arrangements in the Persian Gulf and Red Sea area, was said to be colluding with the imperialists by seeking to scare these states with the 'mythical' Soviet threat.[9]

Soviet concern about Chinese diplomacy increased in 1978 when China established diplomatic relations with Oman and Libya. This appeared as part of a concerted effort to counter Soviet influence. In the sub-Continent and Afghanistan this could take the form of co-operation between Iran, Pakistan and China to weaken a Soviet ally, Afghanistan. Another possibility aired in mid-1978 was that Iran might use her influence with the West as a conduit for the supply of advanced military equipment to China. The prospect of a tacit alliance developing among a belt of states on her periphery encompassing China, Iran, Turkey and the maverick Eastern European states of Yugoslavia and Romania, was deeply disturbing to the USSR, and to inhibit such an alliance she has sought to discourage even the development of bilateral relations between them. With China, her leverage has been limited, and she has had to be content with accusing China of supporting reactionary states, such as Oman (and Egypt), and pro-imperialist initiatives, such as a Persian Gulf security arrangement designed to isolate and extirpate national liberation movements.

In practice Sino-Soviet rivalry has not radically affected Soviet policy in the Persian Gulf itself. It has not, for example, stimulated a competition between the two states to outbid each other in support for revolutionary movements, or resulted in a clear division between Soviet support for one group of states and Chinese support for another. Neither state has identified its interests ideologically with support for revolutionary movements against conservative governments, or *vice versa*; each has pushed them pragmatically.

It is on the periphery of the region (and particularly in Afghanistan) that Soviet policy has most clearly been affected by China's diplomatic activity. Afghan 'non-alignment', a product of political realism arising from weakness and geographical propinquity, has always rested on Soviet sufferance. The semblance of a balance was maintained for many years, even though it had a pro-Soviet coloration, but the success and continuation of this posture was dependent on its acceptability to the major powers and, above all to the USSR. Afghanistan has consequently been a good barometer of Soviet intentions, the latitude and independence she is permitted reflecting the Soviet Union's own insecurities and concessions. The shift represented by the coup which deposed President Daoud in April 1978 saw Soviet predominance replaced by an exclusively Soviet-oriented régime, characterized by much deeper Soviet involvement at all levels of government and finally by the invasion in December 1979.

The earlier coup in Kabul in July 1973, which had deposed the monarchy and brought President Daoud to power, had aroused concern in Iran, China and Pakistan which had not been allayed by the apparent revival of Afghan claims to parts of Pakistan – Pushtunistan – the Pathan inhabitants of which are ethnically related to the Pathans in Afghanistan. This, combined with apparent support for a Baluchi separatist movement in the area of the border between Iran and Pakistan, looked as though it was designed to accelerate the disintegration of Pakistan. But this threat never materialized. The Daoud government cultivated relations with Iran and Pakistan and accepted economic assistance from Iran which hoped, by offering the Afghan government an alternative trade outlet and a new source of income, to reduce Kabul's considerable dependence on the USSR.[10] By 1976, President Daoud had reassured his neighbours and put some distance between Kabul and Moscow. Nevertheless Afghanistan was constrained by Soviet definitions of non-alignment from joining any regional arrangements that had any political content.[11]

The timing of the April 1978 coup has been attributed by some to the Afghan leadership's plans to suppress the Communists within the country, and by others to Daoud's decision to denounce Cuba at the Conference of Non-Aligned Countries scheduled to take place in Kabul. Particularly unclear was the extent of the USSR's covert role in the actual coup; Moscow had foreknowledge at the least, and quite possibly participated in the actual timing and mechanics. The nature of the new regime with its Marxist leadership [12] and rhetoric, and its immediate recognition by the USSR, Cuba and the Peoples' Democratic Republic of Yemen (PDRY), strengthened this suspicion. So did the new régime's rapid alignment with the Soviet attitudes (e.g., supporting Vietnam against Cambodia), the conclusion of numerous new Soviet–Afghan agreements (including a Treaty of Friendship in December 1978), and a tripling of the number of Soviet advisers in the country to over 3,000.

The USSR's willingness to invest heavily in the country and to stake her reputation on the consolidation of the new Government's power was a new policy departure.[13] Any resuscitation of Afghan claims to Pakistan or the promotion of dissidence in Baluchistan are most unlikely at present, owing to Afghanistan's backwardness and the intractability of many of her social and economic problems. Moscow has few immediate interests beyond consolidating its influence in the country and shoring up an increasingly beleaguered government. Soviet statements over the past year indicate unease about the instability of this new client state; the neighbouring states have therefore been accused of sponsoring a 'secret war'; and, as internal dissidence increased in 1979, to the point where massive Soviet military intervention became necessary.

One explanation for the Soviet decision to acquire a new client state (despite the onerous commitments the relationship implies) is to be found in Sino–Soviet rivalry, which had become more extensive throughout Asia. The decision to consolidate Soviet dominance in Afghanistan may be viewed as a decision to forestall any extension of Chinese influence and to deny China any new area in which to operate. The imminent completion of the Karakoram Highway from Pakistan to China may indeed have been an additional influence on the timing of the coup.

Defensive considerations apart, an enhanced presence in an Afghanistan totally responsive to her wishes increased future Soviet strategic options. Neither Iran nor Pakistan looked immune from domestic disturbances in 1978 and neither government was fully in control of its dissident populations. There may have been attractions in the possibility of using Afghanistan as a source of pressure on either or both of these states, both to induce greater 'sensitivity' to Soviet interests and potentially to open a geographical corridor to the Indian Ocean. This increased Soviet presence on the periphery of the Persian Gulf region, together with the potential for the application of co-ordinated pressure from Ethiopia and the PDRY lent credence to the encirclement scenarios which periodically surface in both Riyadh and Teheran.

Within the Gulf itself the competition with China has been muted and has not affected Soviet policy in any particular direction. Neither power has a broad presence in the area, for both lack ties with Saudi Arabia and most of the Arabian peninsula states. Both are atheistic states (and therefore have no ideological attraction), and neither are seen as purveyors of modern technology. Given her limited military capabilities, China might act as a useful diplomatic counter-weight at most, but she is not viewed as a provider of security for the littoral states.

Sino–Soviet rivalry in Asia will continue to influence Soviet policy on the periphery of the Persian Gulf. For example, the use of Iran's airspace for supplying Vietnam in her conflict with China may be repeated in a similar contingency. Soviet interest in access to ports in the Indian Ocean, as part of her communications route to the Far East, will continue, and she would like to be able to station a portion of her growing fleet clear of easily mined straits. Both concerns will ensure continued attention to sea areas near her periphery and, if China's SLBM force develops, the USSR might want to extend surveillance and patrols over sea areas from which China might launch these missiles against the Western USSR.

The Energy Dimension
As the world's largest oil producer (18 per cent of total world production) the Soviet Union has not hitherto been particularly preoccupied with other sources of energy. She has both encouraged and benefited from price rises decided by the Organization of Petroleum Exporting Countries (OPEC). She also welcomed, in the early 1970s, the moves by the oil-producing states and their national oil companies in their 'struggle against the oil monopolies'. The USSR has also acted with economic pragmatism, for example, by selling oil supplied to her by Iraq (in exchange for arms) at advantageous prices in Europe, and more recently she has used her capacity as a major oil producer to consolidate relations with politically important states, such as Turkey and India, by guaranteeing supplies at concessionary (non-OPEC) prices.

Although the USSR is still unlikely to become a net importer of oil in the immediate future, she is likely to become one within a decade. As a result, trade with the Persian Gulf states (principally Iran and Iraq), which has hitherto been seen simply as contributing to the stabilization of a political relationship, may in future be transformed by Soviet and the Council for Mutual Economic Assistance (COMECON) energy needs into a real dependency.

Iraq has been the principal supplier of oil to the USSR, providing since 1977 90 per cent of her Middle East imports (5.8 million tons), worth approximately $500 million. It was with Soviet assistance that Iraq built up her national oil industry after 1972, and oil has been the principal currency for the repayment of Soviet assistance in a host of industrial projects and in the supply of arms. The Eastern European states have been equally active in Iraq, trading industrial plant and equipment costing up to $1 billion annually. In 1977 at least 150,000 barrels per day of Iraqi crude flowed to Eastern Europe on commercial account and as repayment for aid.[14] At least 2,300 East European personnel were employed on commercial projects, principally in the oil sector and in irrigation. Czechoslovakia, Romania, Hungary, Poland and Bulgaria all have projects under way in Iraq.

Cemented by two decades of co-operation and a common antipathy to the West, commercial relations between the Eastern bloc and Iraq seem certain to expand. Soviet interest in access to oil and Iraqi interest in arms and technology will ensure that they do. (Iraq sees a particular need for increasing her stocks of weapons for a confrontation with Israel.) But the previous relationship will be modified significantly in two ways. First Iraq's oil revenues allow her much more freedom of choice as to the types and sources of the weapons and technology she requires, and, with adequate foreign exchange available, Soviet bloc goods and barter trade may look less appealing. Secondly, a shift towards pragmatism and away from doctrinaire anti-imperialism has lately been discernible in Iraq, and this may argue for a more balanced political relationship with the West as well. (She has already turned to Western, primarily French, arms suppliers.[15])

Soviet co-operation with Iran in the energy field dates back to the late 1960s. By October 1970 a 1,200-mile gas pipeline had been commissioned, and Iranian gas (which had previously been flared) was fed to the USSR. The construction of the pipeline by the USSR was paid for in natural gas, and by the end of 1978 some 70,000 million cubic metres had been pumped along it, generating (after payment for the pipeline) over $1 billion for Iran, which was spent on Soviet goods.

The arrangement proved satisfactory to both states, providing the USSR with an energy source that was located conveniently for her needs and Iran with a return on a commodity that had been hitherto wasted. But the issue of price was sometimes contentious. The agreed price in 1966 was 18 US cents per 1,000 cubic feet. Reflecting rises in the price of oil, this was increased to 30 cents in 1972; and after the 1973 quadrupling of oil prices Iran sought another increase to 62 cents – still well below market prices. The USSR's reluctance to acquiesce in this request exposed her to criticism that she was exploiting the developing countries, but after some mutual recrimination, a compromise was agreed in 1975. In January 1978 a further 33 per cent increase was agreed. In theory the price of gas is pegged to prevailing world oil prices, though in practice Iran under the Shah did not insist on this rigidly. The issue of a fair price for gas sold to the USSR appears to be assuming greater importance with the overthrow of the Shah.

The success of the 'gas-for-goods' arrangement encouraged the two states to look for further co-operative ventures, and in December 1975 they reached agreement (together with West Germany, France, Austria and Czechoslovakia) on a more ambitious project. In exchange for 13.5 billion cubic metres of Iranian gas (and treble this quantity by 1985) to Soviet industrial centres in the Caucasus and eastern Ukraine, the USSR was to supply gas to West Germany, France and Austria from her western Siberian fields. The USSR was to charge Iran a transit fee of 3 million cubic metres of gas per year, both states were to be paid in hard currency, and the European states were to be assured of gas supplies for 23 years, starting in 1981. The agreement necessitated the construction, at a total cost of $3 billion, of a second trans-Iranian pipeline (IGAT II) extending 950 miles from the gas fields to Astara, on the Soviet border, from where the gas would feed into the Soviet-COMECON (Orenburg) pipeline grid.[16]

The agreement had several distinctive features: the involvement of the two blocs and Iran; its duration; and its sheer scale. The second Iranian pipeline, to be built in part by the USSR, would involve the two countries more closely with each other, though, since the growth in bilateral trade between them already threatened to exceed the availability of Iranian gas, future projects might have to be paid for in Iranian oil. The fulfilment of local Soviet energy needs by Iran and the freeing of the USSR's poorly-located gas resources for export was especially welcome to the USSR, given the anticipated decline of her oil exports in the next decade, and a corresponding increased reliance on gas as an earner of hard currency.[17] The three-way arrangement would also solidify political relationships, giving each of the partners a stake in the stability of the others. This project, however, became a casualty of the Iranian revolution.

After 1973 the USSR steadily increased the price of the oil she supplied to the COMECON states (approximately 80 per cent of their needs) to close to world prices. Since 1976 she has also warned them of limits to her future exports and encouraged them to search for alternative sources. She is expected to supply a decreasing fraction of COMECON's growing energy needs, partly because she prefers to sell oil and gas to the West for hard currency, and partly because she will only have a declining surplus available for export anyway.

Soviet oil supply has been a means of subsidizing and controlling Eastern Europe's development, and diminished reliance on the USSR for oil will inevitably necessitate the broadening of COMECON countries' ties with other states. If oil is to be purchased on the world market, it will require hard currency and financing – and the most logical sources of finance will be international institutions identified with the West, such as the International Monetary Fund (IMF) or World Bank. The USSR, unwilling either to expand her own exports or to encourage COMECON to depend on the West for credits, may turn to the Persian Gulf states as a source of supply for Eastern Europe on dependable and reasonable terms. Indeed in May 1977 she disclosed that she had sought to import oil from Iran but had received no answer for six months. The initial request was for 1 million tons a year, a figure which would subsequently increase. In August 1977 an agreement in principle was reached to barter this amount for Soviet goods and services.

In this evolving setting Iran's (and Iraq's) relations with Eastern Europe will become of great interest to the USSR. Moscow has welcomed and encouraged the development of Iran's relations with the Eastern Bloc, pointing out that co-operation despite different social systems, contributes to peace and has political advantages for all concerned. And Iran, like Iraq, has shown some interest in barter arrangements with the Eastern bloc. Discussions have been held with officials from virtually every state – Czechoslovakia, Poland, Hungary, Yugoslavia, Bulgaria and Romania – but so far no long-term barter contracts have been signed, though relatively small agreements have been concluded with Bulgaria, Poland and East Germany. Large, long-term supply arrangements with Czechoslovakia [18] and Hungary are still being considered, and Romania, Iran's largest East European oil customer, is involved in the Iranian development programme.

Iran has thus begun to emerge as a potentially major oil and gas supplier of Eastern Europe. She is an attractive partner because of her experience with Eastern Europe (dating from the mid-1960s), her co-operation with the USSR over gas since 1970, her projected link-up with the Soviet pipeline in 1981, and because she has been flexible on the means of repayment. Furthermore, she has shown evident interest in the development of economic relations with Eastern Europe by, for example, extending $780 million worth of cash loans in 1975. Under current arrangements oil is supplied to some COMECON states via the Pan-Adriatic oil pipeline, and this flow could be expanded in future.

The importance Eastern Europe attaches to the relationship with Iran has been reflected in the care with which East European Governments have dealt with her. Initially this showed itself in an unwillingness to criticize the Shah, and there is now a great deal of Eastern European concern over future policies of the new régime in Teheran. This may turn out well, for co-operation with advanced third-world countries and Eastern Europe appears to be a policy that the revolutionary government in Iran will seek to promote in order to avoid dependence on great powers and ideological 'contamination' from the West.

The Future of Energy Supplies

Despite considerable debate about its extent and precise timing, there is a substantial and growing consensus that the USSR will face an energy problem within a decade.[19] At the very least, Middle East oil and gas will assume greater importance for Eastern Europe, but it may well also become essential for the Soviet Union herself. Under optimistic assumptions, the USSR could produce 10 million barrels per day – enough to cover her domestic needs in 1985 – but this would mean the loss of petroleum as an export and earner of hard currency and would entail further reduction of supplies to COMECON.

In the event of a significant energy deficit which prevents the USSR from either supplying her East European allies or meeting her own requirements, she will become an importer and therefore a competitor in the international petroleum market. In that case her interest in Persian Gulf politics will assume a new and vital dimension. If, on the other hand, the USSR sees the region as a source of energy supplies to replace her own declining exports to COMECON, this interest, though substantial, will be somewhat less vital. Either way, however, she will have a strong, new incentive to follow developments in the Persian Gulf region closely and to increase her involvement substantially.

What form this new interest will take will be contingent on numerous factors, including the precise date when the USSR becomes a net importer, the political complexion of the region at that time and the miliary balance of power then existing. Given her political and military predominance in the region, the temptation to secure oil on attractive terms through persuasion or coercion must be anticipated. If this 'colonial' route of access to the region's energy supplies is sought, its concomitant will be a policy promoting instability and disorder in the region. The alternative 'commercial' route implies a more peaceful approach in which the USSR would have a stake in a tranquil setting to assure her energy needs.

This dichotomy should not be overdrawn. There are powerful incentives to obtain oil on preferential terms, whether by barter (in order to save hard currency) or at guaranteed concessionary prices, and these provide an adequate inducement to exercise political-military 'influence' so as to convince recalcitrant oil producers of the validity of these requests. In this setting, Soviet pressure, bullying and covert interference might be anticipated against any government unwilling to provide oil on acceptable terms, while the promise of support and internal bolstering of governments could be offered to those amenable to such requests. Even assuming that one state could provide for all her energy needs, it is unlikely that the USSR would want to rely totally on any one Middle Eastern source, so that continued interest in Iraq and an expanded interest in Iran for oil and gas therefore both seem certain.

To physical contiguity has been added potential resource dependency, and this is a new motive for much more intensive Soviet involvement in Persian Gulf politics. What form this is likely to take may be clarified after a discussion of the Soviet perspectives and recent Soviet policy in the region.

II. IRAN AND THE GULF IN SOVIET PERSPECTIVE

Iran, The Neighbour

Proximity to the USSR has been the primary constituent of Iranian foreign policy, since for Iran, as for the USSR, geography is important. Although this 'geopolitical fatality' is immutable, its practical effects can fluctuate; the political-military impact of contiguity varies over time with advances in technology and communications and with the degree of the internal cohesion of the state.

For the USSR, the belt of states on her borders may provide reassurance and defence in depth or opportunities for tactical exploitation. These opportunities will vary with the degree of Soviet power, with the importance that other (contending) states attach to the periphery and with Soviet insecurity or belligerence. In the nineteenth century, for example, Russia used the threat of pressure on British Asian interests as a potential response to adverse developments in Europe.[20]

Whatever the precise policy pursued by the USSR, the fact of her unwavering interest in her neighbours generates intense and sustained pressures on them to reassure her as to their policies. The extent to which these neighbours are prepared to give this reassurance, to assuage Soviet sensitivity or accommodate Soviet interests, will be at least partially dependent on the global balance of power, and their intense interest in the fluctuations in this balance will tend to focus on perceptions of power balance, resolve, momentum, etc. To the extent that the USSR appears a dynamic and irresistible force, and her adversaries passive and indecisive, the balance between accommodation and independence in her neighbour's policies will shift in favour of accommodation.

The Soviet Union's interest in her neighbours is rooted in her desire for stable borders as a means of enhancing her own security. But what does this mean for the security of other states? The Soviet goal, as it affects neighbouring states, is the achievement of preponderant (and preferably also exclusive) influence. This is not necessarily synonymous with seeking territorial control or pursuing a policy of military expansionism. As the example of Afghanistan shows, military occupation is likely to be politically onerous and possibly militarily costly as well; it may suffice to ensure that neighbouring states have compliant governments which are sensitive and deferential to Soviet needs.

In the late nineteenth and early twentieth centuries much energy was spent on preserving Persia as a 'buffer' state, purely in order to assuage Russian insecurities. (Russia even protested against any internal development which might have military utility, such as the building of railroads.) This historical fear of possible attack from the south was transmitted to the new Soviet régime, and was fed by the Allied attack on the southern USSR from Persia in 1919.[21] The Soviet Union's pressure on Persia was thus seen as justified in order to forestall the emergence of dominant foreign influence in a region adjacent to her borders. It was this (at times obsessive) concern for security that led the USSR in the 1920s to conclude a series of Treaties with her southern neighbours – Turkey, Persia and Afghanistan.

In many respects the security problems of all the states adjacent to the USSR are analogous. Contiguity not only ensures persistent Soviet attention; it also confers distinct diplomatic advantages. The USSR can woo the target state through a mixture of concessions, flattery and strength. Physical proximity gives her the means both to engage in co-operative ventures on the common border (to facilitate, for example, overland transit of commerce) and to use the example of one neighbour to impress others. (Turkey, for example, is reminded that she can gain prestige and play a constructive role like Finland 'our neighbour to the north'.)

Iran, like Norway and Turkey, has sought to offset Soviet proximity and, at times, belligerence, by allying herself with a distant countervailing power.[22] The trick for these states has been to strike the proper balance between assuring their own security and independence and responding to the needs and sensitivity of their large neighbour, thus achieving maximum freedom of action without provoking the USSR. In practical terms, policies requiring a mix of deterrence and reassurance, seeking to combine elements of independence with deference on selected issues, require at least a receptivity on the part of the target of that policy. They are founded upon the assumption that the Soviet Union's concern about the security of her frontiers are indeed concrete and 'that there is no unbridgeable ideological gulf which would make mutual trust and the recognition of interests held in common in principle unlikely' – an assumption which, as R. J. Vincent implies, may not be valid.[23] Sensitivity may be interpreted as weakness, concessions as rights, and if this carefully calibrated diplomacy is not to unravel under pressure, it needs what Johan Holst calls 'prudent firmness'. It also requires internal cohesion and cool leadership, a combination which is rare among the Soviet Union's southern neighbours.

Soviet policy towards Iran reflects the pursuit of her overriding right to be secure and reassured. The issue revolves around the 1921 Treaty of Friendship and the possibility that Iranian territory might be used for attack on

the USSR. Under Articles 5 and 6 of that Treaty the USSR gained the right to send troops into Iran should a third party intervene militarily there or use Iranian territory as a base for an attack on Soviet territory. At the time it was understood that the USSR was concerned with a possible threat to her security from Czarist counter-revolutionary elements. Since then, however, Moscow has consistently sought to widen the interpretation of these Articles to restrict military activities (in the broadest sense) of any foreign power in Iran. The Treaty was invoked as justification for the Soviet invasion of Iran in 1941. Later Stalin argued that it gave the USSR the right to send troops into northern Iran if there was a possible danger from an outside source, and much of the friction between the two states in the post-war era (particularly between 1955 and 1962) centred on Soviet attempts to use the Treaty as a lever to cajole Teheran into forgoing military links with the West. In 1959 Iran unilaterally denounced the 1921 Treaty as unequal and inconsistent with the UN Charter, but the USSR continued to insist on its validity.[24] In practice it has been invoked by Moscow as a legal cloak for exerting pressure on Teheran and as an assertion of the legitimacy of Soviet interest in Iranian affairs (it was so used to warn the US against intervention during Iran's upheaval in 1978). Apart from its use as an instrument of pressure, the Treaty, with its undertones of Soviet preclusive interest, reflects the central importance the USSR continues to attach to events in neighbouring states, and also, as Afghanistan has shown she does not regard the 'limited sovereignty' formula as applicable exclusively to her East European satellites.

If the Soviet Union has consistently sought to widen her own rights vis-à-vis Iran, she has also sought to restrict her neighbour's right to achieve security through arms.[25] She has therefore been as implacably opposed to Iran's build-up and military expansion as she has been impervious to the political effects of her own expanding military potential. Iran in turn, eschewing the equidistance between the superpowers which had been cultivated in the preceding decade, pursued after 1973 a military modernization made possible by increased oil revenues and necessary by the Shah's desire to play a wider and more active diplomatic role.

Two points about Iran's short-lived military build-up should be noted. The Shah's quest for a proportional deterrent capability *vis-à-vis* the USSR was of long standing. He told the US Ambassador in Teheran in 1947 that the greater Iran's power of resistance, the more the USSR would hesitate to send troops across the border. If Iran could be occupied by one division the Russians might do so. If several divisions were required, the Kremlin might hesitate.[26] What was new was Iran's growing capacity to achieve this in the 1970s and 1980s. And what was potentially alarming to the Soviet Union was the incipient transformation of a tolerably compliant neighbour into a regionally assertive power. George Kennan sympathized with this concern, which he considered justified historically, for 'there have also been times where Persian behaviour in this relationship left something to be desired from the Russian standpoint'. Kennan admitted that Russia has a 'traditional tendency to border expansion' which has been dormant recently but 'may make itself felt again', but he derived comfort from the fact that it is in any case, an impulse which is regional, not universal, in character.[27]

Iran's arms build-up was the focus of consistent Soviet criticism. In 1973 and 1974 both Iran's Prime Minister and the Shah were privately warned about it during visits to Moscow, and the warning was repeated by the Soviet Ambassador in Teheran in August 1976. Soviet public criticism concentrated on several key themes:

- The arms were said to be 'in excess of Iran's legitimate defence needs' and therefore 'offensive', reflecting a policy by the US of seeking to achieve for itself 'unilateral advantages and military superiority to the detriment of the security of the USSR'.
- Given the proximity to her southern borders, these arms are of serious and legitimate concern to the USSR, which cannot therefore 'remain indifferent' to them.
- The transfer of arms increases Iran's dependence on the West, whose instructors not only teach how, but also advise when to use them.
- They create an explosive situation in the entire region, of concern to all states.
- The Soviet Union poses no threat to Iran, whose arms procurement must be seen in terms of a 'general imperialist policy pursued by Washington in the Persian area'.[28]

Two themes are particularly germane: the recurrent emphasis on the Soviet Union's legitimate direct interest arising from her geographic proximity, and the anxiety relating to the wider strategic role of the military build-up (which is also encountered in Soviet commentaries relating to the other Persian Gulf states). In the Soviet view Iran's military build-up, her more assertive regional diplomacy, her continued participation in CENTO and her efforts to create a security arrangement within the Persian Gulf were all directly related. They stemmed inevitably from a tilt towards the United States which was pushing Iran 'on a dangerous course which has nothing to do with Iran's real national interests', and which could not be justified by reference to an 'imaginary threat to the north'. What particularly agitated Moscow was the possibility – inherent in this tactit alliance – that Iran would be used as an instrument of Western policy and a protector of its interests. One commentator explicitly distinguished the permissible from the impermissible. While Iran's close ties with the West were acceptable, he argued, 'The Soviet Union cannot remain indifferent to the course whereby the US imperialist quarters, under the pretext of wishing to expand co-operation with Iran, are trying to turn Iran into an agent of that policy. This is fraught with danger for the cause of peace. The USSR wishes Iran to be an independent, prosperous and strong country and not the tool for carrying out the adventurist policy of the aggressive forces of imperialism.'[29]

In the Soviet view, the arming of Iran was not due to any fortuitous overlapping of interests between Teheran and Washington, but was rather the product of a carefully concerted and planned strategy. It was consistent with the Western policy of replacing a direct military presence, which had become politically vulnerable, by the expedient of cultivating local states to uphold the interests of the West. From this perspective, the infusion of arms, the more dynamic diplomacy of regional states, and the quest for a regional security arrangement were directly connected. Indeed this interpretation was strengthened by the periodic references in Washington after 1971 to the 'twin-pillar' approach to Persian Gulf security and by references to the 'moderating' and 'supportive' role that Iran played in Middle East diplomacy. That Iran's defence build-up was intended for more than merely territorial defence was proved (in this view) by reference to the extension of her security perimeter to the 'approaches' of the Persian Gulf (1972), her involvement in Oman (1973) and by the very scope and pace of her military acquisitions. These policies were seen as reflections of Western powers' interests, and hence stretched Soviet good-neighbourly tolerance to the limits.

More direct than the regional consequences of Iran's arms build-up were its implications for the USSR as an immediate neighbour. Extensive in scope and rapid in pace, the expansion planned by the Shah encompassed all three services. Most critical for the USSR was the air force, which was exclusively US-supplied and included 80 F–14s (with *Phoenix* missiles); the Shah had explicitly noted that these gave Iran the stand-off capability to engage an enemy outside Iran's airspace. The Shah had planned to augment Iran's capacity to deter the Soviet Union's habitual intrusions into Iran's airspace with the proposed purchase of seven AWACS early-warning aircraft and the construction of an electronic intelligence system for surveillance and monitoring of the 1,200-mile border. These intrusions had included periodic flights by Soviet MiG–25s over Iran since 1973.[30]

In addition, the trends in military co-operation between Iran and the US, the complementarity of the two states' weapons systems, the degree of US military assistance (involving several thousand advisers) and the parallel policies pursued by the two states in the region until 1978, suggested that in times of crisis or war Iranian facilities would be available for unrestricted Western use. The depth of Western presence in Iran could create another military front for the USSR, and the Iranian arsenal might be available to the Western powers.

This potential no longer exists as a result of the removal of the Shah and Iran's economic difficulties. In consequence, Soviet concern for Iranian military capabilities has been substantially diminished. Whereas the thrust of the Shah's policy was designed to inhibit Soviet probing and restrict infringements of Iranian sovereignty by posing a credible risk of retaliation, his successors have eschewed this course, while eliminating Western access to Iranian facilities. The granting of overflight rights for Soviet transport aircraft in future crises comparable to those in the Middle East in 1973 and the Horn of Africa 1977–8 is thus appreciably more likely. Indeed, given the present combination of weak leadership and a neutralist orientation, it is difficult to envisage any practical resistance to Soviet assertion of overflight rights.

The change in regime and the shift away from the military build-up and pro-Western orientation will have allayed previous Soviet anxieties for a considerable period. Apart from the curtailment and cancellation of military purchases, one immediate consequence has been the restriction of American military activities. Curiously, Soviet comments on Western monitoring facilities in Iran have always been sparse, and reactions to the Shah's plans to build an electronic intelligence capability, *Project Ibex*, were desultory, although in 1976 Radio Moscow conceded that there were circles in the US 'who express regret at the lack of the possibility of using the strategic significance of this border to the advantage of the CIA and the Pentagon'.[31] The five American stations in Iran which included two run by the CIA, at Kabkhan and Behshar, had two distinct functions: to monitor the radio traffic of the Soviet forces in the southern USSR (in part at least for evidence of heightened military activity), and to monitor Soviet missile testing. When they were closed, as a result of the 1979 Iranian revolution, the Soviet Union reported the fact, but without any conspicuous sense of celebration.

The termination of Iran's arms build-up and the elimination of a strong Western military presence with access to bases and monitoring facilities there was an important gain for the USSR, and has transformed the strategic environment in her favour. What is less clear is whether it represents a gain in Soviet influence. The decline of Western influence may be followed, not by a corresponding increase in Soviet influence, but by a loss of influence for *all* outside powers.

The Persian Gulf States
Despite lying rather close to the USSR, the Persian Gulf has been effectively insulated from

Soviet influence since World War II. With growing power and expanding interests the USSR has sought to remedy this situation since the British withdrawal, yet she has been careful to avoid precipitate actions lest they provoke a Western response. Her primary object in the past decade has been to hasten the decline of Western power and influence and break the Western political monopoly in the region. A minimal objective has therefore been to obtain a voice in Gulf affairs in order to assure her own access to the region. While accepting the concept of 'mutual access' she is unwilling to accept Western dominance, or indeed the 'equal exclusion' of outside powers.

In the Soviet view, the concept of equality of influence in the region is of doubtful validity, given the proximity of the Gulf to Soviet territory and the Soviet Union's 'Asian' dimension. She has therefore resisted any tendency by third powers to equate the super-powers. The prevailing situation seems to her to reflect an inequality of influence in any case, first, because of the residual Western presence through numerous military contract personnel in Saudi Arabia (and, until recently, in Iran) and, secondly, because of Western access to military facilities, (Jufayr in Bahrain, Masirah in Oman). In addition, the West's diplomatic presence in (and commercial relations with) the littoral states are still far more extensive than those of the USSR. Moscow has embassies in only Teheran, Baghdad and Kuwait and her local allies have tended to be either politically isolated (Iraq) or geographically remote (PDRY).

The weakening of the Gulf States' ties with Western countries and the encouragement of alternative governments or policies more congenial to Soviet interests has been an important aspect of Soviet policy. This has coloured the Soviet approach both to a potential regional security arrangement and to the definition of detente in the area. Pro-Western and conservative states comprise a majority in the Persian Gulf, and until recently, encouraged by a pro-Western Iran, they had, in the name of 'excluding outside powers', sought to create a mechanism for conserving the existing order and solidifying Western influence while excluding that of the USSR. Soviet opposition was not due solely to the tacit support which Western powers · extended to the concept; it stemmed rather

from a deep hostility to what was seen as a new pattern of relations between regional states and the West – a pattern which could become a model for other regions. Neither indigenous in inspiration nor local in function, such regional collective arrangements, by creating military links between states, potentially posed new problems for the projection of Soviet power and the extension of Soviet influence.

The second component of the attempt to reduce Western influence in the region lies in the Soviet attitude towards change and her definition of detente. Aware of the political and military realities, the USSR had adopted a benevolent or sanguine approach to change in the region while avoiding confrontations with the West or compromising her state-to-state relations with local powers (which she sees as intrinsically favourable to her interests). In contrast, the Western powers have viewed the prospect of rapid change as potentially disruptive, as inviting exploitation or intervention by outside powers, and have therefore looked for procedures and institutions to arrest and manage change. Although the Soviet Union sees detente as necessary for the avoidance of dangerous confrontations, she does not accept the Western view that equates detente with the stabilization of politics in specific regions.[32]

The faith that any change will favour Soviet interests is understandable in the context of the Persian Gulf, where, until 1978, the Soviet presence was confined to a narrow foothold. But the natural Soviet propensity for assisting change has in practice been limited and cautious. As a means of countering Western ideas, the USSR has promoted her own version of a regional security structure – an Asian collective security arrangement, apparently to be built up on a series of bilateral pacts between the regional states and the USSR, as exemplified by Soviet relations with Iraq.

The Soviet view of the region in the light both of its strategic importance and the USSR's growing influence, highlights her major concerns. An understanding of these interests followed by a discussion of contemporary Soviet policy in a later section, provides the basis for an evaluation of trends in future Soviet policy.

As indicated, Soviet perceptions of the region in the recent past have been coloured by a position of inferiority and a lack of historical interaction with, or presence in, most of the littoral states. As a result the USSR has tended to emphasize her opposition to various aspects of the region's politics or initiatives, rather than to propose meaningful initiatives herself. She has been nothing if not consistent in the past decade, and her first reaction to Western ideas for a regional security arrangement in 1968 could be directly applied to US hints at a similar idea in February 1979:

> The ruling circles of the US and Britain have been hatching plans for knocking together a military bloc under the aegis of the Persian Gulf states . . . . The Soviet Union . . . realizing that the above-mentioned plans of neo-colonialism are directed also against the security of the southern frontiers of the USSR, firmly comes out against any new attempts . . . to interfere in the affairs of the Persian Gulf countries and impose their will on them.[33]

Western co-operation with local régimes is viewed as a deliberate policy cultivated to cover Britain's withdrawal, and it is this, in the Soviet view, that accounts for and explains all other developments in Persian Gulf politics. The quest for a 'regional' security arrangement and the maintenance of bases thus appear to the Soviet Union to reflect a policy of maintaining Western domination through local clients when, in the aftermath of Vietnam, a direct US presence is no longer politically feasible.

Soviet concern about the possible establishment of a Western grouping as an extension of CENTO has long been evident. The US policy of reliance on Iran and Saudi Arabia was seen as the first step in a 'military-political alliance' between these states and the West which would complement the US defence umbrella in the region. It was argued that the function of this proposed pact was ambiguous because the USSR posed no threat, and that indeed it was the Western states who maintained bases, militarized the region and flaunted their naval presence.[34]

Neither the formal demise of CENTO nor Iran's turn towards neutralism will have allayed Soviet anxieties about a regional pact. Any military grouping ('bloc' in Soviet parlance) is unacceptable. CENTO gave the USSR a convenient propaganda target in the region – it

could be exploited as a relic of the cold war, it was said to contradict the 'spirit of the times', and it was used to accentuate divisions between the Arabs and Iran and indeed its disbandment was, in the Soviet view, a precondition for the establishment of harmonious relations in the region.[35] But it was not necessarily a sufficient condition. The USSR's paramount concern was the movement towards the creation of a regional security arrangement, which she saw as aimed at supressing change: 'the plans to set up a closed political-military bloc in the Gulf region may mean the establishment of an alliance between the reactionary forces in the region and imperialism . . . which is against the national liberation movement and the progressive movement of the Arab peoples.'[36]

The reconciliation of Iran and Iraq in March 1975 increased the political momentum towards some type of agreement among the littoral states on concerting their policies and reaching a consensus on a common approach to local conflicts and on the exclusion of outside powers. Despite distrust and rivalry among the three major powers – Iran, Saudi Arabia and Iraq – and their differing orientations towards the super-powers, there existed a core of agreement that regional affairs should be managed autonomously. The Soviet Union's criticisms of the meeting to work on this concept, which was held in Muscat in late 1976, illustrated her view. First, the aim was not the 'genuine security' of the region but a device to 'maintain the *status quo*' in an alliance between 'imperialism and local reactionary forces'. Second, the failure of the conference was a setback for those states who sought to make the region an 'imperialist protectorate' or to create fictitious threats about Communism, or to impose a 'military holy alliance' in the service of counter-revolution on the area.[37]

In the Soviet view, any approach to regional security which sought to maintain a surreptitious Western presence, while promoting conservative policies designed to exclude the USSR and contain change, was thoroughly unacceptable. The first priority was the dismantling of all remnants of a Western presence. A key target here were Western 'bases', which have been criticized as constituting a grave danger to the region. Oman was strongly criticized in 1975 when she seemed ready to offer US aircraft staging rights on Masirah Island. Soviet commentaries noted that public opinion in the region was against this, since it represented 'a direct threat to the security of the countries of the region'.

In contrast, Bahrain's 1977 decision to terminate the agreement under which a small US Naval detachment (MIDEASTFOR) was homeported at Jufayr was welcomed.

The Soviet Union, seeing these bases as links in a much wider strategic network from Taiwan to Diego Garcia in the Indian Ocean, has skilfully fed the endemic distrust of a foreign military presence in the region and increased the inhibitions of states such as Saudi Arabia which, though vulnerable, may be reluctant to expose themselves politically by welcoming, or permitting, foreign bases on their territory.

A related target of Soviet attack has been the military build-up in the Persian Gulf states. Her concerns here are similar to those concerning the Iranian build-up, but without the same proximity of immediacy. The emphasis is not so much on the direct threat to Soviet security as on the impact of the expanding and deepening of the concomitant political relationship with the West. The 'flood of arms' is said to stimulate an 'arms race' to divide the littoral states, to 'pit' some against others, to extinguish national liberation movements, and serve as rewards for military bases. In addition it allegedly increases the recipient's dependence on the supplier state and constitutes a threat to his independence. The arms sales are said to cement a relationship between the West and regional powers, who thereby become extensions of Western influence. Saudi Arabia and Iran were thus seen as actively using financial resources as a means of exercising pressure on other states 'to eliminate the revolutionary essence of their policies'.[38]

Indeed, while the Soviet Union has consistently urged the dissolution of military alliances, she has not therefore renounced support for national liberation movements. In one Soviet commentator's view, while 'continuing to support the elimination of the military presence and military bases in the Persian Gulf region' she would also 'continue to support the people's liberation struggles. This applies completely to the national liberation struggles launched today by the peoples of the Persian Gulf region'.[39]

Soviet analysts concede no contradiction in this. While reserving the right to support national liberation wars (as in Dhofar), they berate Saudi Arabia's support for Oman: 'What the monarchy fears most is the impact of the progressive changes taking place in neighbouring Arab countries'.[40] While parallels between the Dhofari secessionists and Persian Gulf politics were seldom made directly, they were often implicit in commentaries: 'it is still too early to speak of the prospects of the Popular Front in the other Persian Gulf emirates, but Oman is definitely being bogged down more and more in a long and hopeless war against the Dhofar patriots'.[41] In the Soviet view the Dhofar rebellion was an anti-imperialist national liberation movement, enjoying the support of the masses, and therefore fully deserving of assistance; Iran's support for the Oman government was the suppression of a popular movement, not the repulse of an external enemy.

In reality the link between Oman and the other Persian Gulf states had been made by the insurgents who, by changing their name in June 1970 – from the Dhofar Liberation Front to the Popular Front for the Liberation of the Occupied Arab Gulf (PFLOAG) – had expanded their aims to include the overthrow of the 'reactionary' governments in the Gulf as well. Soviet commentaries did not disguise the fact that their support for the 'patriots' in Oman stemmed from their dislike of the government, which they considered pro-Western, and they maintained that the 'Oman patriots have never endangered the security of any Persian Gulf states'. Nevertheless it has been a consistent theme in the Soviet approach to the Persian Gulf region that 'the prime determinant of the entire military and political situation in the Middle East and Persian Gulf area is the Arab anti-imperialist liberation movement'.[42]

In the Soviet view the slow eradication of Western presence, the existence of local rivalries, and the inherent contradictions of a rich but vulnerable region, will in time assure the Soviet Union of increased influence. She has therefore sought to define her own preferences for political relations in the region. In essence these consist of negative and positive elements. The former identifies 'imperialists' as the threat to the region and defines the impermissible – for example, the establishment of local pacts (as a substitute for a military alliance) with regional states assuming greater responsibilities. Her positive suggestions involve less expenditure on arms, the dismantling of foreign bases and alliances, and the conclusion of agreements on non-aggression and respect for sovereignty among the littoral states. In contrast to existing alliances or projected 'regional security arrangements', (viewed as 'closed military political groupings' of right-wing régimes) she advocates a continent-wide system of collective security in Asia. She emphasizes a 'logical and comprehensive' approach based on equality among the participants, and on principles such as the non-use of force and an end to foreign intervention, an approach which emphatically shuns the characteristics of 'military political alliances'.[43]

Originally proposed a decade ago, the Soviet Asian collective security arrangement still has to gain any significant supporters. It does, however, indicate the wider context within which Persian Gulf affairs are viewed, and, although still not defined with any precision, the concept has been sufficiently clarified by commentators to indicate certain elements considered significant by the Soviet government. In essence the proposal urges co-operation among Asian states on the basis of the renunciation of force, respect for sovereignty, non-interference in internal affairs and the development of economic ties. As a substitute for alliances and military bases, which must be terminated, Moscow urges economic co-operation among the Asian states and the conclusion of bilateral and multilateral agreements based on these principles as steps towards the realization of a larger Asian security system.

The primary motivation is to stimulate or accelerate the dissolution of existing alliances and discourage the creation of weaker substitutes. It is argued that these alliances are anachronisms, that they cannot deal with conflicts among Asian states, indeed that they are the source of many of the regional antagonisms which have divided states into 'opposing groupings' and strengthened the influence of outside capitalist states.

The USSR has herself cultivated bilateral agreements on the model of her treaties with Iraq and India, seeing them as the building blocks of a larger continental security edifice rather than as ends in themselves. In practice though, the USSR's support for bilateral co-operation among regional states has been highly selective – India and Iraq are encouraged, while Iran and Saudi Arabia have been criticized – and she has actively discouraged any measures of regional co-operation with potential security implications that appear likely to exclude her. The central theme of her approach is to create the basis for becoming the principal participant in continental affairs and the power that must be consulted on all issues affecting Asia. Her minimum objective is to assure her own unrestricted access to the continent, but the means used seem designed to achieve preponderant and perhaps exclusive influence in Asia.

The 'Asian' formula guarantees the Soviet Union, as an Asian power, membership of, and hence preponderance in, such a security arrangement, and it provides a criterion and a platform for criticism of the presence of non-Asian states. The formula has tactical advantages; in addition to staking out Soviet interests, it facilitates the loosening of alliance structures by offering an alternative security model. Furthermore, it helps the USSR to duck the pressures and painful choices caused by regional conflicts between states she cannot afford to alienate.[44] By being flexible yet comprehensive the proposal can be developed or modified as tactical circumstances dictate. For example, it can be applied not only to the Persian Gulf and Indian sub-continent but to East Asia, to the Indian Ocean, to ASEAN and to ANZUS as well as (until recently) to CENTO. The same themes can be emphasized (the dismantling of foreign bases, etc.) and the same alternatives offered.

There are also defensive considerations. The pursuit of a general agreement on principles of international conduct on non-intervention and respect for territorial integrity reflects an interest in stable border régimes. The right to unconstrained access is also a motive even if the neutralization of regions and the assurance of preponderance are simultaneously emphasized. The formal acceptance of bilateral or even multilateral agreement on the principles of security suggests at least a potential willingness to recognize the necessity of regional security arrangements, but this is strongly undermined by the insistence that any regional co-operation be devoid of any military, or even any practical security, dimension. This is true of the Soviet approach in general. Existing security arrangements are to be replaced by agreements on general principles; foreign military bases and advisers are to be withdrawn, while Soviet involvement in all aspects of Asian affairs is officially recognized.

For some of the Gulf littoral states however, the offer is not altogether attractive. They may not want to trade existing security arrangements for agreement on general principles nor to exchange a countervailing power as an ally in favour of a proximate power. They are asked to prove their good intentions by accepting Soviet political involvement in Asia, relinquishing the right to achieve security through alliances, and acquiescing in the Soviet right to support national liberation wars, however widely defined. If this does not amount to ratifying Soviet hegemony, it is a close approximation to that state of affairs.

III. IRAN AND THE GULF IN SOVIET POLICY

Iran

Soviet policy towards Iran in the post-war era falls into three distinct phases, the last of which ended with the revolution. The tactics and policies employed in these phases have fluctuated but the goal has been unvarying: to detach Iran from her Western alignment and to increase her own influence in Teheran.

1945–62

In the immediate aftermath of the war, Soviet diplomacy was characteristically crude. The reversals in Azerbaijan and Mahabad, where Soviet support for secessionist movements had failed, were followed by threats about the consequences for Teheran of a Western alignment. These threats succeeded only in accelerating Iran's search for a security guarantee – first in the Baghdad pact in 1955,[45] and subsequently in a direct association with the United States, in a loosely worded bilateral mutual security pact which took the form of an Executive Agreement (1959). The principal bone of contention between Moscow and Iran in this period (and indeed throughout the past three decades) was Iran's right to buy arms and obtain military assistance. The Soviet Union viewed the presence of foreign military advisers on Iranian territory during the Cold War as especially provocative. She therefore railed against the construction of 'bases' on Iranian soil, neglecting to define the term precisely but applying it to any military construction she disliked. This expansive definition of her security, combined with a reluctance to specify the conditions under which her own and Iran's security requirements could be reconciled, rendered it difficult for the Iranian government to placate her without jeopardizing Iran's security.

1962–73

In the decade after 1962, Soviet–Iranian relations entered a second phase. The Soviet leadership accepted assurances that Iran's territory would not be used as a missile base and found Teheran eager to take advantage of the thaw in the cold war. The development of technology extending the range of missiles meant that their stationing on the peripheries of the USSR was no longer essential or likely. Furthermore, the Shah, suspicious of the new Kennedy Administration, found it expedient to improve his relations with the USSR, and to diminish his reliance on the US. Soviet criticisms abated, relations improved, official delegations exchanged visits and a new *modus vivendi* was established. Moscow encouraged Iran's interest in bridge-building and welcomed the new equidistance which she adopted *vis-à-vis* the two blocs. This is best illustrated by the growth in trade between the two states, an aim consciously pursued by the Shah in order to give the Soviet Union a stake in a stable and tranquil region, and by the Soviet Union in order to demonstrate to its southern neighbour the tangible benefits accruing from a 'normalized' relationship.

Trade expanded tenfold between 1966 and 1973. The most striking indicator of the changed relationship was the 1966 agreement on arms, under which Iran bought trucks and smaller military vehicles for $110 million of hard currency. In the 1970s, further cross-bloc purchases included SAM–7, SAM–9, RPG–7, ZSU–57–2 and ZSU–23–4 anti-aircraft weapons. Less dramatically visible was the development of solid economic ventures. The centre-piece of co-operation was the Soviet construction of a steel mill in Isfahan (in central Iran) which went into operation in 1972, and has since had its capacity expanded considerably; Iran's payment was in natural gas. A heavy machinery plant with a 50,000-ton capacity was built by the USSR in Arak. In addition to heavy industry, an area in which the USSR has considerable experience, trade has been concentrated where geographical proximity is useful: for example in the development of the joint frontier region near the Caspian, in the construction of electrical power plants, dams and grain silos, and by the provision of overland transit facilities. Soviet economic credits and grants totalling $521 million were extended between 1966 and 1970, a period when the Iranian exchequer had yet to benefit from a large oil income.[46] A large complement of Soviet technicians followed this growth in trade.[47]

Because the industries provided were basic, requiring few intermediate goods, it was argued that Iran's dependence on this trade was limited. Nevertheless, the agreements were politically significant, and Soviet willingness to construct the steel mill was particularly important, for several Western countries had refused to finance it on economic grounds. Soviet commentaries emphasized repeatedly that trade relations with the USSR are mutually beneficial, balanced, non-exploitive, and politically stabilizing, whereas alignment with the West had meant economic and political subservience. A more independent foreign policy, in which relations with the USSR and the Eastern Bloc were expanded and consolidated, assured the development of industries which the imperialists had blocked. Trade was also welcomed for its political effect as a stabilizing factor in the wider, regional context.[48]

The Soviet Union was careful to nurture the improved ties with Iran throughout the 1960s. Unable to support Iran in her dispute with Iraq (because of important commitments in the latter state), she did the next best thing by adopting an impartial stance – for example, when renewed clashes broke out between the two countries after 1969 over their river frontier. She also expressed no opinion on Iran's contentious claim to the Bahrain archipelago (a claim which was finally relinquished in 1970). On the question of the ownership of three islands in the Persian Gulf disputed between Iran, Sharjah and Ras al Khaimah, the USSR again expressed no official

position (though her official encyclopedia identified them as Iranian), and even after Iran occupied the islands in November 1971, which Iraq and Libya condemned as an 'invasion of Arab land', she remained silent.

The temptation to exploit mutual suspicion between Iran and the Arab states was resisted, however, because it would have upset the development of relations with Iran, to which Moscow attached considerable importance. Second, in the transitional phase before Britain's actual withdrawal from the Gulf, any sign of Soviet involvement might have caused a reassessment of policy. Third, overt support for radical states such as Iraq would have propelled the conservative states together and increased the likelihood of concerted policies, while support for Iran would have antagonized the numerous Arab states in and around the Persian Gulf.

For the USSR the improvement in relations with Iran between 1962–73 represented substantial progress. The growth of trade was a factor in this improvement. Representative of peaceful intentions, it was clearly being used to encourage the detachment of Iran (and Turkey, where a parallel process was in progress) from the Western camp. The political cost to the USSR was small, involving only the sacrifice of some Communists in Iran[49] and the avoidance of stands in regional politics likely to antagonize Iran. The gains were considerable and included the loosening of Iran's ties with the West, greater Iranian sensitivity to Soviet interests, and the stabilization of the border region, which corresponded with her own predilection for conservatism and predictability.[50] In 1965 the Shah, with some hyperbole, had told his hosts in Moscow that 'If a state could choose its neighbours itself, we would choose you'. By 1970 the Soviet leadership had become equally adept at flattery, suggesting that alliances were no longer needed for 'Iran is now strong enough to pick her friends'.[51]

1974–9

The third phase of Soviet policy, starting in 1974, began with a reversion to a more hostile and competitive relationship and ended with the overthrow of the monarchy and the ending of Iran's pro-Western orientation, marking a watershed in Soviet–Iranian relations. The hostility arose because of the appearance of a more assertive Iran, which posed for the USSR the problem of adapting to the new dynamism of a previously docile neighbour.

After 1974 the balance in Iran's security policy moved progressively away from accommodation and towards military deterrence and a wider and more ambitious quest for independence. Iran's more broadly activist policy on regional issues, together with growing Soviet involvement in Asia, resulted in increased rivalry and disagreement on a widening number of issues. Foremost among these was the issue of Iran's arms build-up – its scope and its pace, together with its increased political dependency on Western suppliers – which, from the Soviet perspective, was the most concrete indicator of her move from rough equidistance between the blocs to closer integration with the West. Reflecting this shift and flowing from it, Iran's diplomacy in the region was more intelligible. In the Soviet view, Iran's policies supported western interests on a host of issues. For example, Teheran's promotion of a security arrangement in the Persian Gulf, encompassing military co-operation but including only the littoral states, was a recipe for its domination by the pro-Western states. Similarly Iranian military support for the pro-Western Omani government was seen as constituting a warning to national liberation movements, which the conservative states, together with the West (in this case Britain), were determined to punish. Iran's guarantee of Oman's airspace against the PDRY and the institution of joint naval patrols near the Hormuz Straits in 1974–5 appeared to be pretexts for the assertion of Iranian (and Western) dominance in this strategic area.

Indeed, Iran's diplomacy throughout Asia was seen as antithetical to both Soviet interests and those of her allies. For example, the Shah's promotion of an Indian Ocean Common Market, which could gradually become an instrument for co-operation in the security field, was limited in membership to the littoral states and seemed to constitute an alternative concept to the Asian collective security scheme which would include the USSR. Similarly Iranian economic assistance to India and Afghanistan seemed explicitly designed to reduce those states' dependence on the Soviet Union, while support for President Sadat in the Middle East and for Somalia in the

Horn of Africa also ran directly counter to Soviet policies. Finally, Iran's steady cultivation of China after 1974 and the latter's outspoken support for Iran's military build-up touched a particularly sensitive nerve in the leadership of the Soviet Union.

Despite these divergences, which might have been construed as 'provocation', Soviet policy towards Iran retained its mix of firmness and caution. On the issue of Iranian arms procurement, the USSR was well placed to respond, because of her unambiguous interest in the matter (which we have already discussed), because of doubts which she could exploit about the wisdom of the arms build-up among some groups both within Iran and in the West, and because contiguity could be used to make political points. The Shah was repeatedly and bluntly warned about the consequences of a continued arms build-up in 1973, 1974 and 1976. There were consistent Soviet overflights of Iranian territory after 1974 (although Soviet policy was merciless when the issue was infringement of her own airspace [52]), and an ostentatious infringement of Iran's airspace was arranged during the internal upheaval in Iran in 1978.[53] The demonstrative and symbolic use of force to remind neighbours of their vulnerability or to serve notice of her concerns is standard diplomatic practice for the Soviet Union.

In January 1976 the Soviet Union conducted military manoeuvres, *Kavkaz*, which were undoubtedly a hint to Iran. Similarly, the presence of 2,100 tanks (in 12 divisions) in the Transcaucasus Military District 'is not unconnected with Iran's military programmes'.[54] The *Kavkaz* manoeuvres included 2,000 tanks and about 130,000 troops (ten mechanized infantry divisions, one tank division and an airborne division) and penetration operations on the USSR–Iran–Turkey border area were practised.[55]

The Soviet forces in the Transcaucasus 'could certainly overwhelm Iran's capability and defense',[56] and the USSR's qualitative and quantitative improvements across the entire spectrum of military activities, including air and sea lift, her naval programme and her increasing interventionary forces have added a new dimension to her diplomacy. These new capabilities have made easier the accomplishment of tasks previously constrained by geography and space and, furthermore, have enabled the USSR to intervene in new areas which have not hitherto been defined as essential for Soviet security. They have strengthened existing predispositions to define security more widely. Iran's military build-up appears to have been viewed as inherently dangerous, less for its direct effect on Soviet security (for it was more than matched by Soviet military expansion), than for the political and military constraints it seemed to impose on the expansion of Soviet influence, especially in the Persian Gulf.

The Soviet Union, recognizing that military strength may not lead automatically to increasing influence, nonetheless remains sensitive to the proposition that forces in being continue to be a potent factor in the perceptions and calculations of states, particularly neighbouring states. Territorial proximity magnifies the impact of military power. Furthermore, since Stalin she has been conscious that converting military power into political influence requires nimbleness in order to avoid pushing the target further into the other camp (as happened with Turkey and Iran in the 1940s). The prudent exploitation of military power has therefore required neither explicit threats nor ultimata, but rather its retention as a latent threat while more general instruments of pressure or coercive diplomacy are used (e.g., support for internal dissidents, subversion, propaganda attacks, troop manoeuvres, frontier incursions and support for regional opponents). A reputation for bullying and the impression of power can earn political dividends, and regional states' perception of Soviet persistence and irresistible military power encourages caution. At the least, it becomes a new and weighty factor to be taken account of in making decisions, which may increase the incentives for its appeasement.

The conduct of Soviet policy has thus been prudent and firm, exploiting Iran's weakness but acknowledging practical interests. In addition to border pressures and diplomatic *démarches* to demonstrate Iran's vulnerability, she has also taken other initiatives in the region. She armed Iraq, Iran's rival until March 1975, and attacked Iranian participation in CENTO, both to enhance Iran's isolation and to accentuate divisions within the Persian Gulf. She has given indirect support to states antagonistic towards Iran (such as Libya or the PDRY) and material assistance for insurgencies (such as those in Dhofar, or

Baluchistan). The Soviet Union welcomed the April 1978 coup in Afghanistan which deposed President Daoud, who was well disposed towards Iran's diplomacy in the sub-continent, and helped to replace him with a Marxist-Leninist régime more closely aligned with the USSR.

She has, at the same time, sought to allay Iranian fears. For example, after the conclusion of the Soviet Friendship Treaty with Iraq on 9 April 1972, the USSR was careful to point out that it was 'not directed against any other country, it does not infringe upon anybody's legitimate interests', and to place it firmly in the larger context of the Soviet Asian security initiatives. Between 1972 and 1974 she sought to obtain Iran's support for these initiatives. But while agreeing with the Iranian formulation that questions relating to the Persian Gulf should be settled by the Gulf states themselves, the Soviet Union made two provisos: foreign 'bases' in the region were not admissible, and any Gulf security arrangements must be a step towards the creation of an Asian security arrangement (in which the USSR would be involved). No amount of diplomatic drafting in communiqùes could reconcile the differing priorities of the Soviet Union and Iran.[57] Nevertheless, in 1974 the Soviet leadership suggested that her Asian security proposal offered an alternative to the arms race (in which Iran was allegedly engaged with Iraq.) [58]

After 1974 it was clear that the Soviet Union and Iran differed fundamentally on the *membership* of a possible security arrangement ('Asian' versus littoral states), on the *sequence* in which measures were to be achieved (dismantling of bases and the reduction of arms versus prior stabilization) and on the *content* or procedure of a security arrangement (agreement on principles versus practical military co-operation). After 1974 the Soviet Union therefore made no further effort to convince Iran that the two positions were similar.

Despite these political differences, trade relations between the two states grew, and the Soviet Union made much of the theme that co-operation on the joint border reflected the stability of the relationship and contributed to regional security. Although most of the trade generated by Iran's large oil revenues was with the EEC, the US and Japan, commerce with the USSR also grew, and in 1976 a Joint Economic

Commission was established to plan and supervise this expansion. Bilateral trade in 1977 exceeded $1 billion and was growing rapidly (Soviet exports grew by 50 per cent in 1977 alone), so that by the end of the year Iran was the USSR's largest non-military trading partner in the Third World (and her sixteenth largest overall). In addition to the expansion of trade in traditional areas such as coal, steel and heavy industry (some of it believed to have involved deferred payment terms), Soviet assistance was extended to the construction of electrical generating stations in Ramin, Ahwaz and Isfahan. She also provided Iran with electricity in mid-1977 when the latter was faced with power failures and shortages which were causing political problems. The importance to Iran of the Soviet overland transit route for the shipment of goods to and from Europe between 1974 and 1976 – a period of port congestion – can scarcely be exaggerated. Here, as elsewhere in the trade relationship, the pragmatic aspects of interdependence between two unequal neighbours was demonstrated to be a stabilizing influence, even though political interests increasingly diverged.

The Persian Gulf States

In the Persian Gulf, Soviet interests lie in improving access and influence, rather than in achieving the political preponderance sought in Iran. In this region, as elsewhere, how these aims are sought and the extent to which they are achieved depends on both the super–power relationship and on local conditions. The prevailing state of these relations, the military balance, the credibility of security assurances and the solidity of alliances profoundly affect (and may indeed determine) the propensity for risk-taking or probing by the rival power. Unregulated competition between them in the Third World may generate competitive, or preclusive, interventions for access, or denial of access. Yet if the overall super-power relationship is the permissive factor affecting the exercise of power, regional conditions influence its use and effectiveness. Regional tensions may encourage and facilitate, while local harmony may discourage or complicate, external influences and outside intervention.

Local conditions in the Persian Gulf appear advantageous to the Soviet search for influence –

weak governments and institutions, rapid modernization likely to aggravate political discontent, a massive influx of arms, a narrow base of power, and local rivalries which are exploitable and in which surrogate operations may be possible. In addition, Soviet proximity and influence on the peripheries of the region may be counted as advantages. Yet the constraints are equally impressive. Soviet diplomacy has to balance a number of competing desiderata: to exploit targets of opportunity yet at the same time to secure stable borders; to influence allies (which implies entanglement), while also maintaining a free hand; [59] to express commitment to one ally without antagonizing its rival – also an ally – and the policy of pursuing 'controlled tensions', while recognizing the risks arising from loss of control, escalation and confrontation.

In the Persian Gulf the USSR is constrained by the need for caution and the need to hedge her bets against possible reverses. She is not in a position to control or manage domestic trends which are unforeseeable in their ultimate consequences and yet are decisive in shaping the day-to-day politics of this region. Nor are the local states likely to be passive bystanders: they can limit the options and affect the risks of external interventions, and they can compete with outside states for local influence by providing cash or by securing alternative sources of arms, thereby reducing the dependency of the target states on other outside powers.

Soviet diplomacy has been hampered by the lack of historical ties with many of the littoral states. In the era of paramount British power there were no Soviet diplomatic relations, save with Iraq and Iran. Since Britain's withdrawal from the Gulf, only Kuwait (in 1963) has established relations with Moscow (as has the PDRY, outside the Gulf). Soviet policy has been further constrained by the essential conservatism of most of the littoral states and by their deference to the views of Saudi Arabia, which has so far refused to re-establish ties with a 'godless' Communist state.[60] In addition, those Arab states with which the Soviet Union has had close relations, Iraq and the PDRY, have been politically isolated from the mainstream of Arab politics and therefore ill-suited as launching points for Soviet influence. Consequently, although neither of the super-powers has a formal presence in the region other than through embassies, Soviet influence on the Arabian peninsula is circumscribed both by Western diplomatic advantage and by limited commercial or military roles.[61]

In this setting the USSR has interpreted ideology flexibly and pragmatically to further relations with otherwise unattractive reactionary states. She has sought to identify distinctions among the littoral states. Saudi Arabia, Qatar and the United Arab Emirates (UAE) are seen as patriarchal feudal régimes, while the Yemen Arab Republic (YAR) is viewed as one stage more advanced, just entering capitalism.[62] Bahrain and Kuwait are rated higher in the capitalist stage, since they already have a proletariat and incipient class conflict.

Given the absence of a firm basis for influence, a high priority in Soviet policy has been the securing of access to the Persian Gulf and the promotion of the principle of maximum freedom of navigation. This should be contrasted with the joint efforts of Iran and Oman to promote a restrictive legal régime governing the rights of outside powers to transit the Straits of Hormuz; these arise from a profoundly divergent interpretation of the threat facing the region. While Iran (and, tacitly, Saudi Arabia) sought to exclude the navies of both super-powers from maintaining a permanent presence in the Gulf and from unregulated access, Iraq (and the USSR) have seen it differently. Iraq's Information Minister put it baldly:

> Some [littoral states] said we should not have American and Soviet navies here, and we were against this because it was a way to keep only American influence and exclude the Soviets. The Americans are already here . . . . Who is endangering the security of the Gulf? We don't see any present danger, more important is free passage in the Gulf.[63]

The Soviet Union has used Iraq as a vehicle for the dissemination of her own views in the Gulf, and her pressure on the smaller states against a Gulf pact has concentrated on the same theme. She has quoted either Iraq's views or those of some other 'Persian Gulf' source (such as the Bahrain Liberation Movement) to give her propaganda a spurious authenticity, and the smaller states are reminded that a military alliance 'could affect the freedom of navigation' and that imperialist and reactionary states seek to dominate the area 'on the pretext of collective responsibility for freedom of navigation in the Gulf.' In 1975 Soviet Foreign Minister Gromyko told his Kuwaiti counterpart, that, in addition to the elimination of military bases, detente required that 'freedom of shipping should be guaranteed in the Persian Gulf and Hormuz Straits'.[64]

To prevent the aggregation of power through collective arrangements, the Soviet Union has sought to use a receptive regional environment to intensify distrust between Iranians and Arabs and between the Arab states. By so doing, the position of her regional allies (such as Iraq) are also relatively strengthened. Iran's relations with Israel were a natural target, and CENTO was described as an alliance with 'anti-Arab' policies,[65] and, after 1974, references to Iran–Arab rivalry and competition were frequent. Iran's assistance to Oman was cited as an obstacle to the improvement of relations with the Arab states, and her military intervention said to be the criterion by which her intentions should be judged on the Arab littoral. Iran's arms purchases were sometimes singled out as intended for local adventures, while Saudi Arabia was identified as a 'Western tool' in competition with Iran. A US government report that differentiated between Iran and Saudi Arabia was pounced upon as evidence that Washington might 'use' Iran against the Arab states.[66]

In addition to stimulating rivalry between Iran and the Arab states, the Soviet Union has emphasized the (alleged) inherent competition between the larger and smaller states, justifying and encouraging the resistance of the latter to proposals made by their larger neighbours. 'Is it not clear,' Moscow Radio asked rhetorically, 'that what is meant here are the big states in the Gulf which want to establish their military and political domination over the region?' 'The collective security pact', another commentary concluded, 'cannot have any benefit for the small Arab countries'.[67]

Freed from the inhibitions imposed by diplomatic relations, official Soviet comments on Saudi Arabia have been harsh. Yet, while arguing that the plan to set up a security arrangement was connected primarily with Saudi Arabia's 'leadership ambitions and its drive to become the focal point for reactionary . . . forces', the Soviet Union has mixed with her criticisms clear indications that she is prepared to establish diplomatic relations with Riyadh and that differences in outlook, ideology and religion should not preclude it.[68]

However, tactical adjustments and cosmetic changes apart, Soviet interests and policies will continue to diverge fundamentally from those of Saudi Arabia. The basis for Soviet opposition to a Gulf security arrangement, after all, has been put most forthrightly: 'In practice the plans to set up a closed political military bloc in the Gulf region may mean the establishment of an alliance which is against the national liberation movement and the progressive movement of the Arab peoples'.[69]

Whereas Moscow welcomes these movements and retains the right to assist them, it acknowledges that Saudi and other states' views are different: 'Leaders of the reactionary, feudal and royal régimes of the Gulf states fear even the murmur of economic and social changes . . . . Saudi rulers need the arms to quell the national liberation movement in their own country as well as the entire region.'[70]

Soviet criticisms of a regional security arrangement have had the merit of comprehensiveness, in that they connect the aims of its proponents with 'imperialist' objectives, making it difficult for potential adherents to give any public support to the idea. As noted in the preceding section, the objective in any case is not to convert the region but to inhibit it from maintaining any formal Western connection. Iran's change of orientation is doubly significant here. The revolution swept away the Shah, the most active proponent of regional co-operation (and the man who had introduced a formal security arrangement with the West), and his departure provided the USSR with a telling propaganda point. It has also exposed Saudi Arabia to political pressure, as the only remaining pro-Western state of any size in the region.

The inadmissibility of a regional security arrangement has been the primary and consistent theme reflecting Soviet concern. In the Soviet view such an arrangement would be regional only in name. It would act to contain the 'liberation struggle' as a substitute for a direct Western presence. It would be dominated by Saudi Arabia and pre-revolutionary Iran,

working at the behest of the US and Britain, who would control their clients through the arms-supply relationship.[71]

Rather than actively promoting an alternative scheme, however, Soviet policy has focused on discouraging any moves towards regional rapprochement. In this the Soviet Union has been assisted by the latent antagonisms and suspicions within the region which are partly due to historical antipathies, partly to mutual ignorance and partly to structural causes arising from significant disparities in size and power. Kuwait, for example, has sought to use her ties with the Soviet Union as an insurance policy against Iraq's territorial claims and as a means of asserting her own distinctive identity in the Gulf; one result of this was that in 1977 Kuwait became the second Arab Gulf state to purchase Soviet arms.[72] Where the USSR has no formal diplomatic relations, the position of other states is quoted as a means of exerting influence – for example Kuwait's view on freedom of navigation has been commended to Bahrain. Other tactics are to speak of 'growing opposition among public opinion in the Gulf countries', and to remind Gulf states of earlier statements opposing military alliances. (The Soviet Union has for example used the Kuwaiti Deputy Foreign Minister Rashid al-Rashid's comment 'We do not want to enter into any blocs or military alliances and shall never get involved in them' and that of his counterpart in the UAE that 'we are for a neutral policy and against any blocs in this area'.[73])

While specific reference has been made to freedom of navigation, this should be understood in a wider context encompassing the entire spectrum of diplomatic activity. Any form of regulated or conditional access, such as 'innocent passage', or a regional security arrangement, has been opposed. This is not due solely to preponderant Western influence in the region and a reluctance to be frozen out; the very principle of regulated access to sub-regions is particularly unattractive if generalized for a power that has only recently acquired a global reach and seeks commensurate recognition. Furthermore, the USSR prefers to work out zones of abstention for herself, perhaps in consultation with a power of equal standing.[74] To accept a limited role in this strategic region, in which the West is vulnerable and susceptible to pressure in crises, would in any case be to relinquish an important card which might be used for bargaining and should not therefore be given away for nothing. The USSR has sought to spread the view that any regional security arrangement will have the connotation of a 'bloc', thus placing its proponents on the defensive. This has been achieved, despite the limited Soviet diplomatic presence, by the skilful exploitation of the Gulf states' sensitivities to the accepted norms of intra-Arab conduct, and the connotation in Arab politics of 'alliances'. Soviet policy has been to strengthen the inhibitions that exist towards public identification with any 'bloc' by maintaining constant pressure and the threat of public exposure and vilification for any departure from that norm. It would be a mistake to underestimate the susceptibility of the Arab states of the Gulf to this type of pressure.

Soviet policy has also generally been cautious, even if its aims have been ambitious. An active policy of disruption and intervention has been inhibited by two principal factors. The first, between 1968 and 1971, was the possibility that activism might cause Britain to reassess her decision to withdraw militarily (and, later, that it might encourage a US decision to replace her); the second was the fear that such a policy might stimulate the emergence of a united front among the Gulf states. Both considerations still prevail, particularly the latter. The upheaval in Iran encouraged new Western interest in assuring regional security, including more frequent and visible US military deployments in the region, while the perception of enhanced Soviet opportunities after the 1978 coup in Afghanistan and the fall of the Shah in 1979, also galvanized regional co-operation. The moribund discussions on Gulf security were revived in January 1979, and Iraq, uneasy about Soviet advances and sharing a sense of growing vulnerability, closed ranks with the other littoral states.

The self-limiting nature of Soviet successes explains the emphasis on normalization and the pursuit of long-term advantage, rather than immediate returns, in her diplomacy. We are therefore unlikely to see energetic Soviet policies. The need to consolidate relations with Iran, Iraq and Kuwait will require caution; as in the past, the USSR will not risk alienating Iran

and Kuwait, for example, by decisive support for Iraq in territorial disputes.[75] Caution has also been dictated by the risk that regional conflicts close to Soviet territory might escalate and involve other powers. Furthermore, the Soviet tendency has been to treat border disputes conservatively, due to much wider considerations, which seemed, at least for the time being, to have something to do with the need to follow detente policies.[76]

Soviet reluctance to support friendly states for fear of stimulating a united front among the more 'conservative' régimes will continue to operate in the more murky political setting of the Persian Gulf in the aftermath of the revolution in Iran. Political cross-pressures will persist. Support for a revolutionary Iran might be tempting, but the alienation of Iraq and Saudi Arabia may be too high a price to pay, especially if Iran's future is uncertain. Conservative diplomacy is buttressed, too, by Soviet faith in the benefits to be reaped from the inevitable advance of progressive forces in the national liberation struggle in an area characterized by so many tensions and anomalies. The expectation that, in time, local forces will generate a more congenial environment for the extension of Soviet influence can be seen in the USSR's current policy of preventing the consolidation of Western influence and awaiting developments.

Iraq

Soviet policy in the Gulf has rarely been faced with hard choices requiring decisions to increase commitments or risk the loss of influence among friendly states. Only marginally present in the Gulf, the Soviet Union has generally contented herself with seeking a marked diminution of Western influence, an erosion of the adversary's presence. In those cases where Soviet influence does exist, therefore, her policies under pressure are particularly interesting. In both Iraq and the PDRY she has faced difficult choices, and how she has reacted to them merits closer examination.

Relations with Iraq, a friendly state participating both in Arab–Israeli and in Persian Gulf politics, have had considerable importance for the USSR. Although erratic, this friendship has endured for twenty years and, because of the two countries' complementary interests, the relationship now has a solid foundation, which

149

includes exchanges of arms for oil and a Treaty of Friendship and Co-operation (19 April 1972). As a major Arab state, Iraq is of intrinsic interest to the Soviet Union and, with the deterioration of Soviet relations with Egypt (1974) and Syria (1976), those with Baghdad correspondingly expanded. Despite the pressures on Moscow arising from friendship with rival states (Iraq and Syria were rivals until November 1978), this also has its compensations; support for one could be used as leverage against another, as was done in the case of Libya and Egypt after 1974.

If Iraq's value to the USSR transcends her importance in the immediate region, it also antedates the recent rise in strategic significance of the Persian Gulf. Soviet interest in Iraq in the early 1960s illustrated this. The USSR replaced Britain as Iraq's principal arms supplier, and in the mid-1960s, she introduced supersonic aircraft into the Persian Gulf area by supplying Iraq with MiG–21 interceptors. In terms of her size (as defined by population and GNP) Iraq thus became more heavily armed than neighbouring Iran. The 1972 Soviet-Iraqi Treaty of Friendship formalized the relationship and was followed in 1973 by the supply of Tu–22 bombers, and, in 1974, of MiG–23 ground-attack aircraft.

As the Persian Gulf's geopolitical importance grew, so did Iraq's value to the USSR as a friendly littoral state, both because of a growing importance in her own right and as a potential pressure-point on an assertive Iran (which was then arming rapidly and moving closer to the Western camp). Continued investment in Iraq therefore appeared justified, even though complications could be anticipated. Iraq's internal problems, especially with the Kurds, were acknowledged, and her differences with her fellow Ba'athists in Syria, and occasionally with Kuwait, were also recognized. Furthermore, Iraq's views on Palestine and on negotiations with Israel differed significantly from that of the USSR.[77] Nonetheless, despite her political isolation from Persian Gulf politics until 1975 and the Arab mainstream until 1978, and despite her poor location as a potential naval base on the Gulf,[78] Iraq remained the only entry-point for Soviet influence in the region.

Soviet policy towards her volatile ally has been marked by caution and restraint, notably in respect of the extended rivalry and occasional hostilities between Baghdad and Teheran (1969–75), which, although ostensibly centred on an ancient riverine frontier dispute, reflected a much wider competitive relationship. Despite the fact that the Treaty of Friendship with Iraq contained a clause on defence co-operation, Moscow sought to reassure Iran that the agreement was not directed against any third party. The Shah nevertheless interpreted it as anti-Iranian and justified Iran's arms build-up after 1972 by reference to it. At the time of its second anniversary, when relations between Iran and Iraq had further deteriorated, Moscow again reassured Teheran that the treaty 'did not pose a threat to the legitimate interests of anybody'. At the same time it was evident that Iran had extended military assistance to the Kurds within Iraq in their struggle for autonomy from Baghdad. Despite subsequent confirmation of material US assistance to the Kurds, via the Central Intelligence Agency and Iran, Soviet reactions were restrained.[79] Soviet commentaries certainly reflected knowledge of this covert assistance and emphasized that the aim was to 'weaken the progressive régime in Iraq' and to 'slow down the national liberation processes developing' by detaching Iraq 'from its real friends, above all, from the Soviet Union'.[80] They urged moderation, pointed to the common aims of the two states, blamed the imperialists for stirring up trouble, and reiterated Soviet interest in a border settlement. President Podgorny expressed Soviet exasperation with the continued conflict when the Shah visited Moscow that year:

We must say outright that [the] tension existing in relations between Iran and Iraq is not in the interest of peace and we declare in favour of Iranian–Iraqi differences being settled by these countries themselves at a conference table.

The Shah responded that there would be no problem if Iraq behaved like the USSR on border issues.[81]

After the visit hostilities escalated. Two Iraqi planes were shot down by Iran, who expanded her assistance to the Kurds to include artillery support. To counter the range advantage of this artillery (and Iran's air superiority if the conflict widened) Iraq asked for and received Soviet *Scud* surface-to-surface missiles in February

1975. Before the war expanded further, a diplomatic solution was found, and an agreement was signed by the Shah and Saddam Hussein in Algiers on 7 March 1975.

What is one to conclude from Soviet policy towards this conflict? There is little doubt that Iran's arms build-up disturbed the USSR, which, while striving to reassure Iran about the Soviet–Iraqi Treaty, at the same time repeatedly warned her about her arms purchases. Rather than take sides in the frontier dispute, the USSR counselled restraint and urged a peaceful settlement, adopting the position of a concerned but impartial observer. She responded cautiously to Iranian–US assistance to the Kurds, although this must have appeared a tangible provocation.[82] Similar caution characterized her arms transfer policy, for, although extensive, her arms sales to Iraq could be justified in terms of that country's internal security problems and military role against Israel (Iraqi losses in 1973 had been substantial); furthermore, even with Soviet aircraft and missiles, Iraq had no assurance of success in a conflict. Nor is there any persuasive evidence of Soviet willingness to use her own military capabilities to warn, dissuade or influence Iran.

Soviet caution was understandable, given the mixed and complex relationship with Iraq. Differences in priorities and perspective preclude genuine warmth between Moscow and Baghdad, and Moscow's caution regarding Israel and its support for the Communist party within Iraq have been recurrent sources of aggravation. The key factor cementing the uneasy friendship has been a common 'anti-imperialism'. But the extent to which Iraq will be prepared to help the 'progressive' elements in the Persian Gulf, or indeed to interpret events in the same light as the USSR, is uncertain. Iraq's settlement with Iran, though welcome because it defused a crisis, was also disturbing for Moscow because it was reached without Soviet foreknowledge and involved substantial concessions. Foremost among these was an agreement that Iraq would cease support for revolutionary groups in the Persian Gulf region. Equally disturbing for Moscow was the flexibility that Iraq derived from her swollen oil revenues and her apparent decision after 1975 to diversify arms sources.

The Soviet goal after 1975 was to retain influence in Baghdad without entering into any new commitments. The improvement of relations between Iraq and Iran, and Iraq's participation in deliberations on Persian Gulf security, were only guardedly welcomed, for, while bringing Iraq back into the region's politics (possibly as a conduit for Soviet ideas), they involved the risk that the interaction would increase the disposition towards conservatism in Baghdad. After a visit to Iraq by Kosygin in 1976, oblique reference was made to the attempts by some states to 'deradicalize' Iraq, and two months later a major arms agreement was reached, making Iraq the largest recipient of Soviet weapons. The package conservatively estimated at $1 billion, included aircraft (MiG–23s), missiles, artillery, tanks and frigates, and the Soviet Union assumed greater responsibilities for military training and obtained expanded use of Iraq's facilities.[83]

If the arms were intended to consolidate the friendship, the Soviet Union left no doubt as to her hopes. Iraq's success and enhanced international position, Kosygin told Saddam Hussein in February 1977, made it 'possible for Iraq to make a bigger contribution to the cause of national liberation . . . which would determine the development of this region'.[84] On the fifth anniversary of the Soviet–Iraqi Friendship Treaty, its value to Iraq was emphasized by a Soviet commentator who noted that recent years had confirmed 'the strategic nature of the friendly Soviet–Iraqi relations'.[85]

In reality, Soviet–Iraqi relations function within parameters set by a core of overlapping interests; though they may fluctuate, abrupt reversals are unlikely, and practical considerations such as arms supply condition the relationship. For the USSR, experience suggests that Iraq remains the only dependable ally among the Gulf states who can be guaranteed to take her interests into account. The reintegration of Iraq into Persian Gulf politics (and the Arab mainstream) increases the possibilities for the extension of Soviet influence, for which Iraq will remain an important vehicle in the Persian Gulf, both as a potential wedge to block unwelcome initiatives and as a geographical base from which to establish a wider presence perhaps involving greater use of Iraqi naval bases.

The price Iraq may seek to extract for this, however, may be too high if she requires the Soviet Union to show greater militancy *vis-à-vis*

Israel. Moreover, Iraq's growing conservatism may make her less ready to support national literation movements in the Gulf. (The Ba'ath leadership, after eleven years in office, is less intent on incessantly proving its revolutionary credentials). Whether Iraq will prove a reliable 'strategic' ally in the region is also doubtful, for she was alienated by Soviet intervention in the Horn of Africa, strongly criticized it and supported Arab Somalia against Soviet-backed Ethiopia.[86] Soviet activism in Afghanistan, together with Ba'ath suspicions about Soviet-instigated meddling by Communists in her armed forces in mid-1978, further frightened Iraq, and the Shah's fall and the uncertain policies of his successors aggravated feelings of insecurity among her secular Ba'athist leadership, which is vulnerable to opposition – especially among the Shi'ite community, which might be stirred by religious fundamentalism. In short, the USSR's activism and her success in consolidating her influence in nearby regions has complicated relations with Iraq, who sees her growing and proximate power as unconstrained and potentially threatening. Iraq has consequently moved towards consolidating relations with the other littoral states and has sought (and may still seek) reconciliation with Damascus.

The Soviet Union will attempt to use her ability to influence the Arab–Israeli issue as a lever on relations with Iraq. Any trend towards Iraqi conservatism will be checked by reference to the interaction of the Persian Gulf with the strategy of the imperialists in the Arab–Israeli confrontation,[87] and Soviet support for the 'rejectionists' will continue to be used as currency for influence in the Gulf. But even in the relationship with Iraq, Moscow's influence has narrowed. Soviet influence on the Arab–Israeli issue has not been impressive. Baghdad's conservatism on issues affecting the Persian Gulf (and, recently, even in OPEC) is a new, though reversible, factor which limits Soviet relevance. In addition, Iraq's oil wealth has had the effect of diluting Soviet dominance in commercial matters by bringing in competition from elsewhere.

The prospects for Soviet influence in Iraq are cloudy and it seems likely than ever that it will be either stable or synonymous with control. The prognosis must be one of tactical exploitation of indigenous change by the Soviet Union, rather than the instigation and manipulation of change. The mixed nature of Soviet interests, in which the impulse towards exploitation competes with a more conservative instinct, are more than matched by those of some regional states like Iraq, which demand unlimited support on one range of isues (Israel) but seek to maintain their own autonomy in areas closer to home.

The PDRY

The USSR's other regional ally has been the PDRY. Poor in resources and natural wealth with a population of only 1.8 million, the Aden régime has been hostile to its neighbours, suspicious of the West, and isolated by its. extremism from the main currents of Arab politics. Implacably opposed to Israel, the PDRY has become almost totally dependent on the USSR. For Moscow this relationship has had two advantages: first, the USSR has gained access to the fine natural harbour of Aden near the straits of Bab el-Mandeb and overlooking the Red Sea; and, second, she has secured a base for operations in the Arabian peninsula and the Horn of Africa.

The Soviet Union has retained the general right to support wars of national liberation, and in practice this has included, most notably, the Dhofari rebellion in Oman. Separated by desert from the major oil-fields in the Upper Gulf, the Dhofari rebels may not have been an ideal cause to support, but they had two advantages for the Soviet Union. Their dispute was indigenous and tribal-based, rather than externally-instigated; and theirs was a movement with a history in which the goal of secession played a part. Starting in the mid-1960s with local grievances in the southern province of Oman, the Dhofar Liberation Front changed its name to the Popular Front for the Liberation of Oman (PFLO). In September 1968, after receiving assistance from the USSR, the neighbouring PDRY (and from China until 1973), it became more ideological, changed its name again to the Popular Front for the Liberation of the Occupied Arab Gulf (PFLOAG) and extended its aims to include the removal of all monarchies in the Persian Gulf.

PFLOAG increased its guerrilla operations in the Gulf states, in the rugged terrain of Dhofar, (which is extremely hospitable to guerrilla operations) and, with sanctuary provided by the

Marxist Government of the neighbouring PDRY, by 1972 threatened the Oman government with a long and costly war. Iran viewed these developments in Oman both as a threat to the Musandam peninsula and the Hormuz Straits, and hence to shipping in the Gulf, and (less concretely) as part of a policy of probing soft spots in the Gulf. Together with Britain and Jordan, she responded by sending military assistance to Sultan Qabous.

The Soviet Union stood to gain much by the overthrow of the pro-Western Government in Oman – not simply in terms of strategic advantage but also in terms of the uncertainty it would create in the Arabian peninsula more generally. Yet here, as with Iraq, she was cautious in deed, if daring in word. Iran, particularly, was regularly denounced for participation in an unjust war designed 'to advance the interests of the imperialists and their puppets'. The Dhofari war was alleged to be 'a cause for concern' to other countries distant from the Gulf, because of the co-operation between 'local reactionary states' and imperialism. Yet practical Soviet assistance was somewhat limited, particularly in relation to that provided to the Omani government by Iran, the West and, later, the Arab states. Iran's assistance from 1973 to 1977 included 2 battalions plus logistical support (maximum manpower at any time being 4,000–4,500, of which 3,500 were combat personnel). Jordan provided 200 army engineers, and Britain provided 300 officers and troops seconded, plus 220 army (including 180 Special Air Service) and 147 RAF on a contract basis. Soviet economic and military assistance to the PDRY, which actively supported the rebels, remained unimpressive. It included SAM–7 anti-aircraft missiles, Kalashnikov rifles, MiG–17 and MiG–21 aircraft and, in the early 1970s, probably no more than 100 Cuban military advisers in Aden, possibly financed by the Soviet Union. Economic credits with grants totalled $60 million. Moscow also provided training for nearly 800 PDRY officers which form the backbone of an air force of 1,300, and an army of 19,000. Soviet officers are believed to have occasionally assisted the PDRY forces in directing artillery fire over the Omani border, and on one occasion the Soviet Union provided a landing ship from Berbera to move supporters of the Dhofari rebellion to Oman.[88] In return for this assistance,

the USSR gained access to naval and air facilities in South Yemen (at Aden and the airfield at Khormaksar) which enhanced her long-range air reconnaisance capabilities. But, especially during the offensive of the pro-Sultan forces in the Autumn of 1976, she was unwilling to increase the level of her commitment either to the Dhofaris or to the PDRY. The revolt was, to all intents and purposes, over by 1977.

The Dhofari rebellion was indigenous in its roots and inspiration. Soviet support for it was largely indirect, limited and of marginal significance. While defining the conflict in terms of national liberation, the Soviet Union also recognized that major involvement and quick success held risks. She therefore sought, through the PDRY, to exploit the rebellion with a limited investment, while retaining the option of either broadening the base of operations or beating a tactical retreat. The indirect nature of the Soviet role – through the PDRY, the Cubans and East Germans – made it *deniable*. The assistance provided undoubtedly exacerbated the essentially local nature of the dispute but it was more an irritant than a direct challenge to the Gulf states. It was seen as an indication of Soviet willingness to help or sponsor local movements in their contest with established authorities rather than as a test of the ultimate value of the Soviet Union as an ally. The decisive and rapid military response (primarily by Iran) unquestionably created a difficult choice for Moscow: either to escalate through expanded support of the PDRY or to settle for inaction and thereby risk the defeat of the revolt. The decision to adopt the latter course assured the winding down of the PFLO (although its recrudesence is a possibility since Iran's military retrenchment). The Soviet Union was therefore content with a sustained verbal barrage, playing on Iran's involvement so as to undermine Iranian relations with the Gulf states, and focusing on Britain's role in Oman and the residual Western presence in the Gulf.

As in the Upper Gulf, the Soviet Union was constrained both by her local allies and by the hazards attendant on success. The Shah's rapid military response in Oman raised the stakes. In addition, the reminder that the region was vulnerable from many directions caused the littoral states to close ranks. Saudi Arabia initiated overtures to the PDRY and in 1977, together with Kuwait and the UAE, invested in Oman [89] and dangled promises of economic assistance in return for the PDRY's good behaviour. The need to create strong states as a buffer against instabilities originating in the south was reinforced by the emergence of conflict in the Horn of Africa. A conference on the security of the Red Sea, held in Taiz in March 1977, was attended by the Gulf states and promoted by Egypt and Sudan. It was directed primarily against the USSR and Cuba.

Soviet influence in the PDRY has grown since 1978, particularly with the consolidation of the Soviet presence in Ethiopia. A coup in Aden in July 1978 strengthened the orientation of the leadership in favour of Moscow and ended the prospect of an early normalization of relations with Saudi Arabia, the Yemen Arab Republic or Washington.[90] After 1977–8 the interconnections between the southern tip of the Arabian peninsula and the Horn were evident. Cuban advisers, already present in Aden, appeared in much larger numbers. Cuban combat units fought in Ethiopia, and Aden contributed 1,000 officers and men and some tanks. Aden's port facilities were used as a staging point for the re-supply of Ethiopia.

The PDRY is the only Arab state with a single party of avowedly Marxist orientation. Control of society by the party is pervasive, giving this backward state a quasi-totalitarian character. In recent years Aden has welcomed increasing numbers of East German and Cuban advisers for the development of her internal security apparatus and the armed forces.[91] The new relationship with the PDRY is important for Soviet policy in the Gulf in a number of ways. First, it allows the Soviet Union to extend her influence on the periphery in Afghanistan or Ethiopia. Second, it acts as a pressure-point on Oman, thus reviving the threat to the Straits of Hormuz. With Iran no longer prepared to undertake military commitments, the regional balance of power is more vulnerable to sudden injections of relatively small increments of military forces, and Aden's capacity for disturbance is therefore considerable. Third, the long-standing rivalry between the Aden (PDRY) and Sanaa (YAR) régimes is politically exploitable, given the extreme sensitivity of Saudi Arabia to her relations with Sanaa.[92] Over the past decade there have been recurrent border clashes between the two Yemeni States but no full-scale conflicts. The presence of foreign military advisers in both Yemen and in Saudi Arabia would give a generalized conflict the aspect of a proxy war. In the March 1979 border clashes, for instance, Eastern bloc advisers were active on the PDRY side (Soviet advisers were also present but passive in the YAR), while the US moved swiftly to arm and train the YAR [93] and to demonstrate her commitment to Saudi Arabia's defence by a number of conspicuous political and military gestures. Washington's firm reaction, despite the fact that Saudi Arabia appears to have held up arms deliveries to the YAR, has been sufficient response for the moment.

As a result of this incipient instability, the US has moved towards a more active role in the region. This may take the form of more substantial and regular deployments of warships, the expansion of the facility at Diego Garcia and the search for greater access to staging facilities. The island of Masirah belonging to Oman and located less than five hundred miles from the Hormuz Straits, may be just such an attractive air-staging post in the future.[94] If the US can maintain a sense of purpose and commitment, together with an impressive military capability proximate to or readily deployable in the area (without being intrusive), the border conflict will have served a purpose. The drawing of lines in the Persian Gulf may be salutary in preventing future miscalculations.

Despite the growth of Soviet influence on the peripheries and the continuing tensions on the Arabian peninsula, which may be exploitable, Soviet influence should not be exaggerated. The PDRY is a small, unstable state, liable to internal convulsions and reversals and so unlikely to pursue a purposeful foreign policy. The war in the Horn of Africa and the fall of the Shah have made the states in the Arabian peninsula more aware of their security problems, and the United States is showing both concern and a greater willingness to assist them. Even limited trouble-making by the Soviet Union therefore carries an increased risk of being met and matched by the US. The USSR will also find that the risks of entanglement and commitment will increase. On the record of previous practice, she seems likely to bide her time and to await changes in the domestic politics of these states which may be favourable to the extension of her influence.

IV. THE USSR AND DOMESTIC CHANGE

As a revisionist power, the Soviet Union has tended to be well-disposed towards change in the Third World. This tolerance has been fed by the lack of either solid Soviet interests which might generate conservatism (as in Eastern Europe) or of interests which might require protection. As a result, the USSR has taken the view that change in the Gulf is both necessary and inevitable, and could only improve the Soviet position in the region. In practice, however, she has found that not every setback for the West is an unequivocal victory for the East. Her interests are also growing, and she needs oil, gas and stable borders. But these needs co-exist uneasily with protestations of support for national liberation wars and the fact that tensions will arise when promoting good relations with some governments while cultivating their opponents. The promotion of change, as opposed to its exploitation, risks fundamental clashes of interests with the West and therefore increases the potential for conflict through escalation.

Nevertheless, in the Persian Gulf region, where Western dominance has been an acknowledged reality for over a century, Soviet faith in the advantages of change is understandable for two reasons. First, the USSR has had relatively little to lose: the erosion of Western influence, even if not matched by a growth in Soviet influence, still represents an improvement, and neutralization of the region is certainly acceptable to her. Second, between the goals of the USSR and the West there is an asymmetry which favours the USSR. While the USSR can accept (and often welcomes) the maximum degree of disruptive, discontinuous change leading to changes in elites and in policy orientations, the Western interest in orderly change and steady development in a stable context is far more difficult to achieve.

In practice the apparent asymmetry in goals is less stark, since today's break-through becomes tomorrow's setback; 'influence' has been found to be evanescent, illusory and more often synonymous with entanglement than with control. As one scholar has noted, influence in the short term is no guarantee of long term influence, and a change favouring one power can easily unleash forces with damaging effects over a wider set of interests.[95] Furthermore, although the Soviet Union's aim is to spread her influence, this is conditioned by two other factors – the essential conservatism of an elderly Soviet elite which demands a measure of predictability in foreign relations, and an endemic optimism which argues that, since (objective) trends favour the USSR, she ought to preserve her freedom of action to benefit from them without risking crises. Both militate against indiscriminate activism and reinforce the Soviet search for formal equality and participation in world affairs, although the invasion of Afghanistan may indicate a much greater Soviet willingness to take risks.

However one looks at the Gulf, since most of the régimes in this region are traditional and pro-Western, there are solid reasons to expect that violent change will upset previous patterns of government, displace ruling elites and divert policies in new and – for the USSR – advantageous directions. From the Soviet perspective, the strains of growth acting on societies with low levels of institutionalization will lead to lop-sided modernization and give rise to a revolutionary situation. In addition to domestic political pressures there are the stresses arising from secessionist or separatist movements, as well as inter-state rivalries which provide an environment favourable for the exercise of Soviet influence, by making Soviet power relevant.

The 'ripeness' of the region for change can, of course, be accelerated by emphasizing the West's failure to shift Israel's policies, by supplying arms to the PDRY, and by creating the image of a strong and steadfast power which must be taken into account. The immediate Soviet aims are clear: to weaken the links of Persian Gulf states with the West; to dissolve existing alliances and agreements; and to end or forestall the granting of basing rights to Western states. If these aims can be achieved, the establishment of diplomatic relations with Eastern bloc states should follow, together with a decisive re-orientation towards non-alignment in the first instance, and, ultimately, towards a pro-Soviet stance.

The different approaches of the two superpowers to change reflect different interests at stake as much as philosophical differences. In the Persian Gulf this is very evident. The USSR has one potential asset in the competition for influence – an extensive global network of Communist parties at its service. Arrayed against this is the barrier of a religious faith – Islam. The competition between Communism and Islam is likely to become an important dimension of Soviet relations with the Gulf states. In this chapter the relationship of these two factors to the Soviet approach to change is assessed, with particular reference to Iran's revolution of 1978–9.

Soviet Policy and Change in Iran: the Background

Like most powers, the USSR looks first to her immediate neighbours to assure her security and, as with most great powers, the degree of assurance she demands strains relations with those neighbours. Since the establishment of the new Soviet state, a priority where Iran is concerned has been the acquisition of the right to intervene to prevent developments unfavourable to the USSR. As already noted, the USSR has consistently interpreted the wording of the 1921 Treaty for this purpose. Not content with formal though vague assurances, she has twice sought to dismember Iran by detaching one of her provinces. In both the Ghilan (1920–21) and Azerbaijan (1944–5) episodes, the Soviet use of force was cloaked in the fiction of assistance to an indigenous separatist movement. However, in the 1950s, during the Iranian political upheaval following the nationalization of oil, the rise of Mohammed Mossadegh and the struggle for power among various factions, Soviet support for the Iranian Communist party (*Tudeh*) was unenthusiastic and limited, suggesting small faith in it as an alternative government (indeed, Soviet energies were directed at infiltration of the armed forces, the presumed likely successor to the monarchy). This coolness was even more evident in the 1960s. As relations with the Shah improved, support for the *Tudeh* party dwindled to the point where some party members were even returned to Iran from Soviet refuge.

But if Moscow preferred to concentrate on state-to-state relations, to avoid attacks on the Shah and to forgo overt support for the *Tudeh*, the option of reviving support for secessionist movements and dissidents against the monarchy

was retained as a particularly effective form of leverage. It was an important determinant of the Shah's centralization of power. His fear that the instigation of secessionist movements by the USSR could lead to fragmentation and Balkanization, or to the creation of an 'Iranistan' province out of Iran, militated against any sharing of power. Similarly, he saw Iran's geopolitical location as working against a totally open political system with a high tolerance for domestic dissent. He was therefore reluctant to allow a multi-party system which would enable the USSR to 'request' the legalization of the *Tudeh* party, which could then act as a Trojan horse for Moscow.

While declining to use the Communist party as a means of putting pressure on Iran between 1967 and 1978, the Soviet Union continued to maintain informal contacts with the Iranian opposition, and, though dropping direct attacks on the Shah, she used semi-official channels for criticism (for example, Radio Peace and Progress, broadcast from Bulgaria and East Germany, and Radio of the Patriots from Libya). She also used regional conflicts to emphasize Iran's vulnerability, sending arms to Baluchistan via Baghdad, and to Dhofar via the PDRY. Cuba's assistance to the PDRY after 1973 led on to the development of ties with the Iranian Communist Party, cemented at the Twenty-third Communist Party Congress in Moscow,[96] and much of the criticism of Iran at the 'non-aligned' conference in Colombo in mid-1976 by the PDRY and Libya was reminiscent of Soviet propaganda.

There appears to have been a turning point in the Soviet attitude towards Iran in 1976. That summer three US military technicians were assassinated by Iranian guerrillas. Indirect Soviet support for revolutionary groups in exile (e.g., the *Fedayin-e-Khalq*) was well known, while financial assistance and training for them were publicly acknowledged by Libya and the Popular Front for the Liberation of Palestine. In that same year Iran was confronted with a diplomatic embarrassment – a request for political asylum from a defecting Soviet pilot. The Soviet Union bluntly threatened to revive her support for dissidents within Iran, and (allegedly) held military exercises on the joint frontier.[97] In 1977 Soviet espionage in Iran's armed forces was revealed, though whether this will prove to have been as extensive as the massive infiltration of the 1950s remains to be seen. It is clear that proximity and power have undoubtedly enabled the USSR to exercise pressure and influence subtly and indirectly, outside the acknowledged instrument of the Communist Party.

Reaction to Iran's Revolution

The Soviet Union had always approached Iran with a degree of ambivalence. She saw Iran as an anomaly – fundamentally weak but strong in some components of power, inherently fragile yet nevertheless run by the most long-lived régime in the Middle East – which did not fit any formula or pattern. Uneasy about the Shah's military expenditures and independent policies, the USSR was also reassured by the predictability of a centralized system of government and the establishment of a *modus vivendi* with a leader who clearly understood international politics.

The crisis that erupted in Iran in mid-1978 took the USSR by surprise and confronted her with a dilemma: to support the opposition risked thoroughly alienating the Shah if he survived, and the benefits that might be derived from his successors were very uncertain; yet to support the Shah might mean losing the opportunity to exploit a set-back for the West and to increase Soviet influence within an enfeebled Iran. She therefore temporized, abstained from direct attacks on the Shah and awaited developments, for she could lose nothing as a result of a crisis which appeared to be the direct result of Iran's Western alignment and selfish Western commercial policies. Only as the wave of popular protest grew, and with it the recognition that Iran was witnessing the end of a political era, did the USSR discard her caution. However, since the fluidity of politics within Iran and the mass disaffection from the imperial régime made it unnecessary to exercise influence from outside, Soviet actions throughout the crisis were limited. For example, no troop manoeuvres were reported. There was some indirect support for the revolution in Iran (through the PLO and Libya) and limited assistance was extended. In addition, Soviet espionage activities within Iran were clearly less constrained after the disintegration of the Government, the disappearance of SAVAK, and the abstention of the United States.

The one decisive Soviet action that was intended to shape the course of the unfolding crisis was Mr Brezhnev's pronouncement on 18 November 1978, which indicated the Soviet Union's direct interest in Iran: 'It must be made clear that any interference, let alone military intervention in the affairs of Iran – a state which has a common frontier with the Soviet Union – would be regarded by the USSR as a matter affecting its security interests'.[98] By affirming Soviet interests in Iran as unequivocally as was prudent, the statement was designed to influence the debate in Washington on an appropriate response to the weakening of the Shah, and, by omitting to define precisely what would constitute unacceptable 'interference', was intended to induce maximum restraint on the part of US Government. In addition, it provided the basis for later exploitation by means of the claim that the Soviet Union had been responsible for deterring Western intervention and hence defending the revolution. Soviet commentaries defined 'intervention' broadly to include the expansion of the staff at the US Embassy, the provision of fuel and equipment to the Iranian armed forces, and consultations between the American emissary, General Huyser, and the Iranian armed forces. The possibility of a military coup (organized with tacit US support) for a restoration of the Shah was repeatedly alluded to as something which would be intolerable for the USSR.[99]

Given the continuing communication between Moscow and Washington, it was clear, even before the statement, that the US had no intention of undertaking a military intervention. The Soviet warning was therefore designed through ambiguity to inhibit a broader range of possible US actions in Iran. The claim that Soviet security interests were intrinsically involved in and affected by developments in Iran (not in itself a novel claim) inhibited potential US responses (which were in any case constrained by the nature of the popular discontent with the Shah's régime). What was new was the widening of this interest to preclude virtually any type of US assistance to the beleaguered government. And, in particular, the implied assertion of a Soviet right of veto over the type of Iranian government was a departure from the evolution of policies towards Iran since 1945. The most significant departure, however, was the

157

United States' apparent acquiescence in these rather broad and vague claims. Washington was not disposed, given the scope of the opposition to the Shah, to intervene actively on the side of the government; it was simpler to do nothing (or very little) than to devise an effective response to a large-scale revolutionary opposition, even though such non-intervention was not neutral in its consequences. Yet the US response to the Soviet warning and claims was to deny any intention to intervene and to issue a counter-warning. If the Soviet claim is seen as the establishment of an important precedent, Washington's response must be viewed as muffled and perfunctory.[100] Despite the large and preponderant Western material stake in Iran, Washington's acceptance of the inherent primacy and legitimacy of the Soviet claim to interest in Iran during a crisis constituted a turning point in Iran's relations with the super-powers.[101]

The Soviet claim to have protected the revolution (depicted as a revolt against pro-Western policies), coupled with the portrayal of herself as the steadfast guardian of the people's right to choose, could be exploited. 'Lessons' could be derived and communicated to other states in the region. Whatever the uncertainty about the ultimate benefits accruing to the USSR, the interim gains – particularly the defeat for the West and the weakening of Iran – were too tempting to ignore. American confusion and vacillation, which gave the appearance of undependability, could be turned to advantage in Soviet relations with the weaker and equally vulnerable states of the Persian Gulf. One analyst of Soviet behaviour has argued that the Soviet Union, 'trusting events', is nowadays more likely to assign her military power at least one task over and above that of simple defence: that of preventing others from interfering with change.[102]

Certainly in the case of Iran, Soviet diplomacy (backed by the proximity of military power) was geared to the prevention of Western interference – to the protection of change, rather than to its initiation. However, the distinction between 'preventing interference with change' (i.e., protecting change) and 'imposing change', while helpful analytically, is confusing politically. If Soviet diplomacy 'protected' change from Western interference in Iran, it prevented it in Afghanistan in 1979 by providing large-scale

military involvement, technicians and airlift to defend a pro-Soviet régime against Moslem dissidents.[103] For the Soviet analyst the distinction would, by definition, be clear.The USSR only supports 'authentic' or 'progressive' change, which may at times require the provision of assistance to revolutionary forces, while at other times governments must be supported against 'counter-revolutionary forces'. The issue is more than one of semantics. *Status quo* versus change poses a policy question; the answer will depend on which *status quo* serves Soviet interests. Sometimes a new *status quo* is preferable, so the opposition to the old order is protected (Iran); at other times the current *status quo* is defended against those who seek to change it (Afghanistan). In practice it is difficult to see any consistent adherence to principles in Soviet policy other than the pursuit of self-interest, which requires considerable flexibility. The Soviet assertion of legitimate interests in the area adjacent to its frontiers was recognized *de facto* by the West in 1978–9. Whether this will be followed by an extension of a similar claim to the right to exert influence over non-contiguous Gulf states, or by the assertion of a claim to paramount (or exclusive) influence in the contiguous states, remains to be seen. But Soviet policy during Iran's revolution, and Western acquiescence in it, contributed in large measure towards the neutralization of Iran.

Consequences of Change

The revolution in Iran has been portrayed as contributing a major gain for Soviet interests in the region. Even though it was neither the result of Soviet policies nor devoid of complications, on balance it represented a Soviet advance. The credits were obvious, and foremost among them was the anti-Western orientation of the new régime – whatever its ultimate complexion. This represented a gain on many levels. The overthrow of a staunch ally was a set-back for the West and strengthened the perception of many that the West was unwilling or unable to help its friends. (And, although the fall of the Shah again posed the question whether a greater Western involvement might not be necessary, it did so in a context where Western influence was gravely undermined.) More concretely, Iran's shift from alignment to neutralism undermined the entire basis of Western planning for security in the Persian Gulf and revealed the hollowness of the two-pillar concept of regional security, raising doubt as to whether local powers were sufficiently stable or powerful to assume such responsibilities.

The loss of monitoring facilities will complicate Western intelligence-gathering (its effects on SALT verification have already been noted), and denial of Iran's bases constitutes a major logistical set-back which has impaired Western access to the region. On the other hand, Iran's weakness will ensure that the prospects for the extension of Soviet influence in Teheran will improve, while Soviet security concerns will be simplified. For example, the decisions to relinquish the role of 'gendarme' in the Gulf, to reduce arms procurement, to relegate the military modernization programme to a lower priority and, possibly, to assume a passive security policy, all strengthen the position of the USSR. Access to the Persian Gulf and Indian Ocean is made much easier by the absence of an effective Iranian air force, and the USSR has appropriated (at least temporarily) the right to unrestricted transit of Iranian airspace. This has for the time being considerably improved the possible Soviet response time in a Persian Gulf or more distant contingency and will force the West to react more quickly in defence of its interests in the Gulf or further afield.[104] Soviet monitoring capabilities of US activities in the Indian Ocean in peacetime will also be simplified. In addition, the new Iranian government, weakened and preoccupied domestically, will be more susceptible to Soviet pressures and blandishments, since the combination of uncertain leadership and military non-alignment will be conducive to a foreign policy that seeks accommodation with the USSR. Both the indigenous element of deterrence and the credibility of former allies have been weakened.

Coming at a time of a reassessment of policy in both Turkey and Pakistan, Iran's new security perspective was especially welcome for the USSR. Iran's decisions to define security as coterminous with her national territory and to withdraw from CENTO (March 1979) were immediate dividends for the USSR. If the changes in political orientation (demonstrated by support for the Arab cause against Israel and more militance in third-world fora) were predictable, the rapid collapse of the army and

the total disintegration of authority were not. The former dramatically changed the political complexion in the Persian Gulf and exposed Saudi Arabia to pressure and increasing isolation because of her links to the West. The latter transformed the balance of power in the Persian Gulf. As a consequence, Iraq's importance in Gulf politics and as a military power increased. With the removal of the Iranian umbrella, the other Gulf states lost their military protection. None felt this more strongly than Oman, although Kuwait in the upper Gulf also felt the loss. The upshot was a distinct inclination, in the absence of a countervailing Western power, to reinsure by accommodation with potential adversaries.

These undoubted gains for the USSR, however, were not without concrete costs and attendant risks. In the winter of 1978–9 the southern provinces of the USSR suffered from the cutting off of gas supplies from Iran. (The new Iranian government's decision to reduce oil production by a third entailed a corresponding reduction in the availability of gas.) The revolution itself disrupted the construction of the second gas pipeline to the Soviet Union (due for completion by 1981). Iran subsequently cancelled the project and made clear her intention to renegotiate the price of gas currently exported to the USSR via the existing pipeline. This reflected a general inclination to reassess the export of gas in the light of decisions to rely on gas for domestic consumption and reinjection into oil fields and to forgo nuclear power, rather than ill-will towards the USSR. However the new régime's greater militance over the use and sale of Iran's natural resources will affect the USSR just as much as the West. Lacking the Shah's view of trade as something essentially political, the Teheran régime will almost certainly eschew barter arrangements in favour of hard-currency sales, seeking to maximize the returns on each barrel of oil, and may well be less disposed to provide oil on preferential or concessionary terms to the USSR and East Europe in the 1980s. As a result the revolution, as well as disrupting the USSR's own energy programme, may have reduced the prospect of her deriving economic rewards from political influence.

Although a weak Iran is in the Soviet interest, an unstable Iran is less clearly so. Indeed, shifting coalitions within weak governments or multiple and contradictory centres of power are not formulae conducive to stable policies, and the Soviet Union likes her neighbours to be predictable. The more extreme possibility of an Iran fragmenting on ethnic or tribal lines is even less welcome to the USSR. The claims of the Kurdish, Turkmen and Arab populations for 'autonomy', although so far limited, must still be seen in the context of a central government lacking both a post-revolutionary consensus and (that traditional requirement of any state) a monopoly of armed force. A disintegrating Iran would have the international effect (especially in Turkey, Iraq and possibly Pakistan) of 'Balkanizing' the region. While it would thus increase the ability of the USSR to put pressure on governments, increased influence over governments that cannot maintain their own unity, let alone manage their internal affairs, would be a dubious achievement. Indeed, it could constitute a considerable risk for the USSR. Fragmentation and separatism could weaken governments that are friendly to her, like those in Afghanistan and Iraq, and might even infect Soviet minorities in the process. For these reasons the precedent of redrawing international boundaries on lines of nationality is not one the USSR is anxious to undertake lightly.

In other respects, too, the consequences of the Iranian revolution for the Soviet Union are mixed. That revolution may provide a model for neighbouring states, where other diverse populations may unite under the banner of Islam to overthrow unpopular régimes. There were clear signs of this in Afghanistan in 1979 and the prospect of greater Shi'a militancy in Iraq, perhaps unseating the Ba'ath régime and further weakening Soviet influence, could not be ignored. The assertion of Islam could just as effectively block Communist advances as unseat pro-Western rulers.

Evangelical militance in the conduct of foreign affairs also spells danger for the USSR. Active intervention in neighbouring states could bring the new Iranian régime into collision with Soviet allies and interests. For example, the border clashes between Iran and Iraq in 1979 had their origins in mutual suspicion and concerns (over possible Iraqi intervention in Iran's heavily Arab-populated province of Khuzestan and over Iran's interest in the condition of the Shi'a majority in Iraq). Similarly,

Iran could extend active assistance to the Muslim rebels against the Soviet-supported government of Afghanistan. The prospect of a fundamentalist Islamic régime adjacent to Soviet territory and anxious to act as a magnet for the Soviet Muslim population must be disquieting for Soviet authorities and must somewhat dull the lustre of the gains made in other areas.

The impact of the Iranian revolution was considerable throughout the Middle East, Asia and the Western world. While undermining Western strategic interests and the credibility of alliances, it also precipitated a Western and regional reaction. The United States geared its rapid and quite powerful response to the PDRY attack on the YAR in March 1979 to the need to demonstrate military commitment to the region's security. The closing of ranks among the Gulf states, evident in hitherto unprecedented co-operation on security between Saudi Arabia and Iraq, also showed that Soviet advances in the area may become more difficult. In sum, in this region of volatile politics, gains are usually accompanied by complications which the exercise of influence from outside can rarely resolve.

If Soviet optimism about change has its origins in Marxist doctrine, it is also fostered by the natural interest of a revisionist state seeking a transformation of a strategic environment in which it is still – in terms of political influence – the underdog. In the general competition for influence, the Soviet Union has traditionally had the asset of the Communist Party through which to promote her interests and defend her cause. Yet this advantage has seldom been decisive, even at the height of the 'anti-colonial' phase of politics in the Third World, where nationalism has been dominant. In the Persian Gulf region, Communist ideology and the Communist Party face another strong potential competitor–Islam. The interaction of Islam and Communism has acquired added significance in recent times as a result, first, of Islam's growth in political salience in the countries on the Soviet Union's southern periphery (and potentially within the USSR herself) and, second, of the USSR's increasing interest in the region.

Islam and Soviet Policies
The Soviet Union has the fifth largest Muslim population in the world, living principally in

her southern provinces, and Islam is the dominant religion of all countries in the Persian Gulf. From the outset, Lenin and the Bolsheviks' attitudes towards the Soviet Muslims was a mixture of tolerance and repression. It was understood that to antagonize them risked alienating Muslims in adjacent states. Consequently, the USSR's policy towards her own Muslims took account of the impact that it could have on foreign relations and resisted the temptation to treat this as an exclusively domestic matter. This Islamic dimension was recognized early on as a potential foreign policy tool and was consciously exploited in the USSR's relations with the Islamic Middle East in the aftermath of the Russian Revolution. For example, the Soviet Union convened an international congress, the First Congress of the Peoples of the East at Baku in 1921; it was intended to rouse the Muslim world against the West. The Islamic dimension was revived again in the mid-1950s. Delegations from the Islamic world were invited to the USSR to see for themselves that Communism was compatible with, and could even contribute to, Islam's values.

Nonetheless, though tactically exploited for foreign relations purposes, true tolerance has never been extended internally. Islam in the USSR has always been controlled and limited. Islamic leaders within the USSR, recognizing the delicacy of their position, have avoided direct clashes with the Soviet authorities, while seeking to use the leeway that existed to revive and, where possible, integrate Islam with Communism. There remains nevertheless a basic tension between Soviet Islamic clerics and the Soviet authorities. Although tolerance of Islam serves their foreign policy aims, Soviet leaders cannot allow this tolerance to be broadened in such a way as to undermine the basic ideology of the Soviet Union or to weaken the fabric of a multinational state. Since intrinsically Islam does provide an alternative to Marxism, and since religion is the best means of maintaining a national identity in the multinational Soviet empire, Islam, if revived, could constitute a rallying point for the Central Asian peoples (the Uzbeks, Tartars, Kazakhs, Turkmens and Tadzhiks), to increase their national consciousness and lead first to the loosening and, ultimately to the disintegration of the Soviet empire. In this connection, another potential disadvantage of this potentially uneasy co-existence between Islam and a Communist state is the susceptibility of the Soviet Muslim population to developments within the rest of the Islamic world, and particularly those in adjacent states, such as Iran and Afghanistan.

This issue has become especially significant in recent years. One of the reasons for this is the growing importance of the non-Russian population within the USSR. Estimates of the number of Muslims in the USSR vary from 40 to 50 million – a fifth of its total population – and, due to differential birth rates, the population of the predominantly Muslim Central Asian Republics (Uzbekistan, Kazakhstan, Tadzhikistan, Turkmenia and Kirgizia) is growing at five times the rate of that in the Slav USSR. By the 1990s Muslims will account for perhaps a third of the total population, and by the year 2000 the Russian Slav population will be a minority. Moreover, employment prospects are poor in the Central Asian republics and this will result in wider problems for the rest of the USSR. By the end of the century, a third of the new recruits for the armed forces could be Muslim.

The second factor causing renewed interest in the Soviet Muslim population is the resurgence of Islam in nearby Muslim states. What makes this especially significant for the USSR in foreign-policy terms (in addition to the growing importance of the Persian Gulf states as oil producers) is that the expression of this assertive and vigorous commitment to Islam appears to have an anti-Western current which might be harnessed to Soviet political ends. But in order to exploit this phenomenon the USSR will have to play down the atheistic aspect of Communism, and to do this effectively will mean giving greater freedom to Muslims in the USSR. Yet such action brings the risk that they will be contaminated by a new religious zeal. There are indications that the USSR has allowed the opening of some new mosques in deference to demographic pressures and the requirements of foreign policy, but controls on religious schools, literature and the pilgrimage to Mecca (*Hadj*) are carefully supervised.

The degree of religious commitment among those of Muslim background is consequently not easy to assess, nor is it clear whether it is in fact declining or increasing. For sixty years religion has been pushed out of people's lives and, as one Soviet commentator noted, 'it would be hard to imagine more than 10 per cent of the once Muslim population actually being religious today'.[105] Yet, while the Islamic element (like the followings of all religious faiths) is understated by the Soviet Union, possibly in response to Western commentaries that identify it as a potential problem, it is emphasized in dealings with the Muslim world. Neighbouring states are told that Islam has the second largest following in the Soviet Union after the Christian Orthodox religion, that freedom of religion is guaranteed by the constitution and that Islamic institutions are free of government interference and have the right to associate with Muslims of other countries. In 1978–9 forty Islamic delegations visited the USSR.

The Soviet Union has also sought to modify her atheistic image in order to establish ties with Saudi Arabia. In an important article, one commentator observed that some have 'tried to attribute King Faisal's negative attitude towards Communism to his excessive religious zeal . . . But if this were true, then where is the logic, since the USSR has always advocated the freedom of belief.'[106] Other commentaries have stressed the compatibility of Communism and Islam by reference to Soviet relations with other Islamic (and monarchic) states.

The Soviet Union has shown a growing disposition in recent months to tackle the potential problem that Communism might pose for her relations with Muslim states by emphasizing their compatibility. However, if the price of improved relations with neighbouring Islamic states is heightened religious consciousness within the USSR, it may well prove too high for her. Reports of a request by Libya for a consulate in Tashkent to proselytize among Soviet Muslims may reflect the beginning of a trend involving requests for greater religious freedom, more liberal policies governing the *Hadj*, and even emigration rights. In such a situation the use of this religious dimension in foreign policy may well turn a potential asset into a vulnerability. The Soviet Union is undoubtedly aware of the potential dangers but remains confident that her capacity to exploit the Muslim connection exceeds the risks that her southern population may be infected by religious zeal or may appeal to neighbouring co-religionists for intercession with Moscow. Nevertheless, a scenario in which Saudi Arabia, for example, ties concessionary oil terms for Eastern Europe to the liberalization of Soviet Muslims' freedom of worship could be a cause for some unease in the 1980s.

Islam and the Iranian Crisis

How did the Soviet Union respond to the Iranian upheaval and to the strong Islamic component driving it, given this potential vulnerability? After all, Baku, capital of the Azerbaijan Republic and, with a population of 1.5 million, the fifth largest city in the USSR, lies only 200 miles from Iranian territory. The Muslims in Baku are predominantly Shi'ite, and some sources report that there are 4.5 million Shi'ites in Soviet Azerbaijan, with close ethnic and in some cases even cultural ties with Iranian Azerbaijanis.

Like other governments (and analysts), the USSR was slow to foresee the impending departure of the Shah. Only in mid-January 1979 did Moscow commit itself against the monarchy. Press commentaries then acknowledged Ayatollah Khomeini as the main figure in the opposition movement and argued that, contrary to Western allegations, Khomeini was not a reactionary. He would be guided by the Koran and establish an Islamic Republic which would be independent of the foreign domination, unlike its predecessor. Soviet commentaries (ironically) accused the West of underrating Khomeini's influence and derived comfort from the traditionally 'progressive' nature of Shi'ism.[107] But Soviet support for Khomeini was reluctant; he had already shown his lack of enthusiasm for the USSR while in Paris, arguing that it had brought Islamic peoples 'forcibly under its domination' and consequently 'had no right to represent itself as an opponent of exploitation and friend of the oppressed'.[108] Nevertheless Soviet support was extended to Khomeini, first because there was no other leader of comparable stature and, second, because of the expectation that he would in due course be replaced by secular forces more amenable to influence. In any case, given Khomeini's age and the dynamics of revolution, it was a reasonable calculation that the least likely of all outcomes was a strong fundamentalist Islamic régime. In the meantime Khomeini's anti-Westernism was exploited, and it was alleged that the West's opposition to him derived from his independence and patriotism.

The great surge of religious consciousness that accompanied the revolution could not fail to have regional repercussions. Islam, already utilized by a military régime in neighbouring Pakistan to safeguard itself, also became a rallying-point for dissident tribesmen in adjacent Afghanistan. The Marxist pro-Soviet régime of Mohammed Taraki and Hafizullah Amin, severely threatened by this revolt, was also undermined by defections in the armed forces. Although Afghan rebels found sanctuary in neighbouring Pakistan and possibly Iran, and took courage from their Muslim neighbours, there is little evidence of material support from those states. However the Soviet Union justified her military intervention by accusing Iran, Pakistan, China and the United States of providing substantial military support to the rebels. With heightened Islamic consciousness in Iran it would have been unrealistic to expect complete indifference to the revolt in Afghanistan against a 'godless' régime. A prominent Iranian religious leader, Ayatollah Shariat-Madari, issued repeated calls for support of the Afghan Muslims and condemned Soviet brutality and support of the Taraki government.[109] At the end of April huge demonstrations were held outside the Soviet Embassy in Teheran protesting against this policy.

In the light of the USSR's strong attachment to the Kabul régime, there was little leeway for Soviet diplomacy. Unwilling to alienate the new régime in Iran, she was also unwilling to watch the Kabul régime fall, or to condone any militant support for the Muslim rebels in a 'Jihad' or Holy War. Knowing that those in the area are susceptible to religious appeals, a senior Soviet Muslim leader broadcast in March 1979 a commentary pointing out the great gains for Afghanistan's Muslim's since the April 1978 revolution. He stressed the compatibility of the Taraki régime with Islam and identified its opponents as oppressors who distorted religion for their own ends.[110] Although early in 1980, the outcome of the Afghan revolt was still uncertain. Yet, it was evident that the USSR's heavy involvement in Afghanistan had soured her potential for influence in Iran. In recognition of this new dimension the USSR started to use Islam in her foreign policy as a defensive measure pointing out, for example, that 'Marxist–Leninists greatly value the great contribution of religious and faithful Moslems in Iran and other countries in arousing the national liberation movement in the struggle against imperialism'.[111]

Whether the Soviet Union will be able to show in her treatment of her own large number of Muslims that Communism and Islam are compatible and even harmonious remains to be seen. On balance, however, it appears that her Muslim population will constitute a liability which can be exploited by her neighbours (at least as a means of stigmatizing Communism), rather than as an asset by which she can demonstrate her own attractiveness as a diplomatic ally.

The Role of Communist Parties

One instrument at the disposal of the Soviet Union in its rivalry with the West is the world-wide network of Communist parties which, with varying degrees of commitment, support Soviet policies while organizing themselves within the framework of national politics. This channel for advocacy in day-to-day politics gives the USSR an asymmetrical advantage in the competition for influence in states where party structures are weak, institutions fragile and the political context fluid. This theoretical asset, which the proximity of Soviet power might be expected to enhance, nevertheless has not proved advantageous in practice in the Middle East. The reasons for this can be elucidated in a brief discussion of two contrasting states – Iran and Iraq.

Iran

In Iran the Communist *Tudeh* (Masses) party, founded in 1941 and banned after 1949, enjoyed a brief spurt of activity during the oil nationalization crisis of 1951–3. After the rapprochement between the USSR and Iran in the mid-1960s the party lost Moscow's support. Based in East Germany, it found itself with a shrunken membership base within Iran and facing an effective campaign of repression by the Iranian authorities. It lost its role as the major protest movement against the monarchy and failed to attract new adherents either within Iran or abroad. Meanwhile, student opposition gravitated towards Marxist groupings that stressed in varying degrees the need for violence, national independence and a return to Islam. They rejected *Tudeh's* passivity, its continual dependence on a USSR which co-operated with the Shah's régime and, in some cases, its atheism.

The *Tudeh*, like everyone else, was very slow to recognize the popular basis of Ayatollah Khomeini's appeal in the movement of opposition to the Shah. Because it had been the first and principal vehicle for opposition to the Shah, its elderly, exiled leaders were reluctant to acknowledge the erosion of its attraction which resulted in part from the demographic shifts in Iran (over 50 per cent of the population are under 20) and in part from changes in the social structure and the material conditions in the country. Nonetheless, in 1975, at the Fifteenth Plenum of the Central Committee, the *Tudeh* agreed to a tactical coalition with the Islamic opposition with the priority of removing the Shah. However, the events of 1978, culminating in the departure of the Shah in January 1979, took this coalition by surprise. The *Tudeh* leader, Iraj Eskandari, who had only recently disparaged Khomeini's importance, was replaced by Nourredin Khianouri, who quickly sought to identify the *Tudeh* with the massive protests that had been organized in Iran. In the last quarter of 1978 the Soviet Embassy in Teheran printed and circulated a publication called *Novid*, which promoted the notion of an Islamic Communist coalition and stressed the common goals of the two opposition groups.

However, the *Tudeh* was at a severe disadvantage in the new era of Iran's political life which opened up after the fall of the monarchy. Handicapped not only by its marginal role in the revolt and its shrunken base of support, its symbolic importance as the protest movement *par excellence* has been perhaps irretrievably eroded. More significant still, it was anathema to Iranian revolutionaries on two grounds: as an atheist movement, and as an agent of a foreign power which contravened both the religious and the nationalist impulses that fired Iran's revolt.[112] The immediate task of the party was therefore to insinuate itself into the opposition movement's mainstream. Khianouri claimed that the *Tudeh* had organized the oil-field workers and was thus in control of the strategic oil sector. He also argued that the new political system in Iran should not discriminate among parties and should provide 'guarantees for all forms of popular

democracy'. On foreign policy he argued that arms were not necessary for Iran's defence: 'A friendly Iran would be the greatest guarantee for the Soviet Union's security'.[113]

Soviet policy, like that of the *Tudeh*, tended to be improvized, to concentrate on identification with the broad current of the revolt and on not foreclosing future options. Its pattern of reporting of *Tudeh* statements is instructive. While opposing the short-lived Bakhtiar government, Moscow did not transmit *Tudeh* exhortations to overthrow it by force. After its fall, a recurrent theme in Soviet commentaries was the need for unity and for recognition of the pluralism of the opposition movement. It broadcast the *Tudeh's* support for the establishment of a provisional government and the proclamation of an Islamic Republic, but, reflecting anxiety that the Communists might be excluded by the Muslim clerics, it also broadcast the *Tudeh's* warning: 'it is necessary to avoid disagreement and not to try to monopolize the revolutionary movement'.[114] The USSR associated herself with the *Tudeh* statement (echoed by other Leftist groups) that the revolution was 'only the completion of the first step on the people's road to a final victory'. She also broadcast the announcement that the *Tudeh* party was trying to form a single 'people's front' which, by including the main elements, would enable the revolutionary movements and Khomeini's supporters to unite.

The *Tudeh* party is now an instrument of doubtful value to the USSR in Iran's current fluid political scene. Depleted in numbers, it is probably the third largest Leftist grouping – after the radical *Fedayin-e-Khalq* (People's Fighters) and *Mujahedin-e-Khalq* (People's Crusaders).[115] While the former is Marxist–secularist, the latter is a radical Islamic grouping claiming to be 'Marxist' in programme but without the atheism. Neither suffer the same stigma of irrelevance and foreign association as the *Tudeh*, both played small but important roles in the revolution, and both are larger, armed and well-organized. (Nevertheless, the *Tudeh* does appear to be well-organized in Kurdistan and Azerbaijan.) All three groups believe that the provisional government is a first step to a complete revolution and a classless society.

Depending on the course of Iranian politics in the immediate future, all three may well co-operate to protect themselves or to promote their overlapping and partially compatible goals. The durability of the Ayatollah Khomeini's government appears doubtful, and, given the wide dispersion of arms and proliferation of factions, combined with the disintegration of authority, the present disoriented régime does remain an inviting and accessible target for any determined group. The utility of the relationship with the *Tudeh* may thus be somewhat higher for the USSR in the present murky post–revolutionary phase, in which only marginal investments could go a long way towards influencing the eventual outcome of the revolution in Iran, than it might be later on as an alternative government.

Iraq

In Iraq, as in Iran, the Soviet Union has been content to emphasize relations with the government of the day – even at the expense of the local Communist party.[116] The agility of the Soviet Union in reversing priorities and sides in practice has been as evident in Iraq as in Iran. Both the Iraqi Communists and the Kurds have been its victims.

Over the past two decades of Republican Iraq, the role of the Communist party has been severely circumscribed. In at least two respects this role has differed from that of its counterpart in Iran. First, its base being primarily in the Kurdish and Shi'ite areas of Iraq, it has represented a threat to the government, which has been dominated by the Sunni minority. Second, it has competed with popular indigenous ideologies and movements, such as Pan–Arabism, Arab Socialism and Ba'athism. By virtue of its source of support and in its ideology the Iraqi Communist Party has therefore posed a potential threat to Iraqi unity and to the Arab identity of the Iraqi régime.

In the immediate aftermath of the 1958 revolution, the Communists in Iraq quickly succeeded in isolating themselves by underestimating the hold of religion on the very elements of the population whom they sought to attract. Within a year of alleged abortive coup attempts, they were suppressed. The advent of a Ba'athist régime in 1963 increased their isolation, for they were seen as opponents of nationalism and national independence. There was common ground in the acceptance of socialism generally,

but Communism, with its political disadvantages, was rejected by most Iraqis. Throughout most of the 1960s Iraqi leaders struggled with the problem of reconciling the needs of a highly fractured society, and the fear of Communist extremism contributed to a reluctance to move towards representative government.[117] As a result the Iraqi Communist Party was harshly dealt with. The tension between a single Arab Socialist Union movement and the requirements of a plural society has indeed never been satisfactorily resolved, for it raises two problems: the fate of the Kurdish Democratic Party, and the issue of the recognition of the Communist party.

In July 1968, the Ba'athists took over the government for the second time and have since retained it. The leadership, which is tightly controlled by a clique from the town of Takrit, is strongly Sunni in composition. It offered other groups, such as Communists and Kurds, a choice between nominal participation in a National Front under the Ba'ath–military hegemony and a total cessation of political activity. Mindful of earlier repression by the Ba'ath, the Communist party went underground. However, reflecting the warmth of relations between Baghdad and Moscow in the afterglow of the 1972 Treaty of Friendship, it was legalized in July 1973 and, not without internal dissent, agreed (with Soviet encouragement) to join a National Front and accept the Ba'ath–military domination. In practice the Communists thereby put their seal of approval on Ba'athist policies and relinquished the possibility of exercising any influence on them. This accommodation reflected Soviet support for the Ba'ath, rather than any Ba'ath tolerance for the Communists.

After the settlement of the dispute with Iran in March 1975, the Ba'ath moved towards both a draconian settlement of the Kurdish question and increased economic ties with the West. Saddam Hussein reassured the Iranians in April 1975 that the Arab world was in favour of nationalism and revolution but would never be Marxist. Indeed, though still often aligned with the USSR (largely because of similar positions on the issue of Palestine), divergences have surfaced in recent years.

The April 1978 military coup in Afghanistan which brought to power an avowedly Marxist régime unsettled the Ba'ath. This was exacerbated by criticism from the Communist party within the National Front directed against Iraq's commercial activities with the West. It also urged reconciliation with Syria, proposed elections for a National Assembly, and called for an 'autonomous' Kurdish area. This conjunction of Soviet advances in the area and criticism from local Communists spurred a rapid Iraqi response. In May 1978, 21 Communists were executed allegedly for plotting with the armed forces. Saddam Hussein affirmed that this action was intended as a warning to those who would try to subvert the state,[118] and the timing of the suppression served not only as a signal to the Communists to support the National Front, but also as a reminder to her major ally of Iraq's concern. A year later these strains had not been dissipated, and the Ba'ath leadership remained anxious. Although the Kurds had been deprived of Communist support when the Communists joined the National Front, the Kurdish issue appeared set for imminent revival in the wake of Iran's political upheaval. If the prospect of renewed Kurdish pressure, combined with a militant Shi'ite government in Teheran, was bad enough, the growth of Soviet influence in a weakened neighbour was almost worse. To strengthen itself to handle the problems with the Kurds and the USSR, the Ba'ath leadership effected a fragile reconciliation with the Syrian Ba'ath in November 1978. Possibly because of renewed activity by the Iraqi Communist Party, which left the National Front in January, the Iraqi leaders again purged the Communists in 1979, arresting 27 members and suppressing the party paper. Ostensibly the prosecutions were of conspirators rather than Communists, but in practice (as in 1978) they were indistinguishable. Again the issue related in part to Soviet power in the region.[119] The Soviet Union was unable to do little more than broadcast (and hence endorse) the Iraqi Communist Party's pleas for unity and co-operation among revolutionary forces and for an end to the widespread persecution of the Communists in Iraq.

The USSR has found that Communist parties have not fared well in either friendly states (Iraq) or unfriendly states (Iran) – though there is no indication of systematic Soviet support for these parties, either independently, or as a condition for relations with the Governments concerned. In Iran the *Tudeh*, once the protest movement *par excellence*, has been overtaken by events and issues and is severely handicapped by Soviet adjacency and past Soviet imperialism. In Iraq the Communist party could have served as a vehicle of protest for the Kurds and Shi'ites who have been suppressed by the Sunni Arabs. Yet it has been undermined by the USSR's general support for the Ba'ath, while spasmodic Soviet support for the party has only encouraged its suppression. In neither country has the Communist party been identified with nationalism or independence. Communist party appeal to the masses, therefore, has been limited. As an outlet for dispossessed minorities, Communism may still prove effective, but it has little prospect of competing with Islam for the loyalty of the masses or of achieving comparable moral authority in the currency of daily life.

As an instrument of Soviet foreign policy, Communist parties have therefore been of only limited value. Soviet reluctance to support the *Tudeh* party (as an agent of change) without relinquishing the option to do so, has been paralleled elsewhere. In Iraq, Moscow has valued relations with the Ba'ath party, even when this has been at the expense of local Communists. This pragmatic precedence bestowed on relations with governments is likely to remain – particularly until relations are established with Saudi Arabia. At the same time, while support for local Communists will not be allowed to interfere with state relations, the option of reviving such support may be exploitable for psychological pressure. And where relations with governments deteriorate (as they have, for example, in Iraq), the temptation to revert to alternative means of attaining influence in a particular country may increase considerably.

CONCLUSIONS

The competition between the super-powers remains a basic fact in international politics. Although the relative balance of military power between the two blocs will not necessarily be a determinant of influence in specific regions, it will condition great-power relations and affect both definitions of 'interests' and the propensity for risk-taking. In the Persian Gulf region, for example, the shifting military balance has had important political consequences. Growing Soviet military power, strategic and conventional, has brought the USSR to a position of overall nuclear parity and (possibly) conventional military superiority in the region. It has enhanced Soviet access to the region, ended the era of cost-free interventions for the West and thus inhibited Western responses. Politically it is more significant still, for it has, for the first time, made the USSR a factor to be taken into account in decisions made in the capitals of the Arabian peninsula. Quick reaction from the north, a foothold on the periphery, and a naval presence in the south now make the USSR a 'relevant' actor in Persian Gulf affairs.

The presence of proximate Soviet power raises the question of how it will be used politically to affect local states' perceptions, and how it can be used politically for 'commensurate geopolitical adjustment' vis-à-vis the United States.[120] This in turn is contingent on Western reactions and local perceptions of the West's long-term tenacity. In this respect the outlook for the West is bleak. The British withdrawal from the Gulf ended the region's insulation from outside pressures, but the United States' policy of selective retrenchment has not yet been buttressed by a consensus on any core of irreducible commitments. Nor, despite Western dependence on this vulnerable region, has the relevance of the Western commitment been demonstrated beyond doubt to the local states. Over-reaction to the YAR–PDRY border dispute, after under-reaction in Ethiopia and Iran, only underlined United States' unpredictability in the eyes of local leaders. Nor will increased naval deployments be a substitute for a sense of long-term purpose, though they may help in providing reassurance. (Standard US practice has been 'occasional deployments' of carrier task-forces three times a year, lasting 30–40 days each, although three such task forces were on station in January 1980.) Nonetheless, while the growth in virtually all dimensions of her military power has made the Persian Gulf states more accessible to the Soviet Union, and tends to constrain Western responses, it is doubtful whether this power can be easily or economically converted into sustained influence in the Gulf –

despite its marked effect on the perceptions of local leaders.[121]

Intensive Soviet activity on the periphery of the region – in the PDRY, Ethiopia and Afghanistan – has emphasized its vulnerabilities without as yet threatening vital Western interests directly. All the same, this probing on the periphery has clearly been co-ordinated, for these three areas serve Soviet strategic interests, and each can be reinforced from the other.[122] Furthermore, a somewhat more direct Soviet role is suggested by arms shipments, (particularly those to the PDRY in 1979, which included MiG–21, SU–20 and MiG–23 aircraft) and by the speed with which the arms were assimilated. Whether this presages a greater willingness to take risks is unclear, but it does appear to represent a Soviet decision to probe and expose Saudi Arabia to further pressure after the revolt in Iran.

The growing intersection of Western and Eastern interests in the Persian Gulf region makes it most important that a regional code of conduct should be elaborated between East and West. The way in which relations are codified and competition regulated and restrained in this volatile arena will be a test case for super-power behaviour in the Third World. The growth of the Soviet Union's military power and her thirst for status as a co-equal global power has defined a widening arc of 'legitimate' interest, while the Western position appears to be more vulnerable. In peacetime, the fact of Soviet political predominance in the region could be used as a hostage to West European good behaviour.[123] The potentially competitive dimension of oil-consuming countries' dependence on the region is also susceptible to exploitation. By exacerbating differing needs and vulnerabilities, Western alliance cohesion could be weakened if allies are tempted to compete for oil in crises. Wartime denial has become a credible instrument. Employed as a lever it could be used in crises elsewhere as an inducement for passivity. The very fact of vulnerability could psychologically inhibit Western policy-makers.

Short of crisis or conflict, however, military power is not a feasible instrument of day-to-day relations. The USSR has found that her own interests in the Persian Gulf are no longer one-dimensional. Her interests in stable borders, in assured supplies of gas (and possibly oil) from Iran, in trade and in predictable neighbours vie with the desire to exploit instabilities that may be construed as set-backs for the West. Yet exploitation is becoming progressively more difficult. The Soviet Union needs technology and trade with the West and she is becoming more entangled and more interested in creating the basis for long-term supply. A web of interests discourages abrupt shifts and dictates sensitivity to a much broader pattern of interactions. For example, buying oil from Iraq and reselling it at a profit has annoyed the Iraqis, and relations with Baghdad also suffer from wider Soviet involvement, for example in Ethiopia; similarly the credit of Soviet support for Afghanistan has a corresponding debit in terms of relations with Iran. In a region of increasingly mixed interests, clear-cut enemies or allies are hard to identify.

The USSR's response has been to hedge her bets (e.g., between Iraq and Syria or between Iraq and Iran). But caution is not a recipe for great break-throughs. Indeed, Soviet experience in the region has underlined the limits of external power. Flux and ferment, the features of politics in this region, are unsteady foundations for strong diplomatic relationships. Moreover, the Soviet Union is twice handicapped: first, by the limited relevance of her technology and ideas in an area that is both rich and religious; and, second, by her narrow political foothold on the Arabian peninsula itself, which constrains expansion. The resulting sense of frustration may encourage the exploitation of such political opportunities as do occur, particularly as these opportunities are likely to favour the USSR as underdog. The Soviet Union has also realized that it is only the military instrument that can affect events decisively. Yet Soviet gains may risk triggering a decisive Western response which would tend to neutralize any advance and accelerate a regional unity that would otherwise be unimaginable.

While it is true that the USSR values stability and predictability on her borders, and that her growing and more diverse interests will strengthen her attachment to them further afield, it is premature to see such trends as determining Soviet policy. Chaos is as much a constraint as an opportunity, but, though change (and particularly disruptive change) could benefit the USSR as a relative newcomer to the region, this is not inevitably the case. Much depends on how change comes about, on the role of outside powers before and during the crisis, on the alignment of the state or states concerned, as well as on the 'final' outcome after the change.

The major threats to the region's stability, and hence to the availability of oil at reasonable prices and in the necessary quantities, have come from internal rather than external sources. The types of régimes in power in the oil-producing states and their character, composition and orientation are of far more importance than scenarios of interdiction of oil on the high seas or at choke-points. The Soviet Union knows this just as she knows that military power is visible, that willingness to use it is remarked, and that the leaders in the Persian Gulf are impressionable. For these leaders the perceived balance between Western reliability, on the one hand, and the momentum of Soviet cumulative gains, on the other, determines the orientation of their foreign policies. And, since these policies are, after all intended to assure the régimes' security, they are susceptible to reversal. Moreover, such reversals need not only occur when a régime falls; redefinitions of interest by elites may swiftly move a state from alignment to neutrality without the precipitant of revolution.

However, the process of rapid modernization which the oil-producing states are undergoing will in any case affect their internal stability. The revenues brought by oil seem bound to undermine traditional structures of power, even as they provide the leadership with the means with which to allay immediate pressures. Young populations will, in a short space of time, seek all the benefits of welfare states and all the freedom of political participation, and the loads on existing institutions will be very great. Change will necessarily mean instability and it will be easier to exploit that instability than to assure stability.

Even though it is likely to find the going difficult, however, it will be particularly important that the West should not define stability as the *status quo* or equate it with 'no-change'. Western interests will be served by seeking to contain and channel disruptive and disorderly change, and by deterring interference whether from within or from outside the region. But the policy will need to be subtle and responsive. The Western thirst for petroleum may accelerate the modernization process, which will in turn tend to destabilize governments. A balance will need to be struck between short- and long-term interests: too much support for an existing régime risks creating an identification with it that will invite retribution from its successor if it is overthrown; too much distance from a régime may only accelerate its demise. An insatiable short-term thirst may unleash the very pressures that undermine long-term oil needs. Interventionary forces may be necessary to deter outside interventions, but they will not be able to deal with the contingencies most likely to affect Gulf security – internal disorders. The Western states will need not only interventionary forces, assured access and staging points, but also a renewed commitment to multi-level involvement.

Yet, if the West is entangled in this volatile region, the USSR will still find it far from easy to gain positions of advantage. Although she does not suffer from the West's handicap of being seen as an intrusive and disruptive agent, she has her own handicap; she is seen as a promoter of atheism and an expansionist power. Her friendship is valued primarily because of the persistence of the Arab–Israeli dispute, and it is here that the greater opportunities lie for Soviet exploitation. A polarization of the Arab world as in the 1960s, a revival of shrillness in intra-Arab politics and increased dependence on the USSR by the rejectionist states will assist in the radicalization of the Arabian peninsula, and active Western (and especially US) diplomacy will be essential if the traditional régimes are to escape the resultant pressures.

If she lacked the toehold the Arab–Israeli dispute provides, the Soviet Union's advantages in the region would be less obvious. Her relevance as an 'anti-colonialist' power is not striking to Muslim states which hold no salt-water theory of imperialism, and as she has little to offer, the governments of states must find ways of meeting the needs and demands of restive peoples by, *inter alia*, devising responsive political institutions. Nonetheless, Soviet policies have met with some success. While benefiting from the Arab resistance to alignment which increases the inhibitions of states like Saudi Arabia and Kuwait from making overt, formal security arrangements and granting bases, the USSR is able meanwhile to promote 'non-alignment' in a self-serving way in the PDRY, for example. She can also provide non-attribut-

able covert assistance (an instrument now eschewed by the West) via the supply of Cuban forces, which can quickly upset a regional balance. Finally, the uneven though inexorable growth of her influence on the periphery of the region provides her with the means for probing and exerting pressure which may encourage a process of 'self-Finlandization' among these weak and exposed states.

If the politics of the region, the balance of forces and the interests at work in it are not conducive to sudden break-throughs and to irreversible changes in control, the issue for outside powers becomes one of the balance of influence obtained at a particular time. Although the two blocs are not symmetrically dependent on the region, both have growing interests in it. Recognition that advantages gained are likely to be of a temporary nature, combined with an understanding of the costs and dangers involved, may create incentives to identify ground rules governing the behaviour of outside powers towards the region, although it has to be admitted that Soviet actions in Afghanistan demonstrate that convergence may be a long way off. Pending such an agreement, tacit or formal, Western states will need to be more rather than less involved. Their lack of covert capabilities will inhibit the range of responses (short of inter-vention) that may be required. A substitute must be found in better intelligence, in more accurate political analysis and by showing greater sensitivity to the inter-related nature of events in the Persian Gulf, the Arab–Israeli zone and Afghanistan. Furthermore, for any single Western country to attempt to gain unilateral advantage at the expense of others would be a recipe for chaos. Though not all equally dependent on the region for their oil, NATO members share an equal stake in a stable region and a harmonious alliance. Any assistance bilateral or multilateral, that individual members can give in assuring access to the Persian Gulf's resources and buttressing its security would therefore diminish the heavy burden on the US. The co-ordination of policy in the West would therefore be helpful in spreading the load throughout the Western Alliance. In sum, the progress of Soviet influence in the Persian Gulf is less likely to result from a hospitable regional environment than from Western failures of conception, unity and will.

NOTES

[1] A major problem in any study of Soviet policy is the relative weight to be attached to public declarations, radio broadcasts and official statements, as opposed to the actual conduct of policy.

There has been little historical contact and even less diplomatic interaction between the USSR and the countries of the Persian Gulf region, apart from Iran. The past is thus a relatively barren source of insights into future behaviour. Of necessity, therefore, considerable reliance has been placed on statements, radio broadcasts and official documents. It is hoped that a judicious use of these rather soft sources has avoided excessive reliance on purely declaratory policy, and that the corresponding analysis of Soviet interests has put them in their proper perspective.

[2] Historically, Russia was not present in naval or political terms, either in or close to the Persian Gulf while British paramountcy guaranteed a degree of political insulation from outside influences.

[3] For example, if the Chah Behar base on the Indian Ocean is ever developed, it would be an attractive site for a Soviet naval base facility.

[4] See, *inter alia*, *Peking Review*, 4 February 1977, p. 24, and 10 February 1978, pp. 20–21.

[5] *Ibid.*, 30 June 1978.

[6] *Ibid.*, 8 September 1978, pp. 5–10.

[7] *Ibid.*, 13 April 1979, pp. 18–20.

[8] See *Krasnaya Zvezda* articles, reprinted in *Pravda* and broadcast by Tass, 2, 3 June (SU/4616/A4/1, 4 June 1974); V. Pavlovsky, 'Asian Security and Peking Policy', *New Times*, No. 23 (July 1974) pp. 25–26; L. Medvedko, 'CENTO: Against the Current', *Pravda*, 1 March 1975 (*Current Digest of Soviet Press* (CDSP), Vol. XXVII, No. 9 p. 22); L. Dadian, 'Peking's Middle-East Policy', *International Affairs* (Moscow), 5 May 1978, p. 52; 'Asian Security and Peking's Intrigues', *Pravda*, 21 April 1974 (CDSP, Vol. XXVI, No. 16 p. 23); article in *Aziya i Afrika Segodnya* broadcast by Tass, 30 July 1976 (SU/5275/A3/1, 2 August 1976).

[9] Moscow Radio in Persian, 21 November 1974 (SU/4763/A4/2 23 November 1974), 30 May 1974 (SU/4615/A4/2, 3 June 1974), 18 June 1978 (SU/5844/C/1, 21 June 1978), 24 June 1978 (SU/5850/A4/1–2, 28 June 1978); Tass in English, 8 July 1978 (SU/5860/A4/3–4, 10 July 1978).

[10] The Soviet Union supplied all arms and training and accounted for 50 per cent of trade. US assistance was small-scale and symbolic, amounting to $15 million in 1975. Even after major OPEC commitments (of up to $800 million) the USSR remained the most important source of economic and military aid and Afghanistan's principal trading partner. Moscow's $1.3 billion economic aid programme created Kabul's natural gas and petroleum industry and is responsible for the infrastructure. See *Communist Aid to less Developed Countries of the Free World 1976* (Washington DC: CIA, July 1977). Soviet assistance includes a north–south highway linking Soviet Central Asia to Northern Pakistan.

[11] The July 1937 Sa'dabad Pact of non-aggression with Iran, Iraq and Turkey 'was the first (and last) regional agreement Afghanistan made'. Vartan Gregorian, *The Emergence of Modern Afghanistan* (Stanford, Calif.: Stanford U.P., 1969), p. 377.

[12] The thirteen-member 'Revolutionary Council' of the new 'Democratic State of Afghanistan' contained eleven known Communists.

[13] By 1979 the USSR had promised $1,000 million over the next five years and had almost doubled the low price paid for natural gas from Afghanistan (from $21 to $37.8 per cubic metre), boosting Afghan revenues from $54 million to nearly $97 million dollars a year. Two-thirds of the Soviet advisers are military.

[14] This data is from *Communist Aid to the Less Developed Countries of the Free World 1977* (Washington DC: CIA, November 1978), p. 32.

[15] 32 *Mirage* F–1C fighters and 4 F–1B combat trainers, 100 AMX–30 tanks and 360 *HOT* anti-tank missiles are on order. See *The Military Balance 1979–1980* (London: IISS, 1979), pp. 40, 104.

[16] In 1976 agreement was reached for the delivery of a further 3.6 billion cubic metres annually to Czechoslovakia bringing the total annual throughout to 17 billion cubic metres.

[17] Up to $2 billion by the mid-1980s, according to one source, see the CIA report, *USSR: Development of the Gas Industry*, quoted in *International Herald Tribune*, August 1978.

[18] This is in addition to the gas-swap arrangement, under which Iran is to supply $2.5 billion worth of gas over 20 years – the largest commercial arrangement Czechoslovakia has ever concluded with a non-socialist state.

[19] See especially the CIA's report, *Soviet Economic Problems and Prospects* (Washington DC: CIA, ER77-10436U, July 1977), and Senate Select Committee on Intelligence, *The Soviet Oil Situation: An Evaluation of CIA Analyses of Soviet Oil Production*, Staff Report 95th Cong., 2nd sess. (Washington DC: USGPO, 28–025, May 1978). More recent analyses corroborate these e.g., a CIA report leaked in 1979 (see *New York Times*, 30 July 1979).

[20] See Giles Bullard, 'The Power of Menace: Soviet Relations with South Asia 1917–1974', *British Journal of International Studies*, Vol. II, No. 1 (April 1976), pp. 51–66. A modern variant is pressure on Iran and the Persian Gulf states as a reply to tensions originating elsewhere, for example in Europe.

[21] For a historical perspective see Richard Ullmann, *Anglo-Soviet Relations 1917–1921*, Vol. III. *The Anglo-Soviet Accord* (Princeton N.J.: Princeton U.P., 1972), pp. 317–94 (esp. 343–4).

[22] All three states sought alliances after World War II, when their policies of neutrality in varying degrees failed. For an especially useful discussion of Norway see Johan Holst, 'Norwegian Security Policy: Options and Constraints' in Johan Holst (ed.), *Five Roads to Nordic Security* (Oslo: Universitetsforlaget, 1973), pp. 76–126.

[23] R. J. Vincent, *Military Power and Political Influence*, Adelphi Paper No. 119 (London: IISS, 1975), p. 27.

[24] In October 1979 the provisional government in the republic of Iran announced its formal abrogation of the Treaty.

[25] For details see my *Iran's Foreign Relations* (Berkeley, Calif: University of California Press, 1974), pp. 60 *et seq.* Moscow sought to avoid any precise definition of what it found offensive and to retain the freedom to object to any activity that it deemed unwelcome. There is an illuminating parallel with Moscow's attempts to define as *rights* Norway's conditional and self-imposed restrictions on foreign troops (and nuclear weapons emplacement) on her soil in peacetime. See Holst, *op. cit.* in note 22, pp. 113–18, and Egil Ulstein, *Nordic Security*, Adelphi Paper No. 81 (London: IISS, 1971), p. 9.

[26] The Shah's views were summarized by George V. Allen in a dispatch to Secretary of State George C. Marshall on 16 June 1947. *Foreign Relations of the US 1947*, Vol. V, *The Near East and Africa* (Washington DC: USGPO, 1971), p. 915.

[27] This extraordinary sensitivity to Soviet security concerns and blindness to those of others is found in the interview with George Kennan in *The New York Review of Books*, Vol. XXIII, No. 20–21 (20 January 1977). pp. 12–13, and in his book *The Cloud of Danger: Current Realities of American Foreign Policy* (Boston: Little Brown, 1977), pp. 88, 178.

[28] For a representative sample of comments consult: *Izvestiya* article, broadcast by Tass, monitored by Foreign Broadcasts Information Service (FBIS, III, 30 August 1976); L. Medvedko, 'Manoeuvres of Oil-Neo-Colonialism' in *Sotsialisticheskaya Industriya* (Tass, 10 August 1976, in SU/5283/A4/1, 11 August 1976); Sergey Losev, 'Who is Kindling the Arms Race', *Pravda Vostoka* (Tashkent), 21 August 1976 (FBIS, III, 10 September 1976, pp. F10–11); S. Losev, Moscow Radio, 10 September 1976 (SU/5311/A4/1, 14 September 1976); *Krasnaya Zvezda* article, broadcast by Moscow Radio, 26 July (SU/5875/A4/3, 27 July 1978); A. Leonidov, 'Dangerous Course', *Izvestiya*, 26 August (SU/5299/A4/2–4, 31 August 1976); A. Chernyshov, 'Peace and Security in the Indian Ocean', *International Affairs* (Moscow), 12 December 1977, pp. 43–4; V. Gan, 'Dangerous Policy' in *Krasnaya Zvezda*, broadcast by Moscow Radio (FBIS III, No. 173, 3 September 1976, p. F–3).

[29] Shamseddin Rakhimov, Commentary, Moscow Radio in Persian, 29 November (SU/5379/A4/1–2, 2 December 1976).

[30] Despite repeated protests the intrusions continued. In 1977 the Shah requested live missile tests for the F–14 crews (see *Aviation Week*, 5 September 1977, p. 14).

[31] Moscow Radio in Persian, 15 December 1976 (FBIS, III, No. 244, 17 December 1976, pp. F1–2). See also 'In order to Eavesdrop', *Pravda*, 4 June 1975, (CDSP, XXVII, No. 22, 15 June 1975, p. 16); Tass in English, 30 August 1976 (FBIS, III, No. 169, 31 August 1976, pp. F6–7).

[32] Soviet commentaries on the Arabian peninsula emphasize this. For example, detente 'does not and cannot possibly mean the freezing of the objective process of historical development in this region. Detente does not represent an insurance policy for rotten régimes, does not confer rights for the suppression of the just struggle of peoples for national liberation and does not obviate the necessity for social changes. This is a problem for the people themselves in each country to solve'. Radio Peace and Progress (RPP), in Arabic, 25 June 1976 (SU/5246/A4/1, 27 June 1976).

[33] Tass, 3 March 1968 (SU/2712/A4/1, 5 March 1968).

[34] See, for example, Moscow Radio in Persian, 28 May 1974 (SU/4613/A4/1, 31 May 1974); Moscow Radio in Arabic, 5 June 1974 (SU/4619/A4/2, 7 June 1974).

[35] See Moscow Radio in Persian, 25 May 1974 (SU/4610/A4/1, 28 May 1974).

[36] RPP in English, 15 August 1974 (SU/4680/A4/1, 17 August 1974); see also Moscow Radio in Arabic, 20 April 1976 (SU/5189/A4/a, 23 April 1976).

[37] See *inter alia*, Moscow Radio in Arabic, 29 November 1976 (SU/5378/A4/1, December 1976); Tass, 28 November 1976 (FBIS, III, No. 231, 30 November 1976); Moscow Radio in Persian, 30 November 1976 (SU/5379/A4/2, 2 December 1976); Moscow Radio in Arabic, 26 November 1976 (FBIS, III, No. 234, 3 December 1976).

[38] D. Volsky, 'King Faysal's Holy War', *New Times*, February 1973, pp. 26–7.

[39] See Moscow Radio in Persian, 14 April 1974 (SU/4576/A4/1, 17 April 1974); D. Dymov, 'Persian Gulf Countries at the Cross-Roads', *International Affairs* (Moscow), March 1973, p. 57.

[40] Moscow Radio in Arabic, 6 July 1976 (SU/5254/A4/1, 8 July 1976).

[41] Alexei Vasiliyev, 'Persian Gulf: Where Epochs Meet', *New Times*, January 1974, p. 29.

[42] Boris Teplinsky, 'The Persian Gulf in Imperialist Plans', *New Times*, September 1972, pp. 23–4.

[43] For representative comments see Moscow Radio in Persian, 29 July 1976 (SU/5275/A4/5, 2 August 1976); Moscow Radio in Arabic, 5 August 1975 (SU/4975/A4/1, 7 August, 1975).

[44] Howard Hensel makes this point in two detailed articles: 'Asian Collective Security: The Soviet View', *Orbis*, XIX, No. 4 (Winter 1976), pp. 1564–80; and 'Asian Collective Security and the Irani-Iraqi Border Dispute: The Soviet View', *Journal of South Asian and Middle Eastern Studies*, I, No. 1 (September 1977), p. 44–64.

[45] This treaty comprised Iran, Turkey, Pakistan, Iraq and Britain, with the US as an associate member. After the 1958 revolution in Iraq it was renamed the Central Treaty Organization (CENTO), and Iraq withdrew.

[46] See Department of State: Intelligence and Research, *Communist States and Developing Countries: Aid and Trade in 1972* (Washington DC: RECS-10, August 1973).

[47] By 1977, 3,850 Soviet economic technicians were in Iran, *op. cit.* in note 14, p. 9.

[48] A. Shuschazhnikev, 'Soviet–Iranian Economic cooperation', *International Affairs* (Moscow), 6 June 1974, pp. 111–12. All these themes were combined in a *Pravda* article, 'Two Approaches to Iran', after the revolution in Iran in 1979; it was broadcast by Tass in English on 13 March and excerpted in SU/6066/A4/1, 14 March 1979.

[49] See Chapter IV.

[50] The loosening of Iran's ties with the West was in part the inevitable result of larger oil revenues (stemming from increased production), which reduced her earlier near total dependency, and in part the result of a deliberate policy of seeking a form of *de facto* non-alignment within a pro-Western alliance. It was evident in the emphasis on an 'independent national' foreign policy

after 1964. Greater sensitivity to Soviet interests did not preclude serious differences. For example, Teheran, mindful of the potential precedent which the invasion of Czechoslovakia and the formulation of the Brezhnev doctrine might set for other Soviet neighbours, condemned the Soviet action. But the Shah refused to cancel a subsequent visit to Moscow, despite appeals from the US and Britain to do so.

51 President Podgorny in Teheran in March 1970. See *Iran's Foreign Relations, op. cit.* in note 25.
52 In June 1978 two Iranian helicopters which strayed across the Turkmenistan border area were shot down, killing eight military personnel. Moscow protested about the incident, demanding that those responsible 'be punished' and that measures be taken to 'prevent any recurrence'.
53 In this incident, in December 1978 there were indications that Soviet espionage was also responsible for disabling the Iranian air force squadrons that might have responded to the intrusion.
54 See John Erickson, 'The Ground Forces in Soviet Military Policy', *Strategic Review*, Vol. 6, No. 1 (Winter 1978), p. 74; Erickson, 'Soviet European Theatre Forces', colloquium on *The British Defence Effort in the 1980s and Beyond* (University of Aberdeen, June 1978), p. 9.
55 See Dennis Chaplin, 'Soviet Oil and the Security of the Gulf', *RUSI Journal*, Vol. 123, No. 4 (December 1978), pp. 50–52.
56 Secretary of Defense Harold Brown, *Annual Report FY 1980* (Washington DC: Department of Defense, 1979) p. 106. Normal deployment on the Soviet–Iranian border consists of some 100,000 troops, including 17 divisions, 4,500 tanks, 500 fighters, 150 long-range bombers and two airborne divisions. Only 3 divisions in the Transcaucasus are reported to be in a high state of readiness (category I status).
57 For representative efforts, see *Pravda*, 22 October 1972 (CDSP, XXIV, No. 42, 15 November 1972, p. 6–7); Radio Moscow, 17 March 1973 (CDSP, XXVI, No. 11; 11 April 1973, pp. 25–6); *Ibid*, 12 August 1973 (FBIS, No. 156, 13 August 1973, pp. B4–6).
58 Speech by President Podgorny to Iranian Prime Minister Hoveyda. Tass, 18 November 1974 (SU/4760/C/4, 20 November 1974).
59 For example co-ordinating policy vis-à-vis Palestine with Iraq or agreeing to differ.
60 The Kremlin severed diplomatic ties with Saudi Arabia in 1939.
61 The arrangement to home-port a US detachment of flagship and two escorts (MIDEASTFOR) at Jufayr (Bahrain) was formally terminated in June 1977. In practice the facilities are still used regularly, but without the stationing of military dependents on shore.
62 The YAR has traditionally maintained diplomatic relations with both the USSR and China (since the 1950s) and has secured military equipment from both. In recent years she has been susceptible to Saudi Arabia's influence and has therefore moved towards arms purchases from the West (financed by Riyadh).
63 Tariq Aziz, *The Middle East*, February 1978, pp. 63–4. Later, Saddam Hussein repeated that a requirement for any Gulf security arrangement was 'respect for the status

on freedom of navigation' (*International Herald Tribune*, 10 July 1978).
64 Tass, 2 December 1975 (SU/5076/A4/1–2, 4 December 1975).
65 Moscow Radio, 11 November 1976 (SU/5363/A4/2); RPP, 14 September (SU/5313/A4/2, 16 September 1976).
66 US Senate Committee on Energy and Natural Resources (Jackson Committee), *Access to Oil – The US Relationships with Saudi Arabia and Iran* (Washington DC: USGPO, 95–70, December 1977) See Moscow Radio, 27 December 1977 (SU/570/A4/3–4, 29 December 1977).
67 Moscow Radio 20 April and 12 October 1976 (SU/5189/A4/2, 22 April 1976, and SU/5337/A4/1, 14 October 1976).
68 Moscow Radio, 4 March 1977 (SU/5456/A4/1–2, 7 March 1977). Overtures for normalization were made in 1975, in 1978 and again in 1979, in the aftermath of Saudi hints of distress at US policy in the region. For illustrative Soviet comments see Moscow Radio, 21 September 1978 (SU/5924/A4/2, 23 September 1978), 22 February 1979 (SU/6053/A4/2, 27 February, 1979), 5 March 1979 (SU/6060/A4/2, 7 March 1979). The lack of relations with Saudi Arabia and all the smaller littoral states save Kuwait has limited Soviet opportunities in the area and a rectification of this must be a high priority for Soviet policy. Official Soviet criticisms have usually been muted, once diplomatic relations are established, and this may eventually constitute an incentive for Saudi Arabia to entertain them. The consistency and reliability of US policy, and the balance of advantage in favour of continued exclusive reliance on Washington must also determine any Saudi decision. The Soviet Union may be expected to continue to exploit Saudi doubts about US reliability and to allay anxieties about her own intentions. Particularly in the wake of diminished US credibility as an ally after the crisis in Iran, Washington's failure to anticipate the strains within Iran, and, once they became apparent, to act decisively to minimize the regional consequences, were widely and trenchantly criticized by her allies within the region, and without.
69 Moscow Radio, 20 April 1976 (SU/5189/A4/2, 22 April, 1976).
70 Moscow Radio, 13 February 1977 (FBIS, III, No. 32, 15 February 1977, pp. F6–7).
71 This perspective is cogently spelled out in a commentary by Viktor Alexsandrov, Moscow Radio, 10 August 1978 (SU/5889/A4/1, 12 August 1978).
72 After two years of rumours an agreement was concluded to buy SAM–7 ground-to-air missiles. Kuwait chose to have Egyptian, rather than Soviet, instructors.
73 Quoted by the Middle East Correspondent of *Pravda*, *op. cit.* in note 41, pp. 24–5.
74 The Soviet Union does not acknowledge an equality of interest in Asia between the super-powers.
75 This was true in the Iran–Iraq dispute of 1969–75 and the periodic Iraqi forays into Kuwait in 1973 and in 1975–6. Only where an ally is in serious danger (e.g., Afghanistan in 1979), or where a dispute involves an insignificant or unfriendly state (as with Oman's border dispute with Ras al Khaimah in 1978) does the USSR take sides. (Soviet dislike of Oman is mainly due to her Western orientation; her establishment of diplomatic relations with Peking was probably the last straw.)

172

[76] Soviet conservatism on border issues is related to the fact that she is a beneficiary of existing territorial arrangements, particularly in East Asia, where both China and Japan seek modifications. In Europe her enthusiasm for the Helsinki conference stemmed from this interest.

[77] This was true until November 1978, when, at the Baghdad summit, Iraq moved towards a tacit acceptance of UN General Assembly Resolution 242 and the notion of negotiations over territories occupied in 1967, and implicitly recognized Israel's existence.

[78] Iraq has a short coastline of some 30 miles. Her principal candidate as a naval base, Umm Qasr is unattractive *inter alia* because its approaches are controlled by two islands, Bubiyan and Warba, over which Iraq is in dispute with Kuwait.

[79] The CIA provided Soviet arms captured by Israel in the 1967 war. The decision to support Iran and weaken Iraq by means of encouraging Kurdish separatism was made by President Nixon and Dr Kissinger in Teheran in 1972. Some of the considerations affecting Washington's deliberations were discussed in the US House of Representatives, Select Sub-Committee on Intelligence and leaked in *Village Voice* (New York) 16 February 1976.

[80] L. Koryavin, *Izvestiya*, 9 April 1974, (CDSP, XXVI, No. 14, 1 May 1974, p. 12 *et seq*.); *Pravda*, 26 April 1974 (CDSP, XXVI, No. 17, 27 May 1974, p. 17).

[81] Tass, 18 November 1974 (SU/4760/A4/4, 20 November 1974); *Kayhan International* 21 November 1974.

[82] It appears that the only concrete reaction was the provision to Iraq, of tactical military intelligence obtained by espionage within Iran. Whether this antedated Iran's assistance to the Kurds or was a reaction to it, however, cannot be confirmed. For a popular summary see Arnaud de Borchgrave, 'Space-Age Spies', *Newsweek*, 6 March 1978.

[83] The most reliable figures for the agreement, and also the most conservative, are those of the CIA (*op. cit.*, in note 10, pp. 3, 30). The number of military technicians from the Communist bloc as a whole numbers 1,200.

[84] Moscow Radio, 1 February 1977 (SU/5429/A4/1, 3 February 1977).

[85] Tass, 9 April 1977 (FBIS, III, No. 69, 11 April 1977, pp. F11–12).

[86] See, especially, the criticism by the Ba'ath party organ *Ath Thawra*, 16 August 1977, in *Arab Report and Record*, 16–31 August 1977, pp. 675–6.

[87] Moscow, for example, interprets US assurances to Saudi Arabia after the Shah's removal as gunboat diplomacy intended to intimidate those states 'refusing to approve an Egyptian–Israeli separate treaty'. See Yuri Glukhov 'Increased US Interference in Middle East Affairs', Tass, 12 March 1979 (SU/6065/A4/1, 13 March 1979).

[88] Michael McGwire, 'Changing Naval Operations and Military Intervention' in Ellen P. Stern (ed.), *The Limits of Military Intervention* (London: Sage Publications, 1977), p. 169.

[89] Saudi Arabia provided $100 million for the development of Dhofar province, and an equal sum for the development of a copper industry in the north. In addition she underwrote Oman's purchases of *Rapier* surface-to-air missiles. Kuwait and the UAE made economic commitments, though the actual disbursements to date are unknown.

[90] Washington had been looking towards the establishment of diplomatic relations with the moderate leader Rubbayat Ali who was deposed and killed in the coup.

[91] By the end of 1977 there was a total of 750, split evenly between Cubans and Soviet Union/East Europe (in contrast the YAR had 100 Soviet/East European military advisers); *op. cit.* in note 14, p. 3. By 1979 there were reports of 500–1,000 Soviet military advisers and between 350–700 Cuban advisers.

[92] This is due not only to the Yemen Civil War (1962–7) and the proximity of the YAR but to the fact that well over a million Yemenis work in Saudi Arabia and could become infected with Marxist ideas, or be used as infiltrators. In addition the prospect of unification of the YAR and PDRY – whatever the resulting states' political orientation – is alarming to Riyadh, since it would be numerically dominant in the Peninsula.

[93] Saudi Arabia had for three years been urging the US to provide the YAR with arms (to be paid for by Riyadh), partly to diminish Sanaa's dependence on Soviet arms and advisers. Finally in February 1979, after the Shah's fall and Saudi alarm, Washington agreed to a package of $1,400 million, including 12 F-5E fighters, 64 M-60 tanks, anti-tank missiles and 70 advisers.

[94] Britain's right to use the island expired after 20 years in March 1977, and since 1975 the US has expressed interest in its use. It is not suitable as a naval base, as the waters are too shallow, but its location, outside but near the Persian Gulf, makes it ideal politically as well as militarily.

[95] Robert Legvold, 'The Nature of Soviet Power', *Foreign Affairs*, Vol. 56, No. 1 (October 1977), pp. 49–71.

[96] In April 1976 Iran severed relations with Cuba as a result of hostile references by the Cuban leadership to the Iranian régime.

[97] See *International Herald Tribune*, 28 September 1976, and *Strategic Mid-East and Africa* III, No. 5, 2 February 1977.

[98] *Pravda*, broadcast by Tass, 18 November (SU/5973/C1/1, 20 November 1978).

[99] Ouchinnikov, 'What then is Interference?', *Pravda*, 13 January 1979; Tass, 12 January 1979 (SU/6016/A4/1, 15 January 1979); Alexsey Petrov, 'US Interference in Iran', *Pravda*, 29 January, broadcast by Tass, 30 January 1979 (SU/6030/A4/1, 31 January 1979).

[100] I refer here to two phenomena. First, the calculated leak and publication of the Soviet–Iranian Treaty of 1921 in Washington, in a manner designed to suggest that the Soviet Union indeed had certain interests to which the US ought to adhere. Second, leaving aside the moral question, the *option* of a military coup existed before Ayatollah Khomeini's seizure of power. That General Huyser strongly discouraged this was due in part to Soviet warnings that it would not be tolerated.

[101] Granted the natural Soviet interest, arising from territorial contiguity and enshrined in various legal documents like the 1921 Treaty, there still remains the issue of defining precisely how extensive the legitimate defensive rights of the USSR are, and how they can be balanced with Iran's sovereignty and her allies' responsibilities. The US reaction *during* the crisis appeared to

minimize, if not waive, the latter. It is interesting to speculate whether the United States would have acquiesced in the Soviet claim if domestic conditions in Iran had been better suited to decisive Western intervention, or if a similar claim had been made regarding a non-contiguous state, say Iraq.

[102] Legvold, *op. cit.* in note 95, p. 65.

[103] This action was undertaken in defiance of US diplomatic notes and objections. The USSR gained both ways in the Iran–Afghanistan events. Her warnings put the US on notice regarding assistance to the Teheran government, while she rejected US expressions of concern, and pursued her assistance to her embattled ally. The impression is unavoidable: the USSR has a legitimate and paramount interest in the states on her periphery that makes unilateral interventions permissible, while denying the West equal rights *vis-à-vis* its allies in the same region. This conclusion is reinforced by the Soviet invasion of Afghanistan in December 1979, which occurred after this Paper was completed.

[104] For two years US defence planners, stimulated principally by the USSR's development of power projection capabilities, have been considering the creation of such forces for possible use in local cases such as in the Persian Gulf. Even though the precise contingencies in which such forces might be used had not been fully analysed, the revolution in Iran gave this force-restructuring programme (involving 110,000 troops including 40,000 combat soldiers) a new impetus in early 1979. See Harold Brown, *Department of Defence Annual Report: Fiscal Year 1979*; *Ibid.: Fiscal Year 1980* (Washington DC: Department of Defense, 1978, 1979).

[105] In his broadcast to the US this source estimated the Muslim population at over 3 million. Vladimir Posner, Moscow Radio, 30 March 1979 (SU/6082/A1/5, 2 April 1979).

[106] Igor Belyayev, 'Saudi Arabia – What Next?', *Literaturnaya Gazeta*, excerpted by Radio Moscow, 3 February 1979 (SU/6035/A4/1, 6 February 1979). See also Moscow Radio, 27 February 1979 (SU/6053/A4/2, 27 February 1979), and 'Around the Arabian Knot', *Sovetskaya Rossiya*, broadcast by Tass, 27 March 1979 (SU/6078/A4/3, 28 March 1979).

The Soviet Union has recently shown a greater inclination to exploit the Islamic connection diplomatically. See especially the interview with a senior Soviet Muslim by Hungarian radio, wherein it is reported, *inter alia*, that 25 pilgrims a year visit Mecca. Radio Budapest, 14 April 1979 (SU/6097/C/1, 21 April 1979), and Moscow Radio, 22 May 1979 (SU/6124/C/1, 24 May 1979).

[107] See Vadim Ardatovskiy, 'On the Situation in Iran', *Izvestiya*, 22 January 1979 (excerpted in SU/6024/A4/1, 24 January 1979), and P. Demchenko, *Pravda*, 24 January 1979.

[108] *Der Spiegel*, 20 November 1978.

[109] See, for example, *New York Times*, 23 March 1979; *International Herald Tribune*, 20 April 1979; *Le Monde*, 17 July 1979. The Soviet Union supported the Afghan government's protest against these and other remarks, observing that they were beneficial to enemies of Afghan-istan, but noting that they did not reflect official Iranian policy. Moscow Radio, 20 March 1979 (SU/6074/A3/4–5, 23 March 1979); see also Moscow Radio, 23 May 1979 (SU/6127/A3/1, 28 May 1979).

[110] Address by the Deputy Chairman of the Moslem board of Central Asia and Kazakhstan, Sheikh Yusubkhan Shakirov, Tass, 21 March 1979 (SU/6074/A3, 2–4, 23 March 1979). For a similar theme see RPP, 21 April 1979 via (SU/6099/A4/1, 24 April 1979).

[111] Moscow Radio, 10 May 1979 (SU/6114/A4/3, 12 May 1979).

[112] After the revolt 'Communists' became an epithet on the Iranian political scene connoting both 'godlessness' and receiving orders 'from outside Islamic frontiers'.

[113] See Khianouri's interview with *Newsweek*, 29 January 1979. The reverse of this proposition was also true but presumably less relevant from the Communist point of view.

[114] Moscow Radio, 13 February 1979 (SU/6043/A4/2, 15 February 1979); Tass 16 February 1979 (SU/6046/A4/2, 19 February 1979).

[115] Notoriously difficult to quantify, *Tudeh* active membership cannot be over 1,000 hard core today.

[116] Apart from pragmatism, one suspects that one motive is an extreme aversion to the possibility of dealing with the types of Communist régimes these countries are likely to produce: i.e., local Communism may be most resistant to Soviet influence.

[117] See Edith Penrose and E. F. Penrose, *Iraq: International Relations and National Development* (London: Benn, 1978), p. 341.

[118] *International Herald Tribune*, 10 July 1978.

[119] Tarek Aziz, a leading Ba'ath government member, observed, 'we cannot sustain a party inside our country which has unnatural ties with foreign blocs . . . . We reject the wide expansion by the Soviet Union in the homeland'. See *International Herald Tribune*, 9 and 25 April 1979; *Arab Report*, 25 April 1979, pp. 11–12.

[120] Helmut Sonnenfeldt and William G. Hyland *Soviet Perspectives on Security*, Adelphi Paper No. 150 (London: IISS, 1979), p. 21.

[121] The decline of Western influence, tends to be connected by observers with growing Soviet military power: Of many comments made by Gulf state leaders, note a pointed remark by Crown Prince Fahd of Saudi Arabia to an interviewer after the Iranian Revolution: 'perceptions of power are crucial when it comes to conditioning minds and affecting the decision-making process in any country' (*International Herald Tribune*, 19 March 1979).

[122] Since December 1978 there have been reports of Soviet use of PDRY bases for anti-submarine and maritime patrol missions by Tu–16 and Il–38 aircraft.

[123] I have argued that a formula of political parity or equality in regions adjacent to Soviet power tends in fact to ratify Soviet political predominance. Other analysts also see predominance as the Soviet goal. See especially John Campbell's writings: e.g., 'The Soviet Union in the Middle East', *The Middle East Journal*, XXXII, No. 1 (Winter 1978), pp. 1–12.

174

Index

WITHDRAWN